Game Theory and Animal Behavior

D0207423

GAME THEORY & ANIMAL BEHAVIOR

Edited by
LEE ALAN DUGATKIN and
HUDSON KERN REEVE

OXFORD UNIVERSITY PRESS
New York   Oxford

Oxford University Press

Oxford   New York
Athens   Auckland   Bangkok   Bogota   Bombay   Buenos Aires
Calcutta   Cape Town   Dar es Salaam   Delhi   Florence   Hong Kong
Istanbul   Karachi   Kuala Lumpur   Madras   Madrid   Melbourne
Mexico City   Nairobi   Paris   Singapore   Taipei   Tokyo   Toronto   Warsaw

and associated companies in
Berlin   Ibadan

First published in 1998 by Oxford University Press, Inc.
198 Madison Avenue, New York, New York 10016

First issued as an Oxford University Press paperback, 2000

Oxford is a registered trademark of Oxford University Press

Library of Congress Cataloging-in-Publication Data
Game theory and animal behavior / edited by Lee Alan Dugatkin and
   Hudson Kern Reeve.
        p.   cm.
     Includes bibliographical references and index.
     ISBN 0-19-509692-4
     ISBN 0-19-513790-6 (Pbk.)
      1. Animal behavior—Mathematical models.   2. Game theory.
   I. Dugatkin, Lee Alan, 1962–   .   II. Reeve, Hudson Kern.
   QL751.65.M3G25   1997
   591.5'015'193—dc21   96-29891

9 8 7 6 5 4 3 2 1
Printed in the United States of America
on acid-free paper

To Dana, Jan, Alex, and Aaron.
They are all too wonderful for words.

Preface

It is always notoriously difficult to identify precisely what constitutes a revolutionary change within a scientific discipline (Kuhn 1962). In the fields of animal behavior (ethology) and behavioral ecology, the introduction of inclusive fitness models (Hamilton 1963, 1964) may qualify as such a change in that they reshaped the manner in which behavioral ecologists and ethologists think about nearly every question they address. The subject of this book, game theory, may rank second to inclusive fitness in terms of its effect on the way animal behaviorists currently approach issues surrounding the evolution of social behavior. However, evolutionary game theory's fundamental principle—that actions taken by one individual have effects on the fitness of others and that all such effects must be accounted for when examining the evolution of a trait—has had a large enough impact that phrases like "payoff matrix" and "evolutionarily stable strategies" are used by virtually all pundits of behavioral ecology and animal behavior and are among the first concepts taught in graduate classes. Furthermore, the idea of an evolutionarily stable strategy (ESS) has surpassed the boundaries of ethology and behavioral ecology and can often be heard being uttered by the likes of political scientists, mathematicians, and psychologists. It is certainly rare for mathematical terminology created by behavioral ecologists to be adopted outside the field, and this stands as a testament to the influence of ethological game theory.

Hardly an issue of such journals as *Animal Behaviour, Behavioral Ecology, Behavioral Ecology and Sociobiology* (to name a few of the top journals in the field), or for that matter *The Journal of Theoretical Biology* is published in which at least one, and usually more, articles cite some reference to evolutionary game theory (most often Maynard Smith's 1982 book, *Evolution and the Theory of Games*). Yet, to date, there is no place where one can turn for a large-scale picture which not only reviews the impact of games on behavioral ecology and ethology, but suggests directions for future research. This volume (and the 1995 *National Animal Behavior Society* symposium on "Game Theory and Animal Behavior" that it is loosely based on) is an attempt to remedy this problem by gathering some of the leading researchers in the field and having them review (and sometimes extend) work in their area in a manner that is accessible to those interested in games and animal behavior, but not necessarily trained in the sometimes tedious mathematics of game theory. This book is intended for all advanced undergraduates, graduate students, and professional biologists interested in the evolutionary analysis of animal behavior. A basic mathematical background in algebra (and some elementary calculus) will be sufficient to allow access to even the most complex models discussed in this volume. However, even in the absence of such training, the vast majority of material will be accessible to the interested reader.

After an opening chapter that provides a lucid attempt to answer the question "What is evolutionary game theory?" (Hammerstein), the following topics are reviewed: the impact of game theory and ESS thinking on the study of social foraging (Giraldeau and Livoreil), cooperation (Dugatkin), animal contests (Riechert), communication (Johnstone), reproductive skew and nepotism within groups (Reeve), sibling rivalry and parent–offspring conflict (Mock et al.), alternative life histories (Gross and Repka), habitat selection (Brown), trophic-level interactions (Sih), learning (Stephens and Clements), and human behavior (Wilson). Gomulkiewicz then reviews the relations among game theory, optimality, and quantitative genetics. In a final chapter, we briefly assess the utility of game-theoretic reasoning in the study of social behavior (Reeve and Dugatkin).

We believe that evolutionary game theory is one of the most powerful analytical tools available to behavioral ecologists and ethologists today and sincerely hope that this volume opens the door to those readers who were tantalized by game theory, but until reading this book believed it to be the domain solely of theoreticians.

References

Hamilton, W. D. 1963. The evolution of altruistic behavior. *Am. Nat.,* 97, 354–356.

Hamilton, W. D. 1964. The genetical evolution of social behaviour. I and II. *J. Theor. Biol.,* 7, 1–52.

Kuhn, T. 1962. *The Structure of Scientific Revolutions.* Chicago: University of Chicago Press.

Maynard Smith, J. 1982. *Evolution and the Theory of Games.* Cambridge: Cambridge University Press.

Spring 1997

L. A. Dugatkin
University of Louisville

H. K. Reeve
Cornell University

Acknowledgments

First and foremost, we would like to thank the contributors to this volume for providing outstanding chapters in a timely fashion. We had very high expectations for this book; and thanks to their talents and effort, even our expectations were surpassed.

In addition to our own comments and suggestions, each chapter in this volume was reviewed by at least two external referees. Reviewing for an edited book is thankless work, and we are indeed indebted to the following individuals for their efforts on this front: Robert Boyd, Phil Crowley, Larry Dill, Jim Gilliam, Peter Hammerstein, David Haskell, Geoff Hill, Don Hugie, Laurent Keller, Steve Lima, Jeff Lucas, Peter Nonacs, David Pfennig, David Queller, Peter Richerson, Jan Shellman-Reeve, David Stephens, and George Uetz.

We thank Dana Dugatkin for proofreading and indexing this entire book. Dana now knows more about behavioral ecology and game theory than any sane person outside the field should. Finally, we are indebted to Kirk Jensen at Oxford University Press for all his time, effort, and encouragement. We are honored to have this volume published by the oldest and most respected academic press in the world.

Contents

Contributors

Joel S. Brown
Department of Biological Sciences
University of Illinois at Chicago
845 W. Taylor St.
Chicago, IL 60607
United States

Kevin C. Clements
School of Biological Sciences
University of Nebraska
Lincoln, NE 68588
United States

Lee Alan Dugatkin
Department of Biology
Life Sciences Building
University of Louisville
Louisville, KY 40292
United States

Luc-Alain Giraldeau
Department of Biology
Concordia University
1455 Ouest Blvd. Maisonneuve
Montreal, Quebec H3G 1 MB
Canada

Richard Gomulkiewicz
Department of Genetics and
   Cell Biology
P.O. Box 644234
Washington State University
Pullman, WA 99164
United States

Mart R. Gross
Department of Zoology
University of Toronto
25 Harbord Street
Toronto, Ontario M5S 3G5
Canada

Peter Hammerstein
Max-Planck-Institut fur
   Verhaltensphysiologie
Abteilung Wickler
82319 Seewiesen
Germany

Rufus A. Johnstone
Department of Zoology
Cambridge University
Downing Street
Cambridge CB2 3EJ
United Kingdom

Barbara Livoreil
Department of Biology
Concordia University
1455 Ouest Blvd. Maisonneuve
Montreal, Quebec H3G 1 MB
Canada

Douglas W. Mock
Department of Zoology
University of Oklahoma
Norman, OK, 73019
United States

Geoffrey A. Parker
Population Biology Group
Department of Environmental and
    Evolutionary Biology
University of Liverpool
Liverpool, L69 3BX
United Kingdom

Joe Repka
Department of Mathematics
University of Toronto
Toronto, Ontario M5S 3G3
Canada

Hudson Kern Reeve
Neurobiology and Behavior
Seeley G. Mudd Hall
Cornell University
Ithaca, NY 14853
United States

Susan E. Riechert
Department of Ecology &
    Evolutionary Biology
University of Tennessee
Knoxville, TN 37996
United States

P. L. Schwagmeyer
Department of Zoology
University of Oklahoma
Norman, OK 73019
United States

Andrew Sih
Department of Biology
University of Kentucky
Lexington, KY 40506
United States

David W. Stephens
Department of Ecology, Evolution
    and Behavior
University of Minnesota
100 Ecology Building
1987 Upper Buford Circle
Saint Paul, MN 55108
United States

David Sloan Wilson
Department of Biology
Binghamton University
P.O. Box 6000
Binghamton, NY 13902
United States

Game Theory and Animal Behavior

PETER HAMMERSTEIN

What Is Evolutionary Game Theory?

1.1 Why Evolutionary Game Theory Exists

When Charles Darwin developed his theory of natural selection, he created a picture of the evolutionary process in which organismic adaptation was ultimately caused by competition for survival and reproduction. This biological "struggle for existence" bears considerable resemblance to the human struggle between businessmen who are striving for economic success in competitive markets. Long before Darwin published his work, social scientist Adam Smith had already considered that in business life, competition is the driving force behind economic efficiency and adaptation. It is indeed very striking how similar the ideas are on which the founders of modern theory in evolutionary biology and economics have based their main thoughts.

Ideally, this similarity of ideas could have led to a permanent interchange between disciplines after Darwin (1859) wrote his *The Origin of Species*. It seems, however, as if the theories of evolution and of economics first needed to mature independently before such an interdisciplinary dialogue could become very fruitful. Biologists, on the one hand, had to explore the mechanisms of inheritance and to achieve their own synthesis of theories about phenotypic and genetic evolution. Economists, on the other hand, had to develop the mathematical backbone of their classical theory of competition. This backbone surely is the theory of games which came into existence with a famous book written by von Neumann and Morgenstern (1944). The intense dialogue between biology and economics started a few decades later. Both disciplines have since tried to systematically explore what their concepts have in common and how biologists and economists can share the effort of further theory development. The field of evolutionary game theory emerged as the major result of this exploration.

What initiated the biological interest in game theory? The important event was a change of paradigm regarding the level of aggregation (i.e., species, population, group, or individual) at which natural selection shows its strongest effects. Until the early 1960s, many biologists had held the view that the evolution of an organismic trait can be explained by identifying the trait's benefit to the species, or to other units above the level of the individual. This view was then deeply shaken (Williams 1966, Maynard Smith 1976). It neither represented Darwin's original thoughts properly, nor did it stand up to scrutiny in the updated theory of evolution (but see Wilson and Dugatkin, both in this volume, for alternative views of this subject).

We are now used to the idea that natural selection tends to act more effectively at the level of individuals than at higher levels of aggregated entities. Therefore, we have a strong inclination to look at natural selection "through the eyes" of the individuals that carry out the Darwinian struggle for existence. This helps us to understand the conceptual link between evolution and the theory of games. Similar to the theory of evolutionary adaptation, the latter theory is also deeply rooted in methodological individualism. After all, we expect businessmen to strive for their own success. Depending on the circumstances, this may or may not increase the well-being of society, very much like natural selection may have a positive or negative effect on the overall performance of animal groups or populations (Riechert & Hammerstein 1983).

1.2 What Is an Evolutionary Game?

A classical game is a model in economic decision theory describing the potential interactions of two or more individuals whose interests do not entirely coincide. The term "game" is chosen because whenever we specify such a model, this resembles the process of creating a new parlor game. We have to make precise (a) who is involved, (b) what are the possible actions, and (c) how individual success depends on the behavior of all participants. Obviously, even a biologist who is not dealing with decision theory, but with functional analysis of animal or plant interactions, needs exactly these three ingredients in order to describe the phenotypic scenario of competition. Therefore, the structure of a game arises naturally in evolutionary studies.

As far as the mathematical representation of a biological game is concerned, the modeler has a choice of several forms. For example, a very explicit description of the phenotypic scenario would be given by a game in *extensive form* (Selten 1983, 1988). Roughly speaking, this is a mathematical decision tree, the branching points (nodes) of which correspond to the players' objective decision situations, and branches stand for the alternative actions that are possible in such a situation. A superimposed structure describes the possible information states of the players, and a strategy is a "list of behavioral instructions" for all the different information states (subjective situations) which may arise during a game. By "behavioral instruction" it is not necessarily meant that in a given situation a single alternative has to be used with probability 1. Therefore, an instruction can be to use several alternatives, each with positive probability. A strategy is called "pure" if none of its instructions are of the latter type. In other words, in a pure strategy no randomization of action takes place.

How can one simplify a game in extensive form? A more condensed way of describing such a game is the so-called *normal form* (also referred to as the *strategic form*). In this description, pure strategies are named by numbers and their instructions are not made explicit in the model. The normal form only contains information about how strategies and payoffs relate to each other. Suppose that there is a finite set of alternative pure strategies and that organisms interact pairwise in a symmetric game. Symmetry means here that both "players" have the same set of strategies and that payoff depends only on strategies and not on the question of who is player 1 and player 2. A payoff matrix $a = (a_{ij})$ then describes what a player would receive if he plays his ith pure strategy against another player who plays his jth pure strategy. The matrix, a, is all one needs in order to specify a symmetric game in normal form. Implicitly, however, there are more strategies than the ones that define rows and columns of this matrix. A general strategy s is a probability distribution over a player's pure strategies. Let $E(s, r)$ denote the expected payoff for playing such a strategy s against another player's strategy r. Biologically speaking, this function describes how an individual's expected fitness is changed according to his performance in the game.

We are now entering the discussion of the dynamic context in which an evolutionary game is imbedded. In order to analyze any kind of a game, one needs a background theory about the process that generates behavior. This is the point where biology and classical economics differ dramatically. Theoreticians in classical economics rely on the process of rational decision making. They idealize the human brain as an apparatus with incredibly powerful cognitive skills and with the dedication to make the best use of them. In contrast, evolutionary biologists tend to invoke natural selection as the principal "decision maker." In their picture, individual behavior is governed by less potent mental procedures which are passed on from generation to generation via genetic inheritance. The biological theory of games is about the evolution of these procedures (strategies). In this approach, sophisticated behavioral adaptations of animals are thought to reflect the calculation power of the evolutionary process, rather than cognitive skills of the individual brain.

The theory of the evolutionary game can be based on fairly different assumptions about the mode of inheritance, and its picture of genetics can be either more or less explicit. Initially, evolutionary game theory was considered to be a phenotypic approach to frequency-dependent selection in which genetics had to be approximated very crudely by the assumption of exact asexual inheritance. Let us have a brief look at such a selection model for a population with discrete nonoverlapping generations. Suppose that n different strategies $s_1, \ldots, s_n$ are initially present in the population. Let x_i denote the relative frequency of strategy s_i in the population, and let $x = (x_1, \ldots, x_n)$ be the population frequency distribution of strategies. Suppose that the expected fitness w_i of an individual "playing i" is frequency-dependent and that it can be defined as a function $w_i(x)$. Let $\overline{w}(x)$ denote the population mean fitness. Then, after one generation the new population state $x' = (x'_1, \ldots, x'_n)$ is given by the following difference equation, known as the *discrete replicator equation with frequency-dependent fitness*:

$$x' = x_i \frac{w_i(x)}{\overline{w}(x)} \qquad \text{for } i = 1, \ldots, n \qquad (1)$$

In order to link this replicator equation with a phenotypic game, one has to be more explicit about the nature of the fitness function $w_i(x)$. Suppose that in every generation, animals interact pairwise in a game-like situation, that pair formation is random with respect to strategies, and that a payoff matrix describes how an individual's expected fitness is changed by the course of actions in the game. The fitness of strategy s_i can then be defined as

$$w_i(x) = w_0 + \sum_{j=1}^{n} x_j E(s_i, s_j) \qquad \text{for } i = 1, \ldots, n \tag{2}$$

where $E(s_i, s_j)$ is the game payoff for playing strategy s_i against strategy s_j, and w_0 is the basic fitness expectation an organism would have if it could avoid playing the game at all.

The first model in evolutionary game theory (Maynard Smith & Price 1973) left it to the reader's intuition to imagine the dynamic context of the evolutionary game. However, it is obvious that either the discrete replicator equation (1) was what Maynard Smith and Price (1973) had in mind, or else a smoother version of this model (Taylor & Jonker 1978), in which the difference equation is replaced by a closely related differential equation (see also Hofbauer & Sigmund 1988). Many biologists feel uneasy with these equations, because they only describe phenotypic change without keeping track of the underlying genetics. Indeed, once genetics is added to the replicator equation, the evolutionary game can strongly change its dynamic properties. Genetics then constrains the course of phenotypic evolution.

Undoubtedly, theoreticians have to face a dilemma in this regard. Genetics is important, but if one studies evolutionary games together with the underlying genetics, this often becomes such a tedious task that the theory loses most of its heuristic power. The only tractable approaches seem to be one-locus models (reviewed in Cressman 1992) and models of quantitative genetics, where many genes with very small effects are considered. Both these approaches are based on strong assumptions and thereby circumvent at least part of the dilemma under discussion. Gomulkiewicz (this volume) gives a very nice review of how far one gets with evolutionary game theory in the framework of quantitative genetics. However, as we shall see later in section 1.4, there is also another philosophy of how to overcome the modeler's dilemma. This is the philosophy of the "streetcar," which works well even in the difficult context of general n-locus genetics, where genes are allowed to have strong effects on phenotypes.

1.3 Nash Equilibrium and Evolutionarily Stable Strategies

Classical game theory (Luce & Raiffa 1957, Fudenberg & Tirole 1991) has two different branches. In *cooperative game theory*, the phenomenon of cooperation is to a certain extent assumed and thus not subject to a complete analysis. *Noncooperative game theory*, on the other hand, seeks to fully explain cooperation as well as noncooperation. This branch is the one that matters in evolutionary biology. It was established in classical game theory by Nash (1951). He suggested that one should study a game by looking for a combination of strategies (one for each player) with the following property. If all players act according to this combination, then "everybody achieves his maximum payoff against the strategies of all other players." This means that nobody would have an incentive to unilaterally deviate from such a combination. The idea can be rephrased in technical terms.

1.3.1 Nash Equilibrium

A *Nash equilibrium* is a *combination of strategies* for the players of a game, such that each player's strategy is a *best response* to the other players' strategies. A *best response* is a strategy which maximizes a player's expected payoff against a fixed combination of strategies played by the others.

In order to illustrate this, let us consider a game taking place in real life. In a psychological experiment, envelopes are distributed to three subjects. They are each asked to put any amount of money between 0 and 100 units in their envelope. Nobody is given a chance to observe what the others contribute. The experimenter then collects the envelopes and proceeds according to the following rule which is known to everybody. All contributions are thrown into the same box. If this box contains 30 money units or more, the experimenter himself will throw 15 additional units into the box and all the accumulated money will be split equally among the three subjects. However, if the box contains less than 30 units, all money goes to the experimenter.

Let us treat this as a three-person game played by the subjects. What would be a Nash equilibrium for them? We only want to ask here for symmetric equilibria, where everybody plays the same strategy and thus gives the same amount. Obviously, (10, 10, 10) is a symmetric Nash equilibrium. The reason is that no player has an incentive to unilaterally deviate from this solution: If the other two players each play 10, the third player achieves his maximum by also playing 10. In this Nash equilibrium, the players cooperatively exploit their resource—the experimenter—and achieve a net equilibrium payoff of 5 units. We now have to ask whether this is the only solution to the game. There is indeed another symmetric Nash equilibrium, (0, 0, 0), in which all three subjects hand over empty envelopes to the experimenter. Obviously, nobody has an incentive to deviate from this solution. Furthermore, no cooperation takes place, the resource remains unexploited, and the equilibrium payoff is zero.

This type of game is well known and has been played in numerous experiments. It is presented here to give the reader a feel for the Nash equilibrium. We observe a phenomenon which is typical for games, namely that there is more than one such equilibrium. One would think that the players should play the cooperative solution. However, imagine a player who worries about the risk involved if other players come to a different conclusion about the choice of equilibrium. If this player plays zero, he is relatively safe and can only miss the small cooperative payoff consisting of 5 units. Otherwise, he might lose the larger amount of 10 units if he cooperates and another player fails to do so. This would be an argument in favor of the noncooperative solution. Obviously, it can be difficult to decide between alternative Nash equilibria.

Turning back now to biology, the important solution concept developed by Maynard Smith and Price (1973), and foreshadowed by Hamilton (1967), is that of an evolutionarily stable strategy (ESS). Intuitively speaking, ESS theory draws the modeler's attention to population states which are resistant against the forces of selection and mutation. An ESS sensu Maynard Smith (1982) is a strategy with the following property: If all members of a population are genetically coded to play this strategy, any initially rare mutant strategy would receive negative selection pressure in this population.

Let us see what this means in the formal context of equation (1). Suppose that the population plays strategy s_1 and that a mutant s_2 arises. Let the strategy frequencies be $x_1 = 1 - \epsilon$ and $x_2 = \epsilon$, so that ϵ is the mutant frequency. The evolutionary stability of s_1 means that for sufficiently small ϵ the difference $w_1(x) - w_2(x)$ must be positive. If we are dealing with random pairwise interactions and if fitness is defined as in (2), this difference can be written as follows:

$$w_1(x) - w_2(x) = (1 - \epsilon)[E(s_1, s_1) - E(s_2, s_1)] + \epsilon[E(s_1, s_2) - E(s_2, s_2)] \qquad (3)$$

We are now able to see how the Nash equilibrium emerges in evolutionary biology. If for some mutant strategy the first square bracket in (3) is negative, then $w_1(x) - w_2(x)$ becomes negative for sufficiently small values of ϵ. In order to exclude this possibility, one has to require for an ESS s_1 that it should be a best response to itself in the phenotypic game. The latter requirement can be rephrased by saying that the symmetric pair of strategies (s_1, s_1) should be a Nash equilibrium.

This is a necessary, but not sufficient, condition for (3) to be positive. Suppose there is another strategy s_2 which is different from s_1, but also a best response to s_1. The first square bracket in (3) then is zero and the second square bracket needs to be positive in order for selection to act against the mutant under consideration. Clearly, this is only the case if $E(s_1, s_2) > E(s_2, s_2)$. In order to ensure evolutionary stability, this second condition needs to hold for all strategies s_2 that are alternative best responses to s_1.

We have now recapitulated Maynard Smith's original thoughts using the language of game theory. Using this language again, his technical definition of an ESS can be described as follows. It relates to a symmetric game in strategic form and to the dynamic context of (1) with fitness function (2). A strategy s_1 is called *evolutionarily stable* if it satisfies the following two conditions:

1.3.2 Properties of an ESS

1. Property of a symmetric Nash equilibrium: s_1 is a best response to s_1. In other words, if an opponent plays this strategy, one receives the highest possible payoff by also playing this strategy.

2. Stability against alternative best responses: If a strategy s_2 is different from s_1 and $E(s_2, s_1) = E(s_1, s_1)$, then the inequality $E(s_1, s_2) > E(s_2, s_2)$ holds. In other words, if another strategy also achieves the highest payoff against s_1, then it is better to play against this other strategy than to play the latter strategy s_2 against itself.

From an economist's point of view, it is interesting to note that we only have to study the phenotypic game model in order to see whether these two ESS conditions hold. The selection equation (1) is completely hidden in the background theory that gave rise to these conditions. Nash himself foresaw the possibility of dynamic interpretations of the Nash equilibrium when he mentioned in his work the "mass action interpretation" of his solution concept as an alternative to decision-theoretic interpretations. However, it surely was Maynard Smith (1982) who first created such a theory. Furthermore, the now famous statement of Nash was buried in his Ph.D. thesis and cannot be found in his publications. It was only rediscovered when Nash received the Nobel Prize in 1994.

1.4 Genetics and the Evolutionary Game

In order to enrich evolutionary game theory with explicit assumptions about the genetics of behavior, one would have to know what genes are involved, how they recombine, and how phenotypes and genotypes relate to each other. It often seems like a hopeless task to try to accomplish this goal empirically. Even if one sequences strands of DNA completely for their molecular structure, this does not yet reveal how genotypes are translated into complex phenotypes by developmental processes. Therefore, it is tempting to study the evolution of phenotypic traits in purely phenotypic models. Organismic biologists are quite impressed with the explanatory power of such models in their empirical studies. This raises an interesting question: Why do we understand many examples of evolutionary adaptation so well without knowing their genetic background?

In the remainder of this section, I shall review a theory which attempts to answer this question. This is the theory of long-term evolution which had its origin in publications by Eshel (1982), Lessard (1984), and most notably by Eshel and Feldman (1984). The development of this theory and its applications is due to a number of further publications, including the work of Liberman and Feldman (1986), Liberman (1988), Lessard (1990), Eshel (1991, 1996), Eshel and Sansone (1991), Matessi and Eshel (1992), Matessi and Di Pasquale (1996), and Weissing (1996). In my view, Ilan Eshel has played a particularly important role in the conceptual development of the theory under discussion.

A streetcar metaphor (Hammerstein 1996) can be used to explain this theory (Fig. 1.1). The moving streetcar is an evolving population. Suppose that in this population an inherited trait is subject to natural selection and is coded for by more than one gene. As Moran (1964) and Karlin (1975) have shown, it can easily happen that phenotypic adaptation of this trait is made impossible by the "reshuffling" of genes due to recombination. Therefore, natural selection may drive the population toward a genotype frequency equilibrium in which phenotypes fail to maximize fitness or to play an ESS. This is the first temporary stop of the streetcar and we now draw our attention to new passengers that may enter it.

It was the ingenious idea of Eshel and Feldman (1984) to extend at this point the classical framework of population genetics and to take a particularly wide range of potential mutations (new passengers) into account. The general idea which emerges from their approach is that if genetics is in the way of phenotypic adaptation, then it is possible to conceive—at least mathematically—a mutant allele which would cause further phenotypic evolution. Imagine, for example, the case of sickle cell anemia. If a mutant allele is able to produce the same effect against malaria as the heterozygote, it may spread and reduce the prevalence of sickle cell anemia in

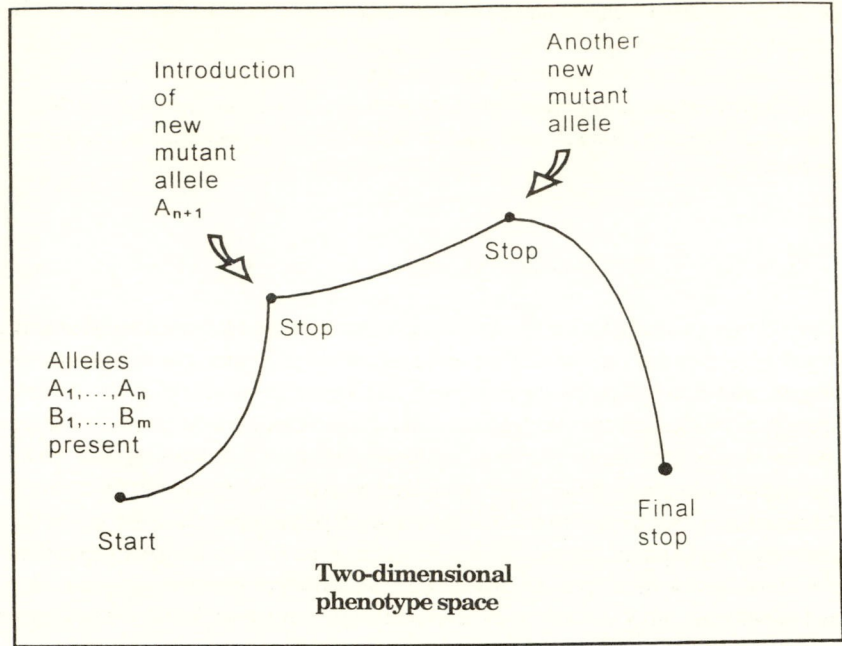

Figure 1.1. Course of an evolving population in phenotype space. The population stops at a genotype frequency equilibrium. Temporary stops are then left after the population is perturbed by an appropriate new mutant allele. A final stop is phenotypically stable against genetic perturbation. At such a stop, phenotypes act according to game-theoretic principles. The streetcar theory compares the course of an evolving population with that of a streetcar and draws the modeler's attention to the analysis of final stops (from Hammerstein 1996).

the population. In other words, if such a passenger enters the streetcar, the streetcar will be moving again. At a subsequent stop, another new passenger may play the same role. In principle, this process may go on forever, or no stop may ever be reached.

A streetcar has a final stop where it comes to a permanent rest. At a final stop, new passengers may enter the streetcar, but it will not move. Suppose that the population has reached such a final stop, where no mutation would be able to initiate new phenotypic evolution. What can be said about the properties of such a final stop? The answer to this question would have pleased Charles Darwin, because it reveals an overwhelming effect of the phenotypic forces of natural selection.

1.4.1 Survival of the Fittest

If selection is frequency-independent, then phenotypic fitness maximization is to be expected at a final stop, and phenotypic optimality theory applies (Eshel & Feldman 1984, Liberman 1988) under a wide range of conditions. The technical term used in the original literature instead of "final stop" is that of "external stability." Any conceivable mutant is here taken into account as a potential passenger, unless it could disturb the basic mechanism of inheritance, such as a segregation distorter would do. The reason not to consider the latter type of mutant is that any stop—be it temporary or final—would be vulnerable to invasion of such genes. Such general invasibility is not the central subject of the theory under discussion. Environmental change also ensures that no final stop is an eternal stop. Eventually, a streetcar will start moving again, and so does an evolving population.

1.4.2 A Streetcar Named Nash

When selection is frequency-dependent and the phenotypic scenario is described by random pairwise interactions in a symmetric two-person game in normal form, the following can be shown. The population mean strategy of any final stop is necessarily a best response to itself in the phenotypic game. Therefore, it corresponds to a symmetric Nash equilibrium (the first ESS condition holds). This is an almost obvious result in light of the conceptual innovation by Eshel and Feldman (1984). Together with a simple proof for the two-locus case of viability selection, this result is formulated in survey articles by Hammerstein and Selten (1994) and Hammerstein (1996), who study mathematical problems with the "interface" between the theories of long-term evolution and of the evolutionary game. They use, in particular, the following subtle adjustment of the concept of external stability. In evolutionary game theory, it is inappropriate to generally require that no mutant allele can invade at a final stop. The simple reason is that different genetic population states may produce the same mean population strategy. This means that alleles may invade without leading to a new phenotypic picture. Therefore, testing for the "final stop property" means looking at genetic perturbation and asking whether the phenotypic trajectory will take the population back to its unperturbed phenotypic state. One could say that the study of final stops is that of "phenotypic stability against genetic perturbation" (Hammerstein 1996).

1.4.3 A Streetcar Named ESS

Consider a final stop which is phenotypically monomorphic in the sense that the same strategy is played by all the individuals of a population (at the genetic level there need not be fixation of all alleles). Such a stop has the following stronger properties. Under assumptions like in the previous paragraph, a phenotypically monomorphic final stop necessarily satisfies the two ESS conditions of Maynard Smith. Conversely, if an ESS is played by a population, no mutant allele can invade if it is unable to generate the ESS with the given genetic background (Hammerstein & Selten 1994, Hammerstein 1996). Weissing (1996) shows how the results about Nash equilibrium and the ESS can be generalized to n-locus models and to nonlinear games.

In the remainder of this section, two mathematical aspects of the model under discussion are described, namely the selection equation and the fitness function. The results about this model and its generalizations are not presented here and can be found in the literature cited above. Let us have a look at the 2-locus case. We consider the standard model describing viability selection in an infinite diploid population with nonoverlapping generations, sexual reproduction, and random mating. Consider in this population an evolving trait which is coded for by two genes, A and B. Suppose that there are n alleles $A_1, \ldots, A_n$ of gene A, and m alleles $B_1, \ldots, B_m$ of gene B. Assume that recombination takes place at a fixed rate r, with $0 < r \le 1/2$.

Let us make a population census at each gametic stage. Let x_{ij} denote the relative frequency of a gamete with haploid genotype $A_i B_j$. At the moment of our census, a population state $x = (x_{11}, \ldots, x_{ij}, \ldots, x_{nm})$ can be conceived as a frequency histogram for the population distribution of possible haploid genotypes $A_i B_j$. Due to the assumption of random mating, the following selection equation describes how this frequency histogram changes from one generation to the next if each diploid genotype, $A_i B_j / A_k B_l$, has a frequency-dependent fitness $w_{ijkl}(x)$:

$$x_{ij} = \frac{1}{\overline{w}(x)} [(1-r)\sum_{kl} w_{ijkl}(x)x_{ij}x_{kl} + r\sum_{kl} w_{ilkj}(x)x_{il}x_{kj}] \tag{3}$$

for $i = 1, \ldots, n$ and $j = 1, \ldots, m$. Here, $\overline{w}$ is the mean fitness of the population:

$$\overline{w}(x) = \sum_{ijkl} w_{ijkl}(x)x_{ij}x_{kl}$$

This equation can be seen as the genetic counterpart of equation (1). It is based on the classical Mendelian laws of inheritance with "fair meiosis." Moran (1964) was the first to show that trajectories of solutions of this equation may easily ignore Wright's fitness landscape in the case of frequency-independent fitness. In his famous example, population mean fitness can decrease over time. This example demonstrates the "survival of the less fit." Similarly, in the case of frequency dependence, equilibrium states of this equation cannot be characterized generally by a Nash equilibrium or an ESS—unless one considers a final stop in the sense of the theory outlined above.

Finally, let us describe the counterpart of (2)—that is, the relationship between game payoff and fitness. Suppose that we look at a symmetric game in normal form which is given by a payoff matrix and for which the expected payoff is denoted by E. Assume that a diploid genotype $A_i B_j / A_k B_l$ causes individuals to "play" a mixed or pure strategy u_{ijkl} in the phenotypic game. If one knows the relative frequencies of phenotypes in a population, one also knows the relative frequencies of strategies with the help of u. This makes it possible to calculate the mean population strategy $\overline{q}(x)$ as follows. The probability with which $\overline{q}(x)$ plays a pure strategy s is $\sum_{ijkl} x_{ij}x_{kl}u_{ijkl}(s)$. The expected fitness of an individual with genotype $A_i B_j / A_k B_l$ can now be defined as

$$w_{ijkl}(x) = w_0 + E(u_{ijkl}, \overline{q}(x)) \tag{4}$$

Like in (2), this means that an individual has a basic fitness expectation w_0 which is changed by the game payoff E. We have now finished the description of the evolutionary game with explicit two-locus genetics (for another approach to genetics, see Gomulkiewicz, this volume).

1.5 Concluding Remarks

Does game theory have its place in the edifice of biological thought, and, if so, where is this place? Obviously, the "methodological individualism" of game theory is the important "preadaptation" for its use in evolutionary biology (but see Wilson and Dugatkin, both in this volume, for alternative views of this subject). As pointed out in section 1.1, the typical picture of phenotypic evolution is one in which nothing matters more than individual performance in reproductive competition. Therefore, game models arise so naturally in biology that it even seems difficult to avoid them. However, what these games describe is only the relationship between behavior and fitness in organismic interactions. For an evolutionary analysis, more than this needs to be specified. Therefore, evolutionary game theory considers the phenotypic game in the wider context of a dynamic model of natural selection.

This dynamic model is based on assumptions about the interaction structure of a population, its mating structure, and the mechanisms of inheritance. In sections 1.2 and 1.3, we discussed a particular selection model, in which interaction partners are randomly chosen and inheritance is assumed to be asexual and exact. Obviously, no mating structure needed to be specified in this case. We then followed Maynard Smith and asked the question of how to characterize for this model an ESS. It turned out that such a strategy must be a "best response to itself" in the phenotypic game. In other words, every ESS corresponds to a particular Nash equilibrium in this context.

This last statement may sound like a very technical remark, but it has a very interesting connotation: The most important concept of classical game theory describes the main characteristic of an ESS. One could hardly imagine a stronger argument in order to defend the important role of game theory in biology. However, let us not forget about all the assumptions made. In real life, the interaction structure can be far from random, the mode of reproduction is usually sexual, and mating can have its assortative and disassortative aspects. All these aspects can, in principle, change the characterization of an ESS.

At the end of section 1.4, we had a brief look at an evolutionary game in which strategies are coded for by two recombining genes in a diploid Mendelian population. This model has a random interaction structure and mating is random as well. A critic of evolutionary game theory would complain that even in such a rather simple model, genetics can impose severe constraints on phenotypic evolution. From this well-founded point of view, it seems naive to analyze an evolutionary game merely at the phenotypic level. If nothing could be held against this view, game theory would already have lost its place in the edifice of biological thought. Fortunately, this is not the case. As discussed in section 1.4, genetic constraints are unlikely to play a major role in long-term evolution. The reason is that evolution not only changes phenotypes, but also alters the underlying genetics. This causes a process of successive removal of such constraints. If this process ever comes to a permanent rest in a given environment, phenotypes will be highly adapted to this environment—the situation in which game theory matters.

ACKNOWLEDGMENTS   I wish to thank Jack Werren, an anonymous referee, and the editors of this volume for a number of very helpful comments on an earlier draft of this chapter.

References

Cressman, R. 1992. *The Stability Concept of Evolutionary Game Theory: A Dynamic Approach.* Berlin: Springer-Verlag.

Darwin, C. 1859. *The Origin of Species.* J. Murray: London.

Eshel, I. 1982. Evolutionarily stable strategies and viability selection in Mendelian populations. *Theor. Pop. Biol.,* 22, 204–217.

Eshel, I. 1991. Game theory and population dynamics in complex genetical systems: The role of sex in short term and in long term evolution. In *Game Equilibrium Models I: Evolution and Game Dynamics,* R. Selten, ed., pp. 6–28. Berlin: Springer-Verlag.

Eshel, I. 1996. On the changing concept of population stability as a reflection of changing problematics in the quantitative theory of evolution. *J. Math. Biol.,* 34, 485–510.

Eshel, I. & Feldman, M. W. 1984. Initial increase of new mutants and some continuity properties of ESS in two locus systems. *Am. Nat.,* 124, 631–640.

Eshel, I. & Sansone, E. 1991. Parent-offspring conflict over the sex-ratio in a diploid population with different investment in male and in female offspring. *Am. Nat.,* 138, 954–972.

Fudenberg, D. & Tirole, J. 1991. *Game Theory.* Cambridge, Mass: MIT Press.

Hamilton, W. D. 1967. Extraordinary sex ratios. *Science,* 156, 477–488.

Hammerstein, P. 1996. Darwinian adaptation, population genetics and the streetcar theory of evolution. *J. Math. Biol.,* 34, 511–532.

Hammerstein, P. & Selten, R. 1994. Game theory and evolutionary biology. In *Handbook of Game Theory with Economic Applications, Volume 2,* R. J. Aumann, & S. Hart. eds., pp. 929–993. Amsterdam: Elsevier.

Hofbauer, J. & Sigmund, K. 1988. *The Theory of Evolution and Dynamical Systems.* Cambridge: Cambridge University Press.

Karlin, S. 1975. General two-locus selection models: Some objectives, results and interpretations. *Theor. Pop. Biol.,* 7, 364–398.

Lessard, S. 1984. Evolutionary dynamics in frequency-dependent two phenotype models. *Theor. Pop. Biol.,* 25, 210–234.

Lessard, S. 1990. Evolutionary stability: one concept, several meanings. *Theor. Pop. Biol.,* 37, 159–170.

Liberman, U. 1988. External stability and ESS: Criteria for initial increase of a new mutant allele. *J. Math. Biol.,* 26, 477–485.

Liberman, U. & Feldman, M. W. 1986. A general reduction principle for genetic modifiers of recombination. *Theor. Pop. Biol.,* 30, 341–371.

Luce, R. D. & Raiffa, H. 1957. *Games and Decisions.* New York: John Wiley.

Matessi, C. & Di Pasquale, C. 1996. Long-term evolution of multilocus traits. *J. Math. Biol.,* 34, 613–653.

Matessi, C. & Eshel, I. 1992. Sex ratio in social hymenoptera: a population genetic study of long-term evolution. *Am. Nat.,* 139, 276–312.

Maynard Smith, J. 1976. Group selection. *Q. Rev. Biol.,* 51, 277–283.

Maynard Smith, J. 1982. Evolution and the Theory of Games. Cambridge: Cambridge University Press.

Maynard Smith, J. & Price, G. R. 1973. The logic of animal conflict. *Nature,* 246, 15–18.

Moran, P. A. P. 1964. On the nonexistence of adaptive topographies. *Ann. Human Genet.,* 27, 338–343.

Nash, J. F. 1951. Non-cooperative games. *Ann. Math.,* 54, 286–295.

Riechert, S. E. & Hammerstein, P. 1983. Game theory in the ecological context. *Annu. Rev. Ecol. Syst.,* 14, 377–409.

Selten, R. 1983. Evolutionary stability in extensive 2-person games. *Math. Social Sciences,* 5, 269–363.

Selten, R. 1988. Evolutionary stability in extensive two-person games—correction and further development. *Math. Social Sciences,* 16, 223–266.

Taylor, P. D. & Jonker, L. B. 1978. Evolutionarily stable strategies and game dynamics. *Mathematical Biosciences,* 40, 145–156.

von Neumann, J. & Morgenstern, O. 1944. *Theory of Games and Economic Behaviour.* Princeton, NJ: Princeton University Press.

Weissing, F. J. 1996. Genetic versus phenotypic models of selection: Can genetics be neglected in a long-term perspective? *J. Math. Biol.,* 34, 533–555.

Williams, G. C. 1966. Adaptation and Natural Selection. Princeton, NJ: Princeton University Press.

Luc-Alain Giraldeau
Barbara Livoreil

Game Theory and Social Foraging

2.1 Introduction

Foraging behavior is central to issues such as the structure and composition of animal communities (Schoener 1987), the abundance and spatial distribution of organisms (Fretwell 1972), the extent to which sociality may evolve (Wilson 1975, pp. 49–57), and intra- and interspecific competition. It is not surprising that this realization in the late 1960s (MacArthur & Pianka 1966) spawned an exponential surge of research into foraging behavior (Schoener 1987). The application of optimality models to the study of foraging behavior led to a number of simple, explicit, economic foraging models that made quantitative, testable predictions. As a consequence, a field known today as "Foraging Theory" quickly emerged in the mid-1970s (Stephens & Krebs 1986).

The use of simple optimality models has been particularly successful in addressing two foraging decisions: whether to attack an encountered prey (prey models) and whether to persist exploiting a patch (patch models; Stephens & Krebs 1986). Simple optimality models, however, are applicable strictly to situations where a behavioral alternative can be assigned a payoff independently of the use of the same or different behavioral alternatives by other population members. In short, they do not pertain to situations of frequency-dependence that characterize many of the population-level phenomena foraging theory purported to address. To embrace these problems, foraging theory must rely more on game theory as an economic modeling tool. We call this area of foraging theory "Social Foraging Theory."

2.2 Social Foraging Theory

Social foraging decisions are characterized by the frequency-dependence of their payoffs. A common example of a social foraging decision is group membership. Social carnivores and some social spiders, for instance, attack their prey in small groups (Giraldeau 1988). In some cases, the success of the attack depends on the number of individuals engaged in the attack (Giraldeau 1988). The payoff that one obtains from joining a hunting group depends on its size and hence the number of other individuals that have made the same decision (Sibly 1983; Pulliam & Caraco 1984; Clark & Mangel 1984; Giraldeau 1988; Giraldeau et al. 1994a). Another commonly studied social foraging decision concerns the distribution of consumers over a number of resource patches, a problem that has been approached using Ideal Free Distribution theory (Fretwell 1972, Milinski & Parker 1991). Social foraging decisions can also involve patch use when groups of foragers exploit a patch concurrently (Parker 1978). The individual payoffs for any patch residence time depend on the number of competitors that have remained in or left the patch (Parker 1978, Sjerps & Haccou 1994) and simple versions have been tested with some success (Beauchamp and Giraldeau 1997, Livoreil and Giraldeau 1997). The competitive patch exploitation game has recently been modeled as an n-person continuous strategy (i.e., a war of attrition) between foragers (Sjerps & Haccou 1994). If the patch contains a number of different prey types, then the foragers must also decide on the best possible combination of types, once again a problem that requires a game theoretic analysis. Finally, a common group foraging decision concerns whether to join the discoveries made by fellow group members. The decision has been associated with a game known as the producer–scrounger (PS) game (Barnard & Sibly 1981), which has been modeled specifically for a foraging system only recently (Vickery et al. 1991, Caraco & Giraldeau 1991).

In this chapter, we introduce readers to the general PS game, its application to a social foraging decision, and some results of experimental testing of the game's predictions. We first present two versions of the PS foraging game; one based on foraging rate maximization (Vickery et al. 1991), the other on shortfall minimization (i.e., risk-sensitive; Caraco & Giraldeau 1991). For each, we review the results of experimental tests of their predictions. In doing so, we pursue two goals: (1) to demonstrate that economic modeling within foraging theory extends beyond patch and prey decisions and (2) to show how game theoretic models can make novel, quantitative, and testable predictions concerning social foraging behavior.

2.3 Joining Other Individuals' Food Discoveries and the PS Game

When individuals search for food in a group, information about the location of a food patch soon spreads to other group members. Traditionally, group foraging behavior has been modeled as an information-sharing process that assumes that all group members search for food independently, and, upon discovery by one group member, all cease searching and move toward the successful individual to gain a share of the food (see, for instance, Clark & Mangel 1984, Mangel 1990, Ranta et al. 1993). This information-sharing scenario has been developed mostly as an evolutionary explanation for group foraging. Information-sharing models merely assume that individuals join all discoveries, but they do not examine whether it is profitable to do so. The question remains whether selection would maintain this high frequency of joining behavior within foraging groups. We propose to study joining as a foraging decision whose ecological determinants can be uncovered through modeling of its economic consequences. We assume that when a group member discovers food, all other group members decide whether they will partake of the discovery or continue searching for food.

Barnard and Sibly (1981) were the first to point out that joining conforms to an alternative-option scramble they called the PS game. The PS game is an n-person game (a scramble) because the outcome of any one play of the game depends on the composition of strategies within the group, not the strategy used by a single opponent. It is an alternative option game, because on any one play of the game the players have only one alternative, producer (P) or scrounger (S). In terms of group foraging, playing P means searching for food while never joining and S means never searching for food while always joining, when an opportunity arises. The proportion of the population playing P is q and the proportion playing S is $(1-q)$. The payoffs of both P and S alternatives are both a function of q: $W(q|P)$ and $W(q|S)$, respectively.

Parker (1984) also identified the ideal free distribution (IFD) as an n-person alternative option game when the decision involves the distribution of n consumers over two resource patches (when j patches are involved, it is an n-person j-option game). However, there are a number of fundamental distinctions between IFD and PS games that are worth pointing out here, if only to indicate the extra complexity of a PS game. In a PS game, the scrounger alternative only exists if there are individuals playing producer. Moreover, the initial value of playing S is not set, but depends on the number of individuals playing the alternative P. The more that play P, the greater the payoff for playing S, because of the greater rate of appearance of exploitation opportunities. In IFD, alternative patches (i.e., strategies) exist independently of whether they are used by any player; and their value is set by their basic suitability, not the number of players using the alternative. In both games the payoffs are negatively frequency-dependent (decrease with increasing frequency of players using the same alternative), but in the PS game, two factors contribute to the frequency-dependence of S payoffs: (1) the initial number of individuals playing the alternative P and (2) the number of competitors playing S. This "compound" frequency-dependence characterizes PS games and not IFD, where the value of any alternative depends only on the number of players using that alternative. In a PS game, the payoff of playing S is highest when playing P is common ($q \to 1$) and lowest when playing S is common ($q \to 0$; Parker 1984; Fig. 2.1). Although the PS game does not specify the details of the producer fitness function, in a foraging context the most likely scenario is that the function declines with increasing proportion of S within the population (Giraldeau et al. 1994b; Fig. 2.1).

In evolutionary terms, the game-theoretic foraging scenario for the PS game invokes some ancestral group with independently searching individuals (P). The first mutant that plays S can exploit the food discovered by all other group members. While group members playing P are constrained by their own intrinsic rate of patch encounter, the mutant S encounters patches much more quickly by exploiting every food patch that one of the P players finds. Because of the compound frequency-dependence that characterizes the payoff of playing S, as the S alternative spreads in the population, its payoff is negatively affected in two ways. First, as S gradually

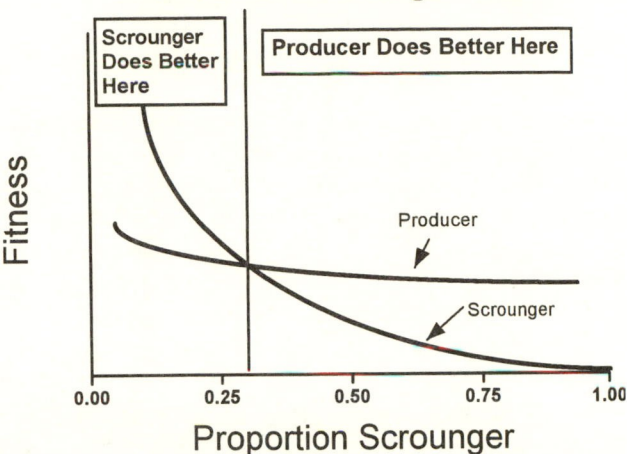

Fig. 2.1. The characteristic fitness functions of a Producer-scrounger game with a stable solution involving both alternatives (proportion of scroungers on x axis $= 1 - q$). The functions meet both conditions required for a mixed stable solution. Consequently, when the proportion of scrounger within a foraging group is low, the fitness of scrounger is higher than the fitness of producer. Conversely, when the proportion of scrounger is high, the fitness of scrounger is lower than the fitness of producer. Given these conditions, the lines will necessarily cross, and hence an equilibrium point exists. A disruption shifting the proportion of scrounger to the right of the equilibrium increases the success of the producer alternative, moving the proportion of scrounger back toward the equilibrium. If a disruption moves the proportion of scrounger to the left of the equilibrium, scrounger is favored and the proportion scrounger increases toward the point of equilibrium. The equilibrium, therefore, is stable. If selection causes the frequency of alternatives to change, the equilibrium is evolutionarily stable (ESS). However, if individuals adjust their use of alternatives through learning, then the equilibrium is developmentally stable (DSS).

replaces P, there are fewer individuals to exploit and the "basic suitability" of the S alternative declines. Second, as the frequency of S increases, each food patch must be shared with a greater number of S competitors. Of course, a population of pure S does very poorly, since no food is ever discovered. In a PS game, pure P can be stable under some conditions, but pure S is never stable. Assuming that all players have equal competitive abilities (i.e., that the game is symmetric), a PS game has an equilibrium solution with proportion $q^$ of P whenever

$$W(q^\wedge|P) = W(q^\wedge|S)$$

and

$$dW(q|P)/dq|_{q-q^\wedge} < dW(q|S)/dq|_{q-q^\wedge}$$

Both of the above conditions must hold if a PS game is to have a stable equilibrium solution (Parker 1984, Caraco & Giraldeau 1991; Fig. 2.1). This mixed solution can take several forms at the individual level (Fig. 2.2). The population may be (1) dimorphic—that is, composed of specialized P and S individuals, (2) monomorphic, wherein each individual plays P and S with probabilities $q^\wedge$ and $(1-q^\wedge)$, respectively, or (3) polymorphic, wherein each individual displays its own frequency of P and S, so long as within the population the average proportion of P corresponds to $q^\wedge$ (Parker 1984; but see Orzack & Sober 1994). It is important to make these alternative mixed solutions to the PS game explicit in order to avoid rejection of the game simply because the population is not dimorphic with respect to P and S roles.

The PS game, as most game models in behavioral ecology, was originally formulated in terms of selection acting on alternative genetic strategies whose solutions, therefore, were called evolutionarily stable strategies (ESS) (Maynard Smith 1982). However, fixed use of an alternative is unlikely in foraging games, where frequently changing conditions favor flexibility (Caraco & Giraldeau 1991). Adjustments of $q^\wedge$ within a group likely involve individual learning in response to the amount of rewards obtained through each foraging alternative. Learned solutions to games have been termed developmentally stable strategies (DSS; Dawkins 1980) or behavioral assessment ESSes (Davies 1982; see Stephens & Clements, this volume, for more on learning and game theory). I will use DSS when solutions to games are reached by learning. Despite some initial enthusiasm for the problem of optimal learning of equilibrium allocation to alternatives (Harley 1981, Regelmann 1984, Milinski 1984, Houston & Sumida 1987), there has been very little recent work devoted to studying how individuals reach a DSS.

2.4 A Rate Maximizing PS Foraging Game

In this section, we determine the conditions under which populations are expected to be pure P and then ask how changes in foraging conditions affect the expected equilibrium proportion of producer ($q^\wedge$). The model is a two-strategy version of Vickery et al.'s (1991) three-strategy PS foraging game (Giraldeau et al. 1994b). It applies to situations where several foragers can exploit the same food clump concurrently, as opposed to when individuals displace each other from food discoveries.

The hypothesized currency of fitness is the mean gross energy intake (I) measured over some time horizon T. The model's decision variable is a population's proportion of producer $q(0 \leq q < 1)$. We assume that the proportions with which individuals use P and S alternatives are learned, but do not specify the learning rule. The optimality criterion therefore is "developmental stability," which is equivalent to evolutionary stability but is expressed within a generation. Keep in mind that in contrast to conventional optimal foraging models, it is incorrect to predict that all

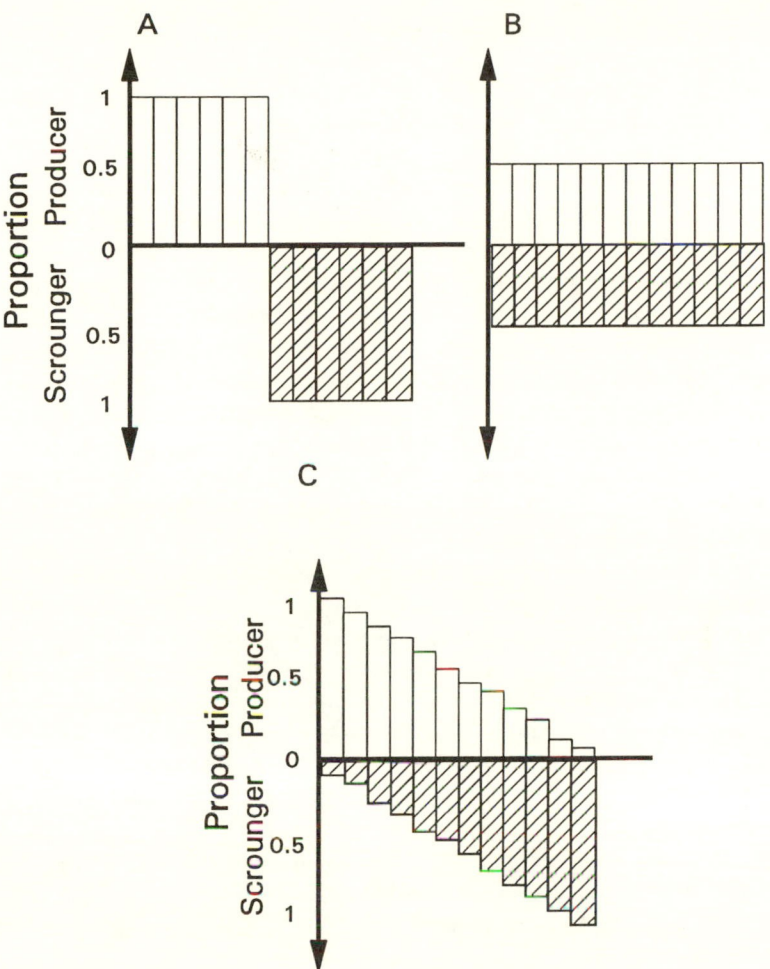

Fig. 2.2. Three theoretically possible frequency distributions of producer and scrounger alternatives within a group of twelve foragers when $q^\wedge = 0.5$. In A, the population is dimorphic with six individuals using only producer and six others using only scrounger. In this case, the frequency of individuals of one and the other type within the population must correspond to the ESS or DSS. In B, the population is monomorphic. Here all twelve individuals use both producer and scrounger alternatives in the same way. In a monomorphic population all individuals must be using frequencies of producer and scrounger that correspond to the ESS or DSS. In C, the population is polymorphic with each individual exhibiting its own combination of frequencies of producer and scrounger alternatives. As in A, the population frequency of producer and scrounger must correspond to the ESS or DSS.

individuals will use the DSS $q\wedge$. The prediction is that the population will exhibit $q\wedge$, and any combination of individual use of P and S that leads to $q\wedge$ at the population level is suitable (see Fig. 2.2). However, not all solutions may be equally stable (Crawford 1989) nor equally acceptable as evidence of adaptation (Orzack & Sober 1994).

A group of G individuals forages such that the $\mathbf{G_S} = (1 - q)G$ individuals playing S always detect and exploit all of the food clumps uncovered by the $\mathbf{G_P} = qG$ individuals playing P. (Note that G here represents the number of individuals maintaining sensory contact; in reality this may be a subset of an actual foraging group). This assumes that the qG foragers search for patches independently, that the time required to encounter patches is long relative to patch exploitation time, and that patches are never exploited concurrently (violations to these assumptions have little qualitative effect.) All food patches contain F items, each of which is eaten whole and cannot be shared. Upon discovering a patch, a P player always obtains a (where $0 \leq a < F$) items for its exclusive use. The term a is referred to as the finder's advantage (Vickery et al. 1991). The mechanism causing a is unspecified by the model but could involve a delay between the actual discovery of the food by P and arrival of the $\mathbf{G_S}$ individuals (Giraldeau et al. 1990). The term a can also reflect some form of positional advantage gained by P that is unaffected by $\mathbf{G_S}$ (Ward & Enders 1985), or a can also be seen as the solution of another game between P and S players. For instance, the time taken by the $\mathbf{G_S}$ individuals to reach the patch may depend on average interindividual distances. This distance may be a compromise between P players trying to be as far away as possible from S players and S players responding by trying to keep an equal distance between themselves and all P players, any one of which may be the next food finder. In any case, here we treat a as a parameter of the game rather than as a decision variable.

Once a P player finds a clump, the $\mathbf{G}$ scroungers arrive in unison. The remaining food ($A = F - a$) is then shared equally among the $n = \mathbf{G_S} + 1$ individuals at the patch. The producer's expected intake (I_P) after T time units of foraging is

$$I_P = \lambda T(a + A/n) \tag{1}$$

where λ is the producer's encounter rate with food patches. The rate of encounter with joining opportunities is a function only of the number of individuals currently playing P. The expected intake of scrounger I_S over some time horizon T is

$$I_S = \lambda qGTA/n \tag{2}$$

where $q\wedge$ can be found by setting I_P equal to I_S and solving for $q\wedge$, which gives

$$a/F + 1/G = q\wedge \tag{3}$$

Note that λqGT, the corporate rate of patch encounter by the $\mathbf{G_P}$ individuals, drops out completely from the solution. This is because the model assumes that the $\mathbf{G_S}$ individuals have no effect on the rate of encounter with patches experienced by individuals playing P. Under those conditions, $1 - q\wedge$, the proportion of the population using scrounger is entirely independent of the rate at which joining opportunities

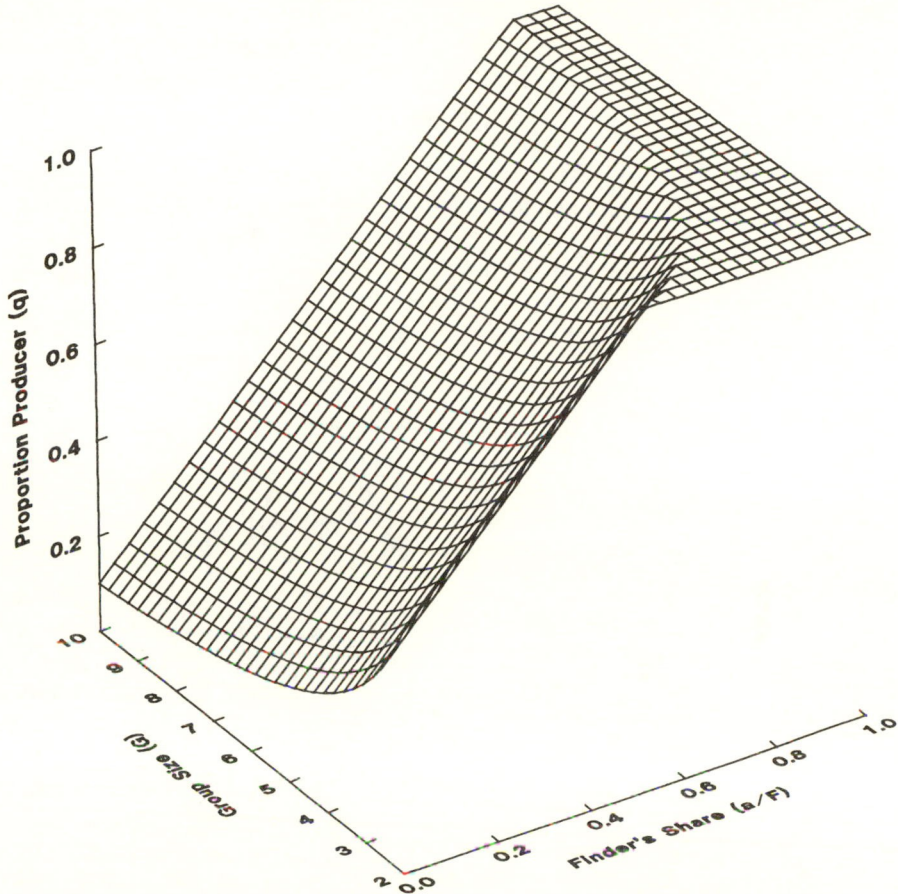

Fig. 2.3. The surface predicting the stable proportion of producer using a two-strategy version of Vickery et al.'s (1991) deterministic rate-maximizing PS game. The proportion of producer increases with the finder's share but decreases with increasing group size. The flat portion on the top righthand side is the producer-only surface where no scrounger could economically exist. At small group sizes, all producer is possible for a wide range of finder's shares. However, as group size increases, the range shrinks of finder's shares for which producer only is stable.

become available. Thus, the proportion using P, and consequently the proportion using S, are predicted to have only two determinants, group size (G) and the finder's share [a/F; equation (3)].

Figure 2.3 depicts how the equilibrium proportion of producer ($q^\wedge$) is affected by the finder's share and group size. The area of the graph for which $q^\wedge = 1$ is the P-only surface. The greater the P-only surface, the greater the range of conditions under which pure P is a DSS. Note that the P-only surface is larger for small G and shrinks with increasing G. This is because as G increases, an individual playing P must monopolize an increasingly large fraction of the patch (a/F) in order to prevent S from providing an economic advantage. It means, for instance, that in a situation where an individual forages with two partners (i.e., $G = 3$), pure P will be a DSS if it could obtain 2/3 or more of the items in the clumps before the arrival of scroungers. For $G = 10$, the fraction increases to 9/10 or more, making it increasingly unlikely to observe pure P as G increases (Vickery et al. 1991).

When formalized as a foraging model, the rate-maximizing PS game makes a number of testable quantitative predictions concerning the extent to which the use of S should be common within foraging groups. In the next sections we look at whether the dynamics of payoffs in the flock-feeding context conform to the compound frequency-dependence required of a PS game. Furthermore, we review the results of an experimental test of whether the proportion of producer within flocks corresponds to proportions expected on the basis of the finder's share [equation (3)].

2.4.1 Testing the Rate-Maximizing PS Foraging Game in a Flock-Feeding Situation

2.4.1.1 Evidence of Compound Negative Frequency-Dependence of Scrounger Payoff

Barnard and Sibly (1981), who first proposed the PS game to account for the flock-feeding behavior of house sparrows (*Passer domesticus*), provided very little experimental evidence that the payoff to S had the characteristic compound negative-frequency dependence required of a PS game. In fact, they noted that S did worst of all when P was most common, the very condition under which S should have done the best.

A rate-maximizing PS game would apply to joining in the context of flock feeding only if joining provides payoffs that are characteristic of those expected by playing S—that is, if $I_S > I_P$ when P is common and $I_S < I_P$ when S is common (Fig. 2.1). An empirical investigation of these conditions in the context of flock feeding would be relatively simple if individuals had unchanging allocation of P and S alternatives, as would be expected by genetic determination of strategies. However, because in most foraging cases we expect that individuals will adjust their use to P and S in order to maximize payoffs, the experimental demonstration becomes problematic. If populations achieve a DSS, then it will be difficult to create a foraging group where excess use of S or P persists long enough to allow for a convincing demonstration that the conditions of a PS game apply. The solution involves coercing individual group members into using uneconomical combinations of P and S alternatives.

The practical problem was resolved at least in part by Giraldeau et al. (1994b) using captive flocks of spice finches (*Lonchura punctulata*), a small, southeast Asian estrildid. By hiding millet seeds under covered wells on a grid, they created a situation where only individuals that had been pretrained to lift lids could find food and hence play P. Other, nontrained individuals could only obtain their food by joining at a discovered patch, hence using S. Giraldeau et al. (1994b) formed "core" flocks characterized by two different proportions of potential P and S individuals: Flock S contained four untrained individuals and Flock P contained four pretrained lid lifters. They observed the behavior of pairs of test subjects, one pretrained the other not, when added to one and then the other core flocks. Hence, in Flock S they expected $q = 0.17$, because one individual would always play P and the five others would play

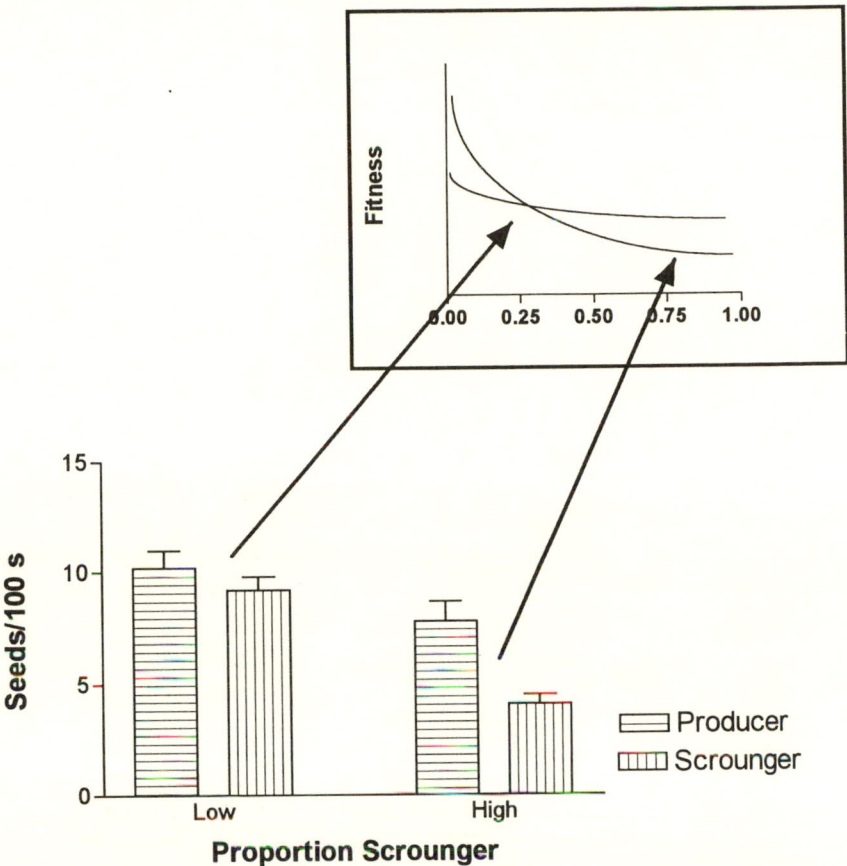

Fig. 2.4. Experimental evidence (histogram) of the frequency-dependence of the scrounger payoff using small flocks of spice finches *(Lonchura punctulata)* compared to expectations of the PS game (inset). When the proportion of scrounger within a flock increased, mean seed intake of all foragers declined, as expected by the PS game. When proportion of scrounger was high, the intake of scrounger was lower than the intake of producer, again as expected by the PS game. However, when proportion of scrounger was low, scrounger did not do better than producer, unlike predictions of the PS game. (Modified from Giraldeau et al. 1994b.)

S. In Flock P they expected $q = 0.83$, because now five individuals were pretrained to play P and only one would play S. If flock feeding in spice finches conforms to a PS game, then I_S was expected to be greater than I_P in Flock P and smaller in Flock S ($I_S > I_P$ in Flock P and $I_S < I_P$ in Flock S).

Giraldeau et al.'s (1994b) results (Fig. 2.4) are only partly consistent with the conclusion that flock feeding allows for the negative frequency-dependence of payoffs, expressed as intake over time, that characterizes a PS game. In the Flock-S condition, playing S provides a significantly lower intake than playing P ($I_S < I_P$). Moreover, when q decreases (i.e., from Flock P to Flock S), the intake of playing both P and S declines significantly and the decline appears more abrupt for individuals coerced into playing S (Fig. 2.4). However, in Flock P the payoffs of playing S are not significantly different from those obtained by playing P. The PS game model predicts that playing S would have done better than playing P in that flock.

Giraldeau et al. (1994b) argued that playing S failed to provide higher payoffs than playing P within Flock P, because, in that specific condition, their methods of coercing finches into the P role failed. Not knowing how to discover food can effectively force an individual into the scrounger role, but knowing how to find food cannot constrain it to playing only producer. Only P individuals (i.e., pretrained lid-lifters) in the Flock-P condition had access to both P and S foraging alternatives. Giraldeau et al. (1994b) noticed that in Flock P, the P individuals obtained an average of 35% of their food through scrounging. Consequently, the P individuals who should have done worse than the S individual when in Flock P increased their use of S, at least to a point where I_S and I_P become statistically indistinguishable, an outcome that is entirely consistent with a DSS solution to a PS game. Giraldeau et al. (1994b) concluded, therefore, that the dynamics of food rewards in a flock-feeding context are compatible with the requirements of a PS game model. If they are correct, then it should be possible to alter each individual's use of P and S roles by changing the foraging conditions. This is the subject of the next section.

2.4.1.2 Testing Predictions of the Rate-Maximizing PS Game

The rate-maximizing PS game predicts that the observed proportion of P, for a given finder's share, is an inverse function of group size. Conversely, the model predicts that for a given group size, the proportion of producer increases as a function of the finder's share. Earlier work on spice finches (Giraldeau et al. 1990) suggested that the finder's share was related to the extent of food patchiness. We took advantage of this to test the rate-maximizing model while observing the P and S behavior of individuals in three flocks of five spice finches while they foraged on a grid that always contained 200 seeds presented under either high, medium, or low patchiness conditions (10, 20, and 40 patches, respectively).

We allowed a flock to feed under one condition five times a day for six consecutive days. Then, we changed patchiness and continued the procedure until all three conditions had been tested for each flock. In all cases, we found that the finder's share (a/F) varied according to patchiness, as anticipated from Giraldeau et al.'s (1990) results. Our results and the predicted $q^\wedge$ are reported in Fig. 2.5. Clearly, all three flocks showed low proportions of producer on the first day of experiments. In all three flocks, however, the proportion playing P moved toward the rate-maximizing PS game's predictions. Note that changing the order of presentation of patchiness condition actually altered the directional change in the proportion of producer within the flocks (Fig. 2.5).

It is important to understand the behavioral mechanism through which individuals manage to alter their use of alternatives. One way in which the proportion of P could have been varied within flocks is if individuals adjusted their tendency to join the discoveries of others. By resisting joining, for instance, a bird increases its chances of finding food itself and hence invests more into the P alternative. The

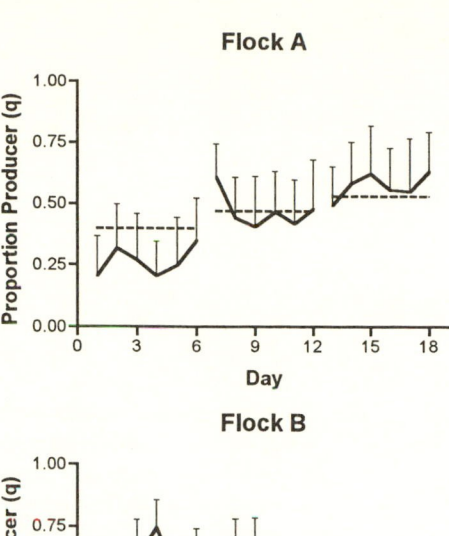

Flock A

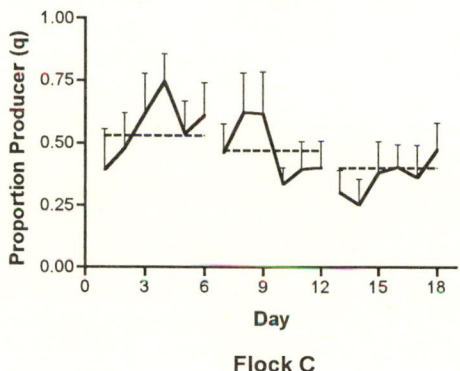

Flock B

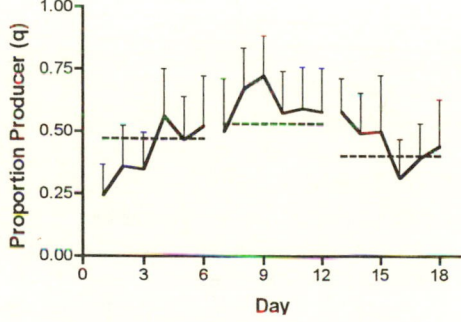

Flock C

Fig. 2.5. The mean ($+$ SEM) observed proportion of producer (solid line) within three flocks of five spice finches foraging on three levels of food patchiness compared to predictions (dashed line) of the mean rate–maximizing PS game. The flocks were tested five times a day for six consecutive days on each patchiness condition. Patchiness levels were low (200 seeds in 10 patches), medium (200 seeds in 20 patches), and high (200 seeds in 40 patches). The effect of patchiness on proportion-using producer was highly significant.

consequence is that the group's proportional use of P increases. Other mechanisms based on adjustments in perceptual distance have also been suggested (Ruxton et al. 1995; but see Beauchamp and Giraldeau 1996). Future work should establish whether all individuals respond similarly to changes in finder's share or whether just a few individuals alter their use of P and S.

2.5 A Shortfall-Minimizing PS Game

The rate-maximizing model presented above hypothesizes that fitness increases linearly with rate of food intake. For some foraging situations this assumption may be unrealistic, since an animal's fitness may not continue to increase once it has obtained enough food to survive to the next foraging bout (Caraco et al. 1980, Stephens 1981). In nonreproductive seasons, maximum fitness can be achieved merely by avoiding an energetic shortfall (Stephens 1981). The probability of an energetic shortfall is a function of both the mean and the variance of payoffs. Fitness in energy shortfall models can be strongly affected by variance in payoffs. For instance, when faced with more and less variable alternatives that provide the same mean payoffs, the probability of an energetic shortfall will be minimized by choosing the variable alternative when requirements are larger than the mean payoffs, but by choosing the less variable alternative when requirements are below the mean payoffs (Fig. 2.6). In both cases the animals should be risk-sensitive (respond to differences in variance), and they are termed risk-prone in the former and risk-averse in the latter case.

Risk sensitivity may be a central concern to group foraging animals because a number of hypotheses claim that the adaptive value of group foraging itself is to provide its members with a reduced foraging risk (i.e., a lower variance in food intake; Thompson et al. 1974, Caraco 1981, Caraco 1987, Ruxton et al. 1995). A PS game based on minimization of the probability of an energetic shortfall has been presented by Caraco and Giraldeau (1991). The shortfall-minimizing game makes many of the same assumptions as the rate-maximizing game presented above. The major differences are the currency of fitness, that foraging is assumed to occur in a stochastic rather than deterministic environment, and that the use of the scrounger strategy entails an energetic cost r. Caraco and Giraldeau (1991) have provided a number of variants of the shortfall-minimization game, but here we will present only one version and refer readers to the original article for details on other variants.

Caraco and Giraldeau (1991) model foraging in a stochastic environment assuming that fitness is maximized by minimization of the probability of obtaining less than some physiological requirement R. In their model they assume that P has higher variance (i.e., is more risky) in rewards than S. So, if both S and P provided equal mean rewards, a risk-prone forager would prefer to use P while a risk-averse forager would prefer S. They assume that patch encounter by a producer is random and occurs at rate λ, so that the number of patches discovered by a producer over a time horizon T, $Y_i(T)$, is Poisson-distributed with expectation λT. They also assume that each of the c indivisible items in a food clump is competed for independently. The producer's probability of obtaining an item is θ $(0 \leq \theta \leq 1)$ and the probability that an item goes to the scroungers is $1 - \theta$. The number of items obtained from a clump by a producer, therefore, is a binomial process with expectation θc. If no group

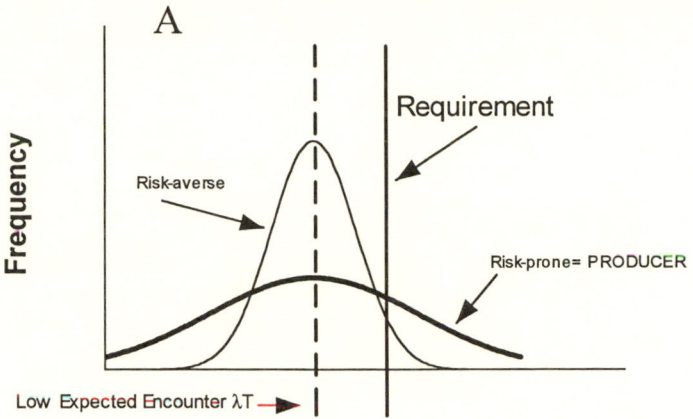

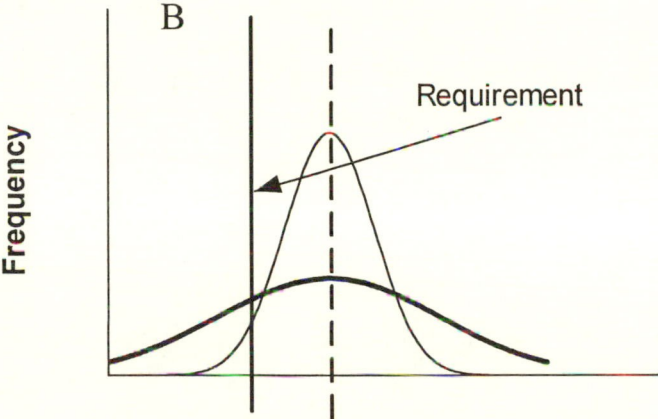

Fig. 2.6. A graphical representation of risk-sensitivity in the context of energy shortfall minimization for two foraging alternatives that offer the same mean but different variance in payoffs. In A, the physiological requirement is higher than the mean payoffs provided by the alternatives. The forager minimizes its chances of an energetic shortfall by being risk-prone and preferring the more variable alternative. In B, the physiological requirement is below the mean payoffs provided by the alternatives. In that case, the forager minimizes its probability of a shortfall by being risk-averse and preferring the less variable alternative.

member plays S (i.e., $\mathbf{G_S}=0$), then an individual playing P obtains all the c items of a clump with certainty. Once $\mathbf{G_S} \geq 1$, the number of food items obtained by playing P is independent of $\mathbf{G_S}$ and depends only on θ. This assumes that the producer gains some advantage, possibly positional or social, over the scrounger that cannot be altered by a scrounger. For each individual playing S, however, the probability of gaining the food item is $(1 - \theta)/\mathbf{G_S}$.

The total number of items eaten $(X_i(T))$ by the ith individual playing P follows a "Poisson-binomial" probability function whose mean and variance are, respectively,

$$E[X_i(T)] = \theta c \lambda T$$

$$V[X_i(T)] = \theta c \lambda T (1 - \theta + \theta c)$$

The animal suffers an energetic shortfall if $E[X_i(T)] < R$. Assuming that $\theta c \lambda T$ is large enough, Caraco and Giraldeau (1991) use a normal approximation and express the probability of an energetic shortfall $\Pr[X_i(T) \leq R]$ using a standardized normal approximation $\Phi(z_P)$, where z_P is

$$z_P = (R - \theta c \lambda T) / \{ \theta c \lambda T (1 - \theta + \theta c) \}^{1/2} \tag{4}$$

Any increase in z_P increases the probability of an energetic shortfall. Hence, the lower the z_P, the greater the producer's fitness.

A similar process characterizes the payoffs to playing S. All $\mathbf{G_S}$ individuals attend each clump discovered by the $\mathbf{G_P}$ individuals. The total number of clumps produced, $Y(T)$, is also Poisson-distributed with expectation $\mathbf{G_P}\lambda T$. Similarly, the number of seeds obtained from each clump by the jth scrounger is binomially distributed. Consequently, the scrounger's payoff is also a Poisson-binomial probability function with respective mean and variance

$$E[X_j(T)] = (1 - \theta) c G_P \lambda T / G_S$$

$$V[X_j(T)] = ((1 - \theta) c G_P \lambda T / G_S)(1 - (1 - \theta/G_S) + ((1 - \theta) c / G_S)) \tag{5}$$

Again, the scrounger's probability of an energetic shortfall $\Pr[X_j(T) \leq R + \rho]$ (recall that ρ is the cost of using S) can be calculated using a standardized normal approximation $\Phi(z_P)$, where z_S is

$$z_s = (R + \rho - \{(1 - \theta) c G_P \lambda T) / G_S\} / \{ V[X_j(T)] \}^{1/2} \tag{6}$$

Here too, minimizing z_S minimizes the probability of an energetic shortfall, so that fitness of playing S increases with decreasing z_S. The variance term can be simplified by assuming that the number of items within a clump (c) grows large so that scroungers get most of the food in the clump (i.e., $\theta << (1 - \theta) c$). In that case the variance approaches $G_P \lambda T \{(1 - \theta) c / G_S\}^2$; and, by substitution of this expression in equation (6), the stability condition for pure producer $(G_P = G; z_P(G_P = G) < z_S(G_S = 1))$ becomes

$$R[(1 - \theta) G_P^{1/2} - 1] + (1 - \theta) c \lambda T - (G_P - G_P^{1/2}) < \rho \tag{7}$$

The Nash equilibrium solution to the game (i.e., the frequency of strategies for which no unilateral deviation can be profitable) is considered the ESS or the DSS in the present context (Caraco & Giraldeau 1991). The equilibrium corresponds to combinations of P and S such that the probability of an energetic shortfall is equal for both P and S players and no player can benefit from its unilateral change in use of P and S. Note that this equilibrium can occur at scrounger frequencies where no player expects to meet its requirement. In that case, presumably, group foragers disband (Caraco & Giraldeau 1991).

Using the above inequality, Caraco and Giraldeau (1991) predict that the proportion of scrounger $(1-q)$ will be small or zero when the cost of scrounging (ρ) and/or the producer's priority (θ) are high, group size (G) is small, and the expected number of patch encounters by producers (λT) is low. Keeping all other parameters constant, the proportion of individuals using scrounger is predicted to increase with expected number of encountered patches (θT). The effect of physiological requirement (R) depends on group size and the extent of producer priority (θ). When producer has a competitive advantage—that is, if $\theta > 1 - (G-1)^{-1/2}$—then the proportion of scroungers should decrease with increasing requirement. When the producer's priority is low—that is, when $\theta < 1 - (G-1)^{-1/2}$—then the proportion of scrounger should increase with increasing requirement.

The predictions can be explained verbally. Increases in expected patch encounter makes it more likely that the physiological requirement will be exceeded. In that case, it pays to be risk-averse (reduce variance) and hence increase the use of the risk-averse scrounger alternative (Fig. 2.6). When requirement increases, foragers are more likely not to meet the physiological requirement. In that case, risk-proneness is more profitable because it increases the probability of meeting the requirement. So, since producer is more risky, the model predicts that P will be used more (and hence S less) when requirement increases. When the producer's priority is low, however, playing P pays so little that as requirement increases, foragers should increase their use of scrounger despite its risk-averse character. The effect is then driven by the large difference in the mean reward that swamps any advantage gained through variance.

2.5.1 Testing Prediction of the Shortfall-Minimizing PS Foraging Game

Experimental tests of the shortfall-minimizing PS game were conducted using flocks of wild-caught starlings (*Sturnus vulgaris*) by Koops (1993; reported in Koops & Giraldeau 1996). Koops (1993) tested two predictions of the risk-sensitive model, namely, whether the proportional use of scrounger increases with increasing number of expected patch encounters (λT) and whether, for a given group size, increased food requirement causes the proportional use of scrounger to change with the extent of the producer's priority.

2.5.1.1 The Effect of Expected Patch Encounter

Koops' starlings foraged in flocks of seven. Each flock was composed of five unchanging core members whose behavior was not recorded and two test subjects added to the core for the duration of a treatment. A total of eight subjects were so tested in a repeated-measures design where they experienced a low and a high expected patch encounter. A flock foraged on an array of 15 patches placed in a checkerboard pattern on the floor of an indoor aviary. A starling used P when it probed in a patch that no other starling was standing on and S when it displaced a resident from a patch.

Koops (1993) manipulated the expected number of encountered patches (λT) by changing the total number of food-containing patches available to the birds while keeping the duration of foraging trials as constant as possible. In the Low Encounter treatment, only 5/15 patches contained food, while in the High Encounter treatment, 10/15 patches contained food. The duration of trials did not differ between treatments. As predicted by Caraco and Giraldeau's (1991) shortfall-minimization PS game, the proportional use of scrounger significantly increased from Low to High Encounter treatments (Fig. 2.7A). Furthermore, 8/8 test starlings changed their proportional use of scrounger in the predicted direction (Fig. 2.7B). The model was therefore successful in qualitatively predicting the effect of expected patch number on the proportional use of scrounger by starlings.

2.5.1.2 The Effect of Future Food Requirement

Koops (1993) did not manipulate the physiological requirement of starlings as defined by the shortfall-minimizing model. Such a manipulation would have required, for instance, altering ambient temperature (Caraco et al. 1990) or the reproductive condition of the birds. Instead, by altering the level of food deprivation, he manipulated the amount of food that the animal required in the future to achieve a positive energy balance by the end of the foraging day. Once again, eight test starlings were added in pairs to core flocks of five individuals experiencing either a low (4-hour deprivation) or a high (18-hour deprivation) requirement. Preliminary measures indicated that starlings should expect a positive energy budget in the low-R treatment but a negative budget in the High-R treatment.

Since Koops (1993) always used groups of seven starlings, the critical value of θ for which the directional effect of requirement is expected to change is 0.59 ($= 1 - 6^{-1/2}$). Koops' (1993) estimate of producer priority was $\theta = 0.42$ in both treatments, a value that is significantly lower than the critical $\theta = 0.59$. The producers, therefore, lacked a competitive advantage, and as such, the model predicts that scrounging should increase with increasing requirement.

As predicted by the game, scrounging increased as requirement increased, but only slightly and insignificantly (Fig. 2.7C). However, 7/8 starlings shifted their proportional use of scrounger in the predicted direction, indicating that, although the quantitative effect of requirement on the proportional use of scrounger was weak, it was significantly consistent (Fig. 2.7D). Koops' (1993) experimental results provide qualitative support for both predictions of the shortfall minimizing PS foraging game.

2.6 Conclusions

In this chapter, we presented two distinct versions of the PS game to group foraging situations. In both cases, the models made testable predictions, which were supported, at least qualitatively, by experimental tests. In one case, spice finch foraging was consistent with rate-maximization; individuals adjusted their joining in response to food patchiness as the rate-maximizing PS game predicted. In the other case, starling

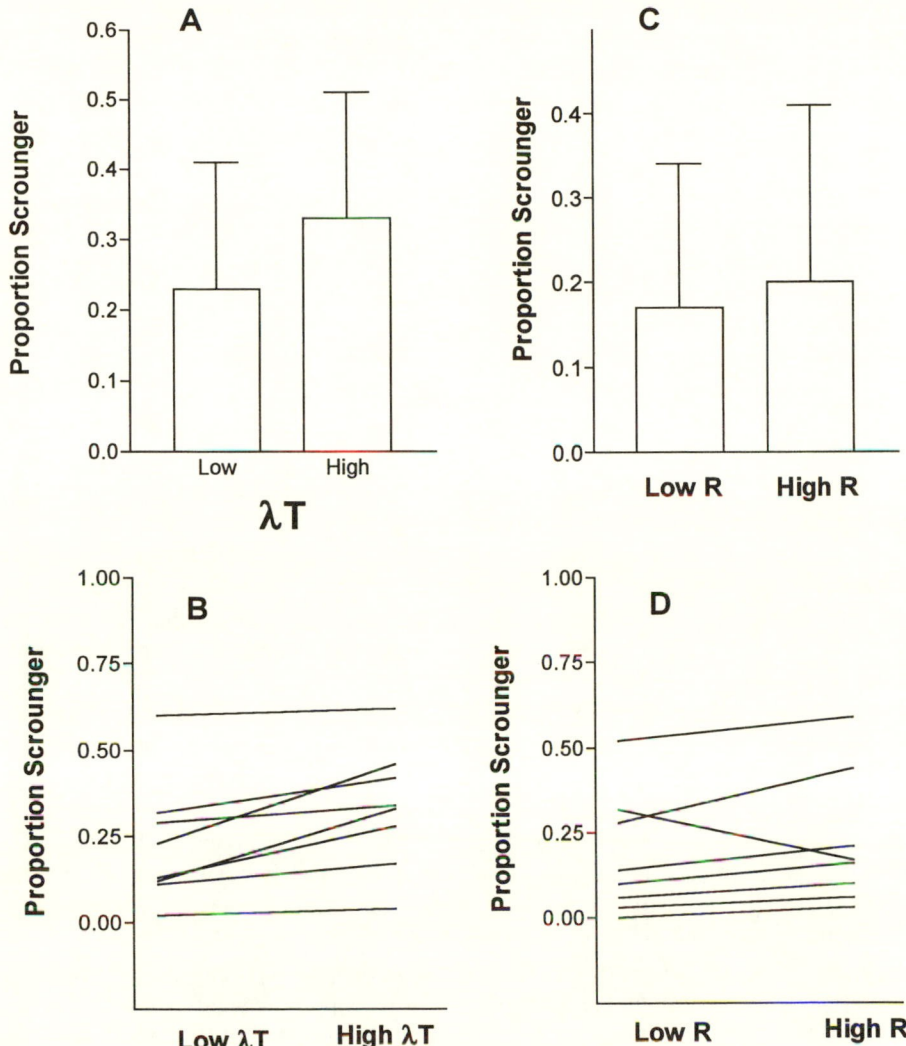

Fig. 2.7. Results of Koops & Giraldeau's 1996 experimental tests of two of the risk-sensitive producer-scrounger game's predictions using flocks of starlings *(Sturnus vulgaris)*. In A, the mean (+ SD) proportional use of the scrounger strategy increases as the expected number of encountered patches (λT) increases. In B, all eight subjects increased their mean proportional use of scrounger as λT increased. In C, the mean (+ SD) proportional use of scrounger increases with increasing requirement (R), but the change is not statistically significant. In D, seven of the eight subjects increased their mean proportional use of scrounger when R increased.

foraging was consistent with shortfall minimization; individuals adjusted their joining in response both to expected patch encounter and food requirement. Our goal here is not to discuss the validity of the experimental tests. However, it is promising to consider that applications of the first two economic models of joining decisions have been successful, suggesting that more research should be devoted to this social foraging decision.

The questions that remain, naturally, are quite numerous and all have the advantage of taking the research in foraging-related matters into a totally new direction. For instance, both games assume that joining opportunities arise as a linear function of the number of individuals playing P. This assumption may be too simplistic if producers interfere with each other, as was found in greenfinches (Hake & Ekman 1988). Moreover, our models assume that individuals playing S arrive as a unit (Beauchamp and Giraldeau 1997). In fact, it is possible that the order of arrival at a discovered food patch depends on position within the group. This possibility implies that work on flock geometry, which to date has focused mostly on predation pressure (Bekoff 1995, Caraco & Bayham 1982), should also include foraging considerations. Furthermore, the way in which food discoveries are divided up among finders and joiners is a critical element in both models. More scrutiny, therefore, must be given to the way group foragers divide their prey or patches. Finally, solid experimental evidence that group feeding actually generates the "compound" frequency-dependence of PS games is still lacking, whether for rate-maximizing or shortfall minimizing games.

The initial success of the PS models also raises a number of questions for more mechanistically oriented researchers. For instance, if one considers that the payoffs in a PS game are frequency-dependent, then learning the appropriate allocation appears to be a daunting task, especially as group size increases. Whenever one individual changes its allocation to P and S, the payoffs to P and S are changed for all other players. What learning rule do group foraging animals use to achieve a DSS in a PS game? Are all foragers equally flexible in their use of alternatives or are only some individuals learning the economical allocation to alternatives? What is certain, however, is that groups of foragers can no longer be portrayed as a collection of individuals independently searching for food and joining opportunistically in each other's discoveries, as is often implied by information-sharing models of group foraging (Clark & Mangel 1984; but see Ranta et al. 1993). It should be clear now that the joining decision, like other foraging decisions, is not preset but is, instead, adjusted to the local foraging conditions.

The results also suggest that foraging systems offer a productive experimental device for testing game models. For instance, consider that the PS game was originally defined in 1981 (Barnard & Sibly 1981). Only three years later, it had already been identified as applicable to a wide number of behavioral systems including cooperative breeding (Vehrencamp 1984), surreptitious matings (Arak 1984), and the evolution of anisogamy (Parker 1984), to name a few. Yet, it was not until the model was adapted to specific social foraging scenarios (Vickery et al. 1991, Caraco & Giraldeau 1991) that it finally generated experimental tests (Koops & Giraldeau 1996; Giraldeau et al. 1994b). If group foraging generates the payoff dynamics that correspond to a PS game, then PS games can be tested using foraging systems. Since foraging is generally more common than say mating or fighting, application of game models to foraging situations may lead to a rapid increase in game theoretic research and tests.

We hope to have demonstrated that application of the appropriate economic modeling techniques (i.e., games; Mesterton-Gibbons 1991) can structure a productive research program in the area of social foraging, much as simple optimality has done for patch and prey models within conventional foraging theory. Social foraging theory offers (a) opportunities for game-theoretic modelers, (b) models for empiricists eager to test new predictions, and (c) a welcome complement to the current body of knowledge derived from conventional foraging theory. Ultimately, it is through the development of social foraging that foraging theory will likely provide the answers to questions raised by the population ecologists who created it.

ACKNOWLEDGMENTS   This research was funded through a Natural Science and Engineering Research Council (Canada) Research Grant. B.L. was supported by a Fyssen Foundation Postdoctoral Fellowship. We thank Guy Beauchamp, Lee Dugatkin, James Grant, David Stephens, and Jeff Lucas for comments.

References

Arak A. 1984. Sneaky breeders. In *Producers and Scroungers, Strategies of Exploitation and Parasitism,* C. J. Barnard, ed., pp. 154–194. London: Croom Helm.

Barnard C. J. & Sibly R. M. 1981. Producers and scroungers: A general model and its application to captive flocks of house sparrows. *Anim. Behav.,* 29, 543–550.

Beauchamp G. & Giraldeau L.-A. 1996. Group foraging revisited: information-sharing or producer-scrounger game. *Am. Nat.* 148, 738–743.

Beauchamp G. & Giraldeau L.-A. 1997. Patch exploitation in a producer-scrounger system: test of a hypothesis using flocks of spice finches (*Lonchura punctulata*). *Behav. Ecol.,* 8, 54–59.

Bekoff M. 1995. Vigilance, flock size, and flock geometry: Information gathering by western evening grosbeaks (Aves, Fringillidae). *Ethology,* 99, 150–161.

Caraco T. 1981. Risk-sensitivity and foraging groups. *Ecology,* 62, 527–531.

Caraco T. 1987. Foraging games in a random environment. In *Foraging Behavior,* A. C. Kamil, J. R. Krebs, & H. R. Pulliam, eds., pp. 389–414. New York: Plenum Press.

Caraco T., Martindale S. & Whitham T. S. 1980. An empirical demonstration of risk-sensitive foraging preferences. *Anim. Behav.,* 28, 820–830.

Caraco T. & Bayham M. C. 1982. Some geometric aspects of house sparrow flocks. *Anim. Behav.,* 30, 990–996.

Caraco T., Blanckenhorn W. U., Gregory G. M., Newman J. A., Recer J. A. & Zwicker S. M. 1990. Risk-sensitivity: Ambient temperature affects foraging choice. *Anim. Behav.,* 39, 338–345.

Caraco T. & Giraldeau L.-A. 1991. Social foraging: Producing and scrounging in a stochastic environment. *J. Theor. Biol.,* 153, 559–583.

Clark C. W. & Mangel M. 1984. Foraging and flocking strategies: Information in an uncertain environment. *Am. Nat.,* 123, 626–641.

Crawford V. P. 1989. Learning and mixed-strategy equilibria in evolutionary games. *J. Theor. Biol.,* 140, 537–550.

Davies N. B. 1982. Behaviour and competition for scarce resources. In *Current Problems in Sociobiology,* King's College Sociobiology Group, ed., pp. 363–380. New York: Cambridge University Press.

Dawkins R. 1980. Good strategy or evolutionarily stable strategy? In *Sociobiology: Beyond Nature/Nurture? Reports, Definitions and Debate,* G. W. Barlow & D. Silverberg, ed. AAAS Selected Symposium, Volume 35, pp. 331–367. Boulder: Westview Press.

Fretwell S. D. 1972. *Populations in a Seasonal Environment.* Princeton, NJ: Princeton University Press.

Giraldeau L.-A. 1988. The stable group and the determinants of foraging group size. In *The Ecology of Social Behavior,* C. N. Slobodchikoff, ed., pp. 33–53. New York: Academic Press.

Giraldeau L.-A., Hogan J. A. & Clinchy M. J. 1990. The payoffs to producing and scrounging: What happens when patches are divisible? *Ethology,* 85, 132–146.

Giraldeau L.-A., Caraco T. & Valone T. 1994a. Social foraging: Individual learning and cultural transmission of innovations. *Behav. Ecol.,* 5, 35–43.

Giraldeau L.-A., Soos C. & Beauchamp G. 1994b. A test of the producer–scrounger foraging game in captive flocks of spice finches, *Lonchura punctulata. Behav. Ecol. Sociobiol.,* 34, 251–256.

Hake M. & Ekman J. 1988. Finding and sharing depletable patches: When group foraging decreases intake rates. *Ornis Scand.,* 19, 275–279.

Harley C. H. 1981. Learning the evolutionarily stable strategy. *J. Theor. Biol.,* 89, 611–633.

Houston A. & Sumida B. 1987. Learning rules, matching and frequency dependence. *J. Theor. Biol.,* 126, 289–308.

Koops M. 1993. Testing Predictions of a Risk-Sensitive Scrounging Model Using European Starlings. M.Sc. thesis. Montréal: Concordia University.

Koops M. & Giraldeau L.-A. 1996. Producer–scrounger foraging games in starlings: A test of mean-maximizing and risk-minimizing foraging models. *Anim. Behav.,* 51, 773–783.

Livoreil B. & Giraldeau L. A. 1997. Patch departure decisions by spice finches foraging singly or in groups. *Anim. Behav.,* in press.

MacArthur R. H. & Pianka E. R. 1966. On the optimal use of a patchy environment. *Am. Nat.,* 100, 603–609.

Mangel M. 1990. Resource divisibility, predation and group formation. *Anim. Behav.,* 39, 1163–1172.

Maynard Smith J. 1982. *Evolution and the Theory of Games.* Cambridge: Cambridge University Press.

Mesterton-Gibbons M. 1991. *An Introduction to Game-Theoretic Modelling.* Redwood City, CA: Addison-Wesley.

Milinski M. 1984. Competitive resource sharing: An experimental test of a learning rule for ESSs. *Anim. Behav.,* 32, 233–242.

Milinski M. & Parker G. A. 1991. Competition for resources. In *Behavioural Ecology: An Evolutionary Approach,* third edition, J. R. Krebs & N. B. Davies, eds., pp. 137–168. Oxford: Blackwell Scientific Publications.

Orzack S. H. & Sober E. 1994. How (not) to test an optimality model. *TREE,* 9, 265–267.

Parker G. A. 1978. Searching for mates. In *Behavioural Ecology: An Evolutionary Approach,* J. R. Krebs & N. B. Davies, eds., pp. 214–244. Sunderland, MA: Sinauer Associates.

Parker G. A. 1984. The producer/scrounger model and its relevance to sexuality. In *Producers and Scroungers: Strategies of Exploitation and Parasitism,* C. J. Barnard, ed., pp. 127–153. London: Croom Helm.

Pulliam H. R. & Caraco T. 1984. Living in groups: Is there an optimal group size? In: *Behavioural Ecology: An Evolutionary Approach,* second edition, J. R. Krebs & N. B. Davies, eds., pp. 122–147. Sunderland, MA: Sinauer Associates.

Ranta E., Rita H. & Lindström K. 1993. Competition versus cooperation: Success of individuals foraging alone and in groups. *Am. Nat.,* 142, 42–58.

Regelmann K. 1984. Competitive resource sharing: A simulation model. *Anim. Behav.,* 32, 226–232.

Ruxton G. D., Hall S. J. & Gurney W. S. C. 1995. Attraction toward feeding conspecifics when food patches are exhaustible. *Am. Nat.,* 154, 653–660.

Schoener T. W. 1987. A brief history of optimal foraging ecology. In *Foraging Behavior,* A. C. Kamil, J. R. Krebs & H. R. Pulliam, eds., pp. 5–67. New York: Plenum Press.

Sibly, R. M. 1983. Optimal group size is unstable. *Anim. Behav.,* 31, 947–948.

Sjerps M. & Haccou P. 1994. Effects of competition on optimal patch leaving: A war of attrition. *Theor. Pop. Biol.,* 46, 300–318.

Stephens D. W. 1981. The logic of risk-sensitive foraging preferences. *Anim. Behav.,* 29, 628–629.

Stephens D. W. & Krebs J. R. 1986. *Foraging Theory.* Princeton, NJ: Princeton University Press.

Thompson W. A., Vertinsky I. & Krebs J. R. 1974. The survival value of flocking in birds: a simulation model. *J. Anim. Ecol.,* 43, 785–820.

Vehrencamp S. L. 1984. Exploitation in co-operative societies: Models of fitness biasing in co-operative breeders. In *Producers and Scroungers: Strategies of Exploitation and Parasitism,* C. J. Barnard, ed., pp. 229–266. London: Croom Helm.

Vickery W. L., Giraldeau L.-A., Templeton J. J., Kramer D. L. & Chapman C. A. 1991. Producers, scroungers and group foraging. *Am. Nat.,* 137, 847–863.

Ward P. I. & Enders M. M. 1985. Conflict and cooperation in the group feeding of the social spider *Stegodyphus mimosarum. Behaviour,* 94, 167–182.

Wilson E. O. 1975. *Sociobiology.* Cambridge: Belknap Press.

3

LEE ALAN DUGATKIN

Game Theory and Cooperation

A hydrogen bomb is an example of mankind's enormous
capacity for friendly cooperation. Its construction requires
an intricate network of human teams, all working with a
single minded devotion toward a common goal. Let us
pause and savor in the glow of self-congratulation we de-
serve for belonging to such an intelligent and sociable species.

R. Bigelow, *The Dawn Warriors*

3.1 Introduction

Philosophers, economists, psychologists, sociologists, anthropologists, political scientists, mathematicians and behavioral ecologists have all pondered over the origin and
stability of cooperative behavior (Axelrod 1984). Despite this, as well as a huge
human literature base and a growing empirical foundation on cooperation in nonhu-
mans, it is actually quite difficult to come up with an accepted definition of cooperation. The opening quote of this chapter is meant to illustrate how the term cooperation can be twisted in ways that seem grossly counterintuitive. In fact, even within
the field of animal behavior and behavioral ecology, attempts to describe terms like
cooperation and altruism sometimes produce almost oxymoronic phrases such as
"self-interested refusal to be spiteful" (Grafen 1984), "quasi-altruistic selfishness"
(West-Eberhard 1975), and "joint stock individualism" (Kropotkin 1908; see Wilson & Dugatkin 1992 for more on these terms and the semantic confusion surrounding them).

To avoid confusion from the start, I will define cooperation as follows: Cooperation
is an *outcome* that—despite potential costs to individuals—is "good" (measured by
some appropriate fitness measure) for the members of a group of two or more individuals and whose achievement requires some sort of collective action. But *to cooperate* can
mean either to achieve that cooperation (something manifest at the group level) or to
behave cooperatively—that is, to behave in a manner making cooperation possible
(something the individual does), despite the fact that the cooperation will not actually

be realized unless other group members have also behaved cooperatively. Here, to cooperate will always mean to behave cooperatively (as in Mesterton-Gibbons & Dugatkin 1992; Dugatkin et al. 1992; also see Stephens and Clements, this volume).

3.2 Paths to Cooperation

Elsewhere my colleagues and I (Dugatkin et al. 1992; Mesterton-Gibbons & Dugatkin 1992) have argued that there are at least three ways that cooperation can evolve among unrelated individuals: reciprocity, group selection, and by-product mutualism. These categories of cooperation are not meant to be mutually exclusive, nor I do believe that it will often be the case that any particular behavior will be explained by invoking one, and only one, of these categories of cooperation. Of course, a fourth category of cooperation is that mediated by kinship. However, the literature on kinship, cooperation, and altruism is mammoth, and I cannot even begin to summarize it in a single chapter.

I now proceed to outline these three categories of cooperation among unrelated individuals, by examining some underlying theory and providing a few examples from nature. Following this, I will attempt to show how empirical work on reciprocity may suggest ways in which the assumptions of game theory models of reciprocity need to be modified and how such modification might occur.

3.2.1 Category I: Reciprocity

The workhorse of games examining the evolution of cooperation via reciprocity (here, the exchange of cooperative acts) is undoubtedly the Prisoner's Dilemma (see Fig. 3.1; also see Stephens and Clements, this volume), introduced to evolutionary biologists and behavioral ecologists by Trivers (1971) and by Axelrod and Hamilton (1981). In this game, each player does better to cheat than to cooperate (i.e., $T > R$ and $P > S$), but the combined payoff for cooperation (R) is greater than the combined payoff for cheating (P)—hence the dilemma.

To examine the evolution of cooperation in such a world, Axelrod and Hamilton (1981) used a two-prong attack. First, they ran computer tournaments in which participants submitted a strategy in the form of a computer program, and strategies competed against one another in games that lasted 200 moves (Axelrod 1984). Fourteen strategies were submitted (Axelrod 1984), and each strategy faced itself and all others in a round-robin tournament. Tit for Tat (TFT), submitted by Anatol Rapoport, emerged as the winner of this tournament. TFT is a strategy that instructs players to cooperate when first meeting an opponent, and to subsequently copy whatever that opponent does (e.g., TFT is one strategic version of Triver's (1971) reciprocal altruism). As such, TFT has three characteristics that allow it to do well in such tournaments: it is nice (always starts off cooperatively), retaliatory (defects in response to defection), and forgiving (does not hold grudges—only remembers one move back). Niceness allows a sequence of possible cooperative exchanges to be initiated, retaliation guards TFT against its partner cheating, and forgiving provides an escape from an endless series of defect/defect exchanges as a result of a single move of defection (which may itself have been an error by one of the players).

Player 2

	Cooperate	Defect
Cooperate	R = 3	S = 0
Defect	T = 5	P = 1

Player 1

Figure 3.1. The Prisoner's Dilemma game. The payoffs presented are for player 1. The game is defined by the following inequalities: Temptation to cheat (T) > Reward for mutual cooperation (R) > Punishment for mutual defection (P) > Sucker's payoff for cooperating when your opponent defects (S), and 2R > T + S.

In addition to these computer tournaments, Axelrod and Hamilton (1981) examined whether TFT and the primitive All Defect (ALLD) strategies were evolutionarily stable—that is, whether they could resist invasion from mutants if they themselves were at a frequency close to 1. They began this task by proving that if ALLD or a strategy that alternates D and C (ALTDC) cannot invade TFT, then no single pure strategy can. They then considered whether ALLD and/or ALTDC can invade TFT.

If we let w equal the probability of interacting with the same player on the next move of a game, then the probabilities of future interaction form a geometric series, and the expected number of interactions with a given opponent is equal to $1/(1-w)$. So, for example, if $w = 0.9$, the expected number of interactions with a given partner is 10 {i.e., $1/(1-0.9)$}. This being the case, when TFT is close to fixation, virtually all TFT players meet other TFTs and their payoff is

$$R + wR + w^2R + w^3R + ... \rightarrow R/(1-w) \tag{1}$$

An ALLD mutant would have all its interactions with TFT and its payoff would be

$$T + wP + w^2P + w^3P + ... \rightarrow T + wP/(1-w) \tag{2}$$

and so TFT can resist invasion from ALLD when

$$R/(1-w) > T + wP/(1-w) \tag{3}$$

Solving the inequality for w, ALLD fails to invade TFT when

$$w > (T-R)/(T-P) \tag{4}$$

Now, ALTDC gets a payoff

$$T + wS + w^2T + w^3S... \rightarrow (T+wS)/(1-w^2) \tag{5}$$

when playing TFT, and thus TFT is resistant to invasion when

$$R/(1-w) > (T+wS)/(1-w^2) \tag{6}$$

Solving the inequality for w, ALTDC fails to invade TFT when

$$w \geq (T-R)/(R-S) \tag{7}$$

and hence Axelrod and Hamilton (1981) concluded that TFT is resistant to any invasion when

$$w \geq \max\{(T-R)/(T-P), (T-R)/(R-S)\} \tag{8}$$

The success or failure of cooperation in the Iterated Prisoner's Dilemma is then clearly dependent on the probability of future play with the same player, or what has been termed "the shadow of the future." When the chances of future play with a given partner are high, but probabilistic, TFT can resist invasion from ALLD and ALTDC. It is important to note, however, as do Axelrod and Hamilton (1981), that ALLD is always resistant to invasion regardless of the value of w. This, of course, poses a problem for the *initiation* of TFT. However, an "initial clustering" of TFT, perhaps, but not necessarily, due to kinship might overcome this threshold problem (Axelrod & Hamilton 1981).

Despite the fact that Axelrod and Hamilton's (1981) article did not spur empirical studies of the Iterated Prisoner's Dilemma (IPD) for about five years, and even though there have been numerous challenges to the use of the Prisoner's Dilemma as a model for the evolution of reciprocity (Rothstein & Pirotti 1987; Noe 1990; Connor 1996), Axelrod and Hamilton's (1981) study immediately tantalized evolutionary theorists who have produced a plethora of articles following up their initial model. Modifications to the IPD include variations in population structure, number of players, number of strategies, relatedness of players, stochasticity of strategies, stochasticity of environment, amount of memory, possibility of individual recognition, norms, ostracism, mobility of players, and mistakes by players. These are summarized in Table 3.1.

Table 3.1 Recent Evolutionary Models of Reciprocity Which Modify Axelrod and Hamilton's (1981) Work[a]

Modification	Result	Reference
N-person game	Increasing group size hinders the evolution of cooperation.	Joshi (1987) Boyd & Richerson (1988)
	Increasing group size hinders the evolution of cooperation, but decreases the threshold frequency of TFT needed to invade ALLD.	Dugatkin (1990) Dugatkin & Godin (1992)
	Predator–prey interactions may result in selfish groups being more vigilant than cooperative groups.	Packer & Abrams (1990)
	Finds mixed ESSs to a synergistic N-person game where individuals "play the field."	Motro (1991)
Population structure	Within social networks, the evolution of TFT is "individual" specific. Players in the most dyads serve as a point of invasion for ALLD.	Pollock (1988)
	Reciprocity can resist invasion in viscous lattice-like populations.	Pollock (1989)
	Group selection can favor cooperation.	Boyd & Richerson (1990a)
	Spatial Prisoner's Dilemmas allow very generous cooperative strategies.	Grim (1995, 1996)
Stochastic environment	Kinship not necessary for food sharing among communal breeders to evolve.	Caraco & Brown (1986)
	Variability in predation risk and value of food patches affects the evolution of food calling.	Newman & Caraco (1989)
	IPD as a Markov chain. Solution contains "never play D after C." TFT is much weaker in a probabilistic world.	Nowak (1990b) Nowak & Sigmund (1990)
	ESSs to the IPD (and other games) may be inaccessible.	Nowak (1990a)
	Stochastic strategies can lead to cycles of reciprocity and defection.	Nowak & Sigmund (1989)
	"Pavlov" strategy outcompetes TFT.	Nowak & Sigmund (1993)
Definition of stability/ suites of strategies	Proves no pure strategy is an ESS to the IPD.	Boyd & Lorberbaum (1987)
	Proves no mixed strategy is an ESS to the IPD.	Farrell & Ware (1989)
	No strategy is an ESS to the IPD.	Loberbaum (1994)
	Sets of strategies exist which do not lose against any other strategy.	Borstnik et al. (1990)
	Generous TFT replaces TFT as best cooperative strategy.	Nowak & Sigmund (1992)
Indirect reciprocity	Networks of indirect reciprocity are unlikely to facilitate cooperation unless groups are fairly small.	Alexander (1986) Boyd & Richerson (1989)
Genetic algorithms	Genetic algorithms come up with TFT-like strategies that are solutions to the IPD.	Axelrod (1987)
	Genetic algorithms are used to examine the relationship between individual recognition and cooperative behavior.	Crowley et al. (1995)

Modification	Result	Reference
Payoff structure	Payment function of next encounter is a random variable. Cooperation may benefit player in that it keeps opponent alive for next play.	Eshel & Weinshall (1988)
	If payoff structure of game changes as the frequency of strategies change, helping behavior can evolve from mutation frequency.	Peck & Feldman (1986)
	Considers dynamic game, where players can opt to play alone and where the game has finite number of moves. Cooperation can evolve even in the face of end-game effects.	Lima (1989)
	Cooperative hunting is examined via a family of models. Cooperation likely when individual is unlikely to capture large prey alone. Individual differences in hunting ability selects against TFT.	Packer & Rutton (1988)
	Cooperator's dilemma allows cooperation to evolve via reciprocity, group selection, kin selection or by-product mutualism.	Dugatkin et al. (1992), Mesterton-Gibbons & Dugatkin (1992)
Kinship	TFT can invade altruistic kin groups, but with respect to other alleles, TFT is an outlaw gene.	Wilson & Dugatkin (1991) Dugatkin et al. (1994)
	Kinship promotes cooperation in small groups.	Aoki (1983)
	When the value of various associates differs, distant kin can easily be selected over close kin for partnerships.	Wasser (1982)
	Hamilton's rule holds for reciprocity, once "coefficients of synergism" are taken into account.	Queller (1985)
Mobility of players	"Roving" defectors hinder cooperation.	Dugatkin & Wilson (1991) Dugatkin (1992) Harpending & Sobus (1987) Enquist & Leimar (1993)
	Partner choice allows cooperation in yucca moth and fig-wasp systems.	Bull & Rice (1991)
Social learning	Observer TFT strategy can invade TFT. Reputation evolves.	Pollock & Dugatkin (1992)
Encounter probabilities	Assortment favors the evolution of cooperation.	Eshel & Cavalli-Sforza (1982) Michod & Sanderson (1985) Toro & Silio (1986)
	"Friendship" can evolve when players can form and re-form partnerships	Peck (1993)
	If opponents are not fixed, population needs to be small for cooperation to evolve.	Mesterton-Gibbons (1991)

(*continued*)

Table 3.1   (continued)

Modification	Result	Reference
Ostracism	Ostracism favors cooperative behavior.	Hirshleifer & Rasmussen (1989)
Punishment of defectors	"Norms" help cooperation spread in a population.	Axelrod (1986) Boyd & Richerson (1992)
Prior experience	If a player's choice of C or D is dependent on its own play on the prior move, cooperation may profit.	Feldman & Thomas (1987) Thomas & Feldman (1988)
Memory/recognition	"Single partner" games are replaced by two parameters that measure encounters with known versus unknown players. Reciprocity can evolve from near zero frequency.	Brown et al. (1982)
	Games with no individual recognition may qualify as a Prisoner's Dilemma under some ecological scenarios.	Mesterton-Gibbons (1991)
Alternating moves	Having opponents alternate moves in a IPD does not change qualitative predictions.	Boyd (1988)
	Generous TFT does well in a game where players alternate moves.	Nowak & Sigmund (1994)
	Challenges the notion that pure Generous TFT does well when players alternate moves.	Frean (1994)
Mistakes	When TFT makes errors, or there is a "cost of complexity" associated with playing TFT, it is no longer robust.	Hirshleifer & Martinez-Coll (1988)
	Mistakes by players allows an ESS to emerge in the IPD.	Boyd (1989)
	Mistakes hinder the evolution of reciprocal strategies like Pavlov.	Stephens et al. (1995)
Cultural transmission	Cultural transmission typically helps cooperation to evolve.	Boyd & Richerson (1982) Boyd & Richerson (1990b)

[a]Some studies fall under more than one heading, but are organized by the primary modification made.

3.2.1.1 Examples of Reciprocity

I. EGG SWAPPING IN HERMAPHRODITIC FISH   While it is probably true that any behavioral act can in principle be reciprocated, if the behavior involves the production and exchange of some physical, measurable good, then reciprocity would be much easier to quantify. In some simultaneously hermaphroditic fishes, just such an exchange takes place, with "egg packets" being the unit of currency.

Among the vertebrates, simultaneous hermaphroditism—the possession by a single individual of both eggs and sperm at the same time—is relatively rare and occurs only in fishes. In the seabasses, individuals spawn daily, as described by Fischer (1988):

> Individuals form pairs late in the afternoon. Before spawning, two mates alternate courtship displays, and the last fish to display releases eggs, while its partner releases

sperm (fertilization is external and eggs are planktonic). Each fish releases only part of its clutch during a given spawning act, and partners regularly alternate release of eggs. (Fischer, 1988, p. 120)

Clutches of eggs in at least eight serranine (seabass) species are divided into parcels and partners exchange roles (producing egg parcels and producing sperm) 80% of the time (Fischer 1984, Fischer 1986). Individuals in one of the better-studied species, *Hypoplectrus nigricans,* fertilize about as many eggs as they parcel out (Fischer 1980). Fischer (1988) refers to such egg swapping as "delayed reciprocity."

The reason that simultaneous hermaphrodites don't cheat (i.e., fail to produce eggs at the appropriate time) in such a game is that they may be trapped in an Iterated Prisoner's Dilemma, and they are using something akin to TFT when paired up with a partner. To examine this possibility, let us first determine if egg traders are trapped in a Prisoner's Dilemma. Following Fischer (1988), define a game as the sequence of mating interactions that occurs during a session of spawning. An "iteration" of the game is then a release of parcels by one player and the subsequent release, or failure to release, eggs by its partner. For example, player 1 releasing eggs and player 2 releasing sperm, followed by player 2 producing eggs and player 1 producing sperm would constitute one possible iteration. Furthermore, it is assumed that sperm is always parceled out when a partner produces eggs and that females are never sperm-limited (i.e., if they don't parcel eggs in the present, they can always get them fertilized later). Now, let us equate cooperation with parceling eggs on your appointed turn and equate defection with the failure to do so. Then, if b is the benefit of fertilizing eggs, c is the cost of producing eggs, and p is the probability that a defector does give up a parcel on its appointed turn, the payoff matrix for such a game would be:

	Cooperator	Defector
Cooperator	$b-c$ (R)	$pb-c$ (S)
Defector	$b-pc$ (T)	$pb-pc$ (P)

This matrix would qualify as a Prisoner's Dilemma if $p<1$ (which allows $T>R$, $P>S$ and $2R>T+S$) and $B>C>0$ (which allows $R>P$). TFT becomes a stable solution to the game when $w \geq c/b$.

Are these inequalities met by egg swappers? By definition $p<1$, and although the cost of producing eggs has not been measured, Fischer (1988) argues that evidence suggests that the cost of producing eggs (c) is relatively small compared to the benefit of fertilizing them (b). If this proves to be the case, then the payoff matrix for egg swapping qualifies as a Prisoner's Dilemma, and the probability of future interaction with the same partner (w) needs to be relatively small for TFT to be one solution to the game.

Although TFT behavior per se has not been explicity studied in simultaneous hermaphroditic egg swappers, some evidence exists that their behavior is consistent with TFT. Fischer (1980; Fischer, unpublished, cited in Fischer 1988) provides some data that suggest black hamlets *(Hypoplectrus nigricans)* and chalk bass *(Serrannus tortugarum)* retaliate against cheating. In these species, mates waited significantly longer to parcel out eggs to a partner that failed to reciprocate compared with partners that had reciprocated in the immediate past (see Connor 1992 for an alternative explanation).

Fischer (1988) notes, however, that "it could be that egg-trading is nicer or more forgiving that simple TFT {TIT FOR TAT}." It seems, in fact, that rather than playing pure TFT, egg swappers use something more akin to Generous TFT (a strategy that does not always retaliate against cheating); (Nowak & Sigmund 1992) in that fish seem to reciprocate only about 80% of the time (i.e., they cheat 20%), yet pairs often stay together for long periods of time.

A remarkably similar form of egg trading and reciprocity occurs in the protandrous, hermaphroditic polycheate worm *Ophryocha diadema* (Sella 1985, 1988, 1991). What makes this case especially fascinating is that as simple a creature as a polycheate worm is able to assess whether its partner is cheating and then respond with an appropriate behavior (Sella 1988).

II. RECIPROCAL GROOMING IN IMPALA   Very strong evidence of reciprocity in the context of allogrooming comes from Hart and Hart's (1992) and Mooring and Hart's (1992) work on impala *(Aepyceros melampus)*. In this species, bouts of reciprocal allogrooming typically occur after one individual begins grooming another near it, rather than via any sort of solicitation. A normal exchange involves three to four such bouts (Hart & Hart, 1992; Fig. 3.2). Grooming appears to reduce the tick load of the individual groomed (Hart & Hart 1992; see Hart et al. (1992) for more on grooming in African ungulates). The benefit of tick reduction may be very great: If data relating

	Females							
	Pair 1		Pair 2		Pair 3		Pair 4	
Bout	A	B	A	B	A	B	A	B
1	6		1		3		15	
2		15		8		3		10
3	4		10		3		12	
4		8		15		8		2
5	12		6		13			6
6		10		10		12		
7	16		8		11			
8		14		10		9		
9	5		8		9			
10		5		2		10		
11					3			
Total episodes delivered	43	52	33	45	42	42	27	18

Figure 3.2. Grooming episodes delivered between four pairs of female impala. Note the strong correspondence between bouts delivered by player A and those delivered in response by player B (after Table 1 in Hart & Hart 1992).

to the effects of ticks on the health of cows (Bennett 1969) is extrapolated to impala, just a few ticks could have very serious effects on impala weight and competitive abilities (Hart & Hart 1992). Grooming itself appears to carry some costs: energy expenditure, electrolyte loss via saliva, decreases in vigilance (Mooring & Hart 1995).

The degree of reciprocity within pairs of impala is quite impressive. Whether pairs are male–male, female–female, female–male, subadult male–adult male or fawn–fawn, individuals inevitably receive almost the same number of allogrooming bouts that they hand out (Figs. 3.3 and 3.4). Although more controlled experiments on individually recognizable impala are needed to provide concrete evidence that impala are playing a conditionally cooperative strategy, the data shown in Figs. 3.3 and 3.4 certainly hint that some sort of conditional behavior is being employed during allogrooming. Of course, it is possible that other factors may play a role in this system (Connor 1995b), if, for example, ticks provide nutrition or allogrooming "builds bonds" between individuals (which is highly unlikely given impala population structure). However, if direct benefits such as this were the driving factor, there would be no reason why bouts should end after one partner stops allogrooming, or why both parties in an allogrooming exchange should receive almost the identical number

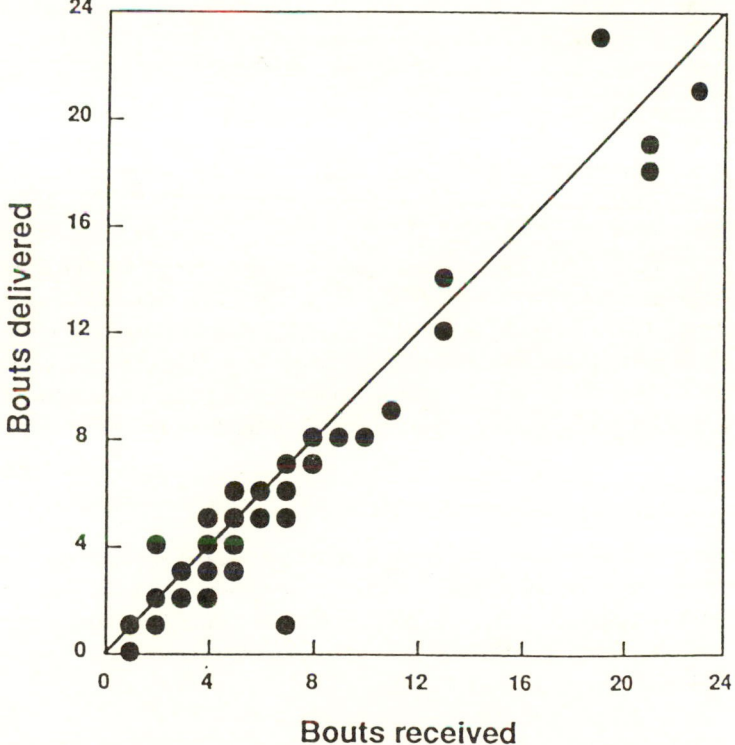

Figure 3.3. The reciprocal nature of allogrooming in female impala. The 45 degree line denotes a perfect match between bouts delivered and bouts received (after Hart & Hart 1992).

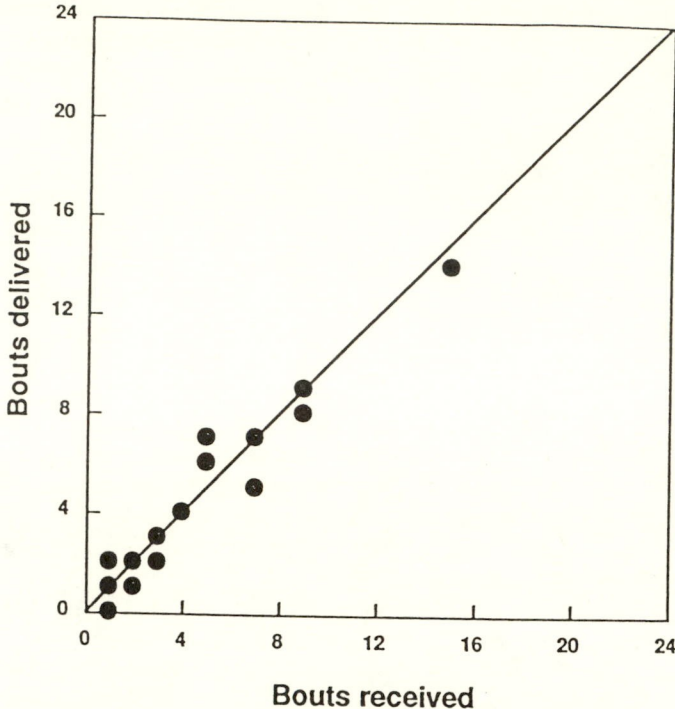

Bouts received

Figure 3.4. The reciprocal nature of allogrooming in male impala. The 45° line denotes a perfect match between bouts delivered and bouts received (after Hart & Hart 1992).

of grooming attempts. This, however, is just what one would expect if reciprocity was the predominant force in allogrooming. The fact that reciprocal allogrooming is seen in neonatal fawns as young as 3 days old, and that young deprived of allogrooming exchanges with adults still display this behavior when put in the appropriate setting suggests, but by no means proves, that the tendency to reciprocate acts of allogrooming may have a genetic component (Mooring & Hart 1992).

3.2.2 Category II: By-product Mutualism

Although group selection, kin selection, and reciprocity have attracted the lion's share of attention in studies of cooperation, it may be the case that by-product mutualism (Brown 1983) is as important, if not more important than, these three other routes. After outlining how the Prisoner's Dilemma works and where it may be applicable, Brown (1983) notes:

> In by-product mutualism, each animal must perform a necessary minimum itself that may benefit another individual as a by-product. These are typically behaviors that a solitary individual must do regardless of the presence of others, such as hunting for

food. In many species these activities are more profitable in groups than alone, so that $CC > CD > DC = DD$. In other words, consistent defection (meaning depending completely on others) is impossible or foolhardy. . . . (Brown, 1983, p. 30)

Following Brown (1983), Connor (1986) introduced the concept of pseudo-reciprocity, which he describes as "investing in by-product mutualism" [but see Mesterton-Gibbons and Dugatkin (1997) for an alternative view]. While pseudoreciprocity may be more likely in the context of interspecific interactions, it is nonetheless an interesting idea that applies as well to intraspecific interactions (Connor 1986, 1995a) and is well worth exploring, particularly because such cooperation appears to be more likely (than noncooperation) in "harsh" environments (Mesterton-Gibbons & Dugatkin 1992). In essence, by-product mutualism and pseudoreciprocity remove the temptation to cheat that cooperators encounter in the Prisoner's Dilemma game, and thus make cooperation the only evolutionarily stable strategy possible.

3.2.2.1 Examples of By-product Mutualism

I. TERRITORIAL DEFENSE IN PIED WAGTAILS   Davies & Houston (1981) outline an illuminating account of Pied wagtail *(Motacilla alba)* behavior which provides behavioral ecologists with much food for thought with respect to the economics of territoriality, the feasibility of simple optimal foraging models, and the evolution of cooperative territory defense. Pied wagtails defend riverside winter territories, foraging on insects that wash up on the banks (Davies 1976). This food source is "renewable" in that after a period of time, prey abundance on a territory again increases after being depleted, and Davies and Houston (1981) show how wagtails systematically search their territories, providing time for depleted resources to again increase.

The story is more complex, however, because intruders often land on such territories, and at times are tolerated (at which point they become "satellites") and at other times are aggressively chased off a territory. What differentiates these situations? Before answering this, it is important to note that a territory may have a different value to an owner than to an intruder who does not know which areas have recently been "cropped." If an owner permits an intruder to stay, it incurs a cost in terms of foraging, but gains assistance in territory defense (Charnov et al. 1976; Davies and Houston 1981). Davies and Houston (1981) devised a model to examine these tradeoffs (what they refer to as "the owner's dilemma") and when owners should allow satellites on their territories. The model does a very respectable job of predicting when intruders should be chased off versus when they should be permitted to remain and engage in cooperative territory defense:

On days of high food abundance, when intruder pressure is greatest, owners tolerate satellites . . . owners increase their feeding rate by this association, because the benefits gained through help with defence outweigh the costs incurred through sharing the food with another bird. On days of low food abundance, when an owner would have a higher feeding rate by being alone, it evicts the satellite from the territory. (Davies & Houston, 1981, p. 157)

This is interesting because it indicates that the costs and benefits of by-product mutualism can vary depending on territory holding status, and this can lead to cooperation under some circumstances, but not others. That is, it appears that intruders, who have no foraging territories of their own, always face a harsh environment with respect to food allocation and are willing to pay the costs of territory defense. When food becomes more limiting for owners, however, they do not allow intruders in. The harsh environment that allows the presence of satellites on territories is not the amount of food on a territory, but the amount of "pressure" from other conspecifics. So, intruders are always willing to undertake cooperative territory defense (in exchange) for food, but the costs and benefits of by-product mutualism does not always select for owners to permit this cooperative act.

II. BY-PRODUCT MUTUALISM AND FORAGING IN BLUEJAYS One critique of much of the work on reciprocity and the Prisoner's Dilemma is that although the inequalities of the Prisoner's Dilemma are often inferred, and sometime qualitatively described, they have never been measured precisely. One way around such a problem is to construct "Skinnerian-like" experiments with precise control over T, R, P, and S. Clements and Stephens (1995) take such an approach when studying foraging in bluejays (*Cyanocitta cristata*). In their experiments, three pairs of bluejays were tested and could peck one of two keys—the cooperate key or the defect key. Two payoff matrices were used: The first was a Prisoner's Dilemma (the P matrix), while the second amounted to a "by-product mutualism" matrix (the M matrix), in which cooperation was the clear best choice, regardless of what the other player did. Birds were exposed to the P matrix, then to the M matrix, and finally to the P matrix once again. Regardless of whether the jays could see each other or not, a predictable pattern emerged. Birds always defected in the first P matrix, cooperated in the M matrix, and reverted to defection during the second time they encountered the P matrix, and hence their cooperation can best be labeled a case of by-product mutualism.

Why didn't some sort of conditional cooperation occur when birds were trapped in a Prisoner's Dilemma? Clements and Stephens (1995) speculate that it may be because bluejays apparently strongly discount future payoffs, even when they play against each other many times (e.g., in this experiment, during the first exposure to the P matrix, birds played against one other an average of 3435 times!), as suggested by much work in the area of operant psychology [see Clements & Stephens (1995) for more on this]. One could, however, argue that jays did not cooperate in this game because it was so removed from how they feed in nature and that natural selection could not possibly have acted on key-pecking. While this is always possible, I think that Clements and Stephens (1995) handle this objection nicely, by noting:

> We do not suppose that natural selection has favored key-pecking in Skinner Boxes. Indeed, we offer no argument that blue jays ever faced Prisoner's Dilemmas in their evolutionary history. Rather, our experiment addresses the general significance of the Prisoner's Dilemma as a model of non-kin cooperation. Supporters of the Prisoner's Dilemma have made sweeping claims about its generality (Axelrod and Hamilton, 1981) and have asserted its status as "the leading metaphor for the evolution of cooperation among selfish agents" (Nowak and Sigmund, 1993, p. 56). Given these

claims, it is reasonable to suppose that natural selection has equipped animals with the ability to recognize and implement cooperative strategies in novel situations, when economic circumstances favor cooperation. (Clements & Stephens, 1995, p. 531)

3.2.3 Category III: Group Selection

Somewhat surprisingly, about the same time that Richard Dawkins (1976) was developing his now well-known "selfish gene" theory, a "new group selection" arose from the ashes. While Dawkins (1976) was presenting his reductionist view that genes, but not groups (or for that matter, individuals), qualified as "replicators" (i.e., enduring units of self-interest), the new group selection school was being spearheaded by D. S. Wilson's trait-group models (Wilson 1975, 1976, 1977) and the empirical and theoretical work of Wade (1977, 1978, 1979).

Two critical features separated Wilson and Wade's view of group selection from that of their predecessors (Wynne-Edwards 1962, Allee, 1951). First and foremost, they provided detailed genetic models which partitioned variance into within- and between-group components. Such models allowed detailed predictions of the circumstances favoring the evolution of individual versus group beneficial traits [see Wilson (1983) for a review]. Secondly, the definition of a group was no longer confined to a reproductively isolated deme. Wilson (1975) introduced the term "trait group" and defined it as a population "within which every individual feels the effect of every other individual" (Wilson 1980, p. 22). As a result, groups do not need to be spatially or temporally isolated for selection to operate, and group selection is not restricted to the narrow cases involving the extinction of entire groups. Furthermore, in these new group selection models, trait groups are embedded within a larger interbreeding population. As such, models of trait-group evolution are sometimes called intrademic selection models, to distinguish them from the interpopulational or interdemic models, such as those implied in the arguments of Wynne-Edwards (1962).

The "trait-group" approach to the evolution of cooperation is very simple, in principle. The core idea is that cooperation can evolve even when it has a cost to the individual performing it, if *within-group cost* is offset by some *between-group benefit*, such that *cooperative groups are more productive than selfish groups.* For such group-level benefits to be manifest, groups must differ in the frequency of cooperators within them, and groups must be able to "export" the productivity associated with cooperation. For example, following Wilson (1990), imagine a metapopulation of social insect colonies (modeled after Rissing et al.'s 1989 study of the ant *Acromymex versicolor*). In the primitive condition there are no "specialized foragers"—those who take the often high risk associated with foraging, but share food with nest mates. How could such a cooperative specialized forager evolve? If we denote the unspecialized strategy as selfish (S), and the specialized strategy as altruistic (A), then

Assume that queens in all-S colonies forage equally, while A forages disproportionately often in colonies of one A and $(N-1)$ S. Let $x<1$ equal A's probability of survival relative to S in colonies all-S and let $y>1$ equal A's effect on her own colonies' chances of prevailing over the other colonies. Globally, the fitness of A will exceed the fitness of S when $xy > 1$. Thus, within-group selection against the trait (represented by x) can be arbitrarily low, as long as the between-group selection for the trait (represented by y) is sufficiently high. (Wilson, 1990, p. 139)

It is important to make a small digression here to note the relationship between the hierarchical approach toward evolution, typified by group selection models, and reciprocity and by-product mutualism. Dugatkin and Reeve (1994) argued that *all* group selection models can be translated into broad-based individual selection models and vice versa. Although there may be cases in which one approach (group or individual selection) is preferred for heuristic or practical reasons, the predictions generated by a broad-based individual selection model and its equivalent hierarchical model must of necessity be the same. In terms of game theory models of cooperation, this means that reciprocal altruism and by-product mutualism can always be translated into some sort of hierarchical model and that group-selected cooperation can always be cast within some broad-based individual selection model.

To illustrate the above, consider the following conversion of TFT into the language of within- and between-group selection. The simplest way to see this is to remember that in any TFT/ALLD pair, TFT always obtains fewer rewards than ALLD $[(S + wP/(1 - w))$ versus $(T + wP/(1 - w))$, respectively]. It is only the existence of TFT/TFT pairs in which TFT gets a relatively high payoff $(R/(1 - w))$ and ALLD/ALLD pairs wherein ALLD does poorly $(P/(1 - w))$ that allows TFT to outdo ALLD. In other words, strong between-group (in this case, between-pair) selection for cooperation outweighs within-group selection against it [for more on this see Wilson (1983), Dugatkin & Reeve (1994), and Wilson & Sober (1994)].

In a similar light, one could claim that by-product mutualism is simply a hierarchical model in which all selection is within groups (versus between groups). Given the relationship amongst group selection, by-product mutualism, and reciprocal altruism, is it valid and/or necessary to view them as three categories of cooperation? I believe that for many of the questions of interest to behavioral ecologists, the answer is yes, for the following reason. The behavioral mechanisms involved in these three categories of cooperation are usually quite different. For example, reciprocal altruism typically requires score-keeping abilities that imply a level of cognition not necessary in group selection models and by-product mutualism models. At the same time, by-product mutualism requires absolutely no direct or indirect interactions between individuals in different groups, while this is critical to group selection models. Given that behavioral ecologists are interested in variability in behavioral mechanisms, in and of themselves, I feel justified in separating these three categories of cooperation.

3.2.3.1 Examples of Group Selected Cooperation

I. RAIDING AND "WARFARE" IN CHIMPANZEES Boehm (1992) notes that "warfare" is often defined as a large-scale, open hostility between groups, in which both sides in the conflict use lethal force against the other. According to this definition, chimpanzees do not engage in war. Yet, between-group interactions often appear to be war-like and in fact resemble the raiding behavior so common among many tribes of humans (Boehm 1992). In humans, "a raid is conducted into enemy territory by a relatively weak force which relies on coordination, stealth, and an element of surprise, either to quickly kill a few of the enemy or to take away readily transportable commodities . . ." (Boehm, 1992, p. 153).

As is often the case, cooperation in this example is tied to competition. That is, cooperation is critical within groups, in order for a group to emerge victorious over its rival. In the context of such behavior, selection between groups favors such raids (as they will likely benefit all group members, not just the raiding party participants), yet, if raiding is dangerous, selection within groups should favor cheating (letting others do the raiding, but reaping the benefits).

During raids, all-male chimpanzee "patrol" groups often travel into areas that border their territorial boundaries (Bygott 1979, Nishida 1979, Goodall 1986). In contrast to group sorties for food, wherein vocalizations are common, patrols move in a more stealthy fashion and remain silent (Goodall 1986), in accordance with the above definition. These raids often (1) involve the killing of a small number of members of the raided group, suggesting strong within-group selection to not be in the patrol party because of the potential costs of fighting, and (2) entail the capture of females. Occasionally, raiding parties from two groups will meet one another. Rather than all-out aggression, both groups engage in hostile vocalizations and then withdraw (Goodall 1986). Despite the fact that all-out warfare does not emerge when two raiding parties meet, raiding can, in the long run, amount to the extinction of one group. Nishida et al. (1985) provide evidence that raiding behavior in the Mahale Mountains of Tanzania amounted to a larger group extinguishing a smaller group of chimps [also see Goodall (1986) for evidence of this at Gombe].

II. PLEOMETROSIS IN THE ANT, *ACROMYMEX VERSICOLOR*   Pleometrosis is a term coined for the case in which a social insect colony is founded by more than a single queen [see Holldobler & Wilson (1990) for more on this]. Cooperative colony foundation during pleometrosis occurs in a number of species of ants (Holldobler & Wilson 1990, Keller 1993); in all species studied, however, cooperating cofoundresses are not closely related, suggesting that selective forces other than kin selection may favor such cooperation in natural populations (Strassmann 1989). Intracolony cooperation in these species appears to be the result of intercolony aggression and territoriality [Bartz & Holldobler (1982); Tschinkel & Howard (1983); Rissing & Pollock (1986, 1987); Rissing et al. (1989); but see Pfennig (1995) for contra evidence from the *field*], such that group productivity is a function of the number of cooperators in a group (Rissing & Pollock 1986)—precisely the sort of situation in which we would predict trait-group selection to play a significant role.

The strongest case of trait-group selected cooperation during pleometrosis is Rissing et al.'s (1989) work on *Acromymex versicolor*. In this species, many nests are found via pleometrosis, no dominance hierarchy exists among queens, queens are unrelated, all queens produce workers, and brood raiding among starting nests appears to be common, with the probability of a nest surviving the brood-raiding period being a function of the numbers of workers produced (Rissing et al. 1989; but see Pfennig 1995).

A. versicolor, however, differs from virtually all other pleometric species, in that queens forage after colony foundation. Increased predation pressure and parasitization make foraging a very dangerous activity for a queen. How a single queen becomes the group's forager is still not well understood. It does appear, however, that this decision is not a coercive one; that is, it is not forced upon a particular queen by other group mates (Rissing et al. 1989). Once a queen becomes the forager, she shares all the food brought into her nest with her cofounders; that is, the forager assumes the risks of foraging and obtains the benefits, while the other queens simply obtain the benefits but pay no costs. Here within-group cooperation (in this instance, on the part of the forager) appears to lead to more workers, which in turn affects the probability that a given nest will be the one to survive the period of brood raiding (Seger 1989; Rissing et al. 1989). One caveat to keep in mind is that the above work on *A. versicolor* was all performed in the laboratory and that the existence of specialized foragers has yet to be demonstrated in nature.

3.3 A Positive Feedback Loop Between Empirical Studies and Game Theory Models of Cooperation?

In the above discussion, the theoretical underpinnings of three different paths to cooperation were outlined, and two examples of each type were provided. In most of the examples given, a particular study was undertaken in order to test some prediction generated by a game theory model. Yet, if game theory is to be a truly valuable tool, it would be gratifying to see the next step in the sequence—namely, empirical studies feeding back on theoretical work and suggesting newer, more fined-tuned models. One possible way such a feedback system might operate is through studies which suggest that some assumption of a game theory model of cooperation is askew and which also suggest that new, testable models be built in which this assumption is then relaxed. Below, I use predator inspection behavior in fish to challenge two basic assumptions of the Prisoner's Dilemma, namely:

1. Players are paired up in a random fashion; that is, individuals do not choose who they interact with, only which behavior they use when interacting with a partner.
2. Cooperation and defection are discrete categories of behavior. No continuum of cooperative (or conversely cheating) behavior exists in the Prisoner's Dilemma. Each action is either cooperative or it is not, and cooperators do not differ in the extent to which they cooperate (also see Stephens and Clements, this volume, for interesting issues regarding the Prisoner's Dilemma game).

During predator inspection behavior in fish (Pitcher et al. 1986), a small group of fish break away from a school to approach and "inspect" a potential predator. Magurran and Pitcher (1987) postulate four potential benefits of inspection behavior: (1) allowing for better judgment of whether the potential danger is in fact a predator, (2) announcing to an ambush predator that it has been spotted, (3) determining the motivational state of the predator (e.g., is it hunting?), and (4) obtaining information on the distance between the school and the predator. Furthermore, Magurran and Higgam (1988) have found that the information obtained by the inspector(s) is either actively or passively transmitted to the noninspectors.

Because of the putative costs and benefits of predator inspection, Milinski (1987) suggested that inspectors were trapped in a Prisoner's Dilemma. Consider a two-person game in which inspection is equated with cooperation and noninspecting is equated with defection. If both fish cooperate and approach the predator, they both obtain the benefit (B) and share the cost (C) such that the payoff to each inspector is ($B - C/2$) (via the dilution effect; because of the nature of predator inspection, predators are rarely, if ever, able to successfully attack both inspectors in a pair). If one fish approaches the predator and the other remains distant, both obtain the benefit while only one obtains the cost, and so the payoff for cooperation is $B - C$ and the corresponding payoff for defection is B. If neither approaches the predator, then the costs and benefits equal zero. If $C > B$, but $B > C/2$, these payoffs satisfy the inequalities of the Prisoner's Dilemma. Experimental work in sticklebacks (*Gasterosteus aculeatus*) and guppies (*Poecilia reticulata*) suggests that individual fish use a TFT-like strategy during inspection (Milinski 1987; Dugatkin 1988, 1991a; Dugatkin & Alfieri 1991a,b, 1992; Milinski et al. 1990a,b; Huntingford et al. 1994; also see Lazarus & Metcalfe, 1990; Masters & Waite, 1990; Milinski 1990a,b, 1992, 1996; Dugatkin 1991b, 1996; Turner & Robinson 1992; Connor 1996 and Stephens et al. 1997 for numerous discussions, critiques, and countercritiques on the issue of predator inspection and the use of TFT).

3.3.1 Challenging the Random Assortment Assumption: Preferential Partner Choice During Predator Inspection in Guppies

Although cooperation can evolve without assuming sophisticated animal cognition, it is more likely to evolve if animals can remember individuals with whom they have interacted, associate past interactions with these individuals, and base future behavior on this information. As such, Dugatkin and Alfieri (1991a) designed a series of experiments to test the hypothesis that guppies remember the previous behavior of their associates during predator inspection and subsequently prefer to associate with the more cooperative individual. Three guppies were placed in the experimental apparatus. Guppies were in visual contact, but clear Plexiglas partitions that created "lanes" for the fish to swim in did not allow the fish to be in physical contact. Adjacent to the experimental tank was a tank containing a predator. Each trial lasted 2.5 minutes, and the position of all three guppies during predator inspection visits was recorded every five seconds.

Immediately following each inspection trial, fish were placed into "preference tanks." First, the fish from the center lane of the inspection trial (the "center" fish) was placed into a tank placed between two smaller side chambers. The two fish from the side lanes (the "side" fish) were placed into the smaller side chambers. The position of the center fish was noted every five seconds. In 24 of the 30 trials, the center fish preferred the side fish which had the average position closest to the predator during the inspection trial, i.e.—the more cooperative of the side fish. There was, however, no significant relationship between how close the more cooperative side fish was to the predator (on average) and the magnitude of preference for that fish. That is, regardless of whether the center fish itself was a cooperator or a cheater, it preferred to associate with cooperative coinspectors. Furthermore, similar results were obtained when the "inspection" and "preference" parts of a trial were separated by four hours, suggesting that fish can remember this information for significant periods of time. Milinski et al. (1990a), using a somewhat different protocol, found that inspecting sticklebacks build up "trust" with one another over time, again supporting the notion that partner choice may not be random.

These results clearly suggest that inspectors are capable of preferentially interacting with more cooperative coinspectors, and provide an empirically based challenge to one of the assumptions of the Prisoner's Dilemma. Two caveats are in order at this point, however. First, these experiments show only that guppies have *the ability* to distinguish between cooperators and defectors, not that they do so in nature. A second, related caveat is that since cooperators and defectors both prefer to associate with cooperative inspectors, it is not at all clear how such preferential assortment would manifest itself in a natural situation. Laboratory and field experiments are underway to address these issues.

3.3.2 Challenging the Discrete Categories of Behavior Assumption: The Relative Nature of Cooperation During Predator Inspection in Guppies

Dugatkin and Alfieri (1991b) examined TFT during predator inspection in guppies, as well as the relative nature of cooperation and defection during predator inspection. In this experiment, individually recognizable males were subject to inspection trials with a given partner, once a day for three days. Each individual was tested with three different partners (for a total of nine days). In addition, each fish was tested alone with a mirror that was placed parallel to the path toward the predator. This mirror created an image of a coinspector that always stayed by the side of a subject, and thus it provided baseline data on what a fish would do if its coinspector always cooperated.

Results indicate that in the trials with a live partner as well as in trials with the mirror, individuals differed in their tendency to inspect, but these differences were consistent over time (in statistical terms, a split plot analysis of variance (ANOVA) found significant differences between individuals, but no significant differences within individuals). Despite the fact that individuals differed in their tendency to inspect, all fish appeared to use the TFT strategy, in that they started off by going out and inspecting some distance x (which again differed across individuals), and then copied the behavior of their partner, in that if the partner failed to go to x, the focal player then went out only as far as its partner did the day before.

What do these results tell us with regard to the Prisoner's Dilemma model's assumption that cooperation and defection are discrete categories? To answer this, consider three fish, all who play TFT and all who show consistent scores in the parallel mirror trials. Suppose fish 1 on average moves x units toward the predator, fish 2 y units, and fish 3 z units, such that $x > y > z$. Now if inspection is equated with cooperation when 1 and 2 meet, 1 is cooperating while 2, in a relative sense, is defecting. In such a case we expect fish 1 to retaliate against fish 2 in the future. If, however, fish 2 is paired with fish 3, 2 is now viewed as cooperating, while 3 is a cheater, and we expect to see 2 retaliate against 3. Clearly, cooperation and defection in this game are relative terms, and they are better viewed as a continuum (i.e. a continuously varying trait) than as discrete categories of behavior.

3.3.3 The Feedback Loop—What's Next?

Now that we have some empirically based challenges to the assumptions of the Prisoner's Dilemma, how can we go about using this data to modify existing game theory models of cooperation? Although a few models exist which allow nonrandom partner choice in the Prisoner's Dilemma (Eshel & Cavalli-Sforza 1982, Michod & Sanderson 1985, Toro & Silio 1986, Peck 1993, Mesterton-Gibbons 1991; also see Table 4.1), none of these models provide clues on how such nonrandom partner choice might manifest itself at the behavioral level (e.g., what rules animals use to determine with whom they will interact). Furthermore, these models treat cooperation and defection as discrete categories of behavior, and thus they only address one of the two questions raised above.

Wilson and Dugatkin (1996) have recently constructed a game theory model in which cooperation is a continuous trait and players are not constrained to choosing partners in a random fashion. Cooperation and defection are made continuous by considering behaviors in which the benefits are shared by all group members, while the costs are paid by cooperators alone. Assuming that costs (C) and benefits (B) are continuous, the degree of cooperation can be modeled by considering how great a cost individuals are willing to pay, which in turn creates a distribution of $B - C$ values. Nonrandom partner choice was incorporated by considering a range of cognitive abilities and the effects of such variables as group size.

Wilson & Dugatkin (1996) found that both nonrandom partner choice and a continuous distribution of traits increased between-group variance and hence favored the evolution of cooperation. The extent of cooperation uncovered depended on the assumptions made about cognition, but incorporating even the most basic elements of memory and individual recognition favored cooperation. Using the appropriate animal system, many of the predictions of Wilson and Dugatkin (1996) can be tested. For example, predator inspection behavior in guppies, in which cooperation and defection appear to be continuous traits (Dugatkin & Alfieri 1991b) and during which partner choice may not be random (Dugatkin & Alfieri 1991a), may prove an ideal test system for this model.

Despite the fact that game theory has a long tradition in the social sciences, and was incorporated into behavioral ecology over 20 years ago, controlled tests of game theory models of cooperation are still relatively rare. It might be argued that this is not the fault of empiricists, but rather due to the fact that much of the theory developed is unconnected to natural systems and thus may be mathematically intriguing but biologically meaningless. Such a critique is not unwarranted with respect to some game theory models of cooperation (not surprising given the number of models listed in Table 4.1).

Historically, there have been two "approaches" to the study of behavioral ecology (and other subdisciplines as well), one which begins with observation and one which begins with theory. I tend to support Darwin's intuition on this question, when he wrote to Wallace in 1867 that "I am a firm believer that without speculation there is no good and original observation." The approach described in this chapter, namely model → controlled tests → revised model → new experiments, reflects my bias on this issue. This approach, however, has rarely been implemented in full. In fact, even work on predator inspection behavior (perhaps the most well-studied case of cooperation) is lacking the last part of this equation, namely, new tests of the revised model. The work outlined in this as well as other chapters of this volume, however, indicates that game theory offers crucial insights into the empirical study of animal social behavior.

ACKNOWLEDGMENTS   I would like to thank M. Alfieri, A. Dugatkin, D. Dugatkin, D. Haskell, P. Nonacs, and H. K. Reeve for comments on this chapter. This work was supported by National Science Foundation grants IBN-9404709 and IBN-9600457 to LAD.

References

Alexander, R. D. 1986. Ostracism and indirect reciprocity: The reproductive significance of humor. *Ethol. Sociobiol.,* 7, 253–270.

Allee, W. 1951. *The Social Life of Animals.* New York: Henry Schuman.

Aoki, K. 1983. A quantitative genetic model of reciprocal altruism: A condition for kin or group selection to prevail. *Proc. Natl. Acad. Sci. USA,* 80, 4065–4068.

Axelrod, R. 1984. *The Evolution of Cooperation.* New York: Basic Books.

Axelrod, R. 1986. An evolutionary approach to norms. *Am. Pol. Sci. Rev.,* 80, 1101–1111.

Axelrod, R. 1987. The evolution of strategies in the iterated prisoner's dilemma. In *Genetic Algorithms and Simulated Annealing,* L. Davis, ed., pp. 32–41. New York: Morgan Kaufmann.

Axelrod, R. & Hamilton, W. D. 1981. The evolution of cooperation. *Science,* 211, 1390–1396.

Bartz, S. & Holldobler, B. 1982. Colony foundation in *Mymecocytus mimicus* and the evolution of foundress associations. *Behav. Ecol. Sociobiol.,* 10, 137–147.

Bennett, G. F. 1969. *Boophilus microplus* (Acarina: ixodidae): Experimental infestations on cattle restrained from grooming. *Exp. Parasitol.,* 26, 323–328.

Bigelow, R. 1969. *The Dawn Warriors: Mankind's Evolution Toward Peace.* Boston: Little, Brown and Company.

Boehm, C. 1992. Segmentary warfare and management of conflict: A comparison of East African Chimpanzees and patrilineal–patrilocal humans. In *Coalitions and Alliances in Humans and Other Animals,* A. Harcourt, & F. B. M. de Waal, eds., pp. 137–173. Oxford: Oxford University Press.

Borstnik, B. B., Pumpernik, D., Hofacker, I. L. & Hofacker, G. L. 1990. An ESS analysis for ensembles of Prisoner's Dilemma strategies. *J. Theor. Biol.,* 142, 195–220.

Boyd, R. 1988. Is the repeated Prisoner's Dilemma a good model of Reciprocal Altruism? *Ethol. Sociobiol.,* 9, 211–222.

Boyd, R. 1989. Mistakes allow evolutionary stability in the repeated Prisoner's Dilemma game. *J. Theor. Biol.,* 136, 47–56.

Boyd, R. & Lorberbaum, J. 1987. No pure strategy is evolutionarily stable in the repeated Prisoner's Dilemma. *Nature,* 327, 58–59.

Boyd, R. & Richerson, P. 1982. Cultural transmission and the evolution of cooperative behavior. *Human Ecol.,* 10, 325–351.

Boyd, R. & Richerson, P. 1988. The evolution of reciprocity in sizable groups. *J. Theor. Biol.,* 132, 337–356.

Boyd, R. & Richerson, P. J. 1989. The evolution of indirect reciprocity. *Social Networks,* 11, 213–236.

Boyd, R. & Richerson, P. 1990a. Group selection among alternative evolutionarily stable strategies. *J. Theor. Biol.*, 145, 331–342.

Boyd, R. & Richerson, P. J. 1990b. Culture and cooperation. In *Beyond Self-Interest*, J. J. Mansbridge, ed., pp. 111–132) Chicago: University of Chicago Press.

Boyd, R. & Richerson, P. 1992. Punishment allows the evolution of cooperation (or anything else) in sizable groups. *Ethol. Sociobiol.*, 13, 171–195.

Brown, J., Sanderson, M. & Michod, R. 1982. Evolution of social behavior by reciprocation. *J. Theor. Biol.*, 99, 319–339.

Brown, J. L. 1983. Cooperation-a biologist's dilemma. *Advances in the Study of Behavior*, 13, 1–37.

Bull, J. & Rice, W. 1991. Distinguishing mechanisms for the evolution of cooperation. *J. Theor. Biol.*, 149, 63–74.

Bygott, J. D. 1979. Agonistic behavior, dominance and social structure in wild chimpanzees of the Gombe National Park. In *The Great Apes*, D. A. Hamburg & E. R. McCown, eds. Menlo Park, CA: Benjamin/Cummings.

Caraco, T. & Brown, J. 1986. A game between communal breeders: when is food sharing stable? *Jour. Theor. Biol.*, 118, 379–393.

Charnov, E. L., Orians, G. H. & Hyatt, K. 1976. The ecological implications of resource depression. *Am. Nat.*, 110, 247–259.

Clements, K. C. & Stephens, D. W. 1995. Testing models of noncooperation: Mutualism and the Prisoner's Dilemma. *Anim. Behav.*, 50, 527–535.

Connor, R. 1986. Pseudoreciprocity: investing in mutualism. *Anim. Behav.*, 34, 1652–1654.

Connor, R. C. 1992. Egg-trading in simultaneous hermaphrodites: an alternative to TIT FOR TAT. *J. Evol. Biol.*, 5, 523–528.

Connor, R. C. 1995a. The benefits of mutualism: A conceptual framework. *Biol. Rev.*, 1–31.

Connor, R. C. 1995b. Impala allogrooming and the parceling model of reciprocity. *Anim. Behav.*, 49, 528–530.

Connor, R. C. 1996. Partner preferences in by-product mutualism and the case of predator inspection in fish. *Anim. Behav.*, 51, 451–454.

Crowley, P. H., Provencher, L., Sloane, S., Dugatkin, L. A., Spohn, B., Rogers, B. & Alfieri, M. 1995. Evolving cooperation: the role of individual recognition. *Biosystems*, 37, 49–66.

Davies, N. B. 1976. Food, flocking and territorial behavior the pied wagtail *Motacilla alba* in winter. *J. Anim. Ecol.*, 45, 235–254.

Davies, N. B. & Houston, A. I. 1981. Owners and satellites: The economics of territory defence in the pied wagtail *Motacilla alba*. *J. Anim. Ecol.*, 50, 157–180.

Dawkins, R. 1976. *The Selfish Gene*, 1st edition. Oxford: Oxford University Press.

Dugatkin, L. A. 1988. Do guppies play TIT FOR TAT during predator inspection visits? *Behav. Ecol. Sociobiol.*, 25, 395–399.

Dugatkin, L. A. 1990. *N*-person games and the evolution of cooperation: A model based predator inspection behavior in fish. *J. Theor. Biol.*, 142, 123–135.

Dugatkin, L. A. 1991a. Dynamics of the TIT FOR TAT strategy during predator inspection in guppies. *Behav. Ecol. Sociobiol.*, 29, 127–132.

Dugatkin, L. A. 1991b. Predator inspection, TIT FOR TAT and shoaling: A comment on Masters and Waite. *Anim. Behav.*, 41, 898–900.

Dugatkin, L. A. 1992. The evolution of the con artist. *Ethol. Sociobiol.*, 13, 3–18.

Dugatkin, L. A. 1996. Tit for tat, byproduct mutualism and predator inspection: A reply to Connor. *Anim. Behav.*, 51, 455–457.

Dugatkin, L. A. & Alfieri, M. 1991a. Guppies and the TIT FOR TAT strategy: Preference based on past interaction. *Behav. Ecol. Sociobiol.*, 28, 243–246.

Dugatkin, L. A. & Alfieri, M. 1991b. TIT FOR TAT in guppies: The relative nature of cooperation and defection during predator inspection. *Evol. Ecol.*, 5, 300–309.

Dugatkin, L. A. & Godin, J.-G. J. 1992. Prey approaching predators: a cost-benefit perspective. *Ann. Zool. Fennici,* 29, 233–252.

Dugatkin, L. A., Farrand, L., Wilkens, R. & Wilson, D. S. 1994. Altruism, TIT FOR TAT and "outlaw" genes. *Evol. Ecol.,* 8, 431–437.

Dugatkin, L. A., Mesterton-Gibbons, M. & Houston, A. I. 1992. Beyond the Prisoner's Dilemma: Towards models to discriminate among mechanisms of cooperation in nature. *Trends Ecol. Evol.,* 7, 202–205.

Dugatkin, L. A. & Reeve, H. K. 1994. Behavioral ecology and the "levels of selection": Dissolving the group selection controversy. *Adv. Study Behav.,* 23, 101–133.

Dugatkin, L. A. & Wilson, D. S. 1991. ROVER: A strategy for exploiting cooperators in a patchy environment. *Am. Nat.,* 138, 687–701.

Enquist, M. & Leimar, O. 1993. The evolution of cooperation in mobile organisms. *Anim. Behav.,* 45, 747–757.

Eshel, I. & Cavalli-Sforza, L. L. 1982. Assortment of encounters and the evolution of cooperation. *Proc. Natl. Acad. Sci., USA,* 79, 1331–1335.

Eshel, I. & Weinshall, D. 1988. Cooperation in a repeated game with random payment functions. *J. Appl. Prob.,* 25, 478–491.

Farrell, J. & Ware, R. 1989. Evolutionary stability in the repeated Prisoner's Dilemma. *Theor. Pop. Biol.,* 36, 161–168.

Feldman, M. & Thomas, E. 1987. Behavior dependent contexts for the repeated plays of the Prisoner's Dilemma II: Dynamical aspects of the evolution of cooperation. *J. Theor. Biol.,* 128, 297–315.

Fischer, E. 1988. Simultaneous hermaphroditism, Tit-for-Tat, and the evolutionary stability of social systems. *Ethol. Sociobiol.,* 9, 119–136.

Fischer, E. A. 1980. The relationship between mating system and simultaneous hermaphroditism in the coral reef fish, *Hypoplectrus nigricans* (Serranidae). *Anim. Behav.,* 28, 620–633.

Fischer, E. A. 1984. Egg trading in the chalk bass, *Serranus tortugarum,* simultaneous hermaphrodite. *Z. Tierpsych.,* 66, 143–151.

Fischer, E. A. 1986. Mating systems of simultaneously hermaphroditic Serranid fishes. In *Indo-Pacific Fish Biology: Proceedings of the Second Conference on Indo-Pacific Fishes,* T. Uyeno, R. Arai, T. Taniuchi & K. Matsuura, eds., pp. 776–784. Tokyo: Ichythological Society of Japan.

Frean, M. R. 1994. The prisoner's dilemma without synchrony. *Proc. R. Soc. Lond, Series B.,* 257, 75–79.

Goodall, J. 1986. *The Chimpanzee of Gombe: Patterns of Behavior.* Cambridge, MA: Belknap Press.

Grafen, A. 1984. Natural selection, kin selection and group selection. In *Behavioural Ecology: An Evolutionary Approach,* J. Krebs & N. Davies, eds., Second edition, pp. 62–84. London: Blackwell Scientific Publications.

Grim, P. 1995. The greater generosity of the spatialized prisoner's dilemma. *J. Theor. Biol.,* 173, 353–359.

Grim, P. 1996. Spatalization and greater generosity in the stochastic Prisoner's Dilemma. *Biosystems,* 37, 3–17.

Harpending, H. & Sobus, J. 1987. Sociopathy as an adaptation. *Ethol. Sociobiol.,* 8, 63s–72s.

Hart, B. L., Hart, L., Mooring, M. S. & Olubayo, R. 1992. Biological basis of grooming behavior in the antelope: The body-size, vigilance and habitat principles. *Anim. Behav.,* 44, 615–631.

Hart, B. L. & Hart, L. A. 1992. Reciprocal allogrooming in impala, *Aepyceros melampus. Anim. Behav.,* 44, 1073–1083.

Hirshleifer, D. & Rasmussen, E. 1989. Cooperation in a repeated prisoner's dilemma game with ostracism. *J. Econ. Behav Org.,* 12, 87–106.

Hirshleifer, J. & Martinez-Coll, J. C. 1988. What strategies can support the evolutionary emergence of cooperation? *J. Conflict Resolution,* 32, 367–398.

Holldobler, B. & Wilson, E. O. 1990. *The Ants.* Cambridge, MA: Harvard University Press.

Huntingford, F. A., Lazarus, J., Barrie, B. D. & Webb, S. 1994. A dynamic analysis of cooperative predator inspection in sticklebacks. *Anim. Behav.,* 47, 413–423.

Joshi, N. V. 1987. Evolution of reciprocation in structured demes. *J. Genet.,* 1, 69–84.

Keller, L. (ed.). 1993. *Queen Number and Sociality in Insects.* Oxford: Oxford University Press.

Kropotkin, P. 1908. *Mutual Aid,* third edition. London: William Heinemann.

Lazarus, J. & Metcalfe, N. 1990. TIT FOR TAT cooperation in sticklebacks: A critique of Milinski. *Anim. Behav.,* 39, 987–989.

Lima, S. 1989. Iterated Prisoner's Dilemma: An approach to evolutionarily stable cooperation. *Am. Nat.,* 134, 828–834.

Lorberbaum, J. 1994. No strategy is evolutionarily stable in the repeated Prisoner's Dilemma. *J. Theor. Biol.,* 168, 117–130.

Magurran, A. E. & Higgam, A. 1988. Information transfer across fish shoals under predator threat. *Ethology,* 78, 153–158.

Magurran, A. E. & Pitcher, T. J. 1987. Provenance, shoal size and the sociobiology of predator evasion in minnow shoals. *Proc. R. Soc. Lond. B,* 229, 439–465.

Masters, M. & Waite, M. 1990. Tit-for-tat during predator inspection or shoaling? *Anim. Behav.,* 39, 603–604.

Mesterton-Gibbons, M. 1991. An escape from the Prisoner's Dilemma. *J. Math. Biol.,* 29, 251–269.

Mesterton-Gibbons, M. & Dugatkin, L. A. 1992. Cooperation among unrelated individuals: Evolutionary factors. *Q. Rev. Biol.,* 67, 267–281.

Mesterton-Gibbons, M. & L.A. Dugatkin 1997. Cooperation and the Prisoner's Dilemma: Toward testable models of mutualism versus reciprocity. *Anim. Behav.,* in press.

Michod, R. & Sanderson, M. 1985. Behavioral structure and the evolution of cooperation. In *Evolution—Essays in Honour of John Maynard Smith,* J. Greenwood & M. Slatkin, eds., pp. 95–104. Cambridge: Cambridge University Press.

Milinski, M. 1987. TIT FOR TAT and the evolution of cooperation in sticklebacks. *Nature,* 325, 433–435.

Milinski, M. 1990a. No alternative to TIT FOR TAT in sticklebacks. *Anim. Behav.,* 39, 989–991.

Milinski, M. 1990b. On cooperation in sticklebacks. *Anim. Behav.,* 40, 1190-1191.

Milinski, M. 1992. Predator inspection: Cooperation or "safety in numbers"? *Anim. Behav.,* 43, 679–681.

Milinski, M. 1996. Is by-product mutualism better than tit-for-tat reciprocity in explaining cooperative predator inspection? *Anim. Behav.,* 51, 458–461.

Milinski, M., Kulling, D. & Kettler, R. 1990a. Tit for Tat: Sticklebacks "trusting" a cooperating partner. *Behav. Ecol.,* 1, 7–12.

Milinski, M., Pfluger, D., Kulling, D. & Kettler, R. 1990b. Do sticklebacks cooperate repeatedly in reciprocal pairs? *Behav. Ecol. Sociobiol.,* 27, 17–23.

Mooring, M. S. & Hart, B. L. 1992. Reciprocal allogrooming in dam-reared and hand-reared impala fawns. *Ethology,* 90, 37–51.

Mooring, M. S. & Hart, B. L. 1995. Costs of allogrooming in impala: Distraction from vigilance. *Animal Behav.,* 49, 1414–1416.

Motro, U. 1991. Cooperation and defection: Playing the field and the ESS. *J. Theor. Biol.,* 151, 145–154.

Newman, J. & Caraco, T. 1989. Co-operative and noncooperative bases of food-calling. *J. Theor. Biol.*, 141, 197–209.

Nishida, T. 1979. The social structure of chimpanzees of the Mahale mountains. In *The Great Apes,* D. A. Hamburg & E. R. McCown, eds. Menlo Park, CA: Benjamin-Cummings.

Nishida, T., Hiraiwa-Hasegawa, M., Hasegawa, T. & Takahata, Y. 1985. Group extinction and female transfer in wild chimpanzees in the Mahale National Park, Tanzania. *Z. Tierpsych.*, 67, 284–301.

Noe, R. 1990. A veto game played by baboons: A challenge to the Prisoner's Dilemma as a paradigm for reciprocity and cooperation. *Anim. Behav.*, 39, 78–90.

Nowak, M. 1990a. An evolutionarily stable strategy may be inaccessible. *J. Theor. Biol.*, 142, 237–241.

Nowak, M. 1990b. Stochastic strategies in the Prisoner's Dilemma. *Theor. Pop. Biol.*, 38, 93–112.

Nowak, M. & Sigmund, K. 1989. Oscillations in the evolution of reciprocity. *J. Theor. Biol.*, 137, 21–26.

Nowak, M. & Sigmund, K. 1990. The evolution of stochastic strategies in the Prisoner's Dilemma. *Acta. Appl. Math.*, 20, 247–265.

Nowak, M. & Sigmund, K. 1992. Tit for tat in heterogeneous populations. *Nature*, 355, 250–252.

Nowak, M. & Sigmund, K. 1993. A strategy of win-stay, lose-shift that outperforms tit-for-tat in the Prisoner's Dilemma game. *Nature*, 364, 56–58.

Nowak, M. A. & Sigmund, K. 1994. The Alternating Prisoner's Dilemma. *J. Theor. Biol.*, 168, 219–226.

Packer, C. & Abrams, P. 1990. Should co-operative groups be more vigilant than selfish groups? *J. Theor. Biol.*, 142, 341–357.

Packer, C. & Rutton, L. 1988. The evolution of cooperative hunting. *Am. Nat.*, 132, 159–194.

Peck, J. & Feldman, M. 1986. The evolution of helping behavior in a large randomly mixed population. *Am. Nat.*, 127, 209–221.

Peck, J. R. 1993. Friendship and the evolution of cooperation. *J. Theor. Biol.*, 162, 195–228.

Pfennig, D. W. 1995. Absence of joint nesting advantage in desert seed harvester ants: Evidence from a field experiment. *Anim. Behav.*, 49, 567–575.

Pitcher, T. J., Green, D. A. & Magurran, A. E. 1986. Dicing with death: Predator inspection behavior in minnow shoals. *J. Fish Biol.*, 28, 439–448.

Pollock, G. 1988. Population structure, spite and the iterated Prisoner's Dilemma. *Am. J. Phys. Anthropol.*, 77, 209–221.

Pollock, G. 1989. Evolutionary stability of reciprocity in a viscous lattice. *Soc. Net.*, 11, 175–213.

Pollock, G. & Dugatkin, L. A. 1992. Reciprocity and the evolution of reputation. *J. Theor. Biol.*, 159, 25–37.

Queller, D. C. 1985. Kinship, reciprocity and synergism in the evolution of social behavior. *Nature*, 318, 366–367.

Rissing, S. & Pollock, G. 1986. Social interaction among pleometric queens of *Veromessor pergandei* during colony foundation. *Anim. Behav.*, 34, 226–234.

Rissing, S. & Pollock, G. 1987. Queen aggression, pleometric advantage and brood raiding in the ant *Veromessor pergandei. Anim. Behav.*, 35, 975–982.

Rissing, S., Pollock, G., Higgins, M., Hagen, R. & Smith, D. 1989. Foraging specialization without relatedness or dominance among co-founding ant queens. *Nature*, 338, 420–422.

Rothstein, S. & Pirotti, R. 1987. Distinctions among reciprocal altruism, kin selection and cooperation and a model for the initial evolution of beneficent behavior. *Ethol. Sociobiol.*, 9, 189–209.

Seger, J. 1989. All for one, one for all, that is our device. *Nature*, 338, 374–375.

Sella, G. 1985. Reciprocal egg trading and brood care in a hermaphroditic polycheate worm. *Anim. Behav.*, 33, 938–944.

Sella, G. 1988. Reciprocation, reproductive success and safeguards against cheating in a hermaphroditic polycheate worm. *Biol. Bull.*, 175, 212–217.

Sella, G. 1991. Evolution of biparental care in the hermaphroditic polychaete worm *Ophryotrocha diadema. Evolution*, 45, 63–68.

Stephens, D. W., Anderson, J. P. & Toyer, K. B. 1997. On the spurious occurrence of tit-for-tat in pairs of predator-approaching fish. *Anim. Behav.*, 53, 113–131.

Stephens, D. W., Nishimura, K. & Toyer, K. B. 1995. Error discounting in the iterated Prisoner's Dilemma. *J. Theor. Biol.* 167, 457–469.

Strassmann, J. 1989. Altruism and relatedness at colony foundation in social insects. *Trends Ecol. Evol.*, 4, 371–374.

Thomas, E. & Feldman, M. 1988. Behavior-dependent contexts for repeated plays of the Prisoner's Dilemma. *J. Conf. Resol.*, 32, 699–726.

Toro, M. & Silio, L. 1986. Assortment of encounters in the two-strategy game. *J. Theor. Biol.*, 123, 193–204.

Trivers, R. L. 1971. The evolution of reciprocal altruism. *Q. Rev. Biol.*, 46, 189–226.

Tschinkel, W. & Howard, D. F. 1983. Colony founding by pleometrosis in the fire ant, *Solenopsis inviticus. Behav. Ecol. Sociobiol.*, 12, 103–113.

Turner, G. F. & Robinson, R. L. 1992. Milinski's tit for tat hypothesis: Do fish preferentially inspect in pairs? *Anim. Behav.*, 43, 677–679.

Wade, M. J. 1977. An experimental study of group selection. *Evolution*, 31, 134–153.

Wade, M. J. 1978. A critical review of the models of group selection. *Q. Rev. Biol.*, 53, 101–114.

Wade, M. J. 1979. The primary characteristics of Tribolium populations group selected for increased and decreased population size. *Evolution*, 33, 749–764.

Wasser, S. 1982. Reciprocity and the trade-off between associate quality and relatedness. *Am. Nat.*, 119, 720–731.

West-Eberhard, M. J. 1975. The evolution of social behavior by kin selection. *Q. Rev. Biol.*, 50, 1–35.

Wilson, D. 1976. Evolution on the level of communities. *Science*, 192, 1358–1360.

Wilson, D. 1977. Structured demes and the evolution of group-advantageous traits. *Am. Nat.*, 111, 157–185.

Wilson, D. S. 1975. A general theory of group selection. *Proc. Natl. Acad. Sci., USA*, 72, 143–146.

Wilson, D. S. 1980. *The Natural Selection of Populations and Communities.* Menlo Park, CA: Benjamin-Cummings.

Wilson, D. S. 1983. The group selection controversy: history and current status. *Annu. Rev. Ecol. Syst.*, 14, 159–187.

Wilson, D. S. 1990. Weak altruism, strong group selection. *Oikos*, 59, 135–140.

Wilson, D. S. & Dugatkin, L.A. 1992. Altruism. In *Keywords in Evolutionary Biology*, E. Fox Keller & E. A. Lloyd, eds., pp. 28–33. Cambridge: Harvard.

Wilson, D. S. & Dugatkin, L. A. 1991. TIT FOR TAT vs nepotism, or, why should you be nice to your rotten brother? *Evol. Ecol.*, 5, 291–299.

Wilson, D. S. & Dugatkin, L. A. 1997. Group selection and assortative interactions. *Am. Nat.*, 139, 336–351.

Wilson, D. S. & Sober, E. 1994. Re-introducing group selection to the human behavioral sciences. *Behav. Brain Sci.*, 17, 585–654.

Wynne-Edwards, V. C. 1962. *Animal Dispersion in Relation to Social Behavior.* Edinburgh: Oliver & Boyd.

Susan E. Riechert

Game Theory and Animal Contests

4.1 Introduction

It is not at all surprising that the first application of game theory to a biological phenomenon dealt with the problem of animal conflict. Here is an area of biology that is pervasive. All animals and even plants, for that matter, compete for resources that may be present in limited supply. A common mechanism of resource defense is to exclude others from access to the resource. This is direct competition, as opposed to exploitation competition in which individuals that are better competitors take more of the limiting resource than do others.

Contests represent the means by which individuals or groups of individuals exclude others from resources. Most of our work on contests has been on male–male competition for mates and individuals fighting for territories or rank in a social hierarchy. It is important to note that contests include a much broader group of interactions than these two classes of disputes. Contests can take place between individuals belonging to closely related species or ecological equivalents that have similar feeding or space requirements (e.g., see discussion in Riechert & Hammerstein 1983). Contests also occur between the sexes (e.g., Petrie & Lipsitch 1994), between juveniles and adults (e.g., Hansen 1986), between parents and their offspring and other close relatives (e.g., Chapais 1985), and between social groups (e.g., McEachron & Baer 1982).

Regardless of which class of individuals is interacting, direct or interference competition is often pairwise (involving two opponents). Thus, the pairwise contest structure typical of classical game theory often fits the pairwise contests observed between animals. Maynard Smith and Price (1973) conceived the idea of applying classical game theory to animal conflict, in part because of the good fit of the method of analysis to the evolutionary context. Perhaps, more importantly, game theory offered a selfish alternative (individual selection) to the traditionally altruistic (group selection) explanation of why dangerous weapons are rarely used in intraspecific contests (see Wilson and Dugatkin, both in this volume, for somewhat different views of this issue). Prior to the publication of this seminal article, studies of animal contests were also approached from a motivational basis. Evolutionary game theory has led away from this focus on motivation and emphasized the tactical aspects of games. As a result, it has contributed much to our understanding of contest structure.

Included among the questions answered by the application of the game theory construct to animal conflict is the problem of why animal contests are so often settled by what game theorists refer to as conventional behavior, rather than by injurious fighting. Conventional behavior involves visual, auditory, olfactory, and/or vibratory displays that often are ritualized or stereotyped and that are noninjurious. Until the development of evolutionary game theory, the common view of the use of conventional behavior in animal conflict was that animals avoided injuring one another for the "good" of their population. This was a group selectionist argument and one that conflicts with the basic tenet of evolution by natural selection operating among individuals. Maynard Smith and Price (1973) used game theory to explain the use of conventional behavior in terms of the selfish interests of the individual contestants. For the evolutionary game, Maynard Smith and Price used fitness as the currency to be maximized and substituted the operation of natural selection in the place of rational thought for the decision process (or causal agent). The solution to this biological game then, the Evolutionarily Stable Strategy (ESS), is the set of behavioral programs an individual is expected to apply to the various contest roles it may find itself in (e.g., a smaller owner of a high-quality site; a larger intruder competing for a poor-quality site). The ESS is that solution which is stable to invasion by any individual that exhibits a mutant strategy (Maynard Smith 1982, Hammerstein, this volume).

Evolutionary game theory has clearly demonstrated that animal conflict can be explained in terms of individual costs and benefits, and this finding has shifted the emphasis of study to the functional rather than the motivational aspects of contests. With the continued development and use of the ESS thinking in the field of animal behavior, we have made inroads into many of the complexities of animal contests. In this chapter I consider these problems, which include: (1) the reasons for inherent variability in contests with respect to the behavior patterns exhibited, contest durations, and levels of escalation reached, (2) what ESS models might best fit animal contests, (3) the problem of payoffs (how do you measure costs and benefits and what currencies are relevant?), and (4) how to use ESS analyses to test predictions (e.g., the function of specific signals and the assumption of adaptive equilibrium).

Although I will discuss other work on each of these subjects where possible, I will rely, in the first place, on the spider system that I and various collaborators have worked on for a number of years, namely territorial disputes between individual *Agelenopsis aperta* Gertsch. *Agelenopsis aperta* (Agelenidae) is a wide-ranging spider in the western United States. It is a sheet-web builder that attaches a silk-funnel retreat to its web-trap. Since this retreat provides protection from unfavorable thermal environments, *Agelenopsis* is a successful aridlands species that ranges from northern Wyoming to southern Mexico and from western California to central Texas. This spider is an annual species that defends an energy-based territory throughout its life, though adult males do give up their territories to search for matings at the end of their lifespans (Riechert 1978a).

4.2 Contest Variability

Ethologists commonly refer to the highly stereotyped nature of animal contests. The head bobs and push-ups typically exhibited by lizards in territorial disputes are excellent examples of this "ritualized" behavior (reviewed in Carpenter 1978). However, contests often show marked variability both within and between populations, let alone between closely related species. DeCourcy and Jenssen (1994), for instance, report that the lizard *Anolis carolinensis* exhibits three distinct head-bob patterns that are emphasized in different contest contexts. They also observed variation in the rates at which these displays were exhibited that were unique to specific contexts.

I have found the behavior exhibited by *A. aperta* fighting over web-sites and associated territories to be even more variable. *Anolis carolinensis* exhibits three behavior patterns that are all variants of head-bobbing. *Agelenopsis aperta,* on the other hand, exhibits as many as 33 different behavior patterns during its territorial disputes. Within one population, these disputes ranged from a few seconds in duration to over 21 hours. At times, contests are settled by displays (conventional behavior) and at other times they involve escalated fighting (Riechert 1978b). To gain some understanding of the nature of this variability, I applied a multivariate mapping technique to the data set, consisting of 81 contests distributed in attribute (behavioral act space). Figure 4.1 shows a three-dimensional representation of the first three axes of this Bray and Curtis ordination. The technique computes similarity indices between each dispute and every other dispute and then uses a Euclidean distance measure to position the sequences relative to one another on axes. The resulting pictorial representation summarizes the interrelationships existing between sequences in terms of their structure. Thus, contests that exhibit similar act-frequency compositions are clustered together on the figure. Each axis accounts for a decreasing proportion of the variance in frequency distributions of the 33 behavior patterns observed among the 81 contest sequences analyzed (first or x axis $= 47.5\%$, second or y axis $= 11.7\%$, and third or z axis $= 11.0\%$). Inspection of the behavior exhibited in sequences with respect to their positions along the various axes (shown in Fig. 4.1) indicates that the variability among sequences explained by the first axis is associated with different estimated contest costs (i.e., a measure of duration and level of escalation), that the spread of sequences along the second axis is associated with different contest complexities (the total number of acts and the number of different action patterns exhibited), and that the spread of sequences along the z axis reflects the degree of complexity in acts exhibited by the winning spider following the withdrawal of its opponent. *Agelenopsis aperta's* territorial disputes are obviously highly variable.

Evolutionary game theory provides an explanation for variability in such aspects of contest structure as cost and duration. It predicts that two factors determine these parameters: (1) the degree to which there is disparity between the contestants in their probability of winning a dispute and (2) the value of the disputed resource. The information presented for the contests listed in Table 4.1 gives some indication of the variability that is exhibited in a diverse array of contests. In many of these studies, authors have concentrated on contest outcome rather than on its underlying structure: Variability in contest duration and levels of escalation are, thus, underestimated.

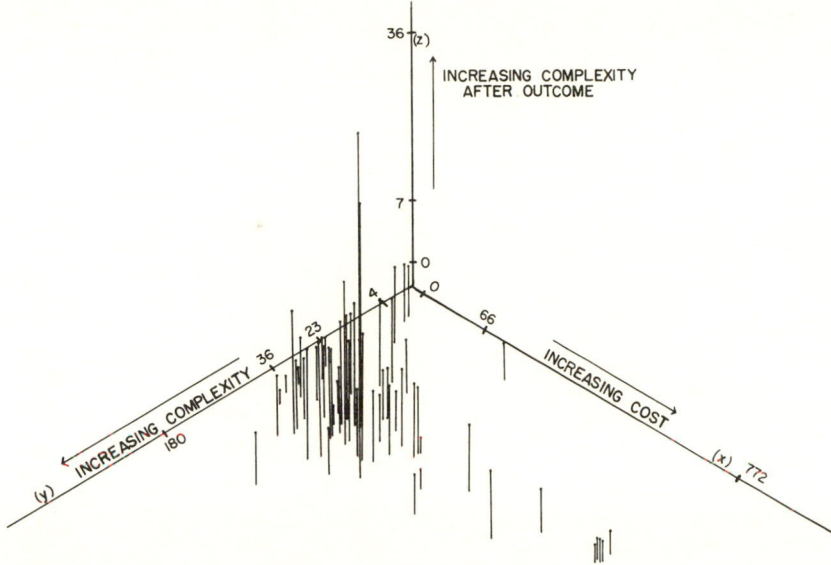

Figure 4.1. Three-dimensional representation of first three axes of a Bray and Curtis ordination of territorial disputes between conspecific *Agelenopsis aperta* (see text for explanation). Plotted on each axis is the contest feature that explains the spread of sequences.

4.3 Disparity in the Probability of Winning: Asymmetric Contests

Often contests are settled without escalated fighting following an initial assessment phase. It is during this period that individuals gain information on potential asymmetries that might determine contest outcome without actual fighting. Most of these are correlated asymmetries, traits, or states that would actually affect an individual's probability of winning the particular contest if a fight were to occur. A difference in payoff, relative to what its opponent would achieve, is another kind of correlated asymmetry because payoffs influence the level of fighting that individuals are willing to engage in. Asymmetries which are not correlated with the potential for winning a fight or that do not reflect differences in payoffs awarded as a result of winning a contest are referred to as uncorrelated asymmetries (Maynard Smith & Parker 1976).

4.3.1 Correlated Asymmetries

For the moment, let's restrict our discussion to the correlated asymmetries. An individual's probability of winning is referred to as its RHP or resource-holding power (Parker 1974). Experience, size, age, and sex are examples of character states that may differ between contestants, thus giving one individual an RHP that is greater than that of its opponent. Table 4.1 shows the degree to which asymmetries of various kinds are known to influence contest outcomes, durations, and levels of escalation.

Table 4.1 Effects of Asymmetries on Various Aspects of Contest Structure

Asymmetry	Contest Features			Reference
	Duration	Escalation	Outcome	
Size disparity				
Prawns[a]			incr[b]	Evans & Shehadi-Moacdieh (1988)
Sea Anemone			incr	Brace (1981)
Velvet swimming crabs	decr[b]	decr	incr	Smith et al. (1994)
Funnel-web spider[a]	decr	decr	incr	Riechert (1987)
Jumping spider	decr	decr	incr	Wells (1988)
Giant damselfly			incr	Fincke (1984)
Dragonfly			incr	Miller (1983), Tsubaki & Ono (1987)
Admiral butterfly[a]			incr	Rosenberg & Enquist (1991)
Damselfly larvae	decr	decr	incr	Crowley et al. (1988)
Trout (two species)		decr		Jenkins (1969)
Blue gourami		decr		Miller (1964)
Pumpkinseed sunfish			incr	Beacham (1988)
Mouthbrooding cichlid[a]		decr	incr	Turner (1994), Turner & Huntingford (1986)
River bullhead			incr	Bisazza & Marconato (1988)
Bullfrogs			incr	Howard (1978, 1984)
Sand lizard (nuptial patch)			incr	Olsson (1994)
Meadow voles			incr	Turner & Iverson (1973)
African elephant (nonmusth)[a]	decr	decr	incr	Poole (1989)
Residency				
Marine isopod crustacean				Shuster (1992)
Prawns[a]			incr	Evans & Shehadi-Moacdieh (1988)
Funnel-web spider	incr		incr	Riechert (1987)
Social spider (retreat residency)[c]			incr	Burgess (1976)
Calopteryx maculata			incr	Waage (1988)
Larval damselfly			incr	Harvey & Corbet (1986)
Damselfly			incr	Gribbin & Thompson (1991)
Admiral butterfly			incr	Rosenberg & Enquist (1991)
Speckled-wood butterfly			incr	Davies (1978)
Mouthbrooding cichlid[a]	incr	incr	incr	Turner (1994)
Anole	decr			Stamps & Kirishnan (1995)
Anole (length of residency)			incr	McMann (1993)
Great tit			incr	Wilson (1992)
Experience				
Dragonfly larvae			incr	Baker (1983)
Black-billed magpies (winter dominance)[c]			decr	Komers (1989)
Physiological state				
Damselfly larvae (hunger)			incr	Crowley et al. (1988)
Damselfly males (fat reserves)			incr	Marden & Rollins (1994)
Fruit fly (males) (developmental temperatures)[a]			incr	Zamudio et al. (1994)
Meadow voles (hunger)			incr	Silbaugh & Ewald (1987)
African elephants (musth)[a]	decr	decr	incr	Poole (1989)
Sex				
Convict cichlids	decr		incr	Koops & Grant (1993)
Coho salmon			incr	Holtby et al. (1993)

| | Contest Features | | | |
Asymmetry	Duration	Escalation	Outcome	Reference
Great tits (males over females)			incr	Wilson (1992)
Duration of food deprivation[b]				
Hermit crab			incr	Hazlett (1966)
Spider crab			incr	Hazlett & Estabrook (1974)
Crayfish		incr	incr	Hazlett et al. (1975)
White rat			incr	Bruce (1941)
Domestic cat		incr	incr	Cole & Shaffer (1966)
Chimpanzee			incr	Nowlis (1941)

[a]More than one relevant contest asymmetry reported for taxon.
[b]incr = increases; decr = decreases.
[c]Paradoxical asymmetries.
[d]Asymmetry that is associated with resource value payoff (see Table 4.2).

As already mentioned in the previous section, one might mistakenly conclude from inspection of the table that asymmetries affect only contest outcome. This is because many workers were only interested in the potential for asymmetries to decide contests. Clearly, though, if asymmetries regularly exist in a given system and animals are able to accurately measure these, then contests may be short and limited to displays. For instance, Fritts (1984) reports a decision rule that exists for male Galapagos tortoises fighting over females: "The taller contestant wins." In addition to having morphological characteristics that permit these tortoises to extend their necks skyward, males seek out rocks and other habitat features that give them height advantages during disputes.

Various workers have demonstrated the significance of asymmetries to contest outcome by manipulating asymmetric relations. In the study of *A. aperta's* territorial disputes, Riechert (1982) altered the weight of intruding individuals by gluing flattened lead shot to their abdomens. This made intruding spiders significantly heavier than the web residents, but without increasing the intruders' apparent sizes (visually). The resident spiders retreated from these manipulated spiders with the same frequency that they exhibited toward naturally heavier opponents (Table 4.2), indicating that visual cues are not used in size determinations but rather relative body mass. Note that weight is a highly significant RHP asymmetry in this spider's contests: 30% of the time, a smaller (lighter) intruding individual withdraws from the dispute following the first few acts without approach or engagement (Riechert 1982).

Size does seem to be the common correlated asymmetry that is used in settling disputes (Table 4.1). This is not surprising, since size is generally correlated with strength and the ability to inflict injury (Archer 1987). If contestants were to engage in actual fighting, then the larger individual would be the probable winner. From Table 4.1, however, it is apparent that this is not always the case. This is because an outcome predicted on the basis of size may be overridden by some other asymmetry such as experience or prior residency. Residence asymmetries are considered to be important determinants of contest outcome, though Grafen (1987) finds fault with a residency bias, particularly in cases of long-term ownership of a resource. He lists two compelling reasons for not considering residency as a valid asymmetry: (1)

Table 4.2 Probability of Territory Owner Showing Initial Retreat Following Encroachment by Intruders Under Weight and Size Bias Categories Shown[a]

	Class Intruder Relative to Owner	
	Apparent Size	P of Initial Owner Retreat
Natural ($N=154$)		
Body mass (mg)		
Advantage > 10%	Larger	0.81
Difference < 10%	Equal	0.22
Disadvantage > 10%	Smaller	0.13
Manipulated ($N=25$)		
Body mass (mg)		
Advantage > 10%	Smaller	0.83

[a]Grassland *Agelenopsis aperta*.

When an individual wins an energy-based territory, it obtains more food, gets larger, and thus is more successful in winning subsequent contests and (2) in many apparent "resident wins" systems, intruders are merely checking for resource occupation. Why should an individual approach an owner at all if the conventional outcome is inevitable and known to both players beforehand (e.g., speckled-wood butterflies: Davies 1978)?

Where more than one asymmetry exists, a size asymmetry is generally overridden or influenced by the other asymmetry. For example, resident biases override weight asymmetries in damselfly (Gribbin & Thompson 1991) and spider (Hammerstein & Riechert 1988) territorial disputes and in prawn (Evans & Shehadi-Moacdieh 1988) and butterfly (Rosenberg & Enquist 1991) agonistic disputes. Residence sometimes overrides weight, because the disputed resource is more valuable to owners than to intruders. Dugatkin and Ohlsen (1990) demonstrated this phenomenon experimentally in pumpkinseed sunfish by offering smaller fish greater food rewards than they offered larger fish at a contested resource: The smaller fish won contests over the contested site in this context.

Experience may also override size considerations, as Beacham (1988) noted in the case of dominance patterns exhibited by pumpkinseed sunfish. So may physiological states: Zamudio et al. (1994) found that smaller male fruitflies won more mating-related contests, because these animals had developed at higher temperatures and as a result were physiologically more active. It was this RHP asymmetry that affected contest outcome rather than size per se. Size determines contest outcome among male elephants that are not in a heightened physiological state of musth (Poole 1989). (Musth is a physiological state in which males exhibit both unique vocalizations and a distinct odor and is associated with heightened male reproductive behavior.) Male elephants in musth win contests over elephants that are larger but that are not in musth. Poole (1989) reports that musth males exhibit heightened aggressiveness and thus would be more likely to win matings if escalated fighting were to occur.

The problem of assessing the relative influence of different asymmetries on contests was solved by Hammerstein (1981) through his partitioning of game payoff matrices into subgames, each of which tests the significance of a potential asymmetry. It is the assumption of perfect information that allows the decomposition of the game into subgames. Hammerstein demonstrated that payoff-irrelevant asymmetries may be used in conventional settlement of contests even when payoff-relevant asymmetric characters exist. He also found that when two strong and opposing RHP asymmetries exist, the contest may not be settled conventionally. He used a class of *A. aperta* contests as an example of this phenomenon: A resident bias versus a size bias that favors an intruder typically leads to fighting in *A. aperta* (Riechert 1978b, 1982).

4.3.2 Uncorrelated Asymmetries

One example of an uncorrelated asymmetry may be "resident wins" games. For instance, Waage (1988) tested for the existence of a "resident wins" asymmetry in the territorial disputes of male damselflies by causing two males to assume ownership of the same territory. He observed a subsequent level of escalation that fit the prediction of a breakdown in a resident wins rule. Other types of uncorrelated asymmetries are also known. Table 4.1 includes two examples of what Maynard Smith (1989) refers to as paradoxical ESSs. (These cases are denoted by footnote *c* in Table 4.1). One example comes from Burgess's (1976) observation of interactions between social spiders over retreats in a communal nest. He found that the normal resident (or bourgeois asymmetry) did not hold in this case. Instead, owners readily abandoned their funnel retreats when challenged by intruding spiders. These losers then went and deposed other owners, creating a domino effect in retreat ownership throughout the colony. Hodge and Uetz (1995) report a similar finding for competition over webs within a tropical colonial spider species. Here, web-sites are abundant and owners leave on the arrival of intruding individuals.

Komers (1989) provides evidence for another paradoxical asymmetry involving residency. During the winter, subordinate black-billed magpies are dominant over breeding birds in obtaining access to food. Breeding birds are typically dominant over nonbreeders, and this is the case in this species for access to food in other seasons. Uncorrelated asymmetries can be evolutionarily stable under conditions in which the value of the resource is low (Maynard Smith 1989). All of the cases mentioned here reflect conditions of resource abundance and low need.

4.3.3 Asymmetries and Contest Structure

Asymmetries influence contest durations and the levels of escalation that are observed in them, in addition to the effect that they have on contest outcome. Contest duration and the degree or probability of escalation are inversely related to the degree of asymmetry (Table 4.1): Where sizes are similar, contests are longer and are more likely to involve escalation. This relationship is nicely demonstrated in examining contest sequences between spiders that vary markedly in body mass (differ by $>10\%$) (Fig. 4.2a) versus those between contestants that are similar in size (difference of $\leq 10\%$)(Fig. 4.2b: Riechert 1984). The assessment phase of contests involving opponents that have large RHP differences is short, escalated behavior is minimal, and withdrawal following retreat from an opponent is much more likely than in contests involving individuals that are similar in weight. Here the animals spend long periods

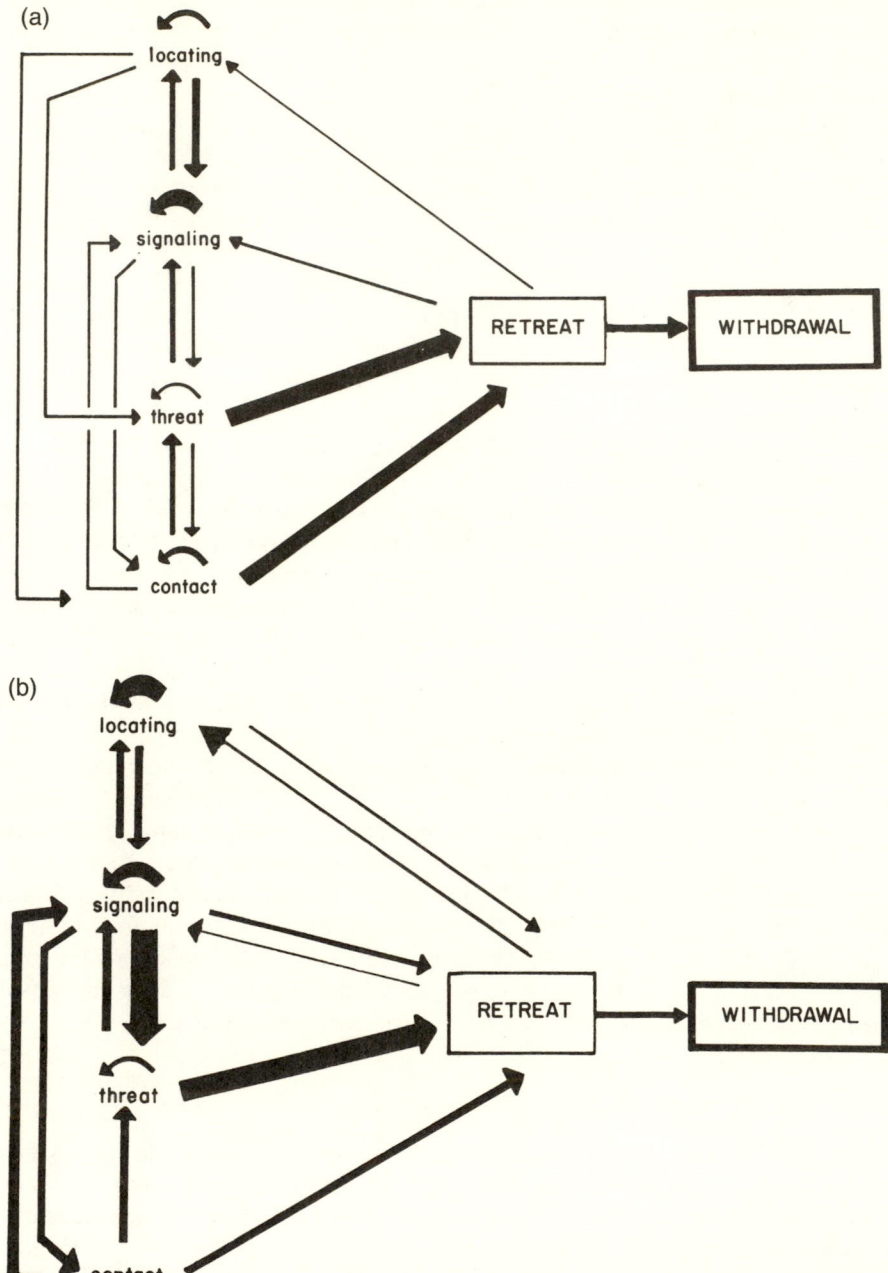

Figure 4.2. Transition probabilities between successively higher cost behavior patterns [locating (assessment)–contact] for territorial disputes of *Agelenopsis aperta:* (a) involving a weight asymmetry $\geq 10\%$; and (b) between individuals that are evenly matched ($<10\%$ size difference). Width of arrows represents relative frequency of transitions indicated.

in assessment with escalation that frequently goes back to display, rather than to withdrawal (Fig. 4.2b). As a result, the latter class of contests are of much longer duration.

4.3.4 Resource Value Asymmetries

As Korona (1991) demonstrates analytically, any number of asymmetries (including correlated asymmetries, such as those in resource value) may affect individual behavior and performance in contests. Resource value is one of these, if winning confers a greater payoff to one contestant than to another. Payoff asymmetries are frequently associated with the feeding state of individuals (e.g., starved versus sated) (Table 4.1). Animals that are more food-deprived (hungrier) tend to win contests, even contests that do not involve escalated fighting.

4.3.5 Resource Value

Examples of the effects that resource value can have on various aspects of contests are presented in Table 4.3. Across a wide range of animals, the contestant that is

Table 4.3 Effects of Resource Value on Various Aspects of Contest Structure

Resource	Contest Duration	Level of Escalation	Outcome	Reference
Duration of food depriva-tion[a]				
Hermit crab			incr	Hazlett (1966)
Spider crab			incr	Hazlett & Estabrook (1974)
Crayfish		incr[b]	incr	Hazlett et al. (1975)
White rat			incr	Bruce (1941)
Domestic cat		incr		Cole & Shaffer (1966)
Chimpanzee			incr	Nowlis (1941)
Limited mating opportuni-ties				
Marine isopod crustacean		incr		Shuster (1992)
Bowl-and-doily spider	incr		Owner incr	Austad (1983)
Dung fly	incr		Owner incr	Sigurjonsdottir & Parker (1981)
Red-spotted newt	incr			Verrell (1986)
Red deer	incr			Clutton-Brock et al. (1979)
Limited food/site availability				
Funnel-web spider	incr	incr	Owner incr	Riechert (1979, 1984)
Digger wasp	incr		incr	Dawkins & Brockmann (1980)
Iguana		incr	incr	Rand & Rand (1976)
Starling			incr	Bruce (1941)
Fulmar		incr	incr	Enquist et al. (1985)
Bald eagle		incr	incr	Hansen (1986)
Grey-breasted silver eye			incr	Kikkawa (1968)
Shrew			incr	Barnard & Brown (1984)

[a]Items also presented in Table 4.1 under RHP asymmetries.
[b]incr = increases.

more food-deprived wins disputes over food. This is expected, because the value of the disputed food is greater to the food-deprived individual than it is to the sated individual. This phenomenon exemplifies a payoff asymmetry.

It is not necessary for a payoff asymmetry to exist for contest value to have important influences on contests. Mating opportunities are resources that vary without necessarily having a payoff asymmetry. Where these are limited, contest durations are longer than where mating opportunities are abundant (Table 4.3). Finally, space may be limited as in nesting or foraging sites. There are numerous examples of the effects of site availability on contest duration, the frequency of escalated contests, and on contest outcome where RHP asymmetries are not honored (Table 4.3). The behavior of *Agelenopsis aperta* in territorial disputes, for instance, fits resource value very closely. These are energy-based territories that are maintained throughout the lifespans of individuals. Because there are a limited number of sites in the desert grassland area studied, which ensure survival to reproduction in most years (Fig. 4.3:

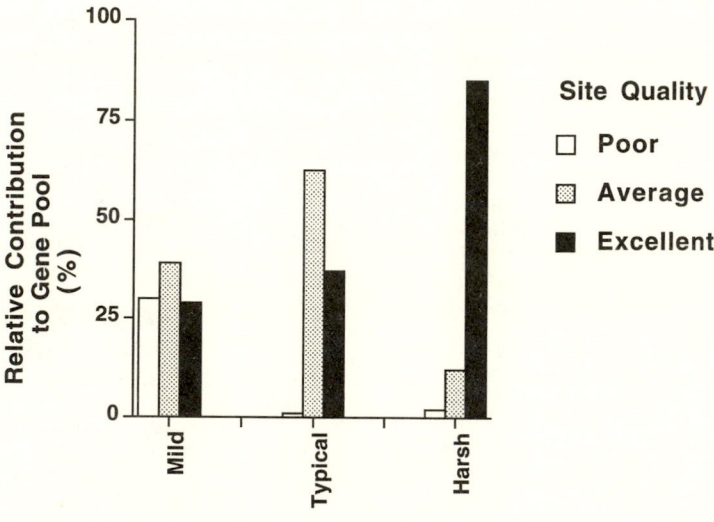

Environmental Conditions

Figure 4.3. Relative contribution (percent of offspring) contributed to gene pool by spiders occupying different quality territories under varying environments in a desert grassland habitat occupied by *Agelenopsis aperta*. Mild, typical, and harsh years refer to prey accessibility, which in turn is dependent on existing temperatures and moistures. Typical years in this study area are characterized by winter and summer precipitation and a hot–dry period between May and July. Mild years reflect greater precipitation and cloudiness, especially in late spring and early summer, while harsh years are drought years with little winter precipitation, no rain in the spring, and very hot and dry conditions between May and July. Data presented represent reproductive success per individual summed for the number of sites occupied by *A. aperta* of respective qualities. Note that 4% of the available web-sites are of excellent quality and 12% are of average quality.

Riechert 1981), *A. aperta* adjusts its conflict behavior to site quality (Riechert 1979). Smaller owners of high-quality sites, for instance, are very persistent at maintaining these sites (Table 4.4), and thus the longest contest durations are in these contexts. On the other hand, contests over poor-quality sites are short in duration and no instances of escalation to fighting has been observed (Table 4.4). I have experimented with the owners of poor-quality sites in the grassland habitat by supplementing individuals at their sites daily for 7 days prior to releasing intruders in the vicinity of their webs. The perceived value of the sites increased to the extent that these owners became markedly more persistent in their contests when compared to a sample of individuals that did not receive this food supplementation regime (Table 4.5: Riechert 1984). Note, however, that the probability of winning disputes did not show a corresponding shift in the supplemented individuals. This most likely reflects their status as poor competitors, which kept them at low-quality sites in the first place.

In addition to affecting individual persistence, contests over valued resources involve more escalation to potentially injurious behavior. Table 4.6 demonstrates this relationship as it pertains to the frequency of fatal injuries observed in a number of different contest systems. Where resources are occupied for only a short time period and offer little fitness advantage [e.g., speckled-wood butterflies competing for sunspots on a forest floor (Davies 1978)], the probability of mortality in contests is 0. Male mammals competing for matings in a system where animals may live to mate another year also exhibit limited serious injury. For instance, Clutton-Brock and Albon (1979) report a probability of serious injury of only about 0.02 among male red deer competing for matings. On the other hand, honeybee and bumblebee queens competing for control of the colonies they are born into (an all or nothing contest) are reported to exhibit a probability of death of 1.0 [Wilson (1971) and Alford (1975), respectively]. That is, in every contest between two queens, one suffers mortality. Another example of high mortality (62%) comes from gall insect larvae who fight over sole access to the plant galls they occupy (Aoki & Makino 1982). As larvae cannot move between galls, their resource is extremely spatially limited.

Table 4.4 Comparison of Various Contest Characteristics of Disputes Involving Territories of Different Quality (RHP Bias Constant, Favoring Intruder)[a]

| Contest Measure (Means + SE) | Quality of Territory | | | |
	Poor ($N=48$)	Average ($N=52$)	Excellent ($N=54$)	Test and Significance Level
Number of bouts	1.8 ± 0.4	3.2 ± 1.3	$3.8 + 0.5$	χ^2 $P < 0.025$
Number of acts	16.3 ± 4.4	48.6 ± 20.9	74.2 ± 13.7	Kruskal–Wallis $P < 0.001$
Richness (number of kinds of acts)	4.8 ± 0.6	7.3 ± 1.0	$12.0 + 1.0$	Kruskal–Wallis $P < 0.001$
Estimated cost (rank score)	94 ± 20	620 ± 233	$1226 + 208$	Kruskal–Wallis $P < 0.001$
Relative representation of "warlike" behavior (threat and contact)	0.07 ± 0.03	0.18 ± 0.07	$0.19 + 0.03$	Kruskal–Wallis $P < 0.001$
Estimated contact cost (rank score)	0 ± 0	0 ± 0	$92 + 3.8$	

[a]Desert grassland *Agelenopsis aperta*.

Table 4.5 Comparison of Contest Statistics Disputes Over Energy-Based Territories Involving Supplemented Versus Unsupplemented Owners of Poor-Quality Sites[a]

Measures	Owner Supplemented ($N=25$)	Owner Unsupplemented ($N=25$)	Significance Level	Test
Estimated contest cost (rank score) (mean $\pm$ SE)	62.8 ± 15.0	46.4 ± 18.1	$P < 0.05$	Mann–Whitney
Number of bouts (mean $\pm$ SE)	2.8 ± 0.04	1.8 ± 0.08	$P < 0.25$	Chi square
P of loss given no size advantage	0.77	.08	$P > 0.50$	Chi square

[a]Desert grassland *Agelenopsis aperta.*

The variation in the value of available feeding territories to *Agelenopsis aperta* (Hammerstein & Riechert 1988) and in the opportunity for matings in the bowl-and-doily spider, *Frontinella pyramitela* (Austad 1983), is reflected in corresponding differences in the frequencies of fatal injuries (Table 4.6). The relationship between the payoff of a given contest and contests over an individual's lifetime has been formalized in Enquist and Leimar (1990). They found that role asymmetries, kinship, and relative fighting ability have little influence on contests in which the ratio of value of the future to value of the immediate resource is small. If the value (potential payoff of the resource in question) is very high, then escalated fighting is predicted regardless of potential biases that might influence outcome, and the single contest is all-important.

4.4 Conceptual ESS Models Applied to Animal Contests

Three conceptual models have been applied to animal contests: the Hawk–Dove game and modifications of it (Maynard Smith & Price 1973, Maynard Smith 1982), the War of Attrition model (Bishop & Cannings 1978, Parker & Thompson 1980), and the Sequential Assessment game (Enquist & Leimar 1987). It is clear that each of these models fits some contest situations better than others and that they also differ in the kinds of insight they provide into agonistic behavior.

4.4.1 The Hawk–Dove Game

The Hawk–Dove game was first described in Maynard Smith and Price (1973) as a dyadic tool for explaining the game theory construct. The essential feature of this contest model is that pairwise contests (which can be analyzed in matrix form) take place between two opponents. In the early models, it was assumed that opponents do not differ in any way that is recognized at the start of the contest: The game is symmetric. Maynard Smith and Price (1973) also assumed that there was a finite set of discrete strategies which permits the matrix form of analysis characteristic to classical game theory.

Table 4.6 Relationship Between Value of Disputed Resource and Probability of Severe Injury

Taxon	Resource	P of Severe Injury	Reference
Speckled-wood butterfly	Mating sites	0	Davies (1978)
Larval damselflies	Feeding sites	0	Crowley et al. (1988)
Red deer	Matings	0.02	Clutton-Brock et al. (1979)
Funnel-web spiders	Feeding territories	0.02–0.06	Hammerstein & Riechert (1988)
Old World fig wasp	Matings	0.04	Murray (1987)
African elephants	Matings	0.1	Poole (1989)
Bowl-and-doily spiders	Matings	0.1–0.6	Austad (1983)
Ant: Veromessor pergandei	Colony control	0.44	Rissing & Pollock (1987)
Gall insect larvae	Feeding site	0.62	Aoki & Makino (1982)
Honeybee queens	Colony control	1	Wilson (1971)
Bumblebees	Colony control	1	Alford (1975)

The two strategies that were available to contestants in the basic Hawk–Dove game were "Hawk" (escalate until injured or until opponent retreats) and "Dove" (display, but retreat if opponent escalates). Payoff matrices were developed for each situation an individual might find itself in [e.g., playing H (hawk) against H versus playing D (dove) against H]. The payoffs were based on V (the value of winning) and C (the cost of injury). Of course, this game itself was much too simple to have any real-world validity. However, complexities can be added including assessment of potential RHP asymmetries and the division of the matrix into subgames that reflect the behavioral choices that animals may exhibit given the conditional role that each may find itself in (Hammerstein 1981). For example, *Agelenopsis aperta* exhibits size and residence RHP asymmetries. It also contests sites that vary in quality (payoff). Hammerstein and Riechert (1988) divide these contests into subgames and analyze each payoff matrix to predict the overall conditional strategy of (A) "escalate" if larger or equal in size to an owner of a high-quality site and (B) "display" if smaller or equal in size to an intruder at an high-quality site for desert grassland spiders. This example of the subgame analysis is presented in Fig. 4.4.

Matrix games are best applied in situations where asymmetries are fairly obvious, as when spiders can accurately estimate their weights relative to those of their opponents through vibrations transmitted through the web-trap (Riechert 1978b), or where frogs (e.g., *Bufo bufo*) can tell the depth of opponent's croaks relative to their own (Davies 1978). The roaring and parallel walk assessments that red deer males make in their contests prior to withdrawal or fighting (Clutton Brock et al. 1979) are components of another contest that lends itself to matrix analysis.

4.4.2 The War of Attrition Model

The War of Attrition model of classical game theory applied to evolutionary games by Maynard Smith and Price (1973; see also Maynard Smith 1974, Bishop & Cannings 1978) assumes (1) that a strategy set is continuous rather than discrete, (2) that the contest is settled by conventional behavior or by struggles that rarely lead to injury, and (3) that there is no correlated asymmetry that can be used to quickly settle the dispute. The question the War of Attrition model addresses is how long a contes-

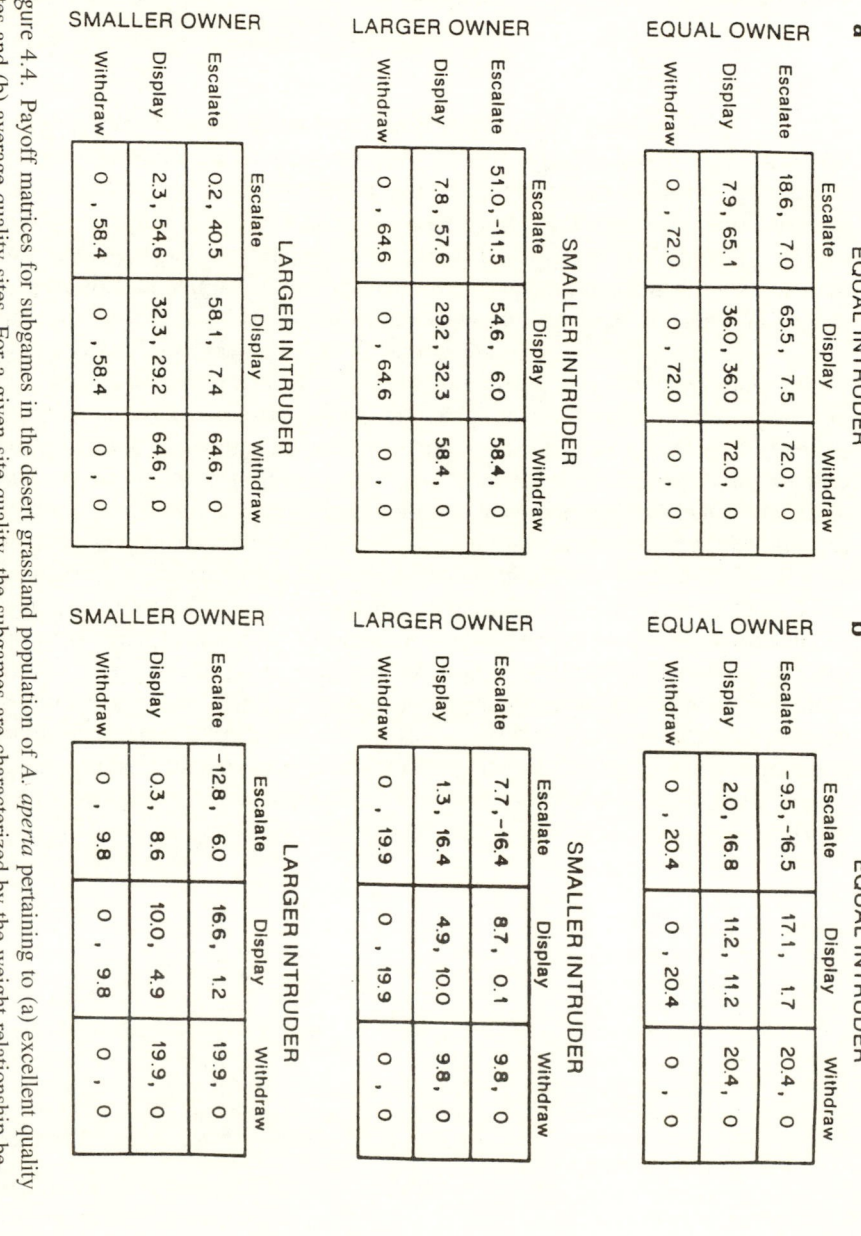

a

EQUAL OWNER / EQUAL INTRUDER

	Escalate	Display	Withdraw
Escalate	18.6, 7.0	65.5, 7.5	72.0, 0
Display	7.9, 65.1	360, 36.0	72.0, 0
Withdraw	0 , 72.0	0 , 72.0	0 , 0

LARGER OWNER / SMALLER INTRUDER

	Escalate	Display	Withdraw
Escalate	51.0, -11.5	54.6, 6.0	58.4, 0
Display	7.8, 57.6	292, 32.3	58.4, 0
Withdraw	0 , 64.6	0 , 64.6	0 , 0

SMALLER OWNER / LARGER INTRUDER

	Escalate	Display	Withdraw
Escalate	0.2, 40.5	58.1, 7.4	64.6, 0
Display	2.3, 54.6	32.3, 29.2	64.6, 0
Withdraw	0 , 58.4	0 , 58.4	0 , 0

b

EQUAL OWNER / EQUAL INTRUDER

	Escalate	Display	Withdraw
Escalate	-9.5, -16.5	17.1, 1.7	20.4, 0
Display	2.0, 16.8	11.2, 11.2	204, 0
Withdraw	0 , 20.4	0 , 20.4	0 , 0

LARGER OWNER / SMALLER INTRUDER

	Escalate	Display	Withdraw
Escalate	7.7, -16.4	8.7, 0.1	9.8, 0
Display	1.3, 16.4	4.9, 10.0	9.8, 0
Withdraw	0 , 19.9	0 , 19.9	0 , 0

SMALLER OWNER / LARGER INTRUDER

	Escalate	Display	Withdraw
Escalate	-12.8, 6.0	16.6, 1.2	19.9, 0
Display	0.3, 8.6	10.0, 4.9	19.9, 0
Withdraw	0 , 9.8	0 , 9.8	0 , 0

Figure 4.4. Payoff matrices for subgames in the desert grassland population of *A. aperta* pertaining to (a) excellent quality sites and (b) average quality sites. For a given site quality, the subgames are characterized by the weight relationship between owner and intruder. Entries in each cell show how the strategies played by the opponents affect an individual's expected reproductive success. These effects on fitness are measured as changes in the expected future egg production (mg wet weight) of a female. Left entry in each cell corresponds to payoff to owner; right entry corresponds to intruder.

tant will display or struggle, given the fact that the one that continues longest wins the disputed resource. Parker and Thompson (1980) derived the distribution of contest lengths as

$$P(x) = (2/V)e^{-2x/V}$$

where $V=$ the payoff value of the disputed resource, x is contest duration, and $P(x)$ is the probability density function. The distribution of contest durations in the War of Attrition model is thus exponential, with a mean of $V/2$. There are, in fact, a number of empirical examples of contests whose durations fit a negative exponential distribution. Parker (1970a,b), for instance, found that the length of time that male dung flies wait on dung for visiting females fits the exponential distribution predicted for War of Attrition, while the length of time that two males struggle over a given female does not (Parker & Thompson 1980). This is despite the fact that superficially the latter contest situation fits a "War of Attrition" interpretation. This latter conclusion was reached because the contests obviously had an asymmetry: owner (had already mated with the female) and intruder (new male who was attempting to displace the owner). Parker and Thompson (1980) found that the distributions of contest durations differed significantly when the data set was partitioned into owner wins versus intruder wins contests. Specifically, the intruder wins category did not fit an exponential distribution, because most contests were much longer than predicted. Ydenberg et al. (1988) demonstrated analytically that it is possible to have an asymmetric War of Attrition game if there are sufficient mistakes in winner versus loser selection of their levels of persistence times. Both classes of individuals then would exhibit similar exponential distributions of strategies.

Crowley et al. (1988) report that contests over feeding sites between equal-sized larval damselflies can be considered wars of attrition because (1) they exhibited extended staring bouts at the cost of loss in feeding, but with no injury or mortality, and (2) contest durations fit negative-exponential distributions. Like Parker and Thompson (1980), however, they found that some classes of these contests failed to meet the assumptions of War of Attrition: If size differences were great enough between individuals, this asymmetry settled the contests. Even with the resident and size asymmetries exhibited in *A. aperta* contests, the individual distributions of two of the three different size classes of contests fit the exponential distribution characteristic of War of Attrition staying times (Fig. 4.5). Such results suggest that a War of Attrition algorithm might be a subgame within the discrete categorical games. Thus individuals would exhibit (A) "escalate" for x_e; or (B) "display" for X_d, where X_e and X_d refer to staying times for fighting and displaying contests, respectively.

4.4.3 The Sequential Assessment Game

The Sequential Assessment Game is a fairly recent development in evolutionary game theory, but it is similar in structure to the Game in Extensive Form of classical game theory (Hammerstein, this volume, Selten 1983). Enquist and Leimar (1987) derived a model that assumes that opponents gain additional information about potential RHP asymmetries with each consecutive exchange of actions. Thus, the error in assessment should decrease as a contest continues, leading to a solution of the game. The greater the

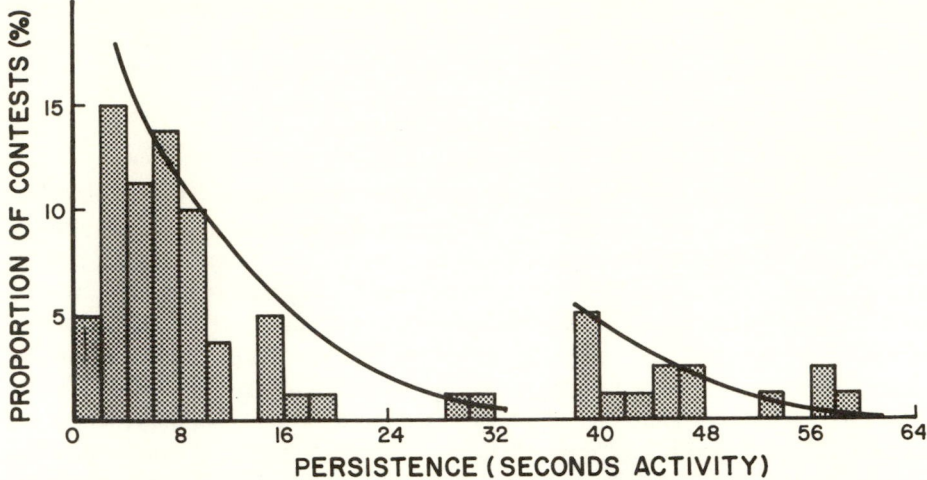

Figure 4.5. Frequency distribution of persistence times (total number of acts) for territorial disputes of *Agelenopsis aperta* over sites in desert grassland habitat. First bar shows disputes between small intruders and much larger owners; adjacent region of graph fitted to negative binomial shows equally weighted opponents; and region at far end of the y axis also fitted to the negative binomial shows small owners vs. larger intruders.

asymmetry between contestants, the more quickly the error in assessment will decrease beyond some critical point, and this will result in a contest of short duration. This model has been applied to Austad's (1983) data on male–male competition for matings in the bowl-and-doily spider, *Frontinella pyramitela* (Linyphiidae) (Leimar et al. 1991). Empirical estimates of grappling contest durations and frequencies of injury with respect to the relative sizes of the competing males show good agreement with the predictions of a sequential assessment analysis using rough estimates of lifetime reproductive success. Additional studies that fully support a sequential contest structure include Marden and Rollin's (1994) investigation of agonistic behavior in damselflies and Mosler's (1985) study of contests between male *Haplochromis burtoni* Pisces.

Along with its prediction of greater information exchange, contestants in sequential assessment games are predicted to show a continuous increase in intensity or escalation, as more detailed information is needed concerning the individual's probability of winning the dispute, if actual fighting were to occur. Smith et al. (1994) found that both the duration and intensity of agonistic interactions between velvet swimming crabs were inversely related to the size differences existing between the contestants. Nevertheless, the authors did not observe the continuous, gradual escalation predicted by the "sequential assessment" model, and contest terminations did not necessarily follow the most intense acts. Nor did Turner (1994) and Koops and Grant (1993) observe gradual increases in escalation during the course of fights between male mouth-brooding and convict cichlids in respective studies. Turner (1994) found that the escalated act rate was highest at the beginning of disputes for mouthbrooding cichlids. Koops and Grant (1993) observed considerable temporal overlap in behavior patterns representing different levels of escalation in convict cichlid fights, as well as contest durations that did not fit sequential assessment predictions. In many real games (e.g., *Agelenopsis aperta* contests over territories (Fig. 4.2a,b), animals change behavior patterns in complex manners that do not necessarily reflect an incremental rise in level of escalation. In fact, Riechert (1978b) found that winners of contests exhibited significantly more variable behavior (an average of 20% lower scores) than did the losers of contests. Humphries and Driver (1967, 1970) coined the term "Protean Displays" to describe those behaviors exhibited by prey that functioned to confuse predators. While this is clearly an amorphous term, the use of as many as 33 different behavior patterns in disputes by *A. aperta* may also have a confusing effect and, thus, could be considered Protean Displays. That the Sequential Assessment Game does not apply to all pairwise contests is also indicated by the fact that assessment obviously occurs early in *A. aperta* contests. For instance, intruding individuals shift their behavior relative to site quality immediately following the first series of acts (i.e., the resident spider inadvertently provides the intruder with site quality information) (Maynard Smith & Riechert 1984). This action by the intruding individual sets the intensity of subsequent events (i.e., high if site quality is high, and low if site quality is low). Experimental manipulations already mentioned indicate that size asymmetries in this spider are determined early in the contest as well (Riechert 1984). Incidental observations indicate the degree to which individual *A. aperta* are locked into this initial weight assessment. During studies of induced encounters in the field between owners of known weight at their own sites and intruders that also had been weighed and paint-marked, there were four occasions when a larger natural intruder invaded the web following a small intruder's retreat. In each instance, the territory owner acted toward the new intruder as if it were the small intruder returning to the contest: The owner retaliated against the individual that it apparently viewed as having failed to obey the rules of RHP asymmetry. On three of the occasions the owner suffered injury as a result of this attack toward a larger intruder. Despite the fact that site quality and RHP assessments are made early in *A. aperta* disputes, these disputes frequently continue for extended periods of time—cycling between "display" and "escalation" and sometimes separated by the retreat of one or both opponents to the web edge or nearby vegetation. These extended contests fit a War of Attrition selection of persistence times, better than they do continuous assessment, throughout the duration of the contest.

It should be apparent from this discussion that each of the three types of conceptual models that have been applied to animal contests has some merit, but that no one type can be considered as better than any other, except in specific contexts. Knowledge of the contest structure of a particular system is needed to determine which model to apply in any particular situation.

4.5 The Problem of Payoffs

One problem with most of the ESS analyses that have been completed to date is with developing realistic payoff matrices. This is actually a difficulty that is common to any kind of optimality model that might be applied to a biological problem. Hammerstein and Riechert's (1988) analysis of agonistic encounters between *A. aperta* fighting over web-sites and associated territories was among the first to consider the payoffs to contestants of a single contest, in terms of lifetime fitness consequences. To complete the ESS analysis desired for the agonistic behavior of individuals belonging to two populations under different levels of competition, it was necessary to determine how individual payoffs (Darwinian fitness) are affected both by the strategies exhibited and by environmental conditions. This type of analysis is complicated, because it is necessary to convert the short-term consequences of behavior (in this case, access to feeding levels gained per day as an owner of a territory of specific quality) into the long-term consequences for reproductive success. Hammerstein and Riechert (1988) modeled only the behavior of female competitors, and, thus, the extension of the immediate payoff to its long-term consequences equaled the gain, x, in expected egg mass that may be laid near the end of an individual's life.

Another difficulty is that V, the value of winning a contest over a web-site, is not a simple measure of prey capture rates at particular sites. One reason for this is that the value of winning must be defined as the difference between the benefit, B_w, a spider can expect if it wins and the benefit, B_a, it would expect if it avoided the contest by withdrawing: $V = B_w - B_a$. In economics, B_a is commonly referred to as "opportunity cost": It represents the loss of other opportunities the winner is giving up as a result of winning this site. If sites are readily available, the opportunity cost is high and the value of winning is low. If sites are present in limited supply, as is the case for $A.$ $aperta$ in desert grasslands, then the opportunity cost is low and the value of winning very high. Thus, in the desert grassland spider system we have been discussing, the value of winning a territory depends not only on the profit from the resource it gains, but also on the availability of other sites. This immediate payoff also influences the future successes of the individual. That is, if a spider gains strength and mass while feeding at a high-quality site, then it gains some advantage in future contests over sites as winners are determined by relative size and strength (see also Korona 1991). Hammerstein and Riechert (1988) measured these parameters in their populations, and the predictive power of their results reflect this.

Another problem with payoffs is with the currencies that are used. A link between energy expenditure and subsequent fitness is generally assumed, since energy expended in activities is energy unavailable for reproduction. It is not surprising then that agonistic behavior is considered to be energetically costly (Hamilton 1964, Rand & Rand 1976, Riechert 1979, Parker & Thompson 1980). Thus, in evolutionary game theory applications, time and energy expenditures are generally assumed to be adjusted to the value of winning the contest and to RHP. But is energy expenditure really the appropriate currency or is it merely correlated, though incompletely, with other currencies that have much greater effects on fitness? Debilitating injury and mortality, exposure to predators, lost feeding opportunities, and physiological stress are other costs of contests that can have major effects on fitness. Only the comparative study of the costs of territorial disputes to individuals representing two populations of the desert spider, $Agelenopsis$ $aperta,$ express all of these costs in a common currency, so that their relative contributions can be examined. Despite the fact that superficially, energy expenditure by this spider in its territorial disputes corresponded to ESS predictions for it (Riechert 1978a,b, 1979, 1986), Hammerstein and Riechert (1988) found that energy expenditure in the contests contributes little to the determination of payoffs in fitness associated with winning or losing particular disputes (Table 4.7a,b). First, $A.$ $aperta$ disputes frequently escalate to fighting in which the

Table 4.7 Payoff Components for Territorial Disputes of Two Populations of the Funnel Spider, *Agelenopsis aperta*[a]

Basic Fitness Parameters	Desert Grassland New Mexico (NM)	Desert Riparian Arizona (AZ)
(a) Payoff Components		
Value of winning average site	16.7	1.6
Cost of leg loss	14.2	6.2
Cost of lethal injury	93.7	84.1
Cost of display	0.1	3
(b) Breakdown of Display Costs Component		
Energy expended	4.8×10^{-5}	2.0×10^{-6}
Loss in food intake	0.1	0.06
Loss to predation	0	2.4

[a]Expected egg-mass increments and decrements respectively (mg wet weight of offspring produced) for events.

probability of injury is as high as 36%. Any energy expenditures made during the course of a dispute are dwarfed by the fitness consequences of being injured: Loss of a single leg decreases foraging success by 10% and the probability of winning future territorial disputes by 25% (Hammerstein & Riechert 1988). Table 4.7a compares these costs expressed in terms of milligrams of future egg production. The energetic costs of disputes are included in the table under the category of display costs. Not only are display costs low relative to injury, mortality costs an individual its entire expected future payoff in reproduction. When display costs are further subdivided into the contributing parts (e.g., energy expenditure itself, loss in feeding, and the potential for suffering predation), it is apparent that the actual energy expended in disputes represents but a small fraction of total display costs (Table 4.7b). Several orders of magnitude higher is the expected loss in food intake resulting from the time spiders are engaged in display contests, and for a riparian population of *A. aperta*, shown in the table, potential predation by birds is an even higher cost of display. This is because (1) displays make individuals more obvious to predators that hunt by motion detection and (2) displaying spiders are far less vigilant than they are when engaged in foraging or web building (Hammerstein and Riechert 1988). Thus, the relative importance of different sources of costs and benefits needs to be expressed in common currencies, and their relative fitness consequences need to be assessed for each system under investigation.

4.6 Predictive Uses of ESS Analyses

The main contribution of ESS thinking to our understanding of contest behavior is to provide a functional, rather than merely a motivational, framework to contests. Historically, it helped us advance beyond "naive" group selection models of contests to one based on the selfish interests of individual contestants, which is more in keeping with our contemporary understanding of evolution by natural selection (see Wilson and Dugatkin, both in this volume, for somewhat different views on this issue). We have since applied this construct to understanding the contexts under which conventional behavior will settle disputes versus those for which escalation is predicted. We have also applied the construct to the question of contest length (e.g., the "War of Attrition" and "Sequential Assessment" models).

4.6.1 Assessment

As with any model development, ESS analyses can be used as tools for understanding what information is transferred and/or is available to contestants during the course of territorial disputes. Through various stages of modeling the contests of *A. aperta,* for instance, we have learned much about the kinds of information this species gains and utilizes in its contest "decisions." In the first published model of this spider's contests, Maynard Smith (1982) assumed that resident spiders had complete information about site quality, while intruding spiders did not. This was because Riechert (1979) contested two intruding spiders over web-sites from which the resident had been removed and found that these spiders did not adjust their behavior to site quality, as was characteristic of animals in natural disputes over web-sites. ESS predictions of *A. aperta* contest behavior, based on this information asymmetry, deviated markedly from the observed empirical strategy. The result led to closer scrutiny of the behavior that occurred early on in these contests. Maynard Smith and Riechert (1984) subsequently found that intruding individuals are the first of the opponents to adjust behavior to site value, and they do so after the first series of acts. We concluded that intruding individuals are gaining information concerning site quality that is inadvertently supplied by the residents, because there is nothing obvious in the actions owners engage in that would cue intruders as to site quality. Game theory also predicts that owners would not intentionally communicate information concerning site quality to visitors, because this would lead them into longer and more escalated fights over high-quality sites. We hypothesize that the amplitude of the signal transmitted through the web varies with a spider's strength and thus feeding history, in addition to body mass itself, which we know spiders are able to detect. Thus, for a given body mass, a spider from a higher-quality site will impose a higher downward force on the web sheet in moving than would a spider that has had a poorer feeding history. This is because body mass is but one component or indicator of recent feeding history; strength is another component.

Another example of how our understanding of what information is available to animals during disputes can be enriched by game theory is provided by Hammerstein and Riechert (1988). In our analysis that first incorporated complete information about site quality, we assumed that an individual was aware of its position in the local population with respect to body mass (e.g., smaller than average, at the heavy end of the population distribution, etc.). The problem was, then, that ESS analyses would predict that small individuals would always escalate because they would have no chance of winning a conventional dispute. This outcome again did not fit the empirical strategy representation we had for *A. aperta* contests. Changing the model to assume that an individual only has information concerning its mass, relative to that of its opponent in a given dispute, provides a much closer fit to the real contests.

4.6.2 The Meaning of Signaling

One of the consuming interests of contest study concerns the meaning of signaling (see Johnstone, this volume). Tinbergen (1959) argued that displays provide honest information about an individual's underlying motivation (e.g., on a fearful–aggressive continuum). Maynard Smith (1974), however, argued that displays should not provide clues as to the degree to which contestants intend to persist, since it is difficult to see the selective advantage of conveying such information. Caryl (1979) attempted to differentiate among these using data from the literature on birds. He did not find any evidence for the transmission of information concerning the probability of attack, but he did find that individuals might convey information about their probabilities of withdrawal.

Round two of the discussion saw contributions favoring honest signaling from Zahavi ("The Handicap Principle," e.g., 1975, 1977, 1993) and game-theoretic analyses demonstrating the instability of display that affects outcome if it transmits intention (Parker 1974, Maynard Smith 1982). More recent contributions (e.g., Gardner and Morris 1989) have applied game-theoretic analyses to understanding the contexts under which bluffing versus honest signaling might be favored. Using extensive form games in which each individual's act at a given point in the contest is assessed relative to the act just offered by the opponent, Gardner and Morris (1989) found that bluffing is predicted (1) for contexts in which the costs of getting caught cheating are low and (2) when the value of the disputed resource is low. Otherwise, an informative signal is favored.

While the basic premise of the Handicap Principle is now widely accepted, its prediction that signal intensity will vary continuously has less empirical support. Johnstone (1994) suggests that perceptual errors lead to discrete "all-or-nothing" displays or stereotypy (also see Johnstone, this volume). This approach is needed to emphasize the differences, for instance, between a high-quality and a low-quality signaler.

I proposed an entirely different function of display in *A. aperta* (Riechert 1978b). The lack of stereotypy in the displays of this spider, along with the fact that the winners of contests exhibited greater variability in displays than did contest losers, suggests that signaling might serve to confuse opponents concerning assessments, for instance. This brings contest signaling under the umbrella of the "protean displays" attributed to prey in the presence of predators. Humphries and Driver (1967, 1970) suggest two reasons for highly changeable behavior in the presence of a predator: (1) The prey confuses the predator, putting it into conflicting states, or (2) confusion slows the approach of the predator. In the context of spider fights, confusion could lead to the retreat of the opponent. Of course, it is possible that more complex and variable behavior is an indication of locomotory agility and stamina (Jackson 1982) and, thus, is honest signaling of RHP.

4.6.3 Tests for Adaptation

Ultimately, ESS analyses might be used to test a major premise of evolutionary biology—that is, that traits (strategy representations in contests) are adaptive and that the local population is at the stable equilibrium. At this stage in ESS model development, we are unable to put statistical confidence intervals around our predictions. We can, thus, only qualitatively compare ESS predictions to empirical strategy representations. Nevertheless, comparisons of empirical deviations from ESS predictions among populations of the same species can lead to an entirely new avenue of research into the phenomena that might limit adaptation (e.g., phylogenetic inertia, genetic structure constraints, and potential interactions between gene flow and selection). This has, in fact, happened in the case of *A. aperta* (Riechert 1993a,b).

Hammerstein and Riechert (1988) identified an ESS for a riparian population of *Agelenopsis aperta* in southeastern Arizona that delineated the actions that individual spiders should take in various contest contexts (conditional evolutionarily stable strategies: Gardner et al. 1987). In the case of the riparian population under investigation, the contexts were related to potential weight biases. The potential actions an individual might exhibit following assessment of its mass relative to that of its opponent were identified as follows: withdrawing from the territory, displaying (visual or vibratory signaling that is noninjurious), and escalating (physical contact that is potentially injurious; Riechert 1984). Because bird predation is a major limiting influence on these riparian spiders (Riechert & Hedrick 1990), predation risk is a major fitness cost to individuals from this population engaged in territorial disputes: Predation events occur when the spiders are out on their web-sheets, where territorial disputes take place. Time exposed to predation is then a major fitness cost to fighting riparian spiders (Table 4.7b), as was the potential for physical injury in escalated contests (Table 4.7a).

The ESS predictions for this population were to display in contexts where the individual had a weight bias or when it was the owner of a site and was equally matched in weight to the intruding individual, but to withdraw from the contest if it was the smaller opponent or the intruding individual and equal in weight to the territory resident (Hammerstein & Riechert 1988). The empirical strategy representation for the AZ riparian (Arizona) population shown in Table 4.8 differed from this predicted ESS in a number of respects. Individuals frequently displayed when it was predicted that they should have withdrawn from contests. There also was considerable escalation to fighting behavior. Since the predictions of the ESS model for the riparian population were robust, Hammerstein and Riechert (1988) concluded that the observed deviation of the real contests from the predicted ESS was not due to inadequacies of the model. No assumptions were made in the model: All parameters were empirically determined. This was also the fourth generation of models developed for the *A. aperta* system and one that we were confident took into account all relevant information exchange and parameters.

Subsequent work on other aspects of the behavior of AZ riparian spiders supported the hypothesis that these animals were not well adapted to local conditions (see review in Riechert 1993a). Tests were conducted for potential phylogenetic inertia and gene flow effects. Because *A. aperta* is primarily an aridlands species (i.e., it characteristically occupies desert grassland and cactus scrub habitats throughout the desert southwest United States), I hypothesized that a major change in the "wiring" of the nervous system of this spider would be required to achieve the predicted ESS. I investigated the potential for gene flow because the AZ riparian habitat is an island in the Chiricahua Mountains of Arizona surrounded by more arid habitats. I tested the phylogenetic argument indirectly by looking at contest behavior in another riparian

Table 4.8 Predicted and Empirical Strategy Representation for *A. aperta*. Field–Induced Contests Over Web-Sites (Relative Proportion)

| | Empirical Strategy Representation | | | | | |
| | Withdraw | | Display | | Escalate | |
Predicted Strategy	AZ	TX	AZ	TX	AZ	TX
Display						
If larger opponent	0.03	0.11	0.6	0.85	0.37	0.04
If equal & owner	0.08	0.11	0.49	0.82	0.43	0.07
Withdraw						
If smaller opponent	0.26	0.53	0.54	0.46	0.2	0.01
If equal & intruder	0.27	0.28	0.53	0.72	0.2	0

population of *A. aperta* that was not exposed to potential gene flow from other local populations that occupy more arid habitats (Riechert 1993b). The empirical strategy representation for this second population located in the hill country of central Texas is presented in Table 4.8. The contest decisions exhibited by TX riparian spiders closely follow predicted behavior for a population existing with unlimited food, but with a risk of predation by visual predators such as birds. Note particularly the lack of escalation and the high frequency of withdrawal from the contests when an individual had a size or ownership disadvantage. The empirical strategy representation exhibited by TX riparian spiders differed significantly from that exhibited by AZ riparian spiders. This finding falsified the phylogenetic inertia hypothesis, and I went on to demonstrate through a combination of field and lab measurements as well as through field experimentation that gene flow accounts for the failure of AZ riparian spiders to be at the ESS predicted for their contest behavior (Riechert 1993c).

4.7 Concluding Remarks

While it is true that population geneticists have considered the problem of frequency dependence in their models long before the publication of this chapter, contest behavior is simply too complex to lend itself to population genetics modeling (perhaps explaining why Maynard Smith and Price's 1973 article sparked both theoretical and empirical interest in the adaptive function of contest structure).

We have made inroads into the four problem areas that I have discussed here. However, many questions remain unanswered.

4.7.1 Contest Variability

We have a good understanding of the contributions of various asymmetries to contest outcome, as well as of the outcome of their interaction. Less work has focused on the effects of context on the sequence of acts that are exhibited in animal contests. Why, for instance, does a lizard species exhibit variations on only three behavior patterns, while a spider has over 30 act types in its agonistic repertoire? The answer may be found with additional cross-taxonomic comparisons, or it may be explained through further theoretical development, particularly in the area of delineating the function of displays in bluffing versus honest signaling.

4.7.2 Conceptual Models

I discussed three different conceptual models that are routinely applied to animal contests: Hawk–Dove, War of Attrition, and Sequential Assessment games. Some researchers designate the model they use as "preferred" (provides a more accurate reflection of reality for all contest applications). I suggest that reality would be better served by considering all of these models as subsets of algorithms within a single game.

In some games the discrete strategy representation of the Hawk–Dove Game might dominate, and in others an extended assessment phase (Sequential Assessment Game) might serve modeling purposes better. Once a strategy is initiated, the opponent might persist in it for some period of time, x, that is predicted by War of Attrition Game structure. It is clear, or should be, that complex, real-world contests have elements (subgames) that fit the structures implicit in all three models. The field would benefit from analyses that predict what factors lead to games that emphasize one game structure over another. Once again, the problem is one of explaining variability.

4.7.3 The Problem of Payoffs

We have borrowed the concept of contest payoffs from classical game theory. Payoffs are simply the value of winning relative to the costs incurred in contests. In classical game theory, the payoff is often economic and the currency of costs and benefits is monetary. Evolutionary biologists view the significance of winning versus losing contests in terms of changes in fitness, with the currency being energy expenditure. Energy expended in contests is not available for conversion into biomass that might ultimately be applied to reproduction, a commonly used measure of fitness. Energy does not merit the prominent position it holds in our models and practical applications of evolutionary game theory, because other factors, such as time lost in foraging and potential for injury, may have orders of magnitude greater effects on fitness. Thus, it is important that investigators identify the constraints on fitness appropriate to their particular system and convey the effects of these constraints in a currency that can reflect the contribution of a single contest outcome to lifetime fitness.

4.7.4 Predictive Uses

I have already mentioned the theoretical contributions that are being made toward our understanding of signaling in contests. Empirical work that tests these predictions is needed, particularly experimental work.

The potential use of ESS analyses to test for adaptation has received less attention. Our models of animal behavior and ecology assume that the populations we are studying are at adaptive equilibrium. Yet, how often is this not the case and what are the consequences of nonequilibrium conditions to our findings? We could perhaps resolve some of the adaptive paradigm controversy by using ESS models to test populations for their empirical approximations to the ESSs predicted for them. This is a call to the statistically inclined among us to develop some protocol for establishing confidence limits around ESS predictions.

In summary, we have come a long way in our understanding of animal contests since the early 1970s. There is still no shortage of work to be done, hopefully through the cooperative efforts of theorists and empiricists.

References

Alford, D. V. 1975. *Bumblebees.* London: Davies Poynter.

Aoki, S. & Makino, S. 1982. Gall usurpation and lethal fighting among foundresses of the aphid *Epipemphigus niisimae* (Homoptera, Pemphigidae). *Kontyu, Tokyo,* 50, 365–376.

Archer, J. 1987. *The Behavioral Biology of Aggression.* Cambridge: Cambridge University Press.

Austad, S. N. 1983. A game theoretical interpretation of male combat in the bowl and doily spider *(Frontinella pyramitela). Anim. Behav.,* 31, 59–73.

Baker, R. L. 1983. Spacing behaviour by larval *Ischmura cervula* Setys: Effects of hunger, previous interactions, and familiarity with an area (Zygoptera: Coenagrionidae). *Odontologica,* 12, 201–207.

Barnard, C. J. & Brown, C. A. J. 1984. A payoff asymmetry in resident-resident disputes between shrews. *Anim. Behav.,* 32, 302–304.

Beacham, J. L. 1988. The relative importance of body size and aggressive experience as determinants of dominance in pumpkinseed sunfish, *Lepomis gibbosus. Anim. Behav.,* 36, 621–623.

Bisazza, A. & Marconato, A. 1988. Female mate choice, male–male competition and parental care in the river bullhead, *Cottus gobio* L. (Pisces, Cottidae). *Anim. Behav.,* 36, 1352–1360.

Bishop, D. T. & Cannings, C. 1978. A generalized war of attrition. *J. Theor. Biol.,* 70, 85–124.

Brace, R.C. 1981. Intraspecific aggression in the color morphs of the sea anemone *Phymactis clematis* from Chile. *Mar. Biol (Berl.),* 64, 85–94.

Bruce, R. H. 1941. An experimental analysis of social factors affecting the performance of white rats. III. Dominance and cooperation motivated by water and food deprivation. *J. Comp. Psychol.,* 31, 395–412.

Burgess, J. W. 1976. Social spiders. *Sci. Am.,* March, 100–106.

Carpenter, C. C. 1978. Ritualistic social behaviors in lizards. In *Behavior and Neurobiology of Lizards,* N. Greenberg & P. D. MacLean, eds., pp. 253–268. Bethesda, MD: DHEW Publ No. 77–491.

Caryl, P. G. 1979. Communication by agonistic displays: What can games theory contribute to ethology? *Behavior,* 68, 136–170.

Chapais, B. 1985. An experimental analysis for a mother–daughter rank reversal in Japanese macaques, *Macaca fuscata. Primates,* 26, 407–423.

Clutton-Brock, T. H. & Albon, S. D. 1979. The roaring of red deer and the evolution of honest advertisement. *Behaviour,* 69, 145–170.

Clutton-Brock, T. H., Albon, S. D., Gibson, R. M. & Guinness, F. E. 1979. The logical stag: Adaptive aspects of fighting in red deer (*Cervus elaphus* L.) *Anim. Behav.,* 27, 211–225.

Cole D. D. & Shaffer, J. N. 1966. A study of social dominance in cats. *Behaviour,* 27, 39–53.

Crowley, P. H., Gillett, S. & Lawton, J. H. 1988. Contests between larval damselflies: Empirical steps towards a better ESS model. *Anim. Behav.,* 5, 1496–1510.

Davies, N. B. 1978. Territorial defense in the speckled wood butterfly *(Parage aegeria):* The resident always wins. *Anim. Behav.*, 26, 138–147.

Dawkins, R. & Brockmann, H. J. 1980. Do digger wasps commit the concorde fallacy? *Anim. Behav.*, 28, 892–896.

DeCourcy, K. R. & Jenssen, T. A. 1994. Structure and use of male territorial headbob signals by the lizard, *Anolis carolinensis. Anim. Behav.*, 47, 251–262.

Dugatkin, L. & Ohlsen, S. 1990. Contrasting asymmetries in value expectations and resource holding power: Effects on attack behaviour and dominance in the pumpkinseed sunfish, *Lepomis gibbosus. Anim. Behav.*, 39, 802–804.

Enquist, M., Plaine, E. & Roed, J. 1985. Aggressive communication in Fulmars *(Fulmarus glacialis)* competing for food. *Anim. Behav.*, 33, 1007–1020.

Enquist, M. & Leimar, O. 1987. Evolution of fighting behaviour: the effect of variation in resource value. *J. Theor. Biol.*, 127, 187–205.

Enquist, M. & Leimar, O. 1990. The evolution of fatal fighting. *Anim. Behav.*, 39, 1–9.

Evans, D. L. & Shehadi-Moacdieh, M. 1988. Body size and prior residency in staged encounters between female prawns, *Palaemon elegans* Rathke (Decapoda: Palaemonidae). *Anim. Behav.*, 36, 452–455.

Fincke, O. M. 1984. Consequences of larval ecology for territoriality and reproductive success of a neotropical damselfly. *Ecology*, 73, 449–462.

Fritts T. H. 1984. Evolutionary divergence of giant tortoises in the Galapagos. *Biol. J. Linn. Soc.*, 21, 165–176.

Gardner, R., Morris, M. R. & Nelson, C. E. 1987. Conditional evolutionarily stable strategies. *Anim. Behav.*, 35, 507–517.

Gardner, R. & Morris, M. R. 1989. The evolution of bluffing in animal contests: An ESS approach. *J. Theor. Biol.*, 137, 235–243.

Grafen, A. 1987. The logic of decisively asymmetric contests: Respect for ownership and the desperado effect. *Anim. Behav.*, 35, 462–467.

Gribbin, S. D. & Thompson, D. J. 1991. The effects of size and residency on territorial disputes and short-term mating success in the damselfly, *Pyrrhosoma nymphula* (Sulzer) (Zygoptera: Coenagrionidae). *Anim. Behav.*, 41, 689–696.

Hamilton, W. D. 1964. The genetical evolution of social behaviour. I and II. *J. Theor. Biol.*, 7, 1–52.

Hammerstein, P. 1981. The role of asymmetries in animal contests. *Anim. Behav.*, 29, 193–205.

Hammerstein, P. & Riechert, S. E. 1988. Payoffs and strategies in territorial contests: ESS analyses of two ecotypes in the spider, *Agelenopsis aperta. Evol. Ecol.*, 2, 115–138.

Hansen, A. J. 1986. Fighting behavior in bald eagles: a test of game theory. *Ecology*, 67, 787–797.

Harvey, I. F. & Corbet, P. S. 1986. Territorial interactions between larvae of the dragonfly *Pyrrhosomma nymphula:* Outcome of encounters. *Anim. Behav.*, 34, 1550–1561.

Hazlett, B. A. 1966. Factors affecting the aggressive behaviour of the hermit crab *Calcinius tibicen. Z Tierpsychol.*, 23, 655–671.

Hazlett, B. A. & Estabrook, G. 1974. Examination of agonistic behaviour by character analysis, I. The spider crab *Microphrys bicornutus. Behaviour*, 48, 131–144.

Hazlett, B. A., Rubenstein, D. I. & Ritschoff, D. 1975. Starvation, aggression, and energy reserves in the crayfish *Orconectes virilis. Crustaceana*, 8, 11–28.

Hodge, M. A. & Uetz, G. W. 1995. A comparison of agonistic behaviour of colonial web-building spiders from desert and tropical habitats. *Anim. Behav.*, 50, 963–972.

Holtby, L. B., Swain, D. P. & Allan, G. M. 1993. Mirror-elicited agonistic behaviour and body morphology as predictors of dominance status in juvenile coho salmon. *Can. J. Fish. Aquat. Sci.*, 50, 676–684.

Howard, R. D. 1978. Influence of male-defended oviposition sites on early embryo mortality in bullfrogs. *Ecology,* 59, 789–798.

Howard, R. D. 1984. Alternative mating behaviors of young male bullfrogs. *Am. Zool.,* 24, 397–406.

Humphries, D. A. & Driver, P. M. 1967. Erratic display as a device against predators. *Science,* 156, 1767–1768.

Humphries, D. A. & Driver, P. M. 1970. Protean defense by prey animals. *Oecologia (Berlin),* 5, 285–302.

Jackson, R. R. 1982. The behavior of communication in jumping spiders (Salticidae). In *Spider Communication,* P. N. Witt & J. S. Rovner, eds., Princeton, NJ: Princeton University Press.

Jenkins, T. M. 1969. Social structures, positions, choice, and microdistribution of two trout species *(Salmo trutta and Salmo gairdnei)* resident in mountain streams. *Anim. Behav. Monogr.,* 2, 57–123.

Johnstone, R. A. 1994. Honest signalling, perceptual error and the evolution of "all-or-nothing" displays. *Proc. R. Soc. London B,* 256, 169–175.

Kikkawa, J. 1968. Social hierarchy in winter flocks of the grey-breasted silvereye *Zosterops lateralis* (Latham). *Jpn. J. Ecol.,* 18, 235–246.

Komers, P. E. 1989. Dominance relationships between juvenile and adult black-billed magpies. *Anim. Behav.,* 37, 256–265.

Koops, M. A. & Grant, J. W. A. 1993. Weight asymmetry and sequential assessment in convict cichlid contests. *Can. J. Zool.,* 71, 475–479.

Korona, R. 1991. On the role of age and body size in risky animal contests. *J. Theor. Biol.,* 152, 165–176.

Leimar, O., Austad, S. & Enquist, M. 1991. A test of the sequential assessment game: Fighting in the bowl and doily spider, *Frontinella pyramitela. Evolution,* 45, 862–874.

Marden, J. H. & Waage, J. K. 1990. Escalated damselfly territorial contests are energetic wars of attrition. *Anim. Behav.,* 39, 954–959.

Marden, J. H. & Rollins, R. A. 1994. Assessment of energy reserves in damselflies engaged in aerial contests for mating territories. *Anim. Behav.,* 48, 1023–1030.

Maynard Smith, J. 1974. The theory of games and the evolution of animal conflicts. *J. Theor. Biol.,* 47, 209–221.

Maynard Smith, J. 1982. *Evolution and the Theory of Games.* Cambridge: Cambridge University Press.

Maynard Smith, J. 1989. *Evolutionary Genetics.* Oxford: Oxford University Press.

Maynard Smith, J. & Price, G. R. 1973. The logic of animal conflict. *Nature,* 246, 15–18.

Maynard Smith, J. & Parker, G. 1976. The logic of asymmetric contests. *Anim. Behav.,* 24, 159–175.

Maynard Smith, J. & Riechert, S. E. 1984. A conflicting-tendency model of spider agonistic behaviour: Hybrid-pure population line comparisons. *Anim. Behav.,* 32, 564–578.

McEachron, D. L. & Baer, D. 1982. A review of selected sociobiological principles: Application to hominid evolution II. The effects of intergroup conflict. *J. Soc. Biol. Struct.,* 5, 121–139.

McMann, S. 1993. Contextual signalling and the structure of dyadic encounters in *Anolis carolinensis. Anim. Behav.,* 46, 657–668.

Miller, P. L. 1983. The duration of copulation correlates with other aspects of mating behaviour in *Orthetrum chrysostigma* (Burmeister)(Anisoptera: Libellulidae). *Odonatologica,* 12, 227–238.

Miller, R. J. 1964. Studies on the social behavior of the blue gourami *Trichogaster trichopterus* (Pisces: Belontidae). *Copeia,* 3, 469–496.

Mosler, H. J. 1985. Making the decision to continue the fight or to flee: an analysis of contests between male Haplochromis burtoni Pisces. *Behaviour,* 92, 129–145.

Murray, M. G. 1987. The closed environment of the fig receptacle and its influence on male conflict in the Old World fig wasp, *Philotrypesis pilosa. Anim. Behav.,* 35, 488–506.

Nowlis, V. 1941. The relation of degree of hunger to competitive interactions in chimpanzee. *J. Comp. Psychol.,* 32, 91.

Olsson, M. 1994. Nuptial coloration in the sand lizard, *Lacerta agilis:* An intra-sexually selected cue to fighting ability. *Anim. Behav.,* 48, 607–613.

Parker, G. A. 1970a. The reproductive behaviour and the nature of sexual selection in *Scatophaga stercoraria* L. (Diptera: Scatophagidae). II. The fertilization rate and the spatial and temporal relationships of each sex around the site of mating and oviposition. *J. Anim. Ecol.,* 39, 205–228.

Parker, G. A. 1970b. The reproductive behaviour and the nature of sexual selection in *Scatophaga stercoraria* L. (Diptera: Scatophagidae). IV. Epigamic recognition and competition between males for the possession of females. *Behaviour,* 37, 113–139.

Parker, G. A. 1974. Assessment strategy and the evolution of fighting behaviour. *J. Theor. Biol.,* 47, 223–243.

Parker, G. A. & Thompson, E. A. 1980. Dung fly struggles: A test of the war of attrition. *Behav. Ecol. Sociobiol.,* 7, 37–44.

Petrie, M. & Lipsitch, M. 1994. Avian polygyny is most likely in populations with high variability in heritable male fitness. *Proc. R. Soc. London Ser. B. Biol. Sci.,* 256, 275–280.

Poole, J. H. 1989. Announcing intent: The aggressive state of musth in African elephants. *Anim. Behav.,* 37, 140–152.

Rand, W. M. & Rand, A. S. 1976. Agonistic behaviour in nesting iguanas: A stochastic analysis of dispute settlement dominated by the minimization of energy costs. *Z. Tierpsychol.,* 40, 279–299.

Riechert, S. E. 1978a. Energy-based territoriality in populations of the desert spider, *Agelenopsis aperta* (Gertsch). *Symp. Zool. Soc. London,* 42, 211–222.

Riechert, S. E. 1978b. Games spiders play: Behavioral variability in territorial disputes. *Behav. Ecol. Sociobiol.,* 3, 135–162.

Riechert, S. E. 1979. Games spiders play. II. Resource assessment strategies. *Behav. Ecol. Sociobiol.,* 6, 121–128.

Riechert, S. E. 1981. The consequences of being territorial: Spiders, a case study. *Am Nat.,* 117, 871–892.

Riechert, S. E. 1982. Spider interaction strategies: Communication vs. coercion. In *Spider Communication,* P. N. Witt & J. S. Rovner, eds., pp. 281–315. Princeton, NJ: Princeton University Press.

Riechert, S. E. 1984. Games spiders play. III: Cues underlying context associated changes in agonistic behaviour. *Anim. Behav.,* 32, 1–15.

Riechert, S. E. 1986. Spider fights as a test of evolutionary game theory. *Am. Sci.,* 4, 604–609.

Riechert, S. E. 1987. Between population variation in spider territorial behavior: hybrid-pure population line comparisons. In *Evolutionary Genetics of invertebrate behavior* (M. D. Huettel, ed.), pp. 33–42. New York: Plenum.

Riechert, S. E. 1993a. A test for phylogenetic constraints on behavioral adaptation in a spider system. *Behav. Ecol. Sociobiol.,* 32, 343–348.

Riechert, S. E. 1993b. Investigation of potential gene flow limitation of behavioral adaptation in an aridlands spider. *Behav. Ecol. Sociob.,* 32, 355–363.

Riechert, S. E. 1993c. The evolution of behavioral phenotypes: Lessons learned from divergent spider populations. *Adv. Anim. Behav.,* 22, 103–134.

Riechert, S. E. & Hammerstein, P. 1983. Game theory in an ecological context. *Annu. Rev. Ecol. Syst.,* 14, 377–409.

Riechert, S. E. & Hedrick, A. V. 1990. Levels of predation and genetically based anti-predatory behavior in the spider, *Agelenopsis aperta. Animal Behav.,* 40, 679–687.

Rissing, S. W. & Pollock, G. B. 1987. Queen aggression, pleometric advantage and brood raiding in the ant *Veromessor pergandei* (Hymenoptera: Formicidae). *Anim. Behav.,* 35, 975–981.

Rosenberg, R. H. & Enquist, M. 1991. Contest behaviour in Weidemeyer's admiral butterfly *Limenitis weidemeyerii* (Nymphalidae): The effect of size and residency. *Anim. Behav.,* 42, 805–811.

Selten, R. 1983. Evolutionary stability in extensive two-person games. *Math. Soc. Sci.,* 5, 269–363.

Shuster, S. M. 1992. The reproductive behaviour of alpha, beta and gamma male morphs in *Paracerceis sculpta,* a marine isopod crustacean. *Behaviour,* 121, 231–258.

Sigurjonsdottir, H. & Parker, G. A. 1981. Dung fly struggles: Evidence for assessment strategy. *Behav. Ecol. Sociobiol.,* 8, 219–230.

Silbaugh, J. M. & Ewald, P. W. 1987. Effects of unit payoff asymmetries on aggression and dominance in meadow voles, *Microtus pennsylvanicus. Anim. Behav.,* 35, 606–608.

Smith, I. P., Huntingford, F. A., Atkinson, R. J. A. & Taylor, A. C. 1994. Strategic decisions during agonistic behaviour in the velvet swimming crab, *Necora puber* (L). *Anim. Behav.,* 47, 885–894.

Stamps, J. A. & Krishnan, V. V. 1995. Territory acquisition in lizards: III. Competing for space. *Anim. Behav.,* 49, 679–693.

Tinbergen, N. 1959. Comparative studies of the behaviour of gulls. *Behaviour,* 15, 1–70.

Tsubaki, Y. & Ono, T. 1987. Effects of age and body size on the male territorial system of the dragonfly, *Nannophya pygmaea* Rambur (Odonata: Libellulidae). *Anim. Behav.,* 35, 528–525.

Turner, B. N. & Iverson, S. L. 1973. The annual cycle of aggression in male *Microtus pennsyvanica* and its relation to population parameters. *Ecology,* 54, 967–981.

Turner, G. F. 1994. The fighting tactics of male mouthbrooding cichlids: The effects of size and residency. *Anim. Behav.,* 47, 655–622.

Turner, G. F. & Huntingford, F. A. 1986. A problem for game theory analysis: Assessment and intention in male mouthbrooder contests. *Anim. Behav.,* 34, 961–970.

Verrell, P. A. 1986. Wrestling in the red-spotted newt *(Notophthalmus viridens):* Resource value and contestant asymmetry determine contest duration and outcome. *Anim. Behav.,* 34, 398.

Waage, J. K. 1988. Confusion over residency and the escalation of damselfly territorial disputes. *Anim. Behav.,* 36, 586–595.

Wells, M. S. 1988. Effects of body size and resource value on fighting behaviour in a jumping spider. *Anim. Behav.,* 36, 321–326.

Wilson, E. O. 1971. *The Insect Societies.* Cambridge, MA: Belknap Press.

Wilson, J. D. 1992. Correlates of agonistic display by great tits *Parus major. Behaviour,* 121, 168–214.

Ydenberg, R. C., Giraldeau, L. A. & Falls, J. B. 1988. Neighbors, strangers, and the asymmetric war of attrition. *Anim. Behav.,* 36, 343–347.

Zahavi, A. 1975. Mate selection: A selection for a handicap. *J. Theor. Biol.,* 53, 205–214.

Zahavi, A. 1977. The cost of honesty. *J. Theor. Biol.,* 67, 603–605.

Zahavi, A. 1993. The fallacy of conventional signalling. *Philos. Trans. R. Soc. London B,* 340, 227–230.

Zamudio, K. R., Huey, R. B. & Crill, W. D. 1994. Bigger isn't always better: Body size, developmental and parental temperature and male territorial success in *D. melanogaster. Anim. Behav.,* 49, 671–677.

RUFUS A. JOHNSTONE

Game Theory and Communication

5.1 Introduction

Communication is said to occur when the acts or cues given by one individual influence the behavior of another (Wiley 1983, Endler 1993). Traits that are specialized for the purpose of communication, which I will refer to as signals or displays, include some of the most striking products of natural selection: Consider the elaborate structures erected by male bower-birds to attract mates, the lengthy and complex songs of whales, or the brilliant colors of venomous coral snakes. These traits, and others like them, are the product of signaler/receiver coevolution. Selection favors signalers that elicit favorable responses from receivers; it also favors receivers that react appropriately to signalers. Game theory, with its emphasis on strategic interaction, is thus a useful tool with which to analyze the evolution of communicative behavior, and biologists have made extensive use of it.

Most interactions between animals involve some kind of communication: For example, offspring may solicit food from their parents, opponents threaten each other during conflict, prey attempt to deter a predator or warn others of its presence, males display to attract females, and so on. Consequently, a large number of different game-theoretic models have been developed, each concerned with just one form of communication. We have, for example, models of offspring solicitation (Godfray 1991, 1995a), models of threat display (Enquist 1985, Adams & Mesterton-Gibbons 1995), models of predator deterrence (Leimar et al. 1986, Vega-Redondo & Hasson 1993), and models of sexual advertisement (Grafen 1990a, Hutchinson et al. 1993). Moreover, any one form of communication may involve a great many more than the minimum of two participants. There are thus many kinds of communicative interaction to consider: competition and cooperation between rival signalers, interaction within a single signaler/receiver pair, interactions between a signaler and the broader audience of potential recipients (McGregor 1993), and so on.

Despite the number and diversity of game-theoretic models of communication, however, even a cursory review reveals that certain issues arise again and again, in many different contexts. Indeed, one of the chief benefits of game theory is that it has helped to reveal the features common to different communication systems and has allowed the development of generally applicable theories of signal evolution (Grafen 1990a, Grafen & Johnstone 1993). In this chapter, rather than attempting a detailed survey of models, I will focus on one of the most important common issues and one to which game theory has contributed much: the problem of honesty. How is informative communication (the transfer of reliable information between two or more individuals) possible when signalers stand to gain by deceit?

5.2 Conflicts of Interest and the Possibility of Deceit

Prior to the development of game theoretical models of communication, honesty was not commonly perceived as a problematic issue. The "traditional ethological" view, as it has since been termed (Dawkins & Krebs 1978; Caryl 1979, 1982), was that animal signals served to facilitate and coordinate social interactions by making information available to be shared (see, e.g., Smith 1977). This information might concern either the external environment or the identity and/or the physiological and motivational state of the signaler. Ethologists were not unaware of the possibility of exploitative signals (see Hinde 1981); studies of mimicry, for example, long predate current debates on honesty in animal communication. However, while it was acknowledged that cooperative sender–receiver relationships might be exploited by third participants (e.g., mimics), little attention was given to the possibility of manipulative communicatory relationships between conspecifics.

The first applications of game theory to animal communication, however, at once called into question the traditional assumption that signals were informative. Maynard Smith (1974, Maynard Smith & Price 1973, Maynard Smith & Parker 1976), using game theory to model conflict behavior, argued that threat displays conveying accurate information about aggressiveness or level of escalation would not be evolutionarily stable. His argument can be summarized as follows: Suppose a population existed in which individuals did convey information about their intentions. If an individual found that its opponent was announcing a higher aggressiveness or level of escalation than its own, it would pay to retreat at once. Consequently, a "deceitful" mutant that invariably announced a very high level of aggressiveness, regardless of its true intentions, would be favored by selection because its opponents would always back down. Before long, everyone would be lying, and it would then pay to ignore the threat display altogether (Maynard Smith 1979).

Although the early models were concerned with aggression and threat display, the above argument can, with slight modification, be applied to any other situation in which there is a conflict of interest between signaler and receiver. It thus appeared that a correlation between signaling behavior (or phenotype) and the underlying state or condition of the signaler would always be disrupted by the spread of a "lying" mutant, which adopted the signaling behavior (or phenotype) typical of individuals in a different state and thereby elicited a more favorable reaction. The conclusion drawn from this was that in many cases communication might be better viewed, not as a cooperative exchange of information but as the focus of an arms race in which signalers attempt to manipulate receivers, and receivers attempt to "mind-read" signalers (Dawkins and Krebs 1978; Krebs & Dawkins 1984). From this perspective, honesty represents only a temporary phase of the arms race in which receivers have successfully overcome the exploitative efforts of signalers, and there is no reason to expect that it will be any more common than deceit (see, e.g., Chapter 4 of Sober 1994). Dawkins and Krebs (1978), the earliest proponents of this view, went so far as to suggest that the term information was itself misleading in such contexts and should be abandoned.

5.3 Mechanisms for the Maintenance of Honesty

Despite the questions raised by early game-theoretic models, the idea of stable, informative communication between individuals with conflicting interests has not been universally abandoned. What can maintain honesty in such cases? One suggestion is that lying may be physically impossible, because there is a direct link between signal and underlying condition (see, e.g., Maynard Smith & Parker 1976, Maynard Smith 1979). A nice example is provided by studies of sexual advertisement in the moth *Utethesia ornatrix* (Conner et al. 1981; Dussourd et al. 1988, 1991). During mating, males of this species transfer protective alkaloids to females by seminal infusion, and these are later used to help defend the eggs. Males also make use of hydroxydanaidal, a compound derived from the same alkaloids, as a pheromone to attract mates. Because the pheromone is derived from the valuable alkaloids, this signal perforce yields honest information about the likely extent of a male's nuptial gift. Only those individuals with high systemic levels of alkaloid, who can provide extensive help with offspring protection, are able to produce large amounts of pheromone.

Displays that are physically constrained to be honest can be found in all signaling modalities: Coloration that is carotenoid-derived, for instance, is thought to provide information about the foraging success and nutritional status of the signaler, because most animals cannot synthesize carotenoids for themselves but must ingest them (e.g., Hill 1991, Kodric-Brown 1989). Similarly, the frequency of vocal signals often reveals the size of the signaler for reasons of physical necessity (e.g., Clutton Brock & Albon 1979). There are thus numerous cases where honesty can be readily understood without recourse to game theory. However, in addition to "assessment signals" like these, there are many systems in which signals do not appear to be inextricably linked to any relevant aspect of the signaler's state. An individual's choice of one threat display rather than another, for instance, is not physically constrained by its fighting ability, aggressiveness, or intention to escalate the conflict. Equally, the length of a bird's tail is not physically dependent on any aspect of its condition. What is needed, therefore, is a strategic explanation for honesty that can be applied to situations where the relationship between signal and state is open to behavioral or evolutionary change.

Zahavi (1975, 1977a,b) was the first biologist to propose such an explanation. He argued that a signal could provide reliable information about the "quality" of signalers, even in the face of a conflict of interest between signaler and receiver, provided that it was costly to produce. The idea, referred to as the "handicap principle," was that a low-quality individual would not make use of the signal even though it could potentially do so, because the costs involved in its production would outweigh the benefits to be gained. Only high-quality individuals, for whom the signal would be cheaper to produce, would benefit by doing so. The handicap principle was similar to the classical economic notion of conspicuous consumption (Veblen 1899): Just as "consumption of valuable goods is a means of reputability to the gentleman of leisure" because it serves as "an evidence of pecuniary strength," the performance of an energetically costly display can serve as evidence of an animal signaler's condition, nutritional status, or foraging efficiency.

At first, the handicap principle was presented as an explanation for the evolution of costly male sexual displays (Zahavi 1975): A population in which males signal their desirability as mates would seem to be vulnerable to invasion by "deceitful" individuals who adopt the display behavior typical of the best individuals, regardless of their own quality. Nevertheless, honesty is possible if the signal used is costly to produce, because only males of superior quality can then afford to employ it—the peacock's train is usually offered as an example (see Petrie 1994). Later, Zahavi developed his idea into a general theory of signal evolution, applicable to many different forms of communication (Zahavi 1977b, 1981, 1987). He suggested, for example, that threat displays could provide information about fighting ability or aggressiveness, because only strong (or strongly motivated) individuals could bear the risks involved in their use. Similarly, contribution to cooperative group activities could advertise social status, since only dominant, high-quality individuals could afford to invest time and energy in such pursuits. In all forms of communication, the process of ritualization, whereby signals tend to become exaggerated, was viewed as an outcome of selection for reliability.

5.4 Game-Theoretic Models of Signaling: A Simple Illustration

Although the handicap principle offers a potential strategic solution to the problem of honesty, it was initially greeted with considerable skepticism (e.g., Maynard Smith 1976). In part, this was because Zahavi presented his theory in verbal form, leaving some doubt as to precisely what was meant. Acceptance of the idea had to await the development of formal models, often using game-theoretic techniques, that clarified the logic of Zahavi's argument [genetic models of male quality advertisement during mating also played an important role in demonstrating the plausibility of honest advertisement; see Kirkpatrick & Ryan (1991) for a brief review]. Evolutionary game theory, which was instrumental in calling the idea of honesty into question, thus played an important role in demonstrating that it could be stable (though classical economic game theory had in fact reached similar conclusions some years earlier; see, e.g., Spence 1973). Below, I give a simple illustration of the game-theoretic approach.

The simplest possible signaling game is formulated as follows: One individual, the signaler, is informed of the value of an uncertain parameter q (in a biological context most commonly representing its own state or type, rather than some aspect of the external environment) and then chooses an action s, referred to as a signal. A second individual, the receiver, observes this signal (but not the value of q) and adopts some response r. The payoff to each individual may depend on the value of q, the signal s given by the signaler, and the response r adopted by the receiver. In the least complicated version, which I will use for the purpose of illustration, there are only two possible state values, q_1 and q_2, two possible signals, s_1 and s_2, and two possible responses, r_1 and r_2. This model is presented graphically in extended form in Fig. 5.1.

The problem of honesty arises when the receiver has an incentive to try to deduce the signaler's type or state from the signal, because it benefits by adopting a different response to signalers of different types, while the signaler has an incentive to mislead the receiver, typically because it benefits by eliciting a certain response irrespective of its type. Suppose, for example, that the payoff to the receiver is 1 if it matches its response to the signaler's type—that is, adopts response r_1 to a signaler of type q_1, or r_2 to a signaler of type q_2—but 0 if it fails to do so. At the same time, the payoff to the signaler is 1 if it provokes the "favorable" response r_2, but 0 if it provokes the "unfavorable" response r_1. How is a separating equilibrium—that is, an equilibrium in which signalers of different types adopt different signals (allowing receivers to respond differently to them)—possible under these circumstances? Any such putative equilibrium appears to be vulnerable to a mutant signaler that, whatever its own type, gives the signal typical of individuals of type q_2, thus eliciting the favorable response r_2.

For a separating equilibrium to exist, individuals of type q_1 must not benefit by adopting the signal typical of individuals of type q_2, even though they would elicit a more favorable response by doing so. The solution suggested by the handicap principle is to make the signal typical of individuals of type q_2 costly to produce, particularly for individuals of type q_1. How can this be formally expressed? Let us restrict our attention to the potential separating equilibrium in which signalers of type q_1 use the signal s_1 while signalers of type q_2 use signal s_2. Assume that s_1 is cost-free, but that use of s_2 incurs a cost, the magnitude of which depends on the type of the signaler. This cost is denoted c_1 for individuals of type q_1, and c_2 for individuals of type q_2. Provided that $c_1 > 1 > c_2$, the cost of s_2 will outweigh the benefits of its production for individuals of type q_1 but not for individuals of type q_2, so that the separating equilibrium does exist [see Hurd (1995) for a more extended analysis].

In the above model, signalers of all types stand to gain the same benefit by eliciting a favorable response. The difference between individuals of type q_1 and q_2 is that the former must pay a higher cost to use signal s_2 than the latter. In the biological literature, analyses of this type have been referred to as models of "quality" advertisement (see, e.g., Grafen 1990a; Johnstone 1994, 1995b). An alternative is to assume that signalers of all types must pay the same signaling costs (i.e., that $c_1 = c_2$), but that signalers of type q_2 stand to gain more by eliciting a favorable response than do signalers of type q_1. If individuals of type q_1 gain b_1 and individuals of type q_2 gain b_2, then provided that $b_2 > c > b_1$ (where c denotes the cost that both types pay to use signal s_2), a separating equilibrium once again exists. Analyses of this type have been referred to as modeling advertisement of "need" (see, e.g., Maynard Smith 1991, 1994; Godfray 1991, 1995a; Johnstone & Grafen 1992a). In reality, of course, signalers may often vary both in their ability to bear the costs of signal production and in the amount they stand to gain by eliciting a favorable response, and recent models have tended to incorporate both factors (e.g., Godfray 1995a, Adams & Mesterton-Gibbons 1995; and see below).

This simple model shows that the handicap principle does provide a potential explanation for the maintenance of honesty. Signal cost can support condition-

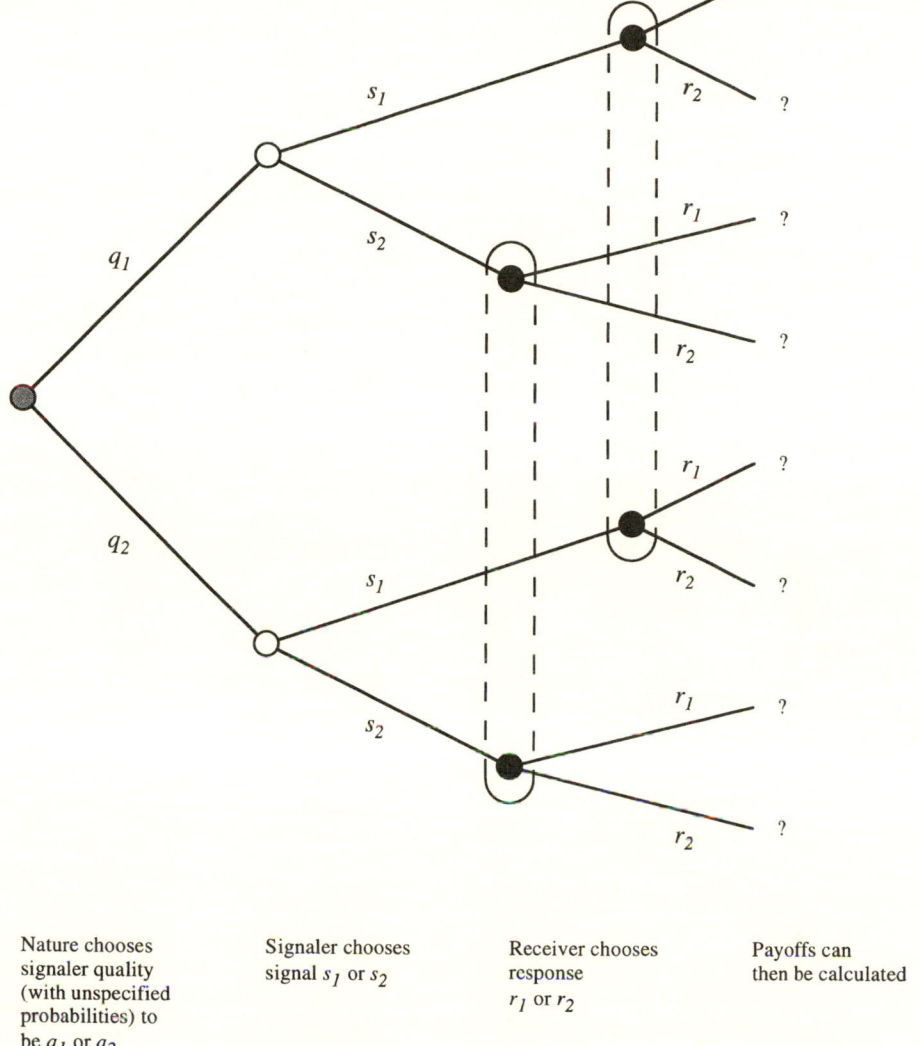

| Nature chooses signaler quality (with unspecified probabilities) to be q_1 or q_2 | Signaler chooses signal s_1 or s_2 | Receiver chooses response r_1 or r_2 | Payoffs can then be calculated |

Figure 5.1. The structure of the minimum signaling game, shown in extensive form. The grey node represents a decision by "nature" (regarding signaler quality); the white nodes represent decisions by the signaler (regarding the signal employed); and the black nodes represents decisions by the receiver (regarding the response adopted). The dotted lines join nodes in the same information set, i.e., nodes that the acting player knows might represent the true state of the game at a particular point in time, but among which he or she cannot discriminate by direct observation. The game is one of imperfect information, because the receiver must choose an action based only on the signal given, without knowledge of the signaler's true quality. Payoffs are not detailed in the diagram; a number of different possibilities are discussed in the text.

dependent expression of a display, provided that either the magnitude of this cost or the benefit to be gained by eliciting a favorable response is also condition-dependent. More complex game-theoretic analyses have shown that the handicap principle can plausibly be applied to a wide range of signaling contexts: In mate choice, as discussed above, males have an incentive to deceive females as to their desirability as mates, but costly signals can nevertheless provide information about male quality (Grafen 1990a; Hutchinson et al. 1993; there are also many genetic models of honest sexual advertisement, notable examples including M. Andersson 1986, Grafen 1990b, Iwasa et al. 1991, and Price et al. 1993). During the period of care, parents need to acquire information about the condition of their young, but because offspring are selected to obtain more resources than parents are selected to give (Trivers 1974, Godfray 1995b), they can only do so by focusing on costly, and hence unfakable, indicators of condition (Godfray 1991, 1995a). Prey animals who possess superior escape abilities stand to gain by advertising them, in order to redirect the attention of predators to more profitable targets; more vulnerable individuals would benefit by misrepresenting their status, but a signal that increases the risk of capture can serve to reliably advertise prey escape capacity (Vega-Redondo & Hasson 1993). Stronger (or more strongly motivated) individuals benefit by advertising their ability to opponents during conflict, in order to deter them from fighting; weaker individuals would benefit by bluffing, but a signal that increases the risk of escalated conflict can provide honest information (Enquist 1985; though see also Adams & Mesterton-Gibbons 1995). Equally, dominant individuals stand to benefit by advertising their status, and while weaker individuals might potentially benefit by adopting high-status signals, costs imposed by the reaction of receivers can maintain honesty (Maynard Smith & Harper 1988; though see Owens & Hartley 1991, Johnstone & Norris 1993, Mock et al., this volume). Many further examples could be given to illustrate the broad applicability of the handicap principle.

5.5 Evidence for Honesty

I will now turn to the issue of how signaling models can be tested. The most basic prediction of these models, and of the handicap principle that inspired them, is that of honesty. Animal signals should provide information about the state of the signaler, because they are expressed in a condition-dependent manner.

Attempts to test the prediction of honesty have most often relied on simple observation, looking for a correlation under natural conditions between the level or intensity of a display and some aspect of the signaler's condition. Some studies, though fewer in number, have involved experimental manipulation of condition, looking for a subsequent effect on the level of display. The advantage of the latter method is that it allows one to control for potential confounding variables [see Johnstone (1995a) for discussion], but it is more restricted in its potential application, since some aspects of the signaler's state are hard to manipulate. In general, both kinds of tests have tended to yield positive results. There is growing evidence that, in a number of different kinds of communication, animal signals often do provide information about the signaler (though the possibility of publication bias means that it is hard to assess how often). I will not attempt a thorough review here, but will simply outline some of the most significant findings, concentrating on those kinds of communication for which the relevant literature is more recent and perhaps less familiar. Evidence concerning the mechanisms by which honesty is maintained will be addressed in a later section of the chapter.

Studies of parent–offspring communication in birds have shown in a number of species that the begging behavior of chicks, and consequently the amount of food they receive from parents, is related to their level of hunger. Redondo and Castro (1992), for example, found that the begging of magpie *(Pica pica)* chicks was strongly influenced by their food intake during the previous hour. Chicks that had received smaller quantities of food (relative to their body mass) exhibited more strenuous posturing and were also more likely to emit begging calls (and to do so for longer); those that did so tended subsequently to obtain more food. Similarly, several studies have found that, following experimental manipulation of the level of chick food deprivation, hungrier birds tend to obtain a position closer to the parent during feeding and acquire more food as a result (Smith & Montgomerie 1991, Kacelnik et al. 1995, Kilner 1995). Parents seem to be influenced both by chick posture and calling and by proximity when allocating food (Kilner 1995).

Hunger is not the only aspect of chick "need" that is advertised. Evans (1988, 1994) has shown that embryonic vocalizations and calling of young chicks in the American white pelican *(Pelecanos erythrorhynchos)* are cold-induced and thus provide honest information about the need for warmth. Moreover, chicks may make use of visual signals, such as bright coloration of plumage, bare patches of skin or the lining of the mouth to advertise their age or level of need (Neuchterlein 1985, Forbes & Ankney 1987, Lyon et al. 1994). Finally, it is worth pointing out that signals of need by offspring to their parents are not restricted to birds, even though most of the existing evidence comes from studies of avian systems. Weary and Fraser (1995) have recently demonstrated that calling of domestic piglets *(Sus scrofa)* provides information in this way; young who have not recently been fed, as well as those with lower long-term rates of weight gain, produce longer, higher-frequency calls that are more likely to elicit parental response.

Turning to pursuit deterrent signals, there is some evidence that the antipredator responses of certain bovids provide predators with information about the physical condition of the prey. FitzGibbon and Fanshawe (1988), for example, found that the stotting of Thomson's gazelles *(Gazella thomsoni)* reflected their ability to outrun coursing predators. Individuals that were chased and killed by wild dogs were less likely to stot during the hunt, and they did so for shorter periods than those which escaped; moreover, the predators appeared to make use of this information, since gazelles that were chased stotted at lower rates than those that were ignored. Caro (1994) subsequently found, in a study of six African bovids (including Thomson's gazelle), that individuals in good condition were not more likely to stot than those in poorer condition, but among those stotting, individual topis *(Damaliscus korrigum)* and Grant's gazelles *(Gazella granti)* in better condition did so more often and, in the latter species, at higher rates. The occurrence of leaping in Impala *(Aepyceros melampus)* was also shown to be related to condition.

Evidence for honest advertisement of escape ability has also been found in birds: Cresswell (1994), looking at singing of skylarks *(Alauda arvensis)* in response to attack by merlins *(Falco columbarius),* showed that a merlin was more likely to catch a nonsinging than a poorly singing skylark and more likely to catch a poorly singing than a full-singing skylark; and once again, the predator was shown to make use of this information, with non- or poorly singing individuals tending to be chased for longer than those that sang well. There are also a number of studies that have found evidence for advertisement of awareness, in which prey indicate that they have detected a predator (see, e.g., Holly 1993, Godin & Davis 1995). I will not detail these here, however, since displays of this kind are examples of "assessment" signals that cannot be faked (the prey being unable to direct a signal at a predator that has not been detected), rather than providing evidence for the handicap principle and strategic maintenance of honesty. Equally, I will not attempt to review the extensive and more well-known literature on aposematism and advertisement of prey unprofitability.

In the context of agonistic interaction, a number of studies have shown that an individual's choice of action conveys information about its probable future behavior, although (as might be expected—see Markl 1985) this behavior is also influenced by the receiver's response. Waas (1991a), for instance, found that the nature of the "threat" call given by burrow-dwelling little blue penguins *(Eudyptula minor)* in response to simulated intrusion conveyed information about the likelihood of subsequent attack (additional instances include Nelson 1984, Hansen 1986, Dabelsteen & Pedersen 1990, but see also Caryl 1979). The information conveyed is probably not about intentions per se, but about factors such as resource-holding potential, or the potential benefit the signaler stands to gain by winning, that influence future behavior. In Hansen's (1986) study of bald eagles *(Haliaeetus leucocephalus),* for example, it was less satiated individuals that were found to more often use displays predictive of future attack. In line with this, some studies have found that the eventual winner of a contest can be predicted from behavior exhibited early on in the interaction (Turner & Huntingford 1986), although there are also cases where early prediction is not possible (Jakobsson et al. 1979). More permanent signals have also been shown in some instances to provide information that can help to settle contests. In particular, studies of several bird species have found that plumage traits can act as "badges of status" (Rohwer 1975). Jones (1990), for example, presents evidence that underpart color in least auklets *(Aethia pusilla)* plays a role in status signaling (and see, e.g., Järvi & Bakken 1984, Møller 1987a, Evans & Hatchwell 1991).

Finally, studies of mate choice and sexual selection have provided the most abundant and familiar evidence for honest advertisement, with male displays being shown to yield information about many different aspects of mate quality. Examples where the male provides information about the magnitude of the direct benefits he has to offer include advertisement of the size of a nuptial gift (Peschke 1987) or the quality of future offspring care (McLennan & McPhail 1989, Norris 1990, Hill 1991), advertisement of health and freedom from transmissible parasites (Clayton 1990) and advertisement of fertility (Robertson 1990, Bourne 1993); numerous other instances could be given. In the last few years, moreover, a small number of studies have found evidence for honest advertisement of the indirect benefits males have to offer, i.e. for advertisement of "good genes" (Norris 1993, Petrie 1994). Given the vast literature on this subject, I will not attempt to provide more detail here (for reviews see Kirkpatrick & Ryan 1991, M. Andersson 1994, Johnstone 1995a).

5.6 Occasional Deceit and the Handicap Principle

The above review, though brief and incomplete, reveals considerable support for the prediction of honesty. There can be little doubt that reliable signaling of condition is possible, even when the interests of the signaler and the receiver are in conflict. However, while most discussion of the handicap principle has focused on the possibility of reliable signaling, it should not be overlooked that models of communication based on Zahavi's theory do not necessarily predict perfect, universal honesty (Grafen 1990a, Johnstone & Grafen 1993, Adams & Mesterton-Gibbons 1995). At a signaling equilibrium, the fact that receivers respond to a signal and are not selected to alter their response means that they must gain some net fitness benefit by doing so. Provided that the signal is honest "on average," however, this does not rule out the possibility of occasional deceit. Suppose, for instance, that there is a rare class of signalers that finds display cheaper (for a given level of quality) than do others; these individuals can then afford to produce the signal typical (in most cases) of a higher level of quality or need than their own, and receivers will consequently respond more favorably to them. Of course, at equilibrium receivers will take into account what fraction of individuals adopting any particular signal belong to this class. Provided that such individuals are rare enough, however, or that responding inappropriately to them is not too costly to the receiver, they need not disrupt the signaling system (Reeve 1989, Grafen 1990a, Johnstone & Grafen 1993, Adams & Mesterton-Gibbons 1995).

What can restrict the frequency of deceit? In some cases, it may be determined by factors external to the signaling interaction. Consider, for instance, the use of deceptive begging signals by avian brood parasites such as cuckoos. As previously discussed, models of signaling of need by offspring to their parents have shown that honest advertisement using costly begging signals can be stable. These models also suggest that young who are less related to others in the brood, or to potential future offspring, will be selected to use more costly begging behavior, since they have less to lose by depriving these others of additional food (Godfray 1995a). In agreement with this prediction, Redondo (1993) found that, for a given level of need, cuckoo chicks in magpie nests beg for food longer and emit more calls per unit time than host chicks, and consequently they tend to be fed more by parents. What prevents this kind of deceit from disrupting the signaling system? The number of brood parasites is constrained by factors such as their high rate of egg mortality (in part due to nest defense and rejection of foreign eggs by hosts), so that low-frequency deception by parasitic chicks can be stable.

Exploitation of host chick-feeding behavior by brood parasites may appear to be an unusual case, since it is based on differences in relatedness of signalers to receivers that cannot be detected by the latter. However, there are other factors that may more commonly give rise to stable deceit. As previously mentioned, models of the handicap principle have been concerned with advertisement of both quality (i.e., the ability of signalers to bear the costs of display) and need (i.e., the extent to which signalers stand to gain by eliciting a favorable response). Since signalers will in reality differ in both respects, signals of either property will be confounded by variation in the other (Johnstone & Grafen 1993, Godfray 1995a, Adams & Mesterton-

Gibbons 1995). Chick begging once again provides a good example: While begging levels can provide parents with information about offspring need (see earlier), a number of studies have shown that food allocation is also influenced by factors such as size and age that affect competitive ability and ease of display (McRae et al. 1993, Price & Ydenberg 1995, Kilner 1995, Mock et al., this volume). Similar arguments applied to other signaling systems include Lotem's (1993) suggestion that older males will exhibit more extravagant and costly sexual displays for a given level of quality than younger males, since they are less concerned with future survival.

In all the above examples, the frequency of "cheats" is determined by factors extrinsic to the signaling interaction (see Reeve, this volume, for a discussion of kinship signaling). Game-theoretic models suggest, however, that low-frequency bluffing may be an outcome of the interaction itself. Adams and Mesterton-Gibbons (1995), for instance, have shown in a model of threat display that low-frequency bluffing can be stable when the signal used is not inherently expensive, but incurs receiver-imposed costs. The basis for their result is that while individuals with superior fighting ability can more easily bear the potential costs of display, they also stand to gain less by deterring their opponent. For the weakest individuals, the potential costs of display are more than made up for by the benefits to be gained, since failure to deter the opponent will lead to a fight that the signaler is very likely to lose. Their model provides an explanation for the occurrence of bluffing in the stomatopod crustacean *Gonodactylus bredini,* a species in which individuals continue to make use of threat displays during the period following moulting, even though they cannot fight effectively at this time (Adams & Caldwell 1990). More generally, it supports the verbal argument of Dawkins and Guilford (1991) that, in systems where the costs of display are receiver-imposed, the potential costs of "probing" to receivers may lead to at least partial corruption of honesty.

5.7 Evidence for Signal Costs

In addition to the prediction of honesty (on average), the handicap principle suggests that when there is a conflict of interest between signaler and receiver, signals are likely to be costly, this cost being necessary for the maintenance of honesty (though see Maynard Smith 1994, Hurd 1995). The most obvious kinds of cost to look for are disadvantages physically concomitant upon display; those that have received most attention are energetic expenditure, decreased locomotory or foraging efficiency, and impairment of the immune response (with most evidence coming from studies of sexual display). Quantitative data concerning the energetic cost of display come mainly from studies of acoustic signaling in insects and anurans, which typically show substantial increases in oxygen consumption during calling [see Ryan (1988) for a review], though there are also studies that provide evidence for an energetic cost of sexual display in birds (Vehrencamp et al. 1989, Höglund et al. 1992, S. Andersson 1994). Turning to the possibility of decreased locomotor and/or foraging efficiency, experimental manipulation has shown in a number of bird species that male sexual ornaments, particularly elongated tail feathers, can reduce flight performance (Møller 1989, Evans & Hatchwell 1992, Evans & Thomas 1992, Møller & de Lope 1995, see Jennions 1993 for a review). Finally, it has been suggested that hormones involved in the development of male sexual display, principally testosterone, may adversely affect immunocompetence (Folstad & Karter 1992; though see Owens & Short 1995).

While the studies mentioned above have shown that some displays do incur a substantial physical cost, there are also cases in which signals have been shown to impose minimal disadvantages of this kind. The energetic costs of acoustic display, for example, may not always be significant: Horn et al. (1995) have recently shown that crowing in roosters *(Gallus gallus domesticus),* which serves as a signal of dominance status (Leonard & Horn 1995), involves less energy expenditure (at the average rate) than low-level activities such as feeding, drinking, and preening. Equally, elaborate and apparently cumbersome plumage ornaments in birds need not always impair flight performance. Aerodynamic models suggest that the costs of tail elongation will depend strongly on tail shape (Balmford et al. 1993), and Norberg (1994) has even shown that elongated tail streamers such as those of male swallows *(Hirundo rustica)* can in theory be aerodynamically advantageous, by allowing tighter turns. Should one conclude in cases such as these that signaling is cost-free? One must first consider the possibility of behaviorally imposed costs.

Two major types of behaviorally imposed costs have been investigated: the potentially deleterious consequences of attracting "eavesdroppers," such as predators or parasites, and increased risk of attack and/or damage by receivers. Beginning with the former, there is good evidence from a number of different species that acoustic sexual signals can attract predators (Tuttle & Ryan 1981, Sakaluk & Belwood 1984) or parasites (Cade 1979). In the context of parent–offspring communication, also, Haskell (1994) recently reported that playback of chick begging calls from artificial ground nests led to higher predation rates (though no such effect was found with tree nests). Turning to visual displays, bright, sexually dimorphic colors have been shown in some cases to increase predation risk: Endler (1980, 1983, 1987), for example, provides strong evidence that this is the case in guppies *(Poecilia reticulata).* More generally, Promislow et al. (1992) showed, in a comparative study of 28 North American passerine bird species, that the ratio of male to female mortality was positively correlated with male plumage brightness. The suggestion has also been made, however, that bright coloration in birds may actually serve to deter predators, acting as a signal of unprofitability (Baker & Parker 1979); and while this hypothesis is controversial (see discussion in Butcher & Rohwer 1989), it has received some support (Götmark 1993).

Costs imposed by the receiver, in the form of an increased risk of attack and/or damage, have been best studied in the context of conflict and status signaling. Waas (1991b), for example, in a study of agonistic communication in the cave-dwelling little blue penguin, found that displays which were more effective in deterring opponents were more dangerous to perform, in that they entailed an increased risk of damage [see Enquist et al. (1985) and Popp (1987) for similar findings in other species]. Similarly, Møller (1987a,b) showed that among male house sparrows *(Passer domesticus),* possession of a large throat patch, which serves as a signal of dominance, leads to a higher frequency of aggressive interaction (with oppponents of similar badge size). Such evidence, moreover, is not restricted to birds: Peschke (1987) has shown that male rove beetles *(Aleochara curtula)* that produce lower levels of female sex pheromones, who tend to be older, dominant, and more well-fed (and who attract more females), incur more aggression from other males. There are also some data to suggest that pursuit-deterrent signals may incur costs of this sort: Caro (1994) found that leaping in impalas, which conveyed information about condition (see earlier), was negatively correlated with flight speed, suggesting that it increases the risk of capture by predators.

Unfortunately, a simple demonstration of either physical or behaviorally imposed costs does not provide clear support for the handicap principle. In order to show that these costs do serve to maintain honesty, one must demonstrate (at least in the case of quality advertisement) that they are condition-dependent. Furthermore, there are a variety of selective pressures, unconnected with the maintenance of honesty, that favor costly signaling of the kind predicted by the handicap principle. Since animal communication takes place in a noisy environment, a certain level of energetic expenditure, predation risk, and so on, may be necessary simply to produce a signal that is detectable (Wiley 1994), and signals that are more costly than is necessary for effective communication (even in a noisy environment) may evolve as a means to exploit sensory biases in receivers (Ryan 1990, Endler 1992, 1993, Arak & Enquist 1993; and see later) or, in the context of sexual selection, via Fisher's runaway process (Lande 1981; Kirkpatrick 1982, 1987; Kirkpatrick & Ryan 1991; Pomiankowski et al. 1991). Consequently, to show that it is selection for reliability that is responsible for the evolution of costly display, one must demonstrate some correlation either between the level of cost and the degree of signaler/receiver or signaler/signaler conflict or between the nature of the cost and the nature of the information conveyed.

Only one study, that of Møller and de Lope (1995), has attempted to demonstrate that signal costs are quality- or condition-dependent. This involved experimental manipulation of tail length in male barn swallows. Survival of individual males was found to decrease with tail elongation and increase with tail shortening, which suggests that the trait is costly (a conclusion borne out by the finding that males with elongated tails captured smaller, less profitable prey items while those with shortened tails captured larger, more profitable prey). Moreover, naturally long-tailed males were better able to survive with an elongated tail, whereas naturally short-tailed males improved their survival following tail shortening. This suggests that tail length normally provides some information about the "quality" of a male, with honesty maintained because "superior" individuals (who are naturally long-tailed) suffer lower costs of tail elongation. It should be noted, however, that the consequences of elongating a male's tail may depend on his natural tail length for physical reasons (e.g., if cost is an accelerating function of tail length) rather than because natural tail length is a reflection of quality; ideally, to provide evidence for quality-dependent cost, one should compare the effects of elongation on males of different qualities (i.e., different natural tail lengths) whose tails have been equalized in length. In any case, this is the only study to provide any evidence for condition-dependent signal cost.

Equally few attempts have been made to compare the cost of signals in systems with different degrees of conflict. The only relevant study is that of Briskie et al. (1994), who showed in an interspecific comparison of 11 passerine birds that loudness of nestling begging calls tended to increase as the frequency of extra-pair parentage increased (and hence as the degree of relatedness among young in the nest decreased). This finding seems to match the prediction of honest signaling models that higher signaling costs are likely in systems with lower relatedness among competing signalers (Godfray 1995b) or between signaler and receiver (Maynard Smith 1991, Johnstone & Grafen 1992a). However, firm evidence that the louder begging of those species with more extra-pair paternity does incur greater costs is lacking (though see Haskell 1994). More comparisons of this kind would be of great value, since it is a key prediction of the handicap principle that signal cost, being a consequence of selection for reliability, should be lower in systems with less conflict (where there is less incentive for deceit).

The final method that might be used to test the importance of selection for reliability in signal evolution is to look for a correlation between the nature of signal cost and the nature of the information conveyed. Zahavi (1977b, 1981, 1987) has argued at some length that signals which are inherently costly can only provide honest information about aspects of signaler condition that affect the ability to bear those costs. There is thus a necessary link between the form of a signal and the information it conveys. Honest advertisement of a male's nutritional condition and energy reserves, for example, will require a signal that is energetically costly. Advertisement of escape ability, on the other hand, will require a signal that increases the risk of capture. This approach, however, has not yet been used to generate testable predictions regarding signal design, for two main reasons. First, the requirement that the cost of a signal be related to the quality it advertises does not allow one to draw detailed conclusions about what the appearance of any given signal will be. Although advertisement of escape ability, for instance, requires a signal that increases the risk of capture, there are many different kinds of display (e.g., stotting, approaching the predator, etc.) that could have this effect. Thus the knowledge that a display provides information about escape ability does not allow one to predict what the precise form of the signal will be. Second, Zahavi's argument can only be applied to instances of quality advertisement in which signal costs are physically concomitant upon display rather than behaviorally imposed. Honest signaling of need may be maintained by any form of cost, and even in the case of quality advertisement, behaviorally imposed costs may be incurred by a signal of any kind, so that the design of a display is in this case conventional and unrelated to the quality advertised (see Guilford & Dawkins 1995).

5.8 The Limits of Game Theory

Before concluding my discussion, I will briefly consider the limitations of the game-theoretic approach to modeling communication. Evolutionary game theory assumes that, at equilibrium, animals behave in a way that maximizes their fitness, given the behavior of other individuals in the population. Unfortunately, the stability of a signaling equilibrium may depend on the response of receivers to out-of-equilibrium signals that are not normally encountered, because these responses determine whether a population is open to invasion by a mutant employing a novel signal type (Grafen 1990a). Fitness maximization cannot single out a particular response to such signals, because selection is blind to responses to stimuli that receivers never encounter (Grafen 1990a, Arak & Enquist 1993). Consequently, simple game theory models often have to make arbitrary assumptions about the nature of these responses. When only one dimension of signal variation is considered, it may not be too difficult to come up with a plausible assumption; for example, Grafen (1990a) uses an approach referred to as "local flat extrapolation," in which signals not given at a candidate equilibrium are assumed, if they are sufficiently similar to a signal that is given, to elicit the same response as that given signal [see Leimar et al. (1986) for an alternative approach]. Where a large space of possible signals is considered, however, so that a high proportion of signal types are never encountered at equilibrium, the problem is greater (Johnstone 1995b). By making various different assumptions, it is possible to construct a great many implausible equilibria.

One solution to the above difficulty is to introduce some randomness into the behavior of the signaler, or the receiver's perception of the signal, so that all possible signal types (or at least all possible perceived signal types) are encountered with at least a small probability, even if signalers never choose to employ some of them at equilibrium. This means that responses to such unused signals are no longer selectively neutral, and fitness maximization can be used to single out a unique best response. Models of biological communication that incorporate perceptual error have shown in this way that there are plausible signaling equilibria that cannot be invaded by novel mutants (Johnstone & Grafen 1992b; Johnstone 1994, 1995a); the approach is similar to the use of "trembling hand" perfectness in economic models [see Rasmusen (1989) for a simple illustration relating to signaling].

The above method, however, places very great faith in the power of natural selection. Perceptual error may resolve the technical problem of response to out-of-equilibrium signals by ensuring that all possible perceived signal types are encountered with a nonzero probability. However, it is perhaps unrealistic to assume that receivers will inevitably evolve fitness-maximizing responses to stimuli that are encountered extremely infrequently. An alternative suggestion is that such responses will drift or fluctuate because they are rarely tested, and thus have minimal fitness consequences (Grafen 1990a, Arak & Enquist 1993). Such random drift would have significant effects on the course of signal evolution, because it could give rise to "hidden preferences" for novel signal types, preferences which would be open to subsequent exploitation (Arak & Enquist 1993, 1995; Krakauer & Johnstone 1995).

In addition to exploitation of random, hidden preferences, signalers may also be able to take advantage of biases that have arisen because of selective pressures unrelated to signaling (Ryan 1990; Ryan & Keddy-Hector 1992; Endler 1992, 1993; Reeve and Sherman 1993). The sense organs and nervous system of an organism serve many functions besides the detection of and reaction to any particular signal, and it is unreasonable to assume that each function can always be independently optimized. Consequently, the evolution of response strategies may often be constrained; if a particular preference serves an important enough role in a nonsignaling context, then it will be maintained even though it gives signalers the opportunity for sensory exploitation (Ryan & Rand 1993). Moreover, even if selection in the context of signaling is sufficiently strong to eliminate a sensory bias once signalers begin to exploit it, the origin and transient exploitation of such biases may nevertheless be a recurrent feature of signal evolution. A good example of a sensory bias is provided by Proctor's (1991, 1992) studies of the water mite *Neumania papillator.* In this species, males attract the attention of females by vibrating their first two pairs of legs, a behavior which appears to exploit the females' preexisting sensory adaptations for detecting the motion of copepod prey.

The small, but growing, number of studies that have found evidence for sensory exploitation of preexisting, hidden preferences [see Ryan et al. (1990) and Basolo (1995) for additional examples] suggest that the evolution of response strategies is in fact constrained. Unfortunately, there is, as yet, insufficient evidence to determine what proportion of signals have arisen in this way. Furthermore, even if a display evolves via sensory exploitation, it may ultimately come to provide reliable information about the signaler. In the túngara frog *(Physalaemus pustulosus),* for instance, females prefer male calls containing lower-frequency chucks. Ryan (1983, 1985) has shown that this preference results in females mating with larger males that fertilize more of their eggs, but also (Ryan 1990, Ryan & Rand 1990, Ryan et al. 1990) that the sensory bias responsible for the preference existed prior to the evolution of the chuck. Sensory exploitation and the handicap principle are thus not incompatible; the former may be responsible for the origin of signals, while the latter determines which ones are eventually eliminated and which ones remain (only those that come to provide reliable information being stable). However, such findings do indicate that the game-theoretic approach alone yields only a partial understanding of signal evolution.

5.9 Conclusions and Suggestions for Future Research

In this chapter, I have attempted to summarize the contribution of game theory to our understanding of information transfer during animal communication. This is a problematic issue, because the logic of natural selection suggests that information transfer is not evolutionarily stable when there is a conflict of interest between signaler and receiver. Selection, it seems, should favor deceit on the part of signalers, and hence a reduction in the amount of useful information receivers can obtain from their signals. The achievement of game theory has been, after raising this problem in the first place, to show that informative communication is possible even in the face of such a conflict. Game-theoretic analyses have verified Zahavi's suggestion that signal cost can maintain honesty and have shown that his handicap principle is theoretically applicable to a wide range of different signaling systems.

The implications of honest-signaling models are potentially of great significance. Not only do they suggest that reliable information transfer is likely to be a ubiquitous feature of communication, they also provide a new perspective on signal evolution. From this persepctive, the "form" or appearance of a signal is influenced not only by selection for efficacy (Guilford & Dawkins 1991) but also by selection for reliability. Since unreliable signals are not evolutionarily stable, the displays we see in the natural world must be designed in such a way that they are not vulnerable to corruption by deceit. This argument provides a potential explanation for the striking and costly nature of many animal signals. It also yields a number of further predictions, discussed below.

Have empirical studies borne out the predictions of honest signaling models? The answer, as one might expect, is both yes and no. There is considerable and growing evidence that many different kinds of signals do provide information about the state of the signaler. Furthermore, the occurrence of occasional deceit is in accord with theoretical expectation. However, the role of signal costs in maintaining honesty has yet to be clearly demonstrated in any case. The possibility thus remains that informative communication depends more on physical constraints than on any strategic mechanism. The course of signal evolution may simply reflect the "discovery" by receivers of a few, key traits that are physically linked to the underlying quality of the signaler. Moreover, the strategic perspective on signal design remains, at present, no more than a set of appealing ideas. There is some evidence (though surprisingly little) that signals can be costly, but this is hardly a unique or surprising prediction. As discussed above, many selective pressures unrelated to reliability can favor the evolution of costly display. What is needed, but still lacking, is evidence that some of the huge variation in signal form seen in the natural world has a strategic explanation.

In order to test any such proposed explanation, one has to be able to determine, for a variety of different signaling situations, two or more of the following things: the degree of conflict between signaler and receiver (or between competing signalers), the information conveyed, and the cost of different kinds of display in that situation. Predictions can be generated by considering the effect of each variable on the signaling system. Changing the degree of conflict should change the equilibrium level of signal cost, with greater conflict associated with more expensive displays. Changing the information conveyed should (at least in some cases) change the nature of that cost; signalers advertising a particular quality should make use of displays that are costly in a way dependent on that quality. Finally, changing the relationship between cost and any particular display should (again, in at least some cases) affect whether or not it is used; at equilibrium, signalers should not employ a cost-free display, since it is unlikely to be reliable. Testing these predictions is difficult, especially since the costs incurred by a signal are not limited to the physical disadvantages concomitant upon it, but may also be socially imposed (see earlier), in which case the physical design of the display becomes far less relevant. Such tests, however, are not impossible (see, e.g., the study of Briskie et al. 1994).

Biological signaling theory is thus at an early, but exciting, stage. Initial tests have yielded favorable results, but a number of fundamental predictions have yet to be verified, which leaves considerable scope for future empirical research. Can the theory itself advance any further? As I discussed in the previous section, there are some basic limitations to the game-theoretic approach. Models that are constructed using game-theoretic techniques typically assume that selection is powerful enough to fine tune all of of a receiver's responses, even those that have minimal fitness consequences. Equally, they ignore the possibility that receivers are constrained by computational limitations or by conflicting selection pressures that result from non-signaling requirements placed on their brain and sense organs. Since these assumptions are clearly unrealistic, additional modeling techniques may be necessary to obtain a full understanding of signal evolution. Nevertheless, the burst of empirical research triggered by the formal verification of the handicap principle has thrown up many intriguing issues that are not addressed by existing signaling models, but do fall within the scope of game theory: Possible subjects of further research include, for example, the use and evolution of multiple signals (see Johnstone 1995b, 1996), the structure of prolonged communicatory interactions (see Godfray 1995b) in which both participants may exchange signals, and the evolution of signaling in a social context, where signalers may compete for the attention of individual receivers [see Greenfield & Roizen (1993) and Godfray (1995a)]. It seems likely, therefore, that game theory still has much to contribute to the study of communication.

References

Adams, E. S. & Caldwell, R. L. 1990. Deceptive communication in asymmetric fights of the stomatopod crustacean *Gonodactylus bredini*. *Anim. Behav.*, 39, 706–716.

Adams, E. S. & Mesterton-Gibbons, M. 1995. The cost of threat displays and the stability of deceptive communication. *J. Theor. Biol.*, 175, 405–421.

Andersson, M. B. 1986. Evolution of condition-dependent sex ornaments and mating preferences: Sexual selection based on viability differences. *Evolution*, 40, 804–816.

Andersson, M. B. 1994. *Sexual Selection*. Princeton, NJ: Princeton University Press.

Andersson, S. 1994. Costs of sexual advertising in the lekking Jackson's widowbird. *Condor*, 96, 1–10.

Arak, A. & Enquist, M. 1993. Hidden preferences and the evolution of signals. *Philos. Trans. R. Soc. Lond. B*, 340, 207–213.

Arak, A. & Enquist, M. 1995. Conflict, receiver bias and the evolution of signal form. *Philos. Trans. R. Soc. London B*, 349, 337–344.

Baker, R. R. & Parker, G. A. 1979. The evolution of bird coloration. *Philos. Trans. R. Soc. London B*, 287, 63–130.

Balmford, A., Thomas, A. L. R. & Jones, I. L. 1993. Aerodynamics and the evolution of long tails in birds. *Nature*, 361, 628–631.

Basolo, A. L. 1995. Phylogenetic evidence for the role of a pre-existing bias in sexual selection. *Proc. R. Soc. London B*, 259, 307–311.

Briskie, J. V., Naughler, C. T. & Leech, S. M. 1994. Begging intensity of nestling birds varies with sibling relatedness. *Proc. R. Soc. London B*, 258, 73–78.

Bourne, G. R. 1993. Proximate costs and benefits of mate acquisition at leks of the frog *Ololygon rubra*. *Behav. Ecol. Sociobiol.*, 31, 173–180.

Butcher, G. S. & Rohwer, S. 1989. The evolution of conspicuous and distinctive coloration for communication in birds. *Curr. Ornithol.*, 6, 51–108.

Cade, W. H. 1979. The evolution of alternative male reproductive strategies in field crickets. In *Sexual Selection and Competition in Insects*, M. S. Blum & N. A. Blum, eds., pp. 343–379. London: Academic Press.

Caro, T. M. 1994. Ungulate antipredator behaviour: preliminary and comparative data from African bovids. *Behaviour*, 128, 189–228.

Caryl, P. G. 1979. Communication by agonistic displays: what can games theory contribute to ethology? *Behaviour*, 68, 136–169.

Caryl, P. G. 1982. Animal signals: A reply to Hinde. *Anim. Behav.*, 30, 240–244.

Clayton, D. H. 1990. Mate choice in experimentally parasitized rock doves: lousy males lose. *Am. Zool.*, 30, 251–262.

Clutton-Brock, T. H. & Albon, S. D. 1979 The roaring of red deer and the evolution of honest advertisement. *Behaviour*, 69, 145–170.

Conner, W. E., Eisner, T., van der Meer, R. K., Guerrero, A. & Meinwald, J. 1981. Precopulatory sexual interaction in an Arctiid moth *(Utethesia ornatrix)*: Role of a pheromone derived from dietary alkaloids. *Behav. Ecol. Sociobiol.*, 9, 227–235.

Cresswell, W. 1994. Song as a pursuit-deterrent signal, and its occurrence relative to other antipredator behaviours of skylark *(Alauda arvensis)* on attack by merlins *(Falco columbarius)*. *Behav. Ecol. Sociobiol.*, 34, 217–223.

Dabelsteen, T. & Pedersen, S. B. 1990. Song and information about aggressive responses of blackbirds, *Turdus merula:* Evidence from interactive playback experiments with territory owners. *Anim. Behav.*, 40, 1158–1168.

Dawkins, M. S. & Guilford, T. C. 1991. The corruption of honest signalling. *Anim. Behav.*, 41, 865–873.

Dawkins, R. & Krebs, J. R. 1978. Animal signals: Information or manipulation? In *Behavioural*

Ecology: An Evolutionary Approach, first edition, J. R. Krebs & N. B. Davies, eds., pp. 282–309. Oxford: Blackwell Scientific Publications.

Dussourd, D. E., Ubik, K., Harvis, C. A., Resch, J. & Meinwald, J. 1988. Biparental defensive endowment of eggs with acquired plant alkaloid in the moth *Utethesia ornatrix. Proc. Natl. Acad. Sci. USA,* 85, 5992–5996.

Dussourd, D. E., Harvis, C. A., Meinwald, J. & Eisner, T. 1991. Pheromonal advertisement of a nuptial gift by a male moth *(Utethesia ornatrix). Proc. Natl. Acad. Sci. USA,* 88, 9224–9227.

Endler, J. A. 1980. Natural selection on color patterns in *Poecilia reticulata. Evolution,* 34, 76–91.

Endler, J. A. 1983. Natural and sexual selection on color patterns in poeciliid fishes. *Environ. Biol. Fishes,* 9, 173–190.

Endler, J. A. 1987. Predation, light intensity and courtship behaviour in *Poecilia reticulata* (Pisces: Poeciliidae). *Anim. Behav.,* 35, 1376–1385.

Endler, J. A. 1992. Signals, signal conditions and the direction of evolution. *Am. Nat.,* 139, S125–S153.

Endler, J. A. 1993. Some general comments on the evolution and design of animal communication systems. *Philos. Trans. R. Soc. London B,* 340, 215–225.

Enquist, M. 1985. Communication during aggressive interactions with particular reference to variation in choice of behaviour. *Anim. Behav.,* 33, 1152–1161.

Enquist, M., Plane, E & Röed, J. 1985. Aggressive communication in fulmars *(Fulmarus glacialis)* competing for food. *Anim. Behav.,* 33, 1007–1020.

Evans, M. & Hatchwell, B. 1991. An experimental study of male adornment in the scarlet-tufted malachite sunbird. I. The role of pectoral tufts in territory defence. *Behav. Ecol. Sociobiol.,* 29, 413–420.

Evans, M. & Hatchwell, B. J. 1992. An experimental study of male adornment in the scarlet-tufted malachite sunbird. II. The role of the elongated tail in mate choice and experimental evidence for a handicap. *Behav. Ecol. Sociobiol.,* 29, 421–427.

Evans, M. & Thomas, A. L. R. 1992. The aerodynamic and mechanical consequences of elongated tails in the scarlet-tufted malachite sunbird: measuring the cost of a handicap. *Anim. Behav.,* 43, 337–347.

Evans, R. M. 1988. Embryonic vocalisations as care-soliciting signals, with particular reference to the American white pelican. *Proc. Int. Ornith. Congr.,* 19, 1467–1475.

Evans, R. M. 1994. Cold-induced calling and shivering in young American white pelicans: Honest signalling of offspring need for warmth in a functionally integrated thermoregulatory system. *Behaviour,* 129, 14–34.

FitzGibbon, C. D. & Fanshawe, J. H. 1988. Stotting in Thomson's gazelles: An honest signal of condition. *Behav. Ecol. Sociobiol.,* 23, 69–74.

Folstad, I. & Karter, A. J. 1992. Parasites, bright males and the immunocompetence handicap. *Am. Nat.,* 139, 603–622.

Forbes, M. R. L. & Ankney, C. D. 1987. Hatching asynchrony and food allocation within broods of pied-billed Grebes, *Podilymbus podiceps. Can. J. Zool.,* 65, 2872–2877.

Godfray, H. C. J. 1991. Signalling of need between parents and offspring. *Nature,* 352, 328–330.

Godfray, H. C. J. 1995a. Signalling of need between parents and young: Parent–offspring conflict and sibling rivalry. *Am. Nat.,* 146, 1–24.

Godfray, H. C. J. 1995b. Evolutionary theory of parent–offspring conflict. *Nature,* 376, 133–138.

Godin, J-G. & Davis, S. A. 1995. Who dares, benefits: Predator approach behaviour in the guppy *(Poecilia reticulata)* deters predator pursuit. *Proc. R. Soc. London B,* 259, 193–200.

Götmark, F. 1993. Conspicuous coloration in male birds is favoured by predation in some species and disfavoured in others. *Proc. R. Soc. London B,* 253, 143–146.

Grafen, A. 1990a. Biological signals as handicaps. *J. Theor. Biol.,* 144, 517–546.

Grafen, A. 1990b. Sexual selection unhandicapped by the Fisher process. *J. Theor. Biol.,* 144, 517–546.

Grafen, A. & Johnstone, R. A. 1993. Why we need ESS signalling theory. *Philos. Trans. R. Soc. London B,* 340, 245–250.

Greenfield, M. D. & Roizen, I. 1993. Katydid synchronous chorusing is an evolutionarily stable outcome of female choice. *Nature,* 364, 618–620.

Guilford, T. C. & Dawkins, M. S. 1991. Receiver psychology and the evolution of animal signals. *Anim. Behav.,* 42, 1–14.

Guilford, T. C. & Dawkins, M. S. 1995. What are conventional signals? *Anim. Behav.,* 49, 1689–1695.

Hansen, A. J. 1986. Fighting behaviour in bald eagles: A test of game theory. *Ecology,* 67, 787–797.

Haskell, D. 1994. Experimental evidence that nestling begging behaviour incurs a cost due to predation. *Proc. R. Soc. London B,* 257, 161–164.

Hill, G. E. 1991. Plumage color is a sexually selected indicator of male quality. *Nature,* 350, 337–339.

Hinde, R. A. 1981. Animal signals: ethological and games-theory approaches are not incompatible. *Anim. Behav.,* 29, 535–542.

Höglund, J., Kålås, J. A. & Fiske, P. 1992. The costs of secondary sexual characters in the lekking Great Snipe *(Gallinago media). Behav. Ecol. Sociobiol.,* 30, 309–315.

Holly, A. J. F. 1993. Do brown hares signal to foxes? *Ethology,* 94, 21–30.

Horn, A. G., Leonard, M. L. & Weary, D. M. 1995. Oxygen consumption during crowing by roosters: Talk is cheap. *Anim. Behav.,* 50, 1171–1175.

Hurd, P. L. 1995. Communication in discrete action–response games. *J. Theor. Biol.,* 174, 217–222.

Hutchinson, J. M. C., MacNamara, J. M. & Cuthill, I. C. 1993. Song, sexual selection, starvation and strategic handicaps. *Anim. Behav.,* 45, 1153–177.

Iwasa, Y. A., Pomiankowski, A. & Nee, S. 1991. The evolution of costly mate preferences. II. The "handicap" principle. *Evolution,* 45, 1431–1442.

Jakobsson, S., Radesäter, T. & Järvi, T. 1979. On the fighting behaviour of *Nannocara anomala* (Pisces, Cichlidae). *Z. Tierpsychol.,* 49, 210–220.

Järvi, T. & Bakken, M. 1984. The function of variation of the breast stripe of the great tit *(Parus major). Anim. Behav.,* 32, 590–596.

Jennions, M. D. 1993. Female choice in birds and the cost of long tails. *Trends Ecol. Evol.,* 8, 230–232.

Johnstone, R. A. 1994. Honest signalling, perceptual error and the evolution of "all-or-nothing" displays. *Proc. R. Soc. London B,* 256, 169–175.

Johnstone, R. A. 1995a. Sexual selection, honest advertisement and the handicap principle: Reviewing the evidence. *Biol. Rev.,* 70, 1–65.

Johnstone, R. A. 1995b. Honest advertisement of multiple qualities using multiple signals. *J. Theor. Biol.,* 177, 87–94.

Johnstone, R. A. 1996. Multiple displays in animal communication: "Backup signals" and "multiple messages." *Philos. Trans. R. Soc. B,* 351, 329–338.

Johnstone, R. A. & Grafen, A. 1992a. The continuous Sir Philip Sidney game: a simple model of biological signalling. *J. Theor. Biol.,* 156, 215–234.

Johnstone, R. A. & Grafen, A. 1992b. Error-prone signalling. *Proc. R. Soc. London B,* 248, 229–233.

Johnstone, R. A. & Grafen, A. 1993. Dishonesty and the handicap principle. *Anim. Behav.*, 46, 759–764.

Johnstone, R. A. & Norris, K. 1993. Badges of status and the cost of aggression. *Behav. Ecol. Sociobiol.*, 32, 127–134.

Jones, I. L. 1990. Plumage variability functions for status signalling in least auklets. *Anim. Behav.*, 39, 967–975.

Kacelnik, A., Cotton, P. A., Stirling, L. & Wright, J. 1995. Food allocation among nestling starlings: Sibling competition and the scope of parental choice. *Proc. R. Soc. London B,* 259, 259–263.

Kilner, R. 1995. When do canary parents respond to nestling signals of need? *Proc. R. Soc. London B,* 260, 343–348.

Kirkpatrick, M. 1982. Sexual selection and the evolution of female choice. *Evolution,* 36, 1–12.

Kirkpatrick, M. 1987. Sexual selection by female choice in polygynous animals. *Annu. Rev. Ecol. Syst.,* 18, 43–70.

Kirkpatrick, M. & Ryan, M. J. 1991. The paradox of the lek and the evolution of mating preferences. *Nature,* 350, 33–38.

Kodric-Brown, A. 1989. Dietary carotenoids and male mating success in the guppy: An envionmental component to female choice. *Behav. Ecol. Sociobiol.,* 17, 199–206.

Krakauer, D. C. & Johnstone, R. A. 1995. The evolution of exploitation and honesty in animal communication: a model using artificial neural networks. *Philos. Trans. R. Soc. London B,* 348, 355–361.

Krebs, J. R. & Dawkins, R. 1984. Animal signals: Mind-reading and manipulation. In *Behavioural Ecology: An Evolutionary Approach,* second edition, J. R. Krebs & N. B. Davies, eds., pp. 380–402. Oxford: Blackwell Scientific Publications.

Lande, R. 1981. Models of speciation by sexual selection on polygenic characters. *Proc. Natl. Acad. Sci. USA,* 78, 3721–3725.

Leimar, O., Enquist, M. & Sillén-Tullberg, B. 1986. Evolutionary stability of aposematic coloration and prey unprofitability: A theoretical analysis. *Am. Nat.,* 128, 469–490.

Leonard, M. L. & Horn, A. G. 1995. Crowing in relation to status in roosters. *Anim. Behav.,* 49, 1283–1290.

Lotem, A. 1993. Secondary sexual ornaments as signals: The handicap approach and three potential problems. *Etologia,* 3, 209–218.

Lyon, B. E., Eadie, J. M. & Hamilton, L. D. 1994. Parental choice selects for ornamental plumage in American coot chicks. *Nature (London),* 371, 240–243.

Markl, H. 1985. Manipulation, modulation, information, cognition: Some of the riddles of communication. In *Experimental Behavioural Ecology and Sociobiology,* B. Hölldobler & M. Lindauer, eds., pp. 163–194. Sunderland, MA: Sinauer.

Maynard Smith, J. 1974. The theory of games and the evolution of animal conflicts. *J. Theor. Biol.,* 47, 209–221.

Maynard Smith, J. 1976. Sexual selection and the handicap principle. *J. Theor. Biol.,* 57, 239–242.

Maynard Smith, J. 1979. Game theory and the evolution of behaviour. *Proc. R. Soc. London B,* 205, 475–488.

Maynard Smith, J. 1991. Honest signalling: The Philip Sidney Game. *Anim. Behav.,* 42, 1034–1035.

Maynard Smith, J. 1994. Must reliable signals always be costly? *Anim. Behav.,* 47, 1115–1120.

Maynard Smith, J. & Harper, D. G. C. 1988. The evolution of aggression: Can selection generate variability? *Philos. Trans. R. Soc. London B,* 319, 557–570.

Maynard Smith, J. & Parker, G. A. 1976. The logic of asymmetric contests. *Anim. Behav.,* 24, 159–175.

Maynard Smith, J. & Price, G. R. 1973. The logic of animal conflict. *Nature,* 246, 15–18.

McGregor, P. K. 1993. Signalling in territorial systems: A context for individual identification, ranging and eavesdropping. *Philos. Trans. R. Soc. London B,* 340, 237–244.

McLennan, D. A. & McPhail, J. E. 1989. Experimental investigations of the evolutionary significance of sexually dimorphic nuptial coloration in *Gasterosteus aculeatus* (L): The relationship between male color and male behaviour. *Can. J. Zool.,* 67, 1778–1782.

McRae, S. B., Weatherhead, P. J. & Montgomerie, R. 1993. American robin nestlings compete by jockeying for position. *Behav. Ecol. Sociobiol.,* 33, 101–106.

Møller, A. P. 1987a. Variation in badge size in male house sparrows *Passer domesticus:* evidence for status signalling. *Anim. Behav.,* 35, 1637–1644.

Møller, A. P. 1987b. Social control of deception among status signalling house sparrows *Passer domesticus. Behav. Ecol. Sociobiol.,* 20, 307–311.

Møller, A. P. 1989. Viability costs of male tail ornaments in a swallow. *Nature,* 339, 132–135.

Møller, A. P. & de Lope, F. 1995. Differential costs of a secondary sexual character: an experimental test of the handicap principle. *Evolution,* 48, 1676–1683.

Nelson, D. A. 1984. Communication of intentions in agonistic contexts by the pigeon guillemot, *Cepphus columba. Behaviour,* 88, 145–189.

Neuchterlein, G. L. 1985. Experiments on the functions of the bare crown patch of downy western grebe chicks. *Can. J. Zool.,* 63, 464–467.

Norberg, R. A. 1994. Swallow tail streamer is a mechanical device for self-deflection of tail leading edge, enhancing aerodynamic efficiency and flight manoeuvrability. *Proc. R. Soc. London B,* 257, 227–233.

Norris, K. 1990. Female choice and the quality of parental care in the great tit *Parus major. Behav. Ecol. Sociobiol.,* 27, 275–281.

Norris, K. 1993. Heritable variation in a plumage indicator of variability in male great tits *Parus major. Nature,* 362, 537–539.

Owens, I. P. F. & Hartley, I. R. 1991. 'Trojan sparrows': evolutionary consequences of dishonest invasion for the badges-of-status model. *Am. Nat.,* 138, 1187–1205.

Owens, I. P. F. & Short, R. V. 1995. Hormonal basis of sexual dimorphism in birds: Implications for new theories of sexual selection. *Trends Ecol. Evol.,* 10, 44–47.

Peschke, K. 1987. Male aggression, female mimicry and female choice in the rove beetle, *Aleochara curtula* (Coleoptera, Staphylinidae). *Ethology,* 75, 265–284.

Petrie, M. 1994. Improved growth and survival of offspring of peacocks with more elaborate trains. *Nature,* 371, 598–599.

Pomiankowski, A., Iwasa, Y. & Nee, S. 1991. The evolution of costly mate preferences. I. Fisher and biased mutation. *Evolution,* 45, 1422–1430.

Popp, J. W. 1987. Risk and effectiveness in the use of agonistic displays by American goldfinches. *Behaviour,* 103, 141–156.

Price, K. & Ydenberg, R. 1995. Begging and provisioning in broods of asynchronously-hatched yellow-headed blackbird nestlings. *Behav. Ecol. Sociobiol.,* 37, 201–208.

Price, T., Schluter, D. & Heckman, N. E. 1993. Sexual selection when the female directly benefits. *Biol. J. Linn. Soc.,* 48, 187–211.

Proctor, H. C. 1991. Courtship in the water mite *Neumania papillator:* males capitalize on female adaptations for predation. *Anim. Behav.,* 42, 589–598.

Proctor, H. C. 1992. Sensory exploitation and the evolution of male mating behaviour: a cladistic test using water mites (Acari: Parasitengona). *Anim. Behav.,* 44, 745–752.

Promislow, D. E. L., Montgomerie, R. & Martin, T. E. 1992. Mortality costs of sexual dimorphism in birds. *Proc. R. Soc. London B,* 250, 143–150.

Rasmusen, E. 1989. *Games and Information.* Oxford: Blackwell.

Redondo, T. 1993. Exploitation of host mechanisms for parental care by avian brood parasites. *Etología,* 3, 235–297.

Redondo, T. & Castro, F. 1992. Signalling of nutritional need by magpie nestlings. *Ethology,* 92, 193–204.

Reeve, H. K. 1989. The evolution of conspecific acceptance thresholds. *Am. Nat.,* 133, 407–435.

Reeve, H. K. & Sherman, P. W. 1993. Adaptation and the goals of evolutionary research. *Q. Rev. Biol.,* 68, 1–32.

Robertson, J. G. M. 1990. Female choice increases fertilisation success in the Australian frog *Uperoleia rugosa. Anim. Behav.,* 34, 773–784.

Rohwer, S. A. 1975. The social significance of avian plumage variability. *Evolution,* 29, 593–610.

Ryan, M. J. 1983. Sexual selection and communication in a neotropical frog, *Physalaemus pustulosus. Evolution,* 37, 261–272.

Ryan, M. J. 1985. *The Túngara Frog, a Study in Sexual Selection and Communication.* Chicago: Chicago University Press.

Ryan, M. J. 1988. Energy, calling and selection. *Am. Zool.,* 28, 885–898.

Ryan, M. J. 1990. Sexual selection, sensory systems, and sensory exploitation. *Oxf. Surv. Evol. Biol.,* 7, 156–195.

Ryan, M. J., Fox, J. H., Wilczynski, W. & Rand, A. S. 1990. Sexual selection by sensory exploitation in the frog *Physalaemus pustulosus. Nature,* 343, 66–67.

Ryan, M. J. & Keddy-Hector, A. 1992. Directional patterns of female mate choice and the role of sensory biases. *Am. Nat.,* 139, S4–S35.

Ryan, M. J. & Rand, A. S. 1990. The sensory basis of sexual selection for complex calls in the túngara frog, *Physalaemus pustulosus* (sexual selection for sensory exploitation). *Evolution,* 44, 305–314.

Ryan, M. J. & Rand, A. S. 1993. Sexual selection and signal evolution: the ghost of biases past. *Philos. Trans. R. Soc. London B,* 340, 187–195.

Sakaluk, S. K. & Belwood, J. J. 1984. Gecko phonotaxis to cricket calling song—a case of satellite predation. *Anim. Behav.,* 32, 659–662.

Smith, H. G. & Montgomerie, R. 1991. Nestling American robins compete with siblings by begging. *Behav. Ecol. Sociobiol.,* 29, 307–312.

Smith, W. J. 1977. *The Behaviour of Communication. An Ethological Approach.* Harvard: Harvard University Press.

Sober, E. 1994. *From a Biological Point of View.* Cambridge: Cambridge University Press.

Spence, M. 1973. Job market signalling. *Q. J. Econ.,* 87, 355–374.

Trivers, R. L. 1974. Parent-offspring conflict. *Amer. Zool.,* 14, 249–264.

Turner, G. & Huntingford, F. 1986. A problem for games theory analysis: Assessment and intention in male mouth brooder contests. *Anim. Behav.,* 34, 961–970.

Tuttle, M. D. & Ryan, M. J. 1981. Bat predation and the evolution of frog vocalisations in the Neotropics. *Science,* 214, 677–678.

Veblen, T. 1899. *The Theory of the Leisure Class.* New York: Macmillan.

Vega-Redondo, F. & Hasson, O. 1993. A game-theoretic model of predator-prey signalling. *J. Theor. Biol.,* 162, 309–319.

Vehrencamp, S. L., Bradbury, J. W. & Gibson, R. M. 1989. The energetic cost of display in male Sage Grouse. *Anim. Behav.,* 38, 885–896.

Waas, J. R. 1991a. Do little blue penguins signal their intentions during aggressive interactions with strangers? *Anim. Behav.,* 41, 375–382.

Waas, J. R. 1991b. The risks and benefits of signalling aggressive motivation: a study of cave-dwelling little blue penguins. *Behav. Ecol. Sociobiol.,* 29, 139–146.

Weary, D. M. & Fraser, D. 1995. Calling by domestic piglets: reliable signals of need? *Anim. Behav.,* 50, 1047–1055.

Wiley, R. H. 1983. The evolution of communication: Information and manipulation. In *Com-*

munication, T. R. Halliday & P. J. B. Slater, eds., pp. 156–189. Oxford: Blackwell Scientific Publications.

Wiley, R. H. 1994. Errors, exaggeration and deception in animal communication. In *Behavioural Mechanisms in Evolutionary Ecology,* L. A. Real, ed., pp. 157–189. London: University of Chicago Press.

Zahavi, A. 1975. Mate selection—a selection for a handicap. *J. Theor. Biol.,* 53, 205–214.

Zahavi, A. 1977a. The cost of honesty (further remarks on the handicap principle). *J. Theor. Biol.,* 67, 603–605.

Zahavi, A. 1977b. Reliability in communication systems and the evolution of altruism. In *Evolutionary Ecology,* B. Stonehouse & C. Perrins, pp. 253–259. London: Macmillan.

Zahavi, A. 1981. Natural selection, sexual selection and the selection of signals. In *Evolution Today. Proceedings of the Second International Congress of Systematics and Evolution,* G. G. E. Scudder & J. L. Reveal, eds., pp. 133–138. Pittsburg: Carnegie-Mellon.

Zahavi, A. 1987. The theory of signal selection and some of its implications. In *International Symposium of Biological Evolution,* V. P. Delfino, ed., pp. 305–327. Bari: Adriatica Editrice.

HUDSON KERN REEVE

Game Theory, Reproductive Skew, and Nepotism

6.1 Introduction

Our understanding of the evolution of cooperative kin groups has been greatly advanced by kin selection models (Hamilton 1964, West-Eberhard 1975) and, more recently, by a melding of such models with game-theoretic models to explain and predict the outcomes of a variety of intragroup conflicts (Trivers & Hare 1976, Grafen 1979, Emlen 1982, Vehrencamp 1983, Reeve 1991, Reeve & Ratnieks 1993, Reeve & Keller 1995, Mock et al., this volume). In this chapter, I focus on potential conflicts within kin groups over both the partitioning of reproduction and the expression of nepotism, the latter conflict arising when resolution of the former leads to reproductive sharing among group members.

In particular, I shall argue that new game-theoretic models are needed to shed light on two fundamental problems: (1) the joint evolution of reproductive partitioning and genetic composition of cooperative groups, especially when potential group-joiners have a choice of groups to join or residents have a choice of joiners to accept, and (2) the selective mechanisms underlying the surprising absence of within-group nepotism in kin groups, most notably in social insect colonies.

6.2 Reproductive Skew and Group Composition with Choosy Subordinates or Choosy Dominants

A critical feature of animal societies is the reproductive skew, a shorthand term for the distribution of direct reproduction among group members (including potentially reproductive nonbreeders) (Vehrencamp 1983). In high-skew societies, actual direct reproduction is concentrated in one or a few dominant individuals in the colony; in low-skew societies, reproduction is distributed more evenly among individuals. Models of "optimal skew" in reproduction attempt to explain the degree of skew by assuming that (1) members of the society differ in dominance and (2) dominant members sometimes yield just enough reproduction to subordinates to induce the latter to stay in the group (Emlen 1982, Vehrencamp 1983, Reeve 1991, Reeve & Ratnieks 1993) and cooperate peacefully (Reeve & Ratnieks 1993), rather than to leave the group and reproduce independently or fight for exclusive control of the group's resources. Reproductive inducements that prevent subordinates from leaving are called *staying incentives;* reproductive inducements that prevent subordinates from fighting to the death for complete control of colony resources are called *peace incentives.*

In spite of what their label suggests, "optimal skew" models are really evolutionary game models (models of "games with alternate moves": Maynard Smith 1982, pp. 137–139), because the solutions to these models (e.g., whether or not a staying incentive is offered by the dominant) are the Nash equilibria for successive interactions (games) between a dominant and a subordinate individual. Optimal skew models also incorporate the second kind of frequency-dependent fitness characteristic of game-theoretic approaches (Reeve and Dugatkin, this volume).

The very first models of the evolution of reproductive skew analyzed how ecological constraints on solitary reproduction, genetic relatedness of potential breeders, and productivity advantages of peaceful association should influence the magnitudes of staying incentives in vertebrate and invertebrate societies (Emlen 1982, Vehrencamp 1983, Reeve 1991). Reeve and Ratnieks (1993) extended these models by examining how relative fighting ability among group members will interact with the above factors to influence the reproductive skew. The general conclusions of these models are that the skew should increase (i.e., the reproductive incentives should decrease in magnitude and thus reproduction should become less equitable) as the relatedness between dominants and subordinates increases, the probability of successful solitary reproduction by the subordinate decreases (i.e., for stronger ecological constraints), the subordinate's contribution to colony productivity increases, and the subordinate's relative fighting ability decreases. Reeve and Keller (1995) also recently showed that the asymmetry in relatedness occurring in mother–daughter associations versus sibling associations will tend to increase the degree of skew in the former [see also Emlen (1996) and Reeve & Keller (1996)]. Recent tests of these predictions have generated striking support for optimal skew theory (review in Keller & Reeve 1994, Bourke & Heinze 1994, Bourke & Franks 1995, Emlen 1995, Reeve & Keller 1995).

Although the first wave of empirical tests indicates that the "classical" skew models described above are extremely promising, these models are incomplete in at least two respects. First, these models assume that subordinate joiners have only two options: Join a single dominant or nest alone. It is possible that a subordinate joiner may be able to sample and choose between two (or more) dominants at different nests, possibly generating a kind of "bidding competition" between the two dominants for the services of the subordinate. Second, the models assume that the dominant interacts with joiners from only one relatedness category, when in fact, it may be able to choose between subordinates of low and high relatedness. Below, I expand the skew models to include the cases of (1) subordinates choosing between multiple dominants and (2) dominants choosing between multiple subordinates. I then integrate (1) and (2) into a general model of the conditions under which cooperative groups should consist of relatives versus nonrelatives, given that reproduction within these groups is regulated as predicted by the classical and expanded skew models.

6.2.1 Choosy Subordinates: Competitive "Bidding" Between Dominants for a Subordinate's Help

As in the classical skew models, we begin with the assumption that two group members differ in dominance, relative dominance position being determined by relative fighting ability (perhaps assessed by relative size) or by conventional cues such as age or order in which they joined the nest. The amount of reproduction yielded by a dominant to a subordinate should depend upon (1) the subordinate's prospects for successful nesting if it leaves the association (i.e., the severity of ecological constraints), (2) the productivity advantages of peaceful association, and (3) the relatedness between dominant and subordinate. [For simplicity, I will ignore the modulation of the precise degree of skew by fighting ability (i.e., peace incentives) and assume that relative fighting ability is important only in deciding who is dominant.] Thus, three parameters enter into the model for dyadic groups: (1) x is the probability of successful nest foundation by a potential subordinate times the proportional expected productivity of such a nest, relative to a standardized reproductive output equal to 1 for an already established solitary nest (lower values of x indicate harsher ecological constraints), (2) k is the ratio of the expected overall productivity of a joined nest to that of an established solitarily founded nest (assumed to be >1), and (3) r is the (symmetrical) relatedness of the dominant to the subordinate.

In the classical skew model, the proportion p_s of overall direct reproduction yielded to the subordinate in a stable association is that which gives the subordinate just sufficient incentive to remain in the association rather than leave and found a nest solitarily. This is the "staying incentive" of Reeve and Ratnieks (1993). If ecological constraints are strong, corresponding to the condition $x < r(k-1)$, the subordinate will stay in the association with no reproduction, that is, $p_s = 0$ (maximum skew). If ecological constraints are moderate [i.e., $r(k-1) < x < k-1$], then the subordinate will receive a staying incentive, the magnitude of which is equal to

$$p_s = [x - r(k-1)]/k(1-r) \tag{1}$$

which is obtained by using Hamilton's rule (see below) to solve for the minimum fraction of reproduction required to make staying favorable for the subordinate. If ecological constraints are weak, corresponding to the condition $x > k-1$, the subordinate is favored to leave and reproduce solitarily (Reeve & Ratnieks, 1993).

Now we pose the new question: If a subordinate can choose between multiple dominants, what will be the evolutionary stable fraction of reproduction received by the subordinate? To answer this question, we will employ Hamilton's rule for deciding which of two strategies will be favored by selection (the same rule was used to derive classical skew theory). That is, strategy i will be favored over strategy j if

$$(P_i - P_j) + \Sigma r(K_i - K_j) > 0 \tag{2}$$

which is equivalent to

$$P_i + \Sigma r K_i > P_j + \Sigma r K_j \tag{3}$$

where r is the coefficient of relatedness between the two interactants, P_i (or P_j) is the personal reproduction associated with strategy i (or j), and K_i (or K_j) is the other party's reproduction if strategy i (or j) is performed. If a strategy affects more than one relative, the fitness effects in (2) and the absolute offspring numbers in (3) are summed over all affected relatives, weighted by the coefficient of relatedness between the actor and each of those relatives. Use of the simple additive version of Hamilton's rule is especially appropriate because dominants and subordinates can be viewed as being in different contexts; the rule appears to work especially well if behaviors are context-dependent—that is, conditional (Parker 1989).

Suppose a dominant is in competition with n other dominants for the services of a single subordinate, which can sample without cost among those dominants (if the subordinate *cannot* sample multiple dominants, then the classical skew model applies). What is the evolutionarily stable fraction of reproduction p^* that the dominant is willing to yield to the subordinate? If we assume that the subordinate can (with negligible cost) sample the $n+1$ dominants (which are initially assumed symmetrically related to the subordinate and each other with relatedness r), the subordinate will associate with the dominant with the highest reproductive "bid" p. The resulting bidding game is an example of a game against the field (Maynard Smith 1982). I assume for simplicity that the productivity ratio k is the same for the different dominants and that $x < k - 1$ (i.e., ecological circumstances favor joining over independent breeding).

Selection will favor continual increases in p (escalated "bidding") as long as the inclusive fitness benefit for attracting a subordinate exceeds that for allowing a subordinate to nest with another relative; increases in p beyond this level will be selectively penalized (Fig. 6.1). Thus, by Hamilton's rule, version (3), p^* satisfies

$$(1-p^*)k + rp^*k + nr = 1 + rk + (n-1)r \qquad (4)$$

The left-hand side is simply the dominant's personal offspring if the subordinate joins + relatedness to the subordinate times the (joining) subordinate's offspring + relatedness to other dominants times offspring of these (unjoined) dominants, and the right-hand side is the corresponding sum if one of the other dominants attracts the joiner. The ESS, p^*, simplifies to

$$p^* = \frac{k-1}{k} \qquad (5)$$

This is the staying incentive in what I will call simply the "bidding game" as opposed to the classical optimal skew model. In the bidding game, there are four novel features of the evolutionary outcome: (a) The staying incentive (5) is always greater than or equal to that when dominants only have to "bid" against a fixed environment (1), which means that especially low skews are expected when helpers can cheaply choose among dominants to join; (b) the skew should *decrease* as the group productivity increases, in dramatic contrast to skews adjusted to a fixed environment; and (c) relatedness does not affect the skew. The fourth, somewhat bizarre consequence, arises if $k > 2$ (dyads are more than twice as productive as unjoined

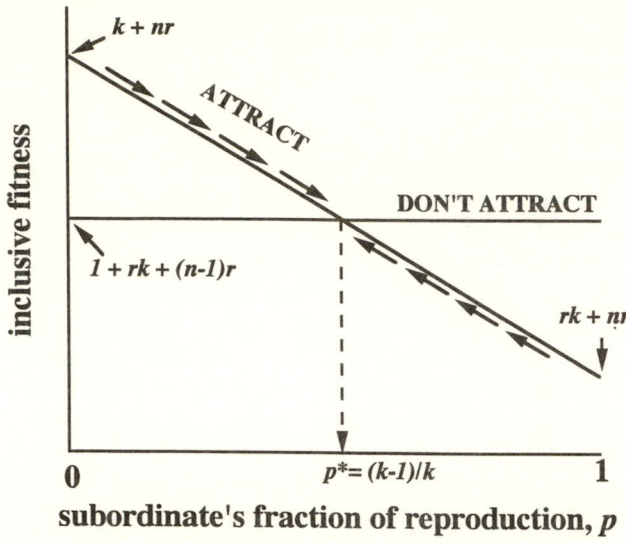

subordinate's fraction of reproduction, p

Figure 6.1. The bidding game. Selection increases the magnitudes of staying incentives (reproductive bids) offered by dominants to attract subordinates, until the point is reached at
which dominants do as well to not attract subordinates as to attract them; r is the coefficient of relatedness, k is the group
output, and $n + 1$ is the number of competing dominants.

dominants). In such a case, it follows from (5) that, at the ESS, the dominant would
receive less than half of the total reproduction. Under such circumstances, it would
actually pay a dominant to leave the group and attempt to become subordinate to
another dominant! Perhaps a more likely outcome is that dominants will be selected
to hide their dominance from joiners and thus dominance hierarchies will be unde-
tectable. In sum, when joiners can choose between multiple dominants, skews should
be quite low and independent of relatedness, and there may be frequent between-
group switching or absence of conspicuous dominance relations.

An interesting feature of the solution to the bidding game is that at the ESS, p^*,
both the joined dominant and the subordinate virtually "break even" by forming (versus not forming) an association. In contrast, in the classical skew model, only the
subordinate is at a break-even point; that is, the subordinate would do nearly as well
to nest solitarily as to join the dominant (because the dominant has given it just
enough direct reproduction to make staying favorable), but the dominant may do
much better to have versus not have the subordinate's help. The gap between these
break-even points for the dominant and subordinate will determine the potential for
intragroup conflict, by setting the upper limit on how much each can selfishly augment its fraction of the group reproduction without jeopardizing the group's stability
(Reeve & Keller, 1997). Thus, low levels of conflict, manifested by low levels of
intracolony aggression, should be characteristic of groups in the bidding game: The
break-even points for dominant and subordinate coincide almost exactly.

The bidding game can be easily generalized to include a sampling cost for the subordinate, and this generalization will automatically yield the conditions under which the bidding game reverts to the classical optimal skew model. To obtain the general model, we assume that a subordinate encounters a dominant resident of a nest and then is faced with the decision of joining that dominant or attempting to seek another dominant, thus establishing a bidding game between the two dominants. If the subordinate seeks to set up a bidding game, its survivorship is equal to $\sigma < 1$, with a reduction in survival resulting from increased predation risk or energetic cost while searching for or switching between dominants.

When will sampling be favored over immediate joining? If the subordinate joins the first dominant immediately and permanently, it receives the classical staying incentive given by (1) for moderate ecological constraints $(r(k-1) < x < k-1)$ and receives no incentive for strong ecological constraints $(x < r(k-1))$. If it receives the classical staying incentive, its total inclusive fitness is $p_s k + r(1 - p_s)k + r$ (= personal offspring + relatedness times offspring of joined relative + relatedness times offspring of unjoined relative) which simplifies to $x + r + r$. Thus, by Hamilton's rule (3), sampling will be favored over immediate joining under moderate ecological constraints if

$$\sigma[p^*k + r(1 - p^*)k + r] + (1 - \sigma)(2r) > x + r + r$$

which simplifies to

$$\sigma > x/(k-1) \tag{6}$$

Similarly, sampling will be favored over immediate joining under strong ecological constraints (no classical staying incentive) if

$$\sigma[p^*k + r(1 - p^*)k + r] + (1 - \sigma)2r > kr + r$$

which simplifies to

$$\sigma > r \tag{7}$$

When condition (6) or (7) applies to the appropriate level of ecological constraints, the subordinate receives the staying incentive of the bidding game. When neither condition applies, the subordinate receives either the lesser staying incentive of the classical skew model (moderate ecological constraints) or no staying incentive at all (strong ecological constraints).

All conditions and their social outcomes are shown in Fig. 6.2, which expands the classical skew models to include the bidding game. Note that the low skews (large staying incentives) predicted by the bidding game model can occur at any level of x, the output of solitary subordinates, but are particularly likely when (1) σ is high, such as when a high density of colonies makes sampling of multiple colonies relatively risk-free and/or a low ratio of potential joiners to dominant residents makes it easier to find dominants without joiners, (2) x is low, and (3) k is high, the latter two conditions corresponding to harsh ecological constraints on solitary nesting. Thus, the low skews and absence of intragroup aggression of the bidding game are

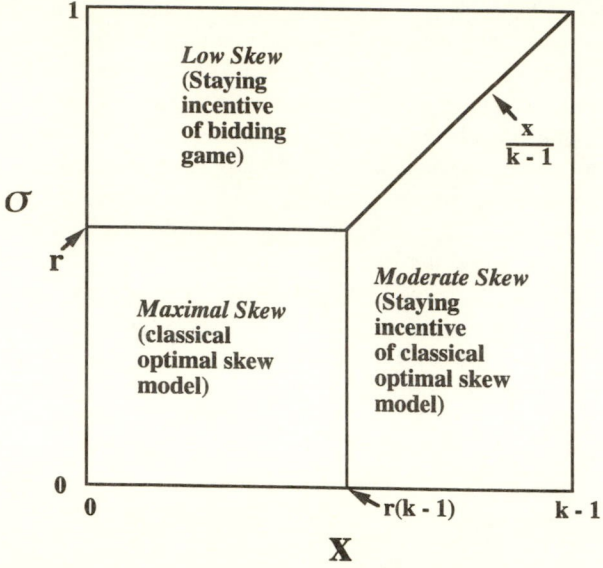

Figure 6.2. Model synthesizing the generalized bidding game and the classical skew model; r is the relatedness between the resident and its relative; k is the standardized group productivity (a lone resident's productivity $= 1$), x is the standardized reproductive output of a joiner if it nests alone, and σ is the probability of survival for a subordinate that tries to sample multiple colonies. Subordinates do not join if $x > k - 1$.

predicted when ecological constraints are harsh, but colonies are present in sufficient density to make sampling multiple colonies feasible.

6.2.1.1 Choices Between Related and Unrelated Dominants in the Bidding Game

In the above bidding game, we assumed that all dominants were uniformly related to the subordinate joiner. What will be the subordinate's preference if it can join either a related or an unrelated dominant? It turns out that the subordinate will be indifferent to its relatedness to dominants. If a subordinate becomes involved in a bidding war between a related and unrelated dominant, then by the same reasoning that led to (4), the evolutionarily stable fractions of reproduction p^* offered by the related dominant and p'^* offered by the unrelated dominant will satisfy the simultaneous equations:

$$(1 - p^*)k + rp^*k = 1 + rp'^*k \tag{8}$$

and

$$(1 - p'^*)k = 1 \tag{9}$$

where equation (8) corresponds to the related dominant's break-even point and equation (9) corresponds to the unrelated dominant's break-even point.

The ESSes are $p^*=p'^*=(k-1)/k$; that is, they are the same as (5) and independent of relatedness. Thus, the subordinate receives the staying incentive (5) in the bidding game from either a related or unrelated dominant. Which bid should the subordinate accept? By Hamilton's rule (3), the subordinate should accept the relative's bid if

$$p^*k + r(1 - p^*)k > p'^*k + r \qquad (10)$$

However, the two quantities on either side of the inequality are exactly equal to each other (both equal $k - 1 + r$), so the subordinate is indifferent to its relatedness to putative dominants in the bidding game.

Finally, we need to consider what a subordinate should do if it first encounters a related versus an unrelated dominant in the generalized bidding game with search costs. Under moderate ecological constraints (in which the subordinate receives the classical staying incentive if it does not sample), a subordinate first encountering the unrelated dominant should sample rather than immediately join the unrelated dominant if, by Hamilton's rule (3), $\sigma(p^*k) + r > x + r$ or $\sigma > x/(k-1)$, the same as condition (6) above. Exactly the same condition holds for the case of the related dominant being encountered first, because the left- and right-hand sides of the inequality are unaltered. Under strong ecological constraints (in which the subordinate receives no staying incentive from the related dominant if it does not sample), a subordinate first encountering the unrelated dominant should sample rather than immediately join the unrelated dominant if, by Hamilton's rule (3), $\sigma(p^*k) + r > x + r$ or $\sigma > x/(k-1)$, exactly as before. However, if the subordinate encounters the relative first, it should sample if $\sigma(p^*k) + r > rk$ or $\sigma > r$, the same as condition (7). In sum, in the bidding game with search costs, the subordinate will prefer the related dominant (and receive no staying incentive) *only* if it encounters the latter first, ecological constraints are strong ($x < r(k-1)$), and $\sigma < r$. All outcomes are summarized in Fig. 6.2.

6.2.2 Choosy Dominants: When to Accept Related Versus Unrelated Subordinates

Next we consider under what conditions dominants should be choosy about the relatednesses of the subordinates they accept. The case of the bidding game is the easiest, and I tackle it first.

6.2.2.1 The Bidding Game

In the bidding game, we found that dominants will be selected to yield the staying incentive $p^*=(k-1)/k$, regardless of the relatedness of the subordinate. Suppose dominants have a choice of accepting a related versus an unrelated subordinate. By Hamilton's rule (3), preference for the related subordinate will be evolutionarily stable over preference for an unrelated subordinate if

$$(1 - p^*)k + rp^*k + r > (1 - p^*)k + rp^*k + r(1 - p^*)k \qquad (11)$$

assuming that (1) dominants will encounter both kinds of subordinates and (2) a rejected related subordinate moves on to nest with a relative of both it and the focal dominant. However, both sides of the inequality are equal to $1 + rk$, and thus dominants in the bidding game should be indifferent to the relatedness of potential joiners. (Both sides will remain equal even if the population contains a *mixture* of dominants with alternative preferences.) In sum, in the bidding game, both dominants and subordinates will tend to be neutral over the genetic relatedness of their partners. Next, we examine the preferences of dominants in the classical skew model.

6.2.2.2 The Classical Skew Model

We first note that an intriguing consequence of the classical model, like that of the bidding game, is that relatedness has either no or a negative effect on a subordinate's decision to join a dominant (Reeve 1991, Reeve & Ratnieks 1993). For example, a subordinate of relatively low relatedness to a dominant receives a lesser indirect kinship benefit by helping the dominant, but it also receives a greater staying (or peace) incentive. It turns out that these two opposing effects of relatedness exactly cancel out in the case of classical staying incentives, leading to the seemingly paradoxical conclusion that subordinates should be indifferent to the relatedness of potential partners.

However, dominants will not necessarily be indifferent to the relatednesses of potentially joining subordinates in the classical skew model (Reeve & Ratnieks 1993). The important consequence of the latter fact is that the relatedness within cooperating dyads in the classical skew model will depend entirely on the optimal choice for the dominant; that is, the relatedness between group members can be predicted solely from a model of how a dominant should choose among subordinates based on their relatedness.

We first examine the case of strong ecological constraints for the related subordinate—that is, $x < r(k - 1)$. The related subordinate (if accepted) would receive no classical staying incentive, but it follows from (1) that the unrelated subordinate would receive a classical staying incentive equal to x/k (since an unrelated subordinate should always require some amount of direct reproductive incentive). If the dominant accepts the related subordinate, it receives a reproductive output k and the subordinate receives 0, but if the dominant accepts the unrelated subordinate, it receives a payoff $k(1 - x/k)$ and the rejected relative receives x. Substituting these values into Hamilton's rule (3) yields the following condition for accepting related subordinates:

$$k - k(1 - x/k) + r(0 - x) = x(1 - r) > 0 \tag{12}$$

Thus, under strong ecological constraints, the dominant would always prefer to choose a related subordinate ($r < 1$) as a joiner, given equal access to both related and unrelated subordinates. The reason for this preference is that the higher skew resulting when the joiner is a relative benefits the dominant more than the joining relative's loss of reproduction hurts the dominant.

Moderate ecological constraints for a related subordinate corresponds to the condition $r(k - 1) < x < k - 1$. Under these conditions, the related subordinate receives the staying incentive given by (1), and the unrelated subordinate again receives a staying incentive of x/k. Thus, the dominant will be favored to choose the related subordinate if

$$k(1-p_s)-k(1-x/k)+r[k(ps)-x]=r(k-1-x)>0 \qquad (13)$$

Since $x<k-1$ by assumption, inequality (13) is necessarily satisfied and again the dominant should prefer to accept a related subordinate because of the benefits of increased skew.

Thus, dominants should always prefer to have related subordinates if dominants regulate reproduction in accordance with optimal skew theory. However, dominants may not always have equal access to related and unrelated subordinates. In particular, a dominant that rejects a nonrelative as a partner runs the risk of obtaining no joiners if relatives are not available. For this reason, it is useful to consider a classical skew model in which choosy dominants sometimes have no related joiners available—that is, a "beggars-can't-be-choosers" game.

6.2.2.3 The Beggars-Can't-Be-Choosers Game

Assume that if a dominant resident in a nest/territory accepts a subordinate, no additional individual subsequently attempts to join the pair because the benefits of being in a group of three are too small and/or the accepted subordinate would aggressively eject the new joiner. A solitary dominant resident confronted with an unrelated potential joiner must decide whether to accept the joiner or to reject it in favor of the future possibility that a related joiner (relatedness $= r$) will arrive. Let s be the probability that a related joiner will later arrive if an unrelated joiner is rejected by the dominant.

We first examine the case of strong ecological constraints for the related subordinate—that is, $x<r(k-1)$. A related subordinate would receive no staying incentive, and the unrelated subordinate would receive a staying incentive equal to x/k. If the dominant accepts the unrelated subordinate, it receives a payoff $k(1-x/k)$ and the relative receives x. If the dominant rejects the unrelated subordinate, its expected payoff (offspring production) is $(1-s)+sk$ and the expected payoff of the relative is $(1-s)x+s(0)=(1-s)x$. Substituting these values into (3), solving for s, and simplifying yields the following condition for accepting the unrelated subordinate:

$$s<(k-1-x)/(k-1-rx) \qquad (14)$$

Thus, when the probability that a relative will arrive is less than the threshold value on the right-hand side of the inequality, the dominant resident is favored to accept the unrelated subordinate. The threshold increases with decreasing x, increasing k, and increasing r. In other words, acceptance of the unrelated subordinate should be especially likely when the ecological constraints are strong (low x), when group benefits are high (high k), and, curiously, when the relatedness r to the related subordinate is high. The latter effect occurs because, under the assumed conditions (strong ecological constraints), the related subordinate receives no staying incentive; thus, as the dominant's relatedness to the latter increases, the dominant is increasingly penalized for depriving this relative of all direct reproduction.

Now suppose that the related subordinate is under moderate ecological constraints—that is, $r(k-1)<x<k-1$. The related subordinate now would receive a staying incentive given by (1), and the unrelated subordinate again would receive a staying incentive equal to x/k. If the dominant accepts the unrelated subordinate, it receives a payoff $k(1-x/k)$ and the relative receives x. If the dominant rejects the unrelated subordinate, its expected payoff is $(1-s)+s(1-p_s)k$ and the expected payoff of the relative is $(1-s)x+s(p_s k)$. Substituting these values into (3), solving for s, and simplifying yields the following condition for accepting the unrelated subordinate:

$$s<1/(1+r) \tag{15}$$

In the case of moderate ecological constraints, accepting the unrelated subordinate is favored if the probability of encountering a related subordinate falls below the threshold on the right side of the inequality, and this threshold decreases (unlike the threshold for strong ecological constraints) as the relatedness increases.

It should be noted that results (14) and (15) actually encompass both the case in which a related subordinate is unavailable because it has died and the case in which it is alive, but unavailable, because it cannot locate the dominant's nest. The component terms in Hamilton's rule (3) differ between the two cases, but the net inequalities (14) and (15) are the same.

What are the relative magnitudes of the two thresholds in (14) and (15)? It is easily shown that $(k-x)/(k-1-rx)>1/(1+r)$ must be true if $x<r(k-1)$—i.e., ecological constraints are strong. That is, the threshold below which unrelated subordinates would be accepted is always higher for strong ecological constraints than for moderate constraints. Thus, the beggars-can't-be-choosers model leads directly to the prediction that associations between nonrelatives will tend to be most frequent when (a) there is a chance that relatives aren't available to join a dominant resident, (b) group benefits of association are especially high, and (c) there are strong ecological constraints on successful independent reproduction. Increased relatedness to related subordinates paradoxically increases the chance that the higher threshold will be in effect (because it becomes increasingly likely that $x<r(k-1)$ as r increases) and increases the magnitude of this threshold under strong ecological constraints (although decreasing its magnitude under moderate constraints). The odd effect of high relatedness occurs because when no staying incentive is offered to a related subordinate (strong constraints), increased relatedness of the dominant to the subordinate increases the kin-selective penalty to the dominant for depriving the subordinate of any reproduction when they are associated.

6.2.3 Group Genetic Composition in the Generalized Bidding Game and Classical Skew Model: A Synthesis

We have seen that both the bidding game and classical skew models make the prediction that *associations of nonrelatives should be more likely when there are stronger ecological constraints—that is, reduced success of solitary breeding* (low x) *and higher benefits for grouping* (high k). The first (but not second) of the two subpredictions is similar to that obtained in a dynamic optimization model of founding decisions by social insect queens (Nonacs 1989). However, in the latter model, reproduction was not adjusted by dominants as in the skew models, and acceptance of unrelated partners occurred either because unrelated dominants were more easily dominated or because further searching was risky: In the bidding game model, unrelated partners are accepted because there is *no* inclusive fitness advantage for preferring related partners, and in the beggars-can't-be-choosers game, nonrelatives are accepted because of the risk that dominants will not subsequently encounter related joiners.

Few studies have quantified the parameters of the bidding and beggars-can't-be-choosers models, so the decisive tests of the models lie ahead. However, the current data appear to be in accord with the overall prediction that associations of nonrelatives will most likely occur under strong ecological constraints. For example, African pied kingfishers exhibit a helper-at-the-nest system in which the relatedness of the helper to the dominant pair is variable (Reyer 1990). At breeding sites near Lake Naivasha, the effect of the helper on the reproductive success of the breeding pair is small (the ratio k is near 1.0), but at Lake Victoria, helpers dramatically increase the survival of nestlings (i.e., k is nearly 2.0). Interestingly, the fraction of helpers that are unrelated to breeders is higher at Lake Victoria, in accordance with the model. (In addition, unrelated helpers at lake Victoria have a higher direct reproduction than do related helpers, in accordance with the classical skew model.)

More supportive evidence comes from data on relatedness within and benefits of belonging to female prides and male coalitions in lions (Packer et al. 1991). The rate at which the overall reproductive output of male coalitions increases with the number of coalition males is high (i.e., k is high) compared to the corresponding rate for females in prides (Packer et al. 1988). As predicted by the models, female pridemates are closely related, whereas male coalitions are often composed of nonrelatives (Packer et al., 1991).

One complication for the above prediction is that, when ecological constraints are strong, offspring of breeders should be more likely to stay in their natal nest (and perhaps help their parents) rather than disperse to start their own nests (Emlen 1995). The latter effect obviously may increase the tendency for groups to be composed of relatives when ecological constraints are harsh (in effect, this is a mechanism by which harsh constraints increase s in the beggars-can't-be-choosers game). For this reason, the strongest prediction of the models is not so much that the proportion of groups consisting of nonrelatives will steadily increase with stronger ecological constraints, but rather that when groups of nonrelatives *occur* with some appreciable frequency, it will be true that ecological constraints are especially harsh. (Another strong prediction is that, *for a given value of s* in the beggars-can't-be-choosers model, the proportion of nonrelative groups should increase with increasing ecological constraints.)

We are now in a position to develop a new, synthetic theory of reproductive skew, group composition, and even intragroup aggression by drawing on the combined predictions of the bidding game (see Fig. 6.2) and the beggars-can't-be-choosers version of the classical skew model. Figure 6.3 diagrams the predicted characteristics of groups as a function of solitary breeding success x, group productivity k, relatedness r_R to group members when groups are composed of relatives, and σ,

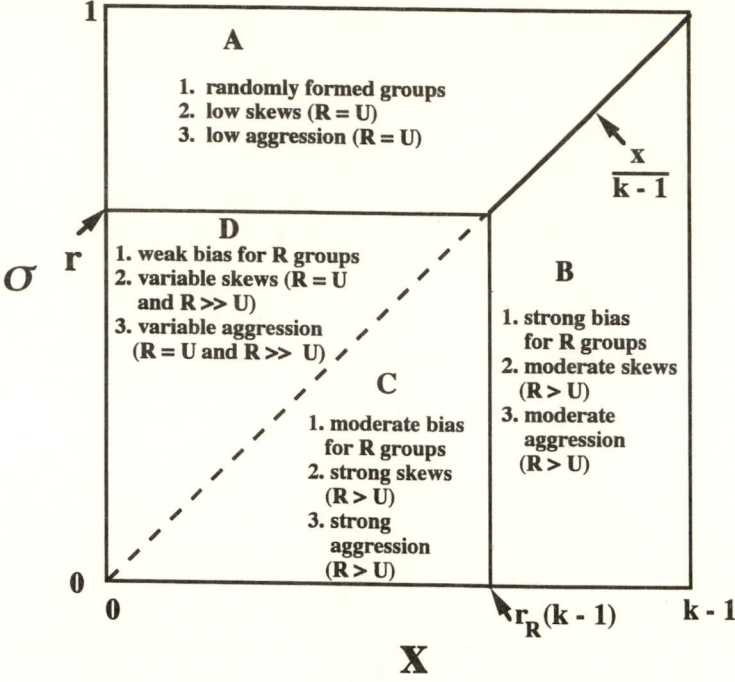

Figure 6.3. A general model of social evolution: the predicted characteristics of groups as a function of solitary breeding success *x,* group productivity *k,* relatedness r_R to group members when groups are composed of relatives, and σ, the survival probability of a subordinate that attempts to sample multiple nests in the generalized bidding game. R refers to groups composed of relatives and U to groups composed of nonrelatives.

the survival probability of a subordinate that attempts to sample multiple nests in the generalized bidding game.

In region A of the diagram, the bidding game applies; and as discussed above, groups should tend to be composed of either relatives (R groups) or nonrelatives (U groups), skews should be very low or zero in both kinds of groups, and intragroup aggression should be low in both kinds of groups (because dominants and subordinates are both at their "break-even points" and *any* intragroup selfishness would threaten colony stability). Strikingly, precisely this combination of characteristics has recently been described in the ant *Myrmica tahoensis:* Skews are low in both U and R groups, both of which occur with high frequency, and aggression is virtually nonexistent within both kinds of groups (Evans 1996). Such a pattern is inexplicable by classical skew theory and suggests that the bidding game conditions may often be fulfilled in nature. Furthermore, Michelle Scott (1996) has recently discovered that female associations in burying beetles have characteristics strongly consistent with the predictions of the bidding game: Associations consist mainly of nonrelatives, and the reproductive skew is low and decreases as the size of a shared carcass *increases* (i.e., as *k* increases: Scott 1994), as predicted by the bidding game but not by the classical skew model.

In region B, R groups are predicted to predominate strongly, and skews and aggression should be moderate, perhaps as illustrated by many social wasps (Reeve 1991). In region C, there should be a moderate bias in favor of R groups, strong skews, and strong aggression (because the break-even points for dominants and subordinates will be well-separated: Reeve & Keller, 1997) as in some leptothoracine ants (Bourke & Heinze 1994). Finally, in region D, there should be a weak bias in favor of R groups, with (a) low skews and aggression in U groups and some R groups and (b) high skews and aggression in other R groups (when subordinates first encounter relatives while searching for colonies to join—see discussion of generalized bidding game above).

Many more tests of the synthetic model in Fig. 6.3 are desirable, but current evidence suggests that it is at least promising as a unified model for social evolution, one that fully integrates genetic (r) and ecological (x, k, σ) factors.

6.3 Game Theory and Intragroup Kin Discrimination

An important consequence of both the classical skew models and the bidding game model is that reproductive sharing will be a common evolutionary outcome in kin (and nonkin) groups (Fig. 6.3). Once reproduction is shared, a potential for nepotistic conflict exists within the group. In this part of the chapter, I discuss some ways in which existing models of nepotism may need to be supplemented by game-theoretic approaches to make sense of the results of some recent empirical studies of intragroup kin recognition (defined broadly as the differential treatment of group members with respect to relatedness).

The empirical study of kin recognition has been a major research effort in sociobiology since the mid-1970s (Waldman et al. 1988). The theoretical impetus for these studies was, of course, provided by Hamilton's (1964) insight that selection will often favor alleles that target relatives as the recipients of beneficent acts, since relatives will tend to share copies of these alleles. Today an impressive literature exists on kin recognition abilities and their underlying mechanisms in a wide variety of animal taxa (Fletcher & Michener 1987, Hepper 1991, Sherman et al. 1997), although the functional bases for these abilities remain unclear in many cases (Waldman et al. 1988, Grafen 1990a, Sherman et al. 1997).

Recent theoretical treatments of kin recognition have been concerned primarily with how selection will increase kin recognition efficiency, efficiency being measured inversely as the average probability of the two kinds of possible recognition errors— that is, rejection errors (rejecting kin) and acceptance errors (accepting non-kin or less highly related kin). This approach has been used to predict what recognition cues should be used (Crozier & Dix 1979), how the internal templates used to identify kin should develop (Lacy and Sherman 1983), and how these templates should be matched to the cues of encountered conspecifics (Getz & Chapman 1987). These theoretical analyses assumed a fixed setting for the kin-acceptance threshold (i.e., a threshold dissimilarity between the recognition template and the encountered cues, below which individuals are identified as kin and accepted: Fig. 6.4) and then examined the effect on recognition efficiency of varying the other components of recognition (i.e., different kinds of cues, different templates, and matching algorithms).

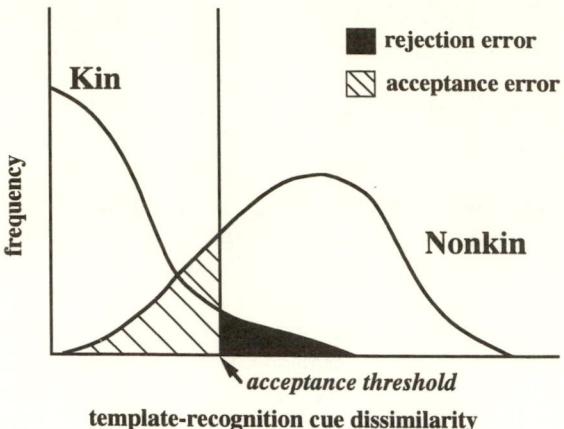

Figure 6.4. Acceptance threshold and the recognition errors generated by this threshold in discrimination between kin and nonkin (or less closely related kin). Shown are the kin and nonkin frequency distributions of the degree of dissimilarity between an actor's kin recognition template and a recipient's recognition cues (modified from Reeve 1989). The position of the acceptance threshold itself will evolve in response to changed frequencies of interaction with, and fitness consequences of rejecting or accepting, kin and nonkin (or less closely related kin). For example, increasing frequency of interaction with less closely related kin can cause the threshold to move left, i.e., become more restrictive (Reeve 1989).

More recently, I argued that the acceptance threshold (i.e., the action component of kin recognition) itself will be subject to selection, since the position of this threshold affects the relative balance of acceptance and rejection errors, and the fitness consequences of these reciprocally related errors will differ in different recognition contexts (Reeve 1989). I showed how the setting of the acceptance threshold should depend on the relative frequencies of interactions with different classes of kin, the fitness consequences of rejecting and accepting the members of these classes, the way the latter fitness consequences combine, and, finally, the extent to which acceptance of a kin alters the ability to accept additional kin. Recent evidence has begun to suggest that kin-acceptance thresholds indeed vary facultatively among recognition contexts in the ways predicted by the optimal acceptance-threshold models, in both vertebrates and invertebrates (review in Sherman et al. 1997).

Most previous theoretical approaches have tended to treat kin recognition as a problem in simple maximization of frequency-independent fitness—for example, asking what recognition template, acceptance threshold, and so on, optimally discriminates between two or more classes of "passive" objects (kin versus nonkin or less highly related kin). Framed in this way, the discrimination problem is much the same as that, for example, faced by an herbivore deciding about the minimum "greenness" of patches acceptable for foraging (Stephens & Krebs 1986).

This simple optimization approach might at first glance appear inherently unsuited to modelling kin recognition, since interactions among kin will generally yield frequency-dependent fitnesses (i.e., the population-genetic "neighbor-modulated fitnesses": Hamilton 1964). However, the simple optimization approach has some justification. For example, in recognition contexts involving pairwise interactions among kin and additive costs and benefits of acceptance and rejection, the evolutionarily stable acceptance threshold for an actor (potentially discriminating individual) is identical to that obtained through frequency-independent optimization if the fitness consequence of accepting a member of a kin class (called the "value" of a member of that kin class to the actor) is set equal to $rb - c$, where r is the actor's relatedness to the member of the kin class, b is the benefit to the recipient of being accepted by the actor, and c is the cost to the actor of accepting the recipient (Reeve 1989). In other words, the left side of the Hamilton's rule inequality $rb - c > 0$ precisely defines the values of the objects to be discriminated, and these values can be substituted directly into frequency-independent fitness expressions to find the optimal acceptance threshold, at least for a large set of kin discrimination contexts.

Unfortunately, members of different kin classes will not always be "passive" objects in the sense required by frequency-independent optimization models. In other words, we sometimes expect the recognition cues or behaviors of recipients themselves to evolve in response to the acceptance thresholds of actors, particularly when the possibility of acceptance errors by actors creates novel reproductive opportunities for recipients (Reeve 1989). For example, the acceptance thresholds of the guards of a social insect colony might coevolve with the propensities for workers to steal resources from nearby, competing colonies: As the permissiveness of a guard worker's acceptance threshold increases, the frequency of acceptance errors will increase, thus increasing the payoffs for attempted robbing. However, as the payoff for robbing increases, the frequency of robbing attempts will increase, which in turn selects for a more restrictive acceptance threshold by guards. Obviously, solving for evolutionarily stable acceptance threshold and robbing rates in this situation requires a game-theoretic approach (Reeve 1989).

Game-theoretic approaches also may be necessary for understanding otherwise puzzling "failures" in kin recognition. A surprising number of studies have failed to detect unambiguous nepotism within social groups composed of different classes of kin (e.g., Carlin et al. 1993). For example, studies of social insect colonies in which multiple queens contribute to the worker force, or a single queen mates multiple times, have generally failed to provide clear evidence of matriline and patriline nepotism, respectively. I shall consider the theoretical possibility that these failures result either from selection for the muting of kin recognition cues by recipients or perhaps even from selection for active "scrambling" strategies—that is, behaviors that effectively scramble intracolonial recognition cues to *prevent* within-group nepotism. The theory of recognition cue muting will simultaneously generate a theory of recognition-cue "amplification" and allow us to consider the evolution of honest signaling in kin recognition systems, thus linking kin recognition theory to modern theories of the evolution of communication (see Johnstone, this volume).

6.3.1 Kin Recognition and Intragroup Communication:
When Should Cues Be Muted, Amplified, or Scrambled?

6.3.1.1 Amplifying Versus Muting of Kin
Recognition Cues: Signalers Versus Nonsignalers

In most kin recognition models, the cues used to identify kin have been treated as fixed attributes. However, it is not trivial to ask under what conditions selection will favor amplification versus muting of cues that increase the probability that a bearer will be correctly assigned to a kin class. This question is interesting because of the possibility of errors in recognition (Fig. 6.4). For example, an individual that amplifies its recognition cues may increase the flow of nepotistic benefits from its true relatives by increasing the accuracy of their discrimination, but may reduce the flow of benefits from nonrelatives by making acceptance errors less likely for the latter.

To analyze this situation, let us assume that individuals encounter two classes of kin of relatedness r and r', respectively, with $r > r'$. If an individual (called the *actor*) identifies another individual (the *recipient*) as one of the more highly related kin (i.e., the recipient's cues fall below the actor's acceptance threshold), the actor delivers a reproductive benefit of magnitude b at a cost c to itself.

Next we consider two strategies, Signaler (S) and Nonsignaler (N). A Signaler amplifies its kin recognition cues (i.e., advertises them less ambiguously), with the result that the more highly related kin deliver benefits to it with increased probability (g_s, versus the smaller value g_n for Nonsignalers) and the less highly related kin deliver benefits to it with reduced probability ($g_{s'}$, versus the larger value $g_{n'}$ for Nonsignalers). Amplification of cues might involve increased exaggeration, emission, or concentration of cues that are genetically polymorphic in the population (e.g., products of MHC loci) or are environmentally variable and shared by kin (e.g., acquired odors from part of the nest). For simplicity, assume that interactions are pairwise and symmetrical and that costs and benefits combine additively. A fraction Ω of an actor's interactions are with the more highly related kin, and a fraction $1 - \Omega$ are with less highly related kin. (Assume these fractions apply to all actors in the population; for example, the pool of interactants consists of multiple sibships of equal size.)

When will mutant Signalers be able to invade a large population of Nonsignalers? An easy way to obtain the solution is to compare the neighbor-modulated fitness of rare Signalers with that of Nonsignalers—that is, focus on reproductive effects *received* rather than reproductive effects *dispensed* by an individual (Hamilton 1964, Queller 1992, Reeve 1998). A rare Signaler will encounter close relatives a fraction Ω of the time and will receive in each interaction a benefit b with probability g_s from such relatives. The Signaler will incur a cost c with probability g_s if the interacting close relative possesses the Signaling allele (probability $= r$) and will incur the same cost with probability g_n if the close relative does not possess the signaling allele (probability $= 1 - r$). A rare Signaler will encounter less closely related individuals a fraction $1 - \Omega$ of the time and will receive in each interaction a benefit b with probability $g_{s'}$ from such relatives. The Signaler will incur a cost c with probability $g_{s'}$ if the less closely related interactant possesses the Signaling allele (probability $= r'$) and will incur the same cost with probability $g_{n'}$ if the less closely related individual does not possess the signaling allele (probability $= 1 - r'$). Summing these fitness effects leads to the following average fitness change for a Signaller in a pairwise interaction:

$$\Omega\{bg_s - c[(1-r)g_n + rg_s]\} + (1-\Omega)\{bg_{s'} - c[(1-r')g_{n'} + r'g_{s'}]\} \tag{16}$$

The mean fitness change of a Nonsignaler is equal to

$$\Omega[bg_n - cg_n] + (1-\Omega)[bg_{n'} - cg_{n'}] \tag{17}$$

The Signalers spread when fitness expression (16) exceeds fitness expression (17)—that is, when

$$\left(\frac{\Omega}{1-\Omega}\right) > \left(\frac{g_{n'} - g_{s'}}{g_s - g_n}\right)\left(\frac{b - r'c}{b - rc}\right) \tag{18}$$

The Signaler strategy spreads if (1) the frequency of interaction with close kin Ω is sufficiently high, (2) the gain in probability of receiving benefits from close kin $(g_s - g_n)$ is sufficiently high, or (3) the loss in probability of receiving benefits from less closely related kin $(g_{n'} - g_{s'})$ is sufficiently low. In addition, the Signaler strategy is more likely to be favored as the relatedness to the less closely related kin r' increases, the relatedness to the close kin r decreases, the benefit b increases, and the cost c decreases (since the altruistic behavior was favored initially, it must be that $rb - c > 0$ and thus both $b - rc$ and $b - r'c$ are greater than zero).

If the Signaler strategy spreads to fixation, the perceptual distance between more and less highly related kin should increase (i.e., the template-cue dissimilarity distribution for close kin will become more "bunched up" toward the left in Fig. 6.4). This in turn should cause subsequent evolution of more restrictive acceptance thresholds (Reeve 1989), with the result that acceptance errors should decline in frequency (i.e., $g_{n'}$ would decline). The latter consequence would make it even harder for Nonsignaling strategists to reinvade. Thus, it seems reasonable that if inequality (18) is satisfied, the Signaler strategy will not only spread, but become evolutionarily stable against invasion by Nonsignalers, once established.

When inequality (18) is reversed, Nonsignaling is the evolutionarily stable strategy. Thus, Nonsignaling (or reduced signaling) is most likely to occur when close relatives are only a small fraction of the total pool of interactants, because accurately signaling kin status would reduce the substantial flow of benefits generated by acceptance errors of the (abundant) less closely related kin. This principle provides one possible explanation for the observed lack or weakness of intracolonial nepotism in social insects: If there are several classes of kin (e.g., matrilines or patrilines) represented within a social insect colony, accurately signaling kin status might shut off benefits from the numerous less closely related kin (e.g., cousins or half-sisters). The reduction in these benefits might be especially large if extensive sharing of common environmental and genetic odors between less closely related kin in the same colony means that acceptance errors will occur with fairly high probability, as long as recognition cues are muted (i.e. as long as the two distributions in Fig. 6.4 overlap substantially). The result might be an incomplete expression or even complete "hiding" of kin recognition cues by colony members. For example, such cue muting might underlie the apparent inability of male parental birds to discriminate against broods that have been sired by extra-pair males (Sherman et al. 1997). Recent evidence from honeybees indicates that workers from different patrilines do differ somewhat in surface hydrocarbons (Arnold et al. 1996), which are potential recognition cues, but patriline recognition is weak or perhaps even absent (Oldroyd et al. 1994), and it is not known whether detectable patriline-related hydrocarbon differences in honeybees are accentuated or reduced relative to those in species without the potential for within-colony nepotism. [*Note:* Recognition cue muting may not be restricted to kin recognition, but may apply sometimes to sex (Nonacs 1993) and mate recognition as well.]

The theoretical situation is very different for between-colony recognition, in which the relative frequency of interaction with nestmates Ω can be very high compared to the relative frequency of interaction with non-nestmates $(1 - \Omega)$ and members of different colonies can differ greatly in environmental and genetic cues. Not surprisingly, highly accurate nestmate recognition systems (usually involving well-developed odor cues) are found throughout the social insects (Fletcher & Michener 1987).

In the above Signaler game, it was assumed that the proportions of the different kin classes are roughly equal. It is useful to consider what will happen when the different kin classes are not equally represented. For example, suppose there are just two groups of siblings, but one group outnumbers the other. Let h and $1 - h$, respectively, be the fractions of the pool of interactants accounted for by the two sibling groups. We make the plausible assumption that individuals have no way of assessing the size of the sibling group to which they will belong prior to developmental generation of the recognition cues. Averaging across individuals, the frequency of interaction with close siblings Ω will be equal to $h^2 + (1 - h)^2$. The latter Ω has a minimum of $1/2$ (for $h = 1/2$) and rapidly increases to 1 as h increasingly deviates from $1/2$. In other words, increasingly disproportionate representation of one kin group relaxes the condition for the evolution of kinship signaling. This yields the prediction that kinship-signaling will most likely occur in societies dominated by one kin class—for example, in multiple-queen social insect colonies in which one matriline predominates. If individuals can assess the size of the kin group to which they belong, before generation of recognition cues, members of the predominant kin group should honestly signal their kinship status, while members of the smaller kin group should produce ambiguous cues, unless uncertainty over kin class membership is sufficiently great to favor honest signaling even by the latter.

6.3.1.2 Honesty in Kinship Signaling

Will kin-recognition signaling be vulnerable to invasion by Dishonest Signalers—that is, individuals that display cues of a kin class to which they do not belong? The possibility of this kind of invasion in competitive signaling (e.g., sexual selection) contexts has led to the controversial notion that evolutionary stability of honest signaling requires that such signals be costly (Zahavi 1977; Johnstone, this volume; but see Maynard Smith 1994).

However, honest signaling can be stable in kin recognition contexts without high signal costs. In the Signaler model, we began by assuming that the different kin classes (e.g., different matrilines) represented in the pool of interactants were roughly of equal size. In such a situation, there would be no net payoff for a Dishonest Signaler: Such a signaler would receive benefits from the "duped" kin group whose signals it mimics, but it would lose the same amount of benefits from its true kin group (which no longer recognizes it). This underlines the key difference between kin-signaling and signaling in other contexts—for example, mate-choice or intrasexual competition: In the former, only a small portion of interactants can be fooled into dispensing benefits, because different kin classes have different internal templates about how kin should appear; in the latter, however, most, if not all, interactants can be fooled into dispensing benefits (i.e., mating with the signaler or retreating from the signaler in a territorial dispute), because most, if not all, interactants can share a common template of how high-quality mates or fierce territorial adversaries should appear. Thus, in the absence of signal costs, the temptation to cheat is much greater in the competitive signaling contexts: Dishonest competitive signalers lose nothing and gain much from their dishonesty, whereas dishonest kinship signalers may lose as much as they gain. This much higher temptation to cheat leads to the necessity for costly signals if competitive signaling systems are to be stable (Zahavi 1977, Grafen 1990b).

This is not to say that dishonest signaling can never occur in kin recognition systems. There can be a net payoff for dishonest signaling if the Dishonest Signaler's own kin group is small in size, relative to a larger kin group that consequently has more benefits to dispense. However, there are still practical problems confronting a would-be dishonestly signaling parasite of the larger kin group. Such a signaler would have to both assess and acquire or produce the cues of the targeted kin group, all *before* members of the kin group make their decisions about whether to dispense benefits to the signaler. Dishonest signalers would have difficulty, not because the signals are costly to produce, but because the correct signals are *unknown* until near the time of interaction. In addition, recognition cues may be difficult to mimic if they are genetically encoded and not easily acquired from the environment; in this case, the cues themselves need not be costly, but the mechanism for facultatively "forging" them on short notice may be quite costly. In most animals, kin recognition cues appear to be chemosensory (Beecher 1988, Waldman 1991). It is interesting to speculate that the use of chemical recognition cues requiring contact or close approach has been favored by selection, precisely because there is so little time to forge these cues before interaction.

Although dishonest kin-signaling may be unlikely to evolve, individuals that reap few nepotistic benefits, because they have relatively few close kin around, may have another option for increasing the flow of benefits to themselves (or other close kin)— that is, by scrambling other individuals' kin recognition cues. We now turn to this possibility.

6.3.1.3 Scrambler Strategies

Within a genetically heterogeneous social group, a potential conflict always exists over allocation of the group's resources (Ratnieks & Reeve 1992). Nepotism will often generate substantial inequities in resource allocation among different kin classes if these kin classes are not equally represented among the individuals that control the distribution of resources. For example, consider a social insect colony with two queens that differ in their production of workers. If workers nepotistically feed and care for their mother queen, the queen that produced more workers will receive more benefits than the less fecund queen. Clearly, the less fecund queen would benefit if she could reduce or eliminate information about kinship within the group, because the resulting increased frequency of acceptance errors by workers of the opposing matriline would increase the fraction of resources flowing to her. In other words, a recognition cue "scrambling" strategy might be favored for the less fecund queen.

How might the less fecund queen scramble information about kinship? One possibility is that she might attempt to homogenize cues within the group. For example, if the brood in one matriline tend to have a clumped distribution within the nest, it will be easier for the brood to learn characteristics of their full sisters by imprinting on cues of nearby brood as they hatch or eclose. A scrambler might attempt to randomize the locations of brood to remove this source of information about kinship. [Interestingly, Bourke (1994) found that in the polygynous ant *Leptothorax acervorum,* eggs from different queens are almost uniformly intermixed in egg clumps.] Alternatively, a scrambler might attempt to blanket all brood with its own chemical cues or add external cues to further reduce information about kinship.

When will such a scrambling strategy spread? Let the scrambler queen's fraction of reproduction be increased from p to $p+b$ if the scrambling is successful, but the scrambling reduces colony productivity from k to $k-a$, where a is the cost of scrambling (costs may result from losses in time or energy that would otherwise be spent in promoting colony growth) (Fig. 6.5). If the relatedness between the scrambler and the other colony member (e.g., the more fecund queen) is equal to r, it is then easy to substitute the above values into Hamilton's rule (3) to obtain as the condition for favored scrambling: $(p+b)(k-a)-pk+r[(1-(p+b))(k-a)-(1-p)k]>0$, which simplifies to

$$b>\frac{a[p(1-r)+r]}{(k-a)(1-r)} \tag{19}$$

The expression on the right defines the critical increase in fraction of reproduction, above which scrambling is favored.

We must also consider whether it would pay the other colony member (e.g., the more fecund queen) to "unscramble" the scrambled cues as a countermanipulation. The unscrambler's fraction of reproduction will be increased from $1-p-b$ to $1-p$ if the unscrambling is successful, but the unscrambling reduces colony productivity from $k-a$ to $k-a-a'$, where a' is the cost of unscrambling (Fig. 6.5). Applying Hamilton's rule again, we obtain

$$b>\frac{a'[(1-p)(1-r)+r]}{(k-a)(1-r)} \tag{20}$$

The expression on the right defines the critical increase in the recovered fraction of reproduction, above which unscrambling is favored.

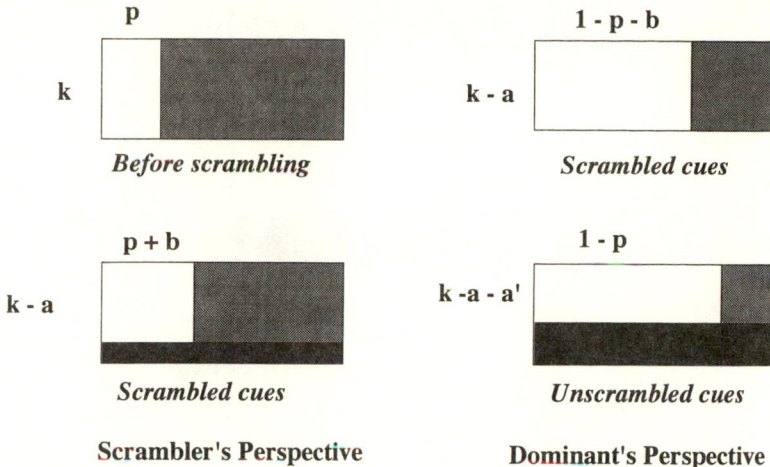

Figure 6.5. Geometric representation of payoffs to recognition cue scramblers (left) and dominant unscramblers (right). The width of the rectangles represents the group reproductive output, and the length of the white region represents the scrambler's or nonscrambler's fraction of the group output (area of the white region is thus the scrambler's or nonscrambler's output). Scrambling reduces group output by a and increases the scrambler's share from p to $p+b$. Unscrambling further reduces the group output by a' and increases the dominant unscrambler's share of the output from $1-p-b$ back to $1-p$.

Whether scrambling occurs will depend on the magnitude of b relative to the two thresholds in (19) and (20). The threshold in (20) will be higher than that in (19) because (i) by assumption, $(1-p)$ is greater than p (since the scrambler begins with a lower fraction of reproduction) and (ii) the cost of unscrambling kin recognition cues a' is likely to be higher than the cost of scrambling cues a, because it should be easier to destroy information than to regenerate it. Thus, the conditions under which scrambled cues will occur (i.e., scrambling by the less fecund queen and not-unscrambling by the more fecund queen will be an evolutionarily stable pair of strategies) corresponds to the black region between the two thresholds in Fig. 6.6.

How will the width of the latter region—that is, the likelihood of scrambling—vary for different values of the parameters? The zone for evolutionarily stable scrambling widens as (1) the increase in the share of reproduction b due to scrambling increases, (2) the difference in cost between a' and a increases, (3) the relatedness r between the scrambler and its partner increases, and (4) the scrambler's fraction of reproduction prior to scrambling p decreases. Thus, kin-recognition cue scrambling is most expected in colonies in which the relatedness is high and the reproductive skew is high (Note that the classical optimal skew models predict that high relatedness will tend to cause high skew).

Recognition cue-scrambling is a possible explanation for the growing number of studies that have failed to detect intracolonial nepotism in the social insects (Carlin et al. 1993). If the hypothesis is true, it should be possible to experimentally increase the degree of nepotism by somehow preventing the potential scramblers from affect-

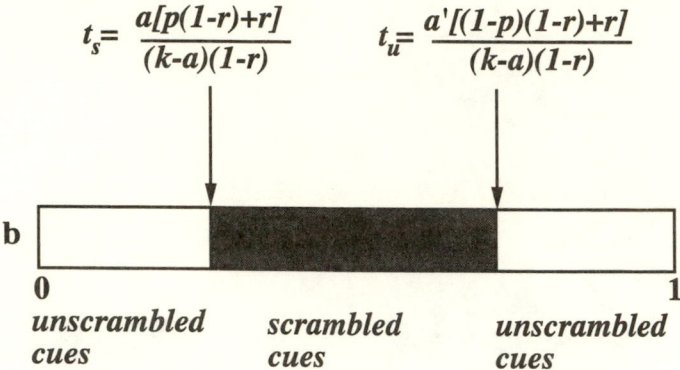

$$t_s = \frac{a[p(1-r)+r]}{(k-a)(1-r)} \qquad t_u = \frac{a'[(1-p)(1-r)+r]}{(k-a)(1-r)}$$

b

0   1

unscrambled   *scrambled*   *unscrambled*
cues   *cues*   *cues*

Figure 6.6. Conditions for evolutionarily stable competitive scrambling. Scrambling is stable for values of b (the proportionate gain in reproduction due to scrambling) that lie between the lower threshold for scrambling t_s and the upper threshold t_u at which unscrambling is favored. r is the genetic relatedness between scrambler and unscrambler. See Figure 6.5 and the text for definitions of other parameters.

ing intracolony kin-recognition cues. Such a recovery of nepotism is predicted in the absence of scrambling, because the selective maintenance of the scrambling strategy requires that at least some colony members have retained the potential for intracolonial nepotism; otherwise, scrambling would be costly without any compensating benefits.

The scrambling hypothesis is an alternative to the "muted kinship signaling" hypothesis of the previous section. In the latter, individuals fail to amplify or even reduce the clarity of their own recognition cues; in the former, a subset of individuals interfere with or mask the recognition cues of others. Fortunately, the two hypotheses make different predictions about the conditions under which intracolonial nepotism will be weakened or absent. The muted kinship signaling hypothesis predicts that absence of nepotism will most likely occur when different kin classes are equally represented within the colony (because, as we saw above, accurate signaling of kinship is most likely to evolve when there is a disproportionately high representation of one kin class), whereas the scrambler hypothesis predicts that absence of nepotism will most likely occur when there is a disproportionate representation of certain kin classes (because scrambling will be most beneficial when members of some kin classes would acquire a relatively small fraction of colony resources if colony members were nepotistic). Both of these hypotheses are alternatives to the previous hypothesis that nepotistic behavior will be directly disfavored by kin selection because of losses in colony efficiency and productivity, particularly when nepotists make frequent recognition errors (Reeve 1989, Ratnieks & Reeve 1991). In the latter hypothesis, kin recognition cues are present but not utilized, because selection has favored highly permissive acceptance thresholds (a rightward-shifted threshold in Fig. 6.1)—that is, "universal acceptance" of different kin classes (Reeve 1989).

6.3.2 Competitive Versus Cooperation-Inducing Scrambling

The scrambler model just considered is fundamentally competitive: Scrambling occurs by one group member to divert more resources to itself at the expense of another group member. The only requirements for the temptation to scramble in any social group are that (1) at least one individual exists that would lose from competitive, intracolonial nepotism, and (2) such an individual can *assess* that it would lose from nepotism.

Scrambling might also evolve to *prevent* competition over intracolony allocation of resources. For example, consider a social insect colony in which the single queen mates with multiple males and simultaneously uses the sperm of more than one of these males. A potential conflict exists among the workers over which queens will get reared, with workers of a given patriline preferring to distribute resources to future queens of their own patriline (Ratnieks and Reeve 1991). If rampant nepotism among the workers reduces colony productivity—for example, by generating interpatriline aggression or simply by taking time away from performance of tasks that augment colony growth—the queen may be selected to scramble patriline-membership cues. Such scrambling would benefit the queen, if it caused different patrilines to share enough cues that workers of different patrilines would now be "fooled" into behaving as if they all belonged to the same patriline (i.e., all reproductive brood would fall under each worker's acceptance threshold). I call this *cooperation-inducing scrambling* because its benefit to the scrambler results from increased overall colony productivity, rather than from an increase in the scrambler's share of the resources. Again, the high costs of unscrambling could make the scrambling an evolutionarily stable strategy.

6.3.3 Organismal Versus Intragenomic Scrambling

Scrambling need not be restricted to interactions between organisms. It may also occur intragenomically to prevent some elements in the genome from "nepotistically" increasing their representation in gametes at the expense of others. For example, in segregation distorter systems, a distorter allele at a distorter locus (e.g., *Sd* locus in *Drosophila*) biases its own transmission by preventing a nondistorting allele on the homologous chromosome from becoming represented in gametes (Wu & Hammer 1991). How does a distorter allele recognize copies of itself in homologues so that it does not harm these copies? The "kin-recognition cue" is the presence of a particular allele (the *insensitive* allele) at another locus (e.g., the *Responder* or *Rsp* locus) that is tightly linked to the distorter locus. This tight linkage is crucial, because it allows the presence of the insensitive allele to be a statistical indicator of the presence of the distorter allele (the two loci are in linkage disequilibrium): If the two loci were loosely linked or unlinked, the two alleles would not be statistically associated, and the *insensitive* allele would be a poor kin-recognition label.

Haig and Grafen (1991) have argued that alleles causing recombination are essentially pursuing the scrambler strategy and that the scrambling is of the cooperation-inducing variety, because it reduces the organismal-level fitness costs inflicted by segregation distortion. By inducing crossing-over between distorter and recognition (e.g., *Rsp*) loci, recombination alleles that are unlinked to these loci can increase the chance that they will occur in genomes which do not carry distorter alleles and which also are resistant to such distortion. There are no organismal-level fitness costs for the latter genomes, because such genomes neither cause nor fall prey to segregation distortion, and thus the recombination (scrambling) allele receives a selective boost. Here, the organism itself is the "group" whose "productivity" is increased by scrambling.

Intriguingly, intragenomic conflicts can have important implications for kin recognition at the organismal level. I shall discuss just two possibilities. It is increasingly clear that the expression of at least some alleles depends on whether they are maternally or paternally inherited; that is, such alleles exhibit *genomic imprinting* (Haig & Westoby 1989). Genomic imprinting generates intragenomic conflicts that may influence the evolution of kin recognition.

First, consider the case of a hymenopteran society with a single queen inseminated by multiple males. The daughter workers of different patrilines will share no paternally inherited alleles by descent, but they will share half of their maternally inherited alleles by descent. Moreover, the probability that two workers share a given maternally inherited allele is the same whether they are from the same or different patrilines. Thus, paternally inherited alleles could benefit by causing patriline-based nepotism, whereas maternally inherited alleles would not and indeed would suffer if such nepotism reduced colony efficiency. Thus, it is possible that maternally and paternally inherited alleles will be in conflict over whether patriline discrimination should occur. In particular, it is possible that maternally imprinted alleles will be favored to suppress or scramble recognition cues (or other components of the recognition system) that are produced by paternally inherited alleles for patriline discrimination. Here, intragenomic conflict leads ultimately to the absence of nepotism among individuals; that is, conflict within organisms leads to direct suppression of conflict between organisms! This constitutes a fourth hypothesis for the lack of nepotism within insect societies.

Second, consider the case of a hymenopteran society with a single queen mated by a *single* male. All worker daughters (100% full sisters) are identical for the paternally inherited allele at a given locus, but they are not necessarily identical for the maternally inherited allele. Maternally inherited alleles theoretically might benefit by nepotism directed toward full sisters that are especially likely to carry these copies of alleles, but paternally inherited alleles obviously could not benefit from such nepotism and indeed would only suffer if the nepotism reduces colony productivity. Thus, we might again expect conflict between maternally inherited and paternally inherited alleles over whether nepotism should occur, but now it is the maternally imprinted alleles that would benefit from nepotism. In fact, *this* potential conflict is unlikely to be expressed, because recombination ultimately destroys most statistical associations between maternally inherited alleles and any genetic markers that might produce cues for detecting the presence of these alleles [the failure to understand this point has been christened by Dawkins (1979) as the "ace of spades fallacy"]. In other words, would-be maternally imprinted nepotism alleles simply have no practical way of detecting copies of themselves in full sisters. In this case, intragenomic scrambling that reduces conflict within an organism (i.e., recombination) has, as an *epiphenomenal* consequence, the suppression of a conflict between organisms.

6.4 Summary

I suggest some new ways in which game-theoretic approaches may illuminate the evolution of reproductive skews and genetic composition of kin groups, as well as the nature of kinship communication within these groups. A "bidding game" model, in which subordinate helpers accept the highest reproductive bid from competing dominants from different nests, predicts (in contrast to classical skew models) that low reproductive skews and low intracolony aggression, as well as frequent associations of nonrelatives, will evolve when ecological constraints are harsh, but high colony density makes repeated sampling of dominants by subordinates feasible. In this model, contrary to the classical skew model, reproductive skew should decrease as group productivity benefits increase. A "beggars-can't-be-choosers" extension of the classical skew model, in which dominants can choose between related and unrelated subordinates, also predicts that associations of nonrelatives will most likely occur under strong ecological constraints. Both of the above models can be fused to create a comprehensive theory of reproductive skews, group genetic composition, and levels of intragroup aggression, as a function of relatedness, constraints on solitary reproduction, group benefits, and opportunities for sampling multiple colonies (Fig. 6.3).

A game-theoretic analysis indicates that kinship signaling (amplification of pre-existing cues of kinship) can easily be honest and stable without being costly. Such signaling will most likely occur when (1) contacts with close kin are especially frequent and (2) there is only a small loss of benefits flowing from distant relatives or nonrelatives via acceptance errors. I propose three hypotheses for the puzzling absence of nepotism within genetically diverse social groups: (1) Selection favors muted (partly ambiguous) recognition cues, because of the benefits received from acceptance errors committed by nonkin (or less closely related kin); (2) selection favors individuals that scramble intragroup recognition cues because the resulting recognition errors increase group productivity (*cooperation-inducing scrambling*) or the scrambler's share of the group resources (*competitive scrambling*); and (3) selection favors genomically imprinted alleles that suppress nepotism-causing alleles imprinted on the opposite parent (*intragenomic scrambling*). These hypotheses are alternatives to the hypothesis that intracolonial nepotistic behavior is directly disfavored because of resulting reductions in colony efficiency (Ratnieks & Reeve 1991) and suggest new lines of research into kin recognition mechanisms.

ACKNOWLEDGMENTS   I thank Lee Dugatkin, Steve Emlen, Peter Nonacs, John Peters, David Pfennig, Jan Shellman-Reeve, Phil Starks, and Paul Sherman for valuable discussion and comments.

References

Arnold, G., Quentet, B., Comuet, J., Masson, C., De Schepper, B., Estoup, A. & Gasqui, P. 1996. Kin recognition in honey bees. *Nature,* 379, 498.

Beecher, M.D. 1988. Kin recognition in birds. *Behav. Genet.,* 18, 465–482.

Bourke, A. F. G. 1994. Indiscriminate egg cannibalism and reproductive skew in a multiple-queen ant. *Proc. R. Soc. London B.,* 255, 55–59.

Bourke, A. F. G. & Heinze, J. 1994. The ecology of communal breeding: the case of multiple-queen leptothoracine ants. *Philos. Trans. R. Soc. London B.,* 345, 359–372.

Bourke, A. F. G. & Franks, N. 1995. *Social Evolution in Ants.* Princeton, NJ: Princeton University Press.

Carlin, N., Reeve, H. K. & Cover, S. P. 1993. Kin discrimination and division of labor among matrilines in the polygynous carpenter ant, *Camponotus planatus.* In *Queen Number and Sociality in Insects,* L. Keller & D. Cherix, eds., pp. 362–401. Oxford: Oxford University Press.

Crozier, R. H. & Dix, M. W. 1979. Analysis of two genetic models for the innate components of colony odor in social Hymenoptera.*Behav. Ecol. Sociobiol.,* 4, 217–224.

Dawkins, R. 1979. Twelve misunderstandings of kin selection. *Z. Tierpsychol.,* 51, 184–200.

Emlen, S. 1982. The evolution of helping I & II. *Am. Nat.,* 119, 29–53.

Emlen, S. 1995. An evolutionary theory of the family. *Proc. Natl. Acad. Sci. USA.,* 92, 8092–8099.

Emlen, S. 1996. Reproductive sharing in different kinds of kin associations. *Amer. Nat.,* 148, 756–763.

Evans, J. D. 1996. Competition and relatedness between queens of the facultatively polygynous ant *Myrmica tahoensis. Anim. Behav.,* 51, 831–840.

Fletcher, D. J. C. & Michener, C. D. 1987. *Kin Recognition in Animals.* Chichester: Wiley.

Getz, W. M. & Chapman, R. F. 1987. An odor discrimination model with application to kin recognition in social insects. *Int. J. Neurosci.,* 32, 963–978.

Grafen, A. 1979. The hawk–dove game played between relatives. *Anim. Behav.,* 27, 905–907.

Grafen, A. 1990a. Do animals really recognize kin? *Anim. Behav.,* 39, 42–54.

Grafen, A. 1990b. Biological signals as handicaps. *J. Theor. Biol.,* 144, 517–546.

Haig, D. & Grafen, A. 1991. Genetic scrambling as a defence against meiotic drive. *J. Theor. Biol.,* 153, 531–558.

Haig, D. & Westoby, M. 1989. Parent-specific gene expression and the triploid endosperm. *Am. Nat.,* 134, 147–155.

Hamilton, W. D. 1964. The genetical evolution of social behavior, I & II. *J. Theor. Biol.,* 7, 1–52.

Hepper, P. G. 1991. *Kin Recognition.* Cambridge: Cambridge University Press.

Keller, L. & Reeve, H. K. 1994. Partitioning of reproduction in animal societies. *Trends Ecol. Evol.,* 9, 98–102.

Lacy, R. C. & Sherman, P. W. 1983. Kin recognition by phenotype matching. *Am. Nat.,* 116, 489–512.

Maynard Smith, J. 1982. *Evolution and the Theory of Games.* Cambridge: Cambridge University Press.

Maynard Smith, J. 1994. Must reliable signals be costly? *Anim. Behav.,* 47, 1115–1120.

Nonacs, P. 1989. Competition and kin discrimination in colony founding by social Hymenoptera. *Evol. Ecol.,* 3, 221–235.

Nonacs, P. 1993. Male parentage and sexual deception in the social Hymenoptera. In *Evolution and Diversity of Sex Ratio in Insects and Mites,* D. L. Wrensch & M. A. Ebbert, eds., pp. 384–401. New York: Chapman and Hall.

Oldroyd, B., Rinderer, T., Schwenke, J. & Buco, S. 1994. Subfamily recognition and task specialisation in honey bees (*Apis mellifera* L.) (Hymenoptera: Vespidae). *Behav. Ecol. Sociobiol.,* 34, 169–173.

Packer, C., Gilbert D. A., Pusey, A. E., Cairns, S. & O'Brien, S. J. 1988. Reproductive success in lions. In *Reproductive Success,* T. H. Clutton-Brock, ed., pp. 363–383. Chicago: University of Chicago Press.

Packer, C., Gilbert D. A., Pusey, A. E. & O'Brien, S. J. 1991. A molecular genetic analysis of kinship and cooperation in Africanlions. *Nature,* 351, 562–565.

Parker, G. 1989. Hamilton's rule and conditionality. *Ethol. Ecol. Evol.,* 1, 195–211.

Queller, D. C. 1992. A general model for kin selection. *Evolution,* 46, 376–380.

Ratnieks, F. L. & Reeve, H. K. 1991. The evolution of queen-rearing nepotism in social Hymenoptera: effects of discrimination costs in swarming species. *J. Evol. Biol.,* 4, 93–115.

Ratnieks, F. L. & Reeve, H. K. 1992. Conflict in single-queen hymenopteran societies: The structure of conflict and processes that reduce actual conflict. *J. Theor. Biol.,* 158, 33–65.

Reeve, H. K. 1989. The evolution of conspecific acceptance thresholds. *Am. Nat.,* 133, 407–435.

Reeve, H. K. 1991. The social biology of *Polistes.* In *The Social Biology of Wasps,* K. Ross & R. Matthews, eds., pp. 99–148. Ithaca, NY: Cornell University Press.

Reeve, H. K. 1998. Acting for the good of others: Kinship and reciprocity, with some new twists. In *Evolution and Human Behavior,* C. Crawford & D. Krebs, eds. Hillsdale, NJ: Lawrence Erlbaum Associates.

Reeve, H. K. & Keller, L. 1995. Partitioning of reproduction in mother–daughter versus sibling associations: A test of optimal skew theory *Am. Nat.,* 145, 119–132.

Reeve, H. K. & Keller, L. 1996. Relatedness asymmetry and reproductive sharing in animal societies. *Am. Nat.,* 148, 764–769.

Reeve, H. K. & Keller, L. 1997. Reproductive bribing and policing as mechanisms for the suppression of within-group selfishness. *Amer. Nat.,* 150, 542–550.

Reeve, H. K. & Ratnieks, F. A. 1993. Queen–queen conflict in polygynous societies: mutual tolerance and reproductive skew. In *Queen Number and Sociality in Insects,* L. Keller & D. Cherix, eds., pp. 45–85. Oxford: Oxford University Press.

Reyer, H.-U. 1990. Pied kingfishers: Ecological causes and reproductive consequences of cooperative breeding. In *Cooperative Breeding in Birds,* P. B. Stacey & W. D. Koenig, eds., pp. 527–558. Cambridge: Cambridge University Press.

Scott, M. P. 1994. Competition with flies promotes communal breeding in the burying beetle, *Nicrophorus tomentosus. Behav. Ecol. Sociobiol.,* 34, 367–373.

Scott, M. P. 1996. Communal breeding in burying beetles. *Amer. Sci.,* 84, 376–382.

Sherman, P. W., Reeve, H. K. & Pfennig, D. W. 1997. Recognition systems. In *Behavioral Ecology: An Evolutionary Approach,* J. Krebs & N. Davies, eds., pp. 69–96, fourth edition. Oxford: Oxford University Press.

Stephens, D. W. & Krebs, J. R. 1986. *Foraging Theory.* Princeton: Princeton University Press.

Trivers, R. & Hare, H. 1976. Haplo-diploidy and the evolution of the social insects. *Science,* 191, 249–263.

Vehrencamp, S. L. 1983. Optimal degree of skew in cooperative societies. *Am. Zool.,* 23, 327–335.

Waldman, B., Frumhoff, P. C. & Sherman, P. W. 1988. Problems of kin recognition. *Trends Ecol. Evol.,* 3, 8–13.

Waldman B. 1991. Kin recognition in amphibians. In *Kin Recognition,* P. Hepper, ed., pp. 162–219. Cambridge: Cambridge University Press.

West-Eberhard, M. J. 1975. The evolution of social behavior by kin selection. *Q. Rev. Biol.,* 50, 1–35.

Wu, C.-I. & Hammer, M. F. 1991. Molecular evolution of ultraselfish genes of meiotic drive systems. In *Evolution at the Molecular Level,* R. K. Selander, A. G. Clark, & T. S. Whittam, eds., pp. 177–203. Sunderland, MA: Sinauer Associates.

Zahavi, A. 1977. The cost of honesty. (Further remarks on the handicap principle). *J. Theor. Biol.,* 67, 603–605.

Douglas W. Mock
Geoffrey A. Parker
P. L. Schwagmeyer

Game Theory, Sibling Rivalry, and Parent–Offspring Conflict

7.1 Introduction

Because family members are quintessentially "kin," most theoretical models exploring the evolutionary significance of intrafamily social dynamics are rooted firmly in Hamilton's Rule.[1] Depending on the biological foci of interest, one can then splice into the model any number of other embellishments that may or may not require genetic relatedness, including such aspects as cooperation versus selfishness (e.g., sexual conflict over biparental care), effects of group size (the family as a Selfish Herd), life-history traits (e.g., parental effort as a function of future reproductive prospects), logic of asymmetric contests (e.g., asynchronous hatching in siblicidal birds), and so on. For example, though we cannot take the space to address how sexual conflict between two supposedly cooperating parents might lower the total food budget for offspring, such outcomes obviously can reshape the economic bases of sibling rivalry and parent–offspring conflict (Parker 1985). In short, there may be numerous connections between the themes featured in this chapter and those showcased elsewhere in this volume and beyond. We shall focus on genetic relatedness per se because it is an essential and rather special component of families.

Evolutionary games within even a simple family can become complicated very quickly. We start with a small family facing an uncertain environment (i.e., one in which resources often prove insufficient, such that one offspring, the "victim" may die) and follow the heuristic device of O'Connor (1978) in identifying three principal classes of players in a family as Parents, Victim, and Surviving Sib(s). We modify this approach slightly by keying in on three "social dimensions" of the nuclear family, thereby emphasizing the relationships between (1) the two parents (we assume biparental care, otherwise this dimension vanishes), (2) the offspring (concurrent siblings or the more abstract consideration of future siblings), and (3) these two generations. In sexual diploid taxa, the typical coefficient-of-relatedness, r, between the two parents is zero (assuming outbreeding), r between the siblings is 0.50 (assuming mate-fidelity by the parents; 0.25 for half-sibs), and r between the generations is 0.50.[2] From our requirement that some resource limitation constrains family size, there is often a backdrop of competition among family members. It follows that there will often be tradeoffs between the welfare and evolutionary interests of Self versus his/her kin, regardless of which "Self" we scrutinize. Here we shall dwell on the selfish aspects of intrafamily dynamics, though we appreciate that full understanding of such a system involves complex balancing of both shared and unshared evolutionary interests within the external constraints imposed by extrafamily factors (e.g., the food base).

The suitability of ESS (Evolutionarily Stable Strategy) approaches to the study of family social dynamics should be evident. In a tight and interdependent group, each individual player's best move is often shaped not only by the payoff to personal fitness, but also by the impact on others. In such games, selfish incentives are automatically tempered by the potential loss of indirect fitness. Our three social dimensions and the burgeoning literature on how to model them have been reviewed and expanded at length elsewhere (Mock & Parker 1997). Because we have already treated the parental dimension (sexual cooperation/conflict) with what we hope is a user-friendly introduction to the relevant ESS models (Mock et al. 1996), our goal in this chapter is to provide similar access to the remaining two family dimensions, sibling rivalry and parent-offspring conflict.

Historically, the problem of parental neglect and partial-brood loss within nonhuman families goes back at least 23 centuries to Aristotle's report that eagles lay three eggs, hatch two, and raise only one chick. His explanation, that the mother rejects the other hatchling because raising it would require her to impose too much predation pressure on small mammal populations, may strike us as quaint—and, for that matter, his suggestion that the orphan is subsequently raised by vultures seems like putting a happy face on a grim situation—but we can acknowledge that he offered a puzzle for future naturalists. Current interest in the problem began with Lack's (1947, 1954) theory of optimal clutch size, which was very much centered on the phenomenon of partial-brood losses in birds. Hamilton's (1964) theory of inclusive fitness clarified the relevance of genetic relatedness among family members. In fact, Hamilton laid out several clear, but mostly overlooked, predictions about sibling rivalry. Then came Trivers' (1974) theory of parent–offspring conflict. O'Connor (1978) pulled all these threads together into a reasonably comprehensive picture of family structure.

Here we selectively review models from the past two decades, during which the influence of ESS reasoning has been applied, formally or intuitively, to sketch where things stand at present. As mentioned above, a fuller treatment of this material has been prepared (Mock & Parker 1997), but even that is only a partial review of the many models and arguments that have been advanced. We also hasten to point out that there are alternative modeling approaches that have been used with great success on many of these same issues (e.g., Forbes 1990, 1993, Forbes & Ydenberg 1992; Pijanowski 1992, Lamey & Lamey 1994, Mock & Forbes 1994), but this volume's emphasis on game theory absolves us of having to cover them all.

7.2 ESS Models of Sibling Rivalry

The sib–sib social dimension is conceptually much simpler than that of parent-offspring conflict, because it is a fairly straightforward economics problem. It is also much easier to study empirically, because one can apply the usual criteria for testing whether demand outstrips supply. For example, if food is suspected of being the critical limiting resource (as is often the case for nestling birds, larval parasitoids, plant seedlings, and many other groups), one can look for signs of starvation (lethal or sublethal) in the victim siblings. Experimentally, one can seek to alleviate the mortality by offering supplemental food (or fertilizer). In other taxa, the key competition is over something else, including repro-ductive rights (e.g., cooperatively breeding birds, mammals, and insects: see Reeve, this volume), uterine space (e.g., swine), sole usage of a dispersal vehicle (e.g., pod-seeded plants), use of a sibling's body tissues (e.g., sib-cannibals in general), and so on. These competitions can be modeled either as *scrambles* (races to out-consume one's rivals), *contests* (one-on-one confrontations, often involving aggression), or combinations of both (e.g., socially enforced starvation).

O'Connor (1978) considered avian brood reduction in terms of how the death of one nestling affects the inclusive fitnesses of three classes of family members: par-ents, surviving sibs, and the victim itself. His approach identified three levels of density-dependent mortality at which each class of player comes to favor sacrificing an offspring to gain the competitive release for the others. These "brood reduction thresholds" brought several points to light, including the fact that the effects are stronger (and more divergent among the players) for small broods than for large ones.

Formal game-theoretic frameworks have been applied to sibling rivalry by sev-eral authors (e.g., Parker & Macnair 1978, 1979; Macnair & Parker 1978, 1979; Parker 1985; Harper 1986; Dickins & Clark 1987; Parker et al. 1989; Godfray 1991, 1995a; Godfray & Harper 1990; Godfray & Parker 1992). We identify two general approaches, based on contest and scramble competitions, respectively.

7.2.1 Sibling Rivalry as a Contest: Hierarchy Models

Here we are interested in the upper limit of selfishness for totally empowered sib-lings, an exercise equivalent to seeking the point at which kinship alone brakes self-promoting actions. The first model considers a simple two-chick avian brood, in which one sib has utter and complete ontrol over the allocation of a set amount, M, of parentally delivered food or some other critical form of parental investment. This superior individual (hereafter the "A-chick") has the power to take whatever propor-tion, p, it chooses, leaving the remainder, $1 - p$, for its B-chick sibling. In particular, A's decision on how selfish to be is assumed not to be constrained in any way by effective resistance from B. So the amount of food that A ends up ingesting is simply

$$m_A = pM \tag{1a}$$

and by default, B's amount ends up as

$$m_B = (1 - p)M \tag{1b}$$

The question of interest is the optimal value of p; that is, we seek to determine which value of p (between 0 and 1.0) maximizes A's inclusive fitness. It is easy to see intuitively that if A takes "too much," the gain to its personal prospects (i.e., the *direct component* of its inclusive fitness: *sensu* Brown and Brown 1981) may not compensate for the loss its close kin suffers (thus lowering the *indirect component* of A's inclusive fitness); conversely, if A takes "too little," the opposite occurs. To give this an evolutionary heart, we can imagine there to be a genetic basis to A's choice of p, a gene or gene complex in which the particular alleles make the difference between A taking varying proportions of the food, so we are seeking the value of p that maximizes the replication rate of its underlying allele(s).

To do this, we need a realistic function to represent how parental investment, here food ingestion, affects fitness. Logically, this must have some minimum value $(m_{\text{min}},)$, which can be thought of as a type of down payment that a nestling needs in order to achieve any fitness at all. Beyond that, additional units of food are highly valuable at first (the fitness curve rises relatively steeply), but they become less so until, eventually, the fitness curve asymptotes. In short, we expect a positive but decelerating cumulative gain curve (Fig. 7.1). There are several formulae for such curves, from which we have chosen an exponential version (to simplify the calculus later):

$$f(m) = 1 - \exp[-k(m - m_{\text{min}})] \tag{2}$$

Here k is a shape constant reflecting the efficiency/speed with which parental invest-ment translates into offspring fitness. This constant can be interpreted in two ways, namely, as a parameter modeling variable conditions either within one species or between multiple species. In the first context, suppose we envisage parental invest-ment as a unit of foraging activity. If prey density is high, many prey are caught and a high increase in offspring growth/fitness is achieved, which is caused by a high k in equation (2). When prey density is low, the reverse occurs and we need a low k in equation (2). In the second context, we might contrast fast-growing passerines, where parents supply food for a mere 2–4 weeks before offspring have to make their own way without further assistance (here, k would be high) with eagles, where parental care may last a year or more, presumably indicating a gradual accumulation of off-spring size, strength, and skills necessary for full independence (low k).

Finally, we assume for simplicity that all nestmates are full siblings $(r = 1/2)$ and that all members of our hypothetical species follow the same cumulative gain curve. That is, A-chicks do not benefit any differently from B-chicks on a given food ration. There are, of course, some taxa in which all kinds of developmental polymorphisms can kick in (e.g., amphibians whose larval siblings become either slow-growing om-nivores or fast-growing carnivores, depending on their early diets); in such cases the model could be amended with distinct expressions for $f_A(m_A)$ and $f_B(m_B)$. Less extraordinarily, simple differences in physiology, parasite loads, and so on, might generate interesting variations in gain curve shapes. [For modeling such cases, see Parker et al. (1989) and Haig (1990).]

We now imagine a rare mutant allele[3] for some value of p and can see that its replication rate is proportional to

$$f(m_A) + \tfrac{1}{2} f(m_B) \tag{3}$$

To find the value of p at which this fitness function is maximized, we take the first partial derivative with respect to p and set that expression equal to zero[4]:

$$\frac{\partial[(f(m_A) + \tfrac{1}{2} f(m_B)]}{\partial p} = 0 \tag{4}$$

which, remembering (1a) and (1b), simplifies to

$$f'(m_A) = \tfrac{1}{2} f'(m_B) \tag{5}$$

where the prime denotes the first derivative with respect to the amount m attained, at m_A and m_B.

In other words, the A-chick should always take the next unit of parental investment (PI) until that unit would enhance B's personal fitness by more than twice as

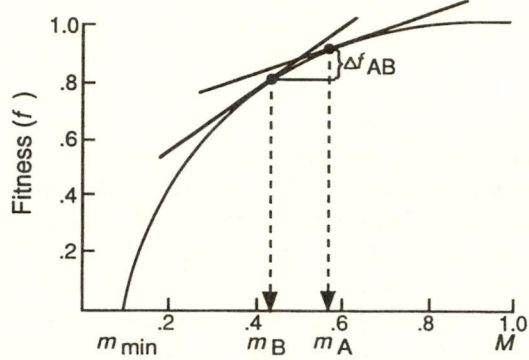

Figure 7.1. Offspring fitness plotted against parental investment projects as a decelerating cumulative gain curve. The fitness value of the next unit of investment can be represented as the tangent directly above a given offspring's current investment total. Here we have plotted the tangents for two siblings, with the despotic A-chick's tangent touching the curve directly above m_A and the subordinate B-chick's tangent touching directly above m_B. The 2-sib Hierarchy Model predicts that A should always take the next unit until the slope of its tangent falls below one-half the slope of B's tangent. Clearly, if there is an abundance of resources, both sibs move farther and farther up the fitness curve, and the difference between them (Δf_{AB}) shrinks. (From Parker et al. 1989, with permission of *American Naturalist*.)

much as it would A's personal fitness. When that point is reached, A's inclusive fitness is better served by passing on the item and letting it go to B (Fig. 7.1). Or as Hamilton (1964, p. 16) put it, "we expect to find that sibs deprive one another of reproductive prerequisites provided they can themselves make use of at least one half of what they take." As we shall see, things are not quite so simple when the sibship includes more than two players, but before we move on to that consideration, this is an appropriate moment to pause and confess that the argument presented thus far is *not* an ESS model. Up to this point, the only individual allowed to make any decisions, the only one with a "strategy" to consider, is the A-chick. The other player, B, is totally passive. So the 2-sib hierarchy is, by definition, a "Simple" optimality model.[5]

Nonetheless, this result already has some quite interesting biological predictions. For long-lived birds, where chick growth is slow (k is relatively low) and hatching is often markedly asynchronous (such that the A-chick may truly enjoy despotic control from the outset), the developmental distance between the two siblings is expected to be relatively high and m_{min} is pushed far to the right as well. In this light, the existence of early obligate siblicide may make sense, even if key resources seem adequate for the moment. The draconian measure of an irreversible preemptive strike makes even more sense when one takes the future uncertainty of resources into account (e.g., Forbes & Ydenberg 1992), though these points have not always been appreciated fully. Conversely, in very fast-growing birds, there may be little incentive for killing a nestmate, because the whole parental ride is so brief.

As soon as we contemplate broods of three or more nestlings, the problem of optimal sibling selfishness requires a formal game theory approach. We modify our assumptions only slightly for a brood of three. As soon as A has taken its cut q off the top, one imagines the B-chick to face a comparable decision: it is empowered to take any proportion p of the remaining food. So now the shares ingested by the three sibs are

$$m_A = qM \tag{6a}$$

$$m_B = p(1-q)M \tag{6b}$$

$$m_C = (1-p)(1-q)M \tag{6c}$$

Now, holding the same assumptions as before (diploidy, monogamy, and full despotism by rank), the A-chick's fitness function is

$$f(m_A) + \tfrac{1}{2} f(m_B) + \tfrac{1}{2} f(m_C) \tag{7}$$

And the A-chick's ESS level of selfishness is found, as before, by partial differentiation with respect to A's share (now q) and setting that slope equal to zero:

$$\frac{\partial[f(m_A) + \tfrac{1}{2} f(m_B) + \tfrac{1}{2} f(m_C)]}{\partial q} = 0 \tag{8}$$

Remembering (6a), (6b), (6c), and that rule (5) must now apply between the B- and C-chicks, a little algebraic fiddling leads to a slightly ponderous-looking solution:

$$f'(m_A) = f'(m_B)[1 - p/2 + p'(q)\tfrac{1}{2}(1 - q)] = f'(m_C) \frac{[1 - p/2 + p'(q)\tfrac{1}{2}(1 - q)]}{2} \qquad (9)$$

which represents the ESS for each of the three sibs' marginal gain rates. That is, it specifies how much steeper the slopes of B and C have to be relative to that of A. This can be contemplated in a stepwise manner to reach the interesting prediction that, all else being equal, the resource consumption of B should lie closer to that of A than to that of C. This occurs because p is an increasing function of q: As the A-chick gets more selfish, B must also be more selfish (having less remaining after A has taken its cut). One way of seeing this is to consider the point at which the next food item no longer does A half as much good as it will do for A's junior sibs: A passes on the item and B quickly consumes it. This is repeated a few times until a new point is reached at which the *next* food item would do twice as much good for the still-unfed C as for A, but it would not be twice as valuable to B as to A. Here, A's inclusive fitness would be best served by seeing C ingest the food; but, once A passes on any item, the next right-of-refusal falls to B. So, paradoxically, A eats that item too (the food does more good for A's direct component of fitness than for the portion of A's indirect component represented by B). And this little game-within-a-game carries the two senior siblings off to a higher plane of gluttony (to the detriment of C) than one might otherwise expect (Fig. 7.2). We shall skip the formal development of this argument here (see Parker et al. 1989), but it should be clear that one can use the decelerating fitness function in equation (2) and extrapolate the predicted shares for each of three players as a function of food availability (shown in Fig. 7.2). This shows the intuitively appealing result that skew is expected to diminish as the overall family budget rises. Below the area where food is too scarce for C to obtain m_{min}, the lines vanish; this is because when food is that tight, the best policy (for virtually everyone, including possibly C itself: Alexander 1974, O'Connor 1978) is for C to die, in which case we switch back to the 2-sib model.

A 4-sib version of this game has now been developed using this same framework and fitness function (Mock & Parker 1997), which bears out the general prediction from the 3-sib model, namely, that the differences in shares between successive members of a sibling hierarchy should increase as one goes down the hierarchy. That general result has also been found by using an alternative (nonexponential) fitness function that allows the game to be made for any number of siblings (L. S. Forbes, personal communication).

Some data on the average shares of food ingested by 3-sib broods of great egrets *(Casmerodius albus)* show qualitative agreement with the first prediction (A and B differed from each other by only about 6%, while B and C differed by 16%). And similar down-the-hierarchy patterns have been found for great blue herons *(Ardea herodias)* (Mock 1985, Mock et al. 1987a) and cattle egrets *(Bubulcus ibis)* (Ploger & Mock 1986). However, when similar great egret broods were artificially provisioned with extra food (Mock et al. 1987b), we did not observe a decrease in skew (the prediction illustrated in the lower panel of Fig. 7.2).

Many additional aspects of this model could be field-tested with appropriate study systems. For example, one could manipulate p in a 3-sib brood, at least approximately, by provisioning the B-chick selectively. Precisely what one would predict from such a perturbation is likely to hinge on, as well as reveal, the mechanism(s)

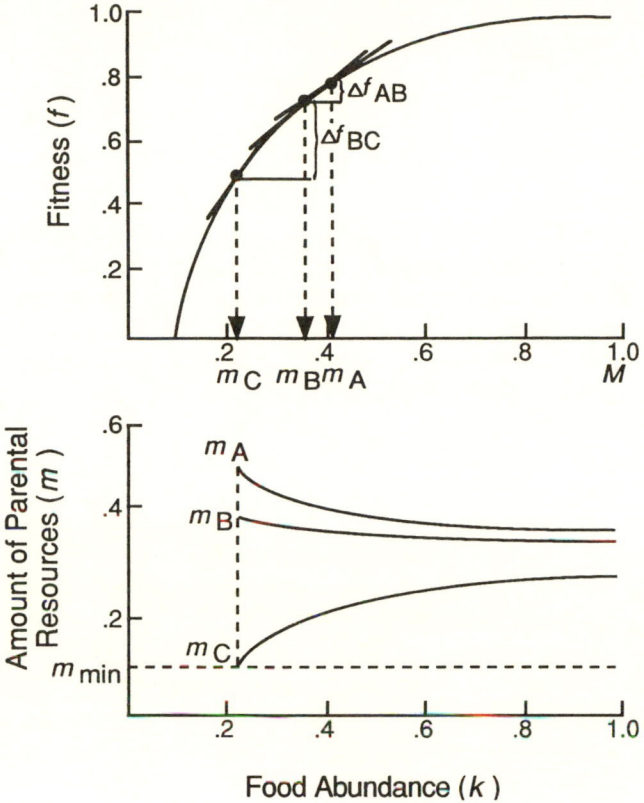

Figure 7.2. Three-sib Hierarchy Model. Note in the upper panel that the fitness difference between the two senior siblings (Δf_{AB}) is predicted to be smaller than that between the two youngest sibs (Δf_{BC}). In the lower panel, shares of parental resources (m) are plotted against food abundance as represented by the shape constant, k. When conditions are severe (low values of k), the weakest sibling is selfishly excluded from food by its senior siblings (m_C is lowest), but the skew is relaxed as conditions improve (higher values of k). (From Parker et al. 1989, with permission of *American Naturalist*.)

by which A normally assesses the conditions of (more specifically, the marginal gain rates of) its junior nestmates. If A appraises the size and vigor of each sib, perhaps relative to itself, experimentally supplementing B with extra food could lead to two rather disparate results: (1) According to the theory sketched here, A should become more generous (as if seeing that a well-fed B would be more prone to pass the opportunity on to C; and/or (2) according to the logic of asymmetric contests, A might perceive B as a greater threat to its own hegemony and escalate (e.g., increase aggression directed at B). In cattle egrets, it has been shown that siblicidal aggression levels are raised sharply when all three nestlings are initially equal in size as the result of having been swapped between nests at hatching (Fujioka 1985, Mock &

Ploger 1987), supporting the latter model. These complicating effects should be possible to tease apart by combining the manipulations of targeted supplements and partial-brood size matching.

7.2.2 Sibling Competition as a Scramble: Begging Models

In species where parental investment is competed for in a relatively nonaggressive manner (surely the case for most taxa that have sibling rivalry at all), one or more neonatal motor skills provides the key to outperforming one's nestmates. The particular skills differ widely across animal groups. For many songbirds, parental food deliveries are typically greeted with clamorous vocalizing, rapid upward stretching, and gaping. It has been shown that the height and speed of the presented gape, in tandem with each individual's two-dimensional position in the nest relative to the parent's point of entry, accounts for much of the variation surrounding which young get fed versus which go hungry. When the brood reaches the age of fledging, the competition may shift to venturing forth so as to intercept the incoming parent before it ever reaches the nest (Bustamente et al. 1992, Nilsson & Svensson 1993, van Heezik & Seddon 1996). By contrast, in wild-caught grasshopper mice *(Onychomys)*, a nursing pup strives to out-race its littermates in draining the small amount of milk released during each given milk letdown, thereby freeing it to move on to an unoccupied nipple and collect that portion, too (J. D. Moodie, unpublished data), a practice called "nipple-switching" and documented originally for domesticated laboratory rodents (Cramer & Blass 1983). In many parasitoids, there may be a simple race to consume more than one's share of the finite host tissues, a pattern of competitive gluttony that may exist very broadly across many taxa exploiting discrete larval food bases (e.g., tree-hole inhabiting insects, puddle-dwelling tadpoles, etc.). In each case, a premium is placed on a few motor skills: Sibs that do slightly better are more likely to survive and, one assumes, to be recruited into the breeding population. For purposes of the next model, we lump all these key motor skills under the label of "begging" and assume that an offspring's fitness is proportional to its begging level relative to that of its whole brood.

Unlike the hierarchy models, we need an ESS approach now even for the simplest 2-sib brood, because each player is making its own strategic decision, namely choosing the level at which to beg (a variable we call x), and because the best choice obviously depends on what its rival does. Now our two imaginary avian nestlings are still called A and B to indicate that they are nonidentical, but A's superiority is now envisioned as being quite modest (emphatically not despotic). We seek the ESS begging efforts, x_A^* and x_B^*, while taking into account that the effectiveness of the sibs' begging is not necessarily scaled identically. For this, we allow the two sibs to differ in their "competitive weights" (*sensu* Parker and Sutherland 1986) and assume that the A-chick's signal is somewhat more telling than that of B. This difference is indicated by use of positive constants, a and b (where $a > b$), such that the A-chick's total signal strength is ax_A and B's total signal strength is bx_B. Now the two sibs' shares of the total resource M can be specified as

$$m_A = \frac{Max_A}{(ax_A + bx_B)} \tag{10a}$$

and

$$m_B = \frac{Mbx_B}{(ax_A + bx_B)} \tag{10b}$$

In words, each offspring is paid its cut of the total M as a function of its *relative signal strength* (its total signal strength divided by whole-brood signal strength). If an ESS exists for these two sibs, their evolutionarily stable efforts (x_A^* and x_B^*) must be resistant to unilateral change by the other (a Nash equilibrium: see Hammerstein, this volume) Thus, to determine the pair of stable optima, we must solve equation (5) for the A-chick while simultaneously solving the equivalent equation from the B-chick's perspective. That is, we need solutions

$$f'(m_A) = \tfrac{1}{2} f'(m_B) \tag{11a}$$

and

$$f'(m_B) = \tfrac{1}{2} f'(m_A) \tag{11b}$$

to coexist. Because these two cannot possibly coexist, our model is clearly lacking some critical element, namely a cost for the begging. As set out to this point, all the signaling by rival nestmates has been implicitly cost-free, but if such signaling (or TV advertising, for that matter) were unchecked by costs, the optimum would always be infinity. But when we insert some signaling costs, we find that stability is achievable. This seems a reasonable thing to do, in light of some actual measurements of avian begging costs. Empirically, it has been shown that eggs placed in artificial nests that emit taped begging calls are more likely to be depredated than eggs in silent nests (Haskell 1994). And studies of cattle egret energetics indicate that two categories of sib-competition motor patterns (namely, the active solicitations toward parents and the pecking directed at nestmates) require substantial increases in oxygen consumption, hence energy expenditure (St. Clair & Mock, in preparation; see also McCarty 1996; Mock, Kenagy, & Visser, in preparation). To work this factor into our model as simply as possible, we focus here on the energetics type of cost, which we assume to be a simple subtraction, a drain on energy reserves, that can be represented as a function of begging level, $E(x)$. We now see the *net gains* for each chick as

$$m_A = \frac{Max_A}{(ax_A + bx_B)} - E(x_A) \tag{12a}$$

and

$$m_B = \frac{Mbx_B}{(ax_A + bx_B)} - E(x_B) \tag{12b}$$

From this step, things can move quickly and in a familiar way. We can use these calculations of m_A and m_B to identify the stable pair of begging rates, x_A^* and x_B^*, which are found once again by differentiating equation (12a) with respect to x_A and equation (12b) with respect to x_B, setting each equal to zero and doing some rearranging of the results, so as to derive a ratio of the two stable begging rates (for more details see Parker et al. 1989, p. 858). This shows that

$$\frac{x_A^*}{x_B^*} = \frac{f'(m_B)E'(x_B^*)[f'(m_A) - \frac{1}{2}f'(m_B)]}{f'(m_A)E'(x_A^*)[f'(m_B) - \frac{1}{2}f'(m_A)]} \tag{13}$$

which can be simplified with a couple of substitutions if we let:

1. $E(x_i) = jx_i$, where j is a positive constant (that is, we convert the begging effort into a linear function, which means that its slope, $E'(x_i)$, is a constant and equal to j; it cancels from equation (13) and
2. $f(m_i) = 1 - \exp(-km_i)$, which is just a streamlined version of the exponential fitness curve.

With a little tidying, we find now that our ratio of stable begging rates has become

$$\frac{x_A^*}{x_B^*} = \frac{2 - \exp[k(m_A - m_B)]}{2 - \exp[-k(m_A - m_B)]} \tag{14}$$

which can be satisfied. When this is solved numerically, we can draw both curves (Fig. 7.3; see Parker et al. 1989 for details) plus a few conclusions that may be useful as testable predictions for empirical studies:

1. Not surprisingly, A-chick should always spend less effort on begging than B-chick (Fig. 7.3, upper graphs); that is, $x_A^* < x_B^*$.

2. As the asymmetry in competitive ability between the two sibs increases, so does their difference in begging effort. Basically, a vastly superior A-chick needs to invest far less in rivalry than an A-chick that is only marginally more effective at begging than its nestmate.

3. If resources are limited ($k = 1$ in Fig. 7.3), the A-chick is expected to take the greater share. Rather counterintuitively, however, if resources are not particularly limited ($k = 5$), A may reduce its begging (and conserve that effort) to such a degree that it actually consumes less than its more active nestmate. At the risk of sounding anthropomorphic, we might say that under conditions of relative bounty, A can relax while B must continue to hustle. Note that at the ESS, the A-chick still has more net energy available for growth and survival (dashed lines) than B.

4. If the asymmetry in competitive ability is sufficiently extreme ($a >> b$), the conclusions from this scramble (Begging) model converge rapidly toward those of the contest (Hierarchy) model. An example of this can be found in crested penguins (*Eudyptes* spp.), where second-hatched chicks emerge from their eggs at such enormous size disadvantages (from having to remain longer inside a much smaller shell)

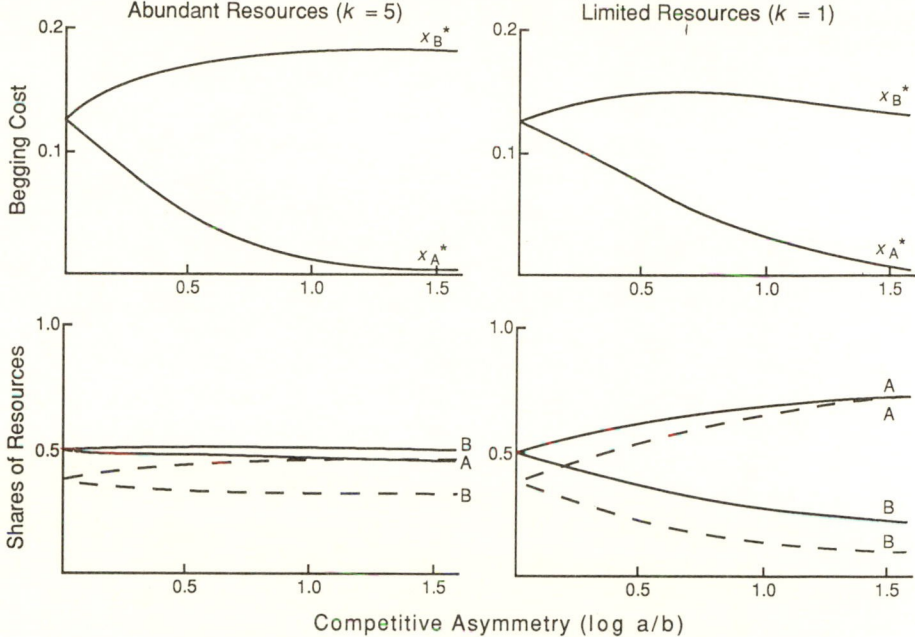

Figure 7.3. Numerical analyses from the 2-sib Begging Model. The horizontal axis is always the competitive asymmetry (expressed as the log a/b), such that a value of zero (extreme left margin of each graph) depicts two evenly matched nestmates and the greater effectiveness of the A-chick's begging is more exaggerated as one moves to the right. The lefthand pair of graphs represents abundant resources ($k = 5$); the righthand pair represents limited resources ($k = 1$). It can be seen that once the rivals are mismatched, A's begging effort (top pair of graphs) is always lower than that of B and that this difference is greater when resources are plentiful (basically because B cannot afford as much begging effort when conditions are lean). In the lower pair of graphs, the resource shares consumed are depicted in two ways: the solid lines show the gross shares and the dashed lines show the net shares (after effort has been subtracted). Not surprisingly, when resources are scarce, A takes more than B (especially when its advantage is largest). But when resources are bountiful, A may consume less than B, but still come out ahead in terms of net shares, because of saved begging effort. (From Parker et al. 1989, with permission of *American Naturalist*.)

that they usually die very soon, but without suffering any of the physical abuse that characterizes virtually all other obligate brood-reducing birds (Lamey 1990, Lamey & Mock 1991).

We know of no published empirical results that apply directly to these predictions, though there are some currently active projects attempting to measure the energetics of begging under field conditions. One obvious empirical challenge in testing these predictions (and those from other models of begging) is getting a handle on the energetic and nonenergetic costs of sibling competition. On the energetics side, a secondary challenge will be to evaluate whether the kilojoules of effort expended are biologically trivial or serious constraints that shape how rivalries work.

7.3 Parent–Offspring Conflict Models

Trivers's (1972) original definition of *parental investment* was strict, assuming both positive effects on the fitness of recipient offspring and a zero-sum game for parental fitness. Despite this clear indication of tradeoffs between resources given to one offspring and those available for the next, his follow-up article, simply titled "Parent–offspring conflict" (Trivers 1974), caught many by surprise. There he posited that natural selection might favor a higher PI optimum when acting on an offspring than when acting on a parent, specifically because of asymmetries in r. A songbird parent delivering worms to a brood of two was expected to prefer an exactly equal allocation pattern, because it is identically related ($r = 0.50$) to each chick. By contrast, a given nestling was expected to prefer a skew in PI toward Self because it is twice as "related to itself" ($r = 1$) as to even a full sibling. If either nestling has the wherewithal to affect such a selfish bias consistently, it might enhance its own fitness at the sib's expense. Such would constitute a case where the offspring "won" the parent–offspring conflict, because the parent's fitness is consequently lowered.

That argument sounded good at first and it seemed to explain immediately why one observes begging behavior (including expensive-looking "tantrums") in dependent young. Offspring were seen as employing potent "psychological weaponry" against the sales resistance of the physically more robust parents.[6] This verbal and graphical model was quickly rejected by Alexander (1974), who argued that any mutant individual that begged "too well" during the nestling phase of its life might achieve a short-term gain, but could not win in the long run. He reasoned that this eventual failure was inevitable because of its own maturation into a parent, at which time its own superavaricious offspring would tax it harshly. In brief, Alexander reasoned that parent–offspring conflict cannot be important, because offspring cannot "win": Their temporary gains are later stripped from them by the same mechanism that helped them initially.

This exchange attracted much attention and serves our purposes well, because it demonstrates some pitfalls inherent in purely verbal arguments. Such a case can *sound* convincing, even when it is directly at odds with a different, but equally convincing, argument. For example, the next volley in the POC debate came from Dawkins (1976) in *The Selfish Gene,* whose verbal form left many readers confused.

Happily, the air cleared considerably when a barrage of quantitative models hit the presses (e.g., Blick 1977; Stamps et al. 1978; Parker & Macnair 1978, 1979; Macnair & Parker 1978, 1979; Parker 1985), from which we have chosen one elegant representative (Box 7.1) to illustrate. Among other things, these models showed that POC is most clearly understood from the perspective of genic selection: Offspring *can* evolve phenotypic traits that impair overall parental fitness because selection need operate only on one (or a few) loci, which may be active only during the first ("receiving") period of parental care. If *those* alleles profit from skewing PI toward the body they occupy, their replication rate may accelerate relative to alleles that do not skew PI. The fact that the body they inhabit may be penalized later to some degree by the next generation is likely, as Alexander stressed, but the *magnitude* of that later penalty need not necessarily cancel out the early benefits; if the deferred penalty is less, the early selfishness is likely to be evolutionarily stable.

So far, this shows only that POC *can* exist, specifically that parentally harmful levels of offspring selfishness *can* spread via natural selection. In the parlance of Godfray & Parker (1992), the "battleground" for POC has been established. However, the matters of how often one side really gains the upper hand and what factors most likely affect the outcome of the POC game are separate issues, requiring completely different models of "resolution." We may agree that the potential for phenotype-shaping selection pressures exists, without having to concede that a given phenomenon (e.g., tantrums and milder forms of begging) arose from POC (reviewed in Mock & Forbes 1992). Other explanations may exist (including some that are more parsimonious) without POC.

As an example of one resolutions model, we sketch the basic components of a model for begging by nestling birds. In truth, limited space prevents our showing more than the bare bones of even the simplest model, so we must refer the interested reader to the original formulation (Parker & Macnair 1979), to an early attempt to clarify (Parker 1985), to an excellent recent review (Godfray 1995b), and to a forthcoming effort to explain the approach in considerable detail (Mock & Parker 1997, Chapter 8). We assume that the two categories of players (parents and offspring) choose a value from a continuous array of strategies; specifically, a parent picks some level of investment, m, that it will provide (in response to a given level of offspring begging) and an offspring must decide on some level of begging, x, it will use for extracting resources from the parent. There are many ways to model the details of the parent–offspring interaction. In Parker and Macnair's (1979) resolution model, parents allocate food in proportion to an offspring's begging level (which is relative to the brood's mean level of begging). If a mutation alters the parent's food allocation strategy, this changes the offspring's immediate *behavioral bid* (begging level), but not its *genetic bid* (which then alters over evolutionary time). An analogous dynamic applies for a mutation in offspring strategy. An alternative approach is based on begging as a signal of an offspring's true need (Godfray 1991); here, if a mutation changes the parent's strategy, nothing happens to the offspring's immediate begging level, though there will again be evolutionary changes in offspring strategy.

The basic idea is that one must seek the twin optima for parent and offspring when the opposing party has made its best choice. This is pursued by specifying formally the fitness of:

Box 7.1 A Battleground model of parent–offspring conflict
(Stamps & Metcalf 1980).

Imagine a species in which parents provide considerable postzygotic care and have two nonconcurrent offspring. One of the parents bears a rare allele causing selfish behavior when present in an offspring. Thus, there are four equiprobable sibships involving the possible permutations of the two offspring genotypes. A standard ("wild-type") offspring has genotype aa and receives m resources from its parents. Fitness is assumed to be directly linked to this investment, so m also represents offspring fitness. The battleground for POC will be demonstrated if a selfish allele (mutant genotype Aa), which enables its bearers to get some additional amount of parental investment and fitness (a total of $m+b$), is able to invade the population. Because the two siblings are not contemporaries, the fitness achieved by an offspring raised in the second and final reproductive cycle is affected by the first sib's removal of finite parental resources: Specifically, if the first offspring was a selfish mutant, the later sib has to make do with what remains (a total of $m-c$). Clearly, the order in which the genotypes are born makes all the difference. The four family combinations and payoffs (indicated by the horizontal arrows) are:

Birth order	Family 1	Family 2	Family 3	Family 4
First	$aa \to m$	$aa \to m$	$Aa \to m+b$	$Aa \to m+b$
Second	$aa \to m$	$Aa \to m$	$aa \to m-c$	$Aa \to m-c$
Total Fitness	$2m$	$2m$	$2m+b-c$	$2m+b-c$

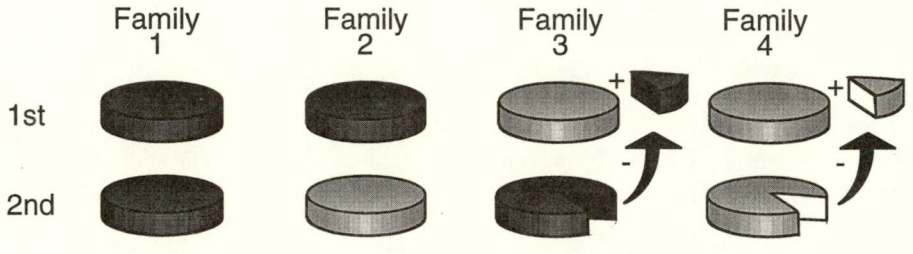

	Family 1	Family 2	Family 3	Family 4
1st				
2nd				

The selfish allele will spread if it outcompetes a comparable wild-type allele. The selfish allele gains $m + b$ when first born (families 3 and 4) and m (family 3) or $m - c$ (family 4) when second born. Thus, the four copies, which occur in the equally probable families, have a total fitness of $4m - 2b - c$. In contrast, an arbitrarily lablelled wild-type allele present in a parent in the rest of the population will achieve a total fitness of $4m$. The selfish allele spreads if $b > 0.5c$. Whether this selfishness will impair parental fitness (as required for it to be POC) depends on the relative magnitudes of b and c. From the "Total Fitness" row, it can be seen that offspring selfishness can be beneficial to parents (when $b > c$), harmful to parents (when $c > b$), or irrelevant (when $b = c$ exactly).

- a mutant parent that provides some amount of m that *differs* from the parental ESS (m^*) when the offspring is begging at its ESS value (x^*); this mutant parental fitness is $W_p (m, x^*)$; and
- a mutant offspring that begs at some level of x that *differs* from the offspring ESS (x^*) when the parent is delivering at its ESS value (m^*); this mutant offspring fitness is $W_o (x, m^*)$.

When each fitness function is differentiated and set equal to zero:

$$\left[\frac{\partial W_p(m,x^*)}{\partial m}\right]_{m=m^*}=0 \tag{15a}$$

$$\left[\frac{\partial W_o(x,m^*)}{\partial x}\right]_{x=x^*}=0 \tag{15b}$$

then solved at either $m=m^*$ [equation (15a)] or $x=x^*$ [equation (15b)], we can obtain expressions for the ESS values for investing (m^*) and begging (x^*), respectively.

From here, we can explore the two "mechanisms" by which each player conducts its end of the bilateral negotiations. Mechanism I, the *Demand Function* (Hussell 1988), specifies how a strategic change (i.e., a long-term change, over evolutionary time) in parental delivery can alter the realized or short-term begging level. And Mechanism II, the *Supply Function,* covers the other side by showing how a strategic change in offspring begging affects the realized investment level.

To model Mechanism I, we represent the realized begging level as X, with a monotonic negative cost function S(X). Thus survival, S, of an offspring decreases with the amount of begging, X, that it performs. The fitness of a mutant parent becomes

$$W_p(m,x^*)=\frac{M}{m}f(m)S(X)$$

and, applying equation (15a) to find the parent's ESS m^*, we get

$$f'(m^*)=\frac{f(m^*)}{m}[1-U] \tag{16}$$

where

$$U=m^*\left[\frac{S'(X)}{S(X)}\right]X'(m^*)$$

Here, $X'(m^*)$ is *Mechanism I*—that is, the rate of change in realized begging with m in the vicinity of m^*. Similarly, $S'(X)$ is the rate of change in survival with X, when X is close in value to x^*.

The effect of *Mechanism I* on the parental strategy depends on the sign of U, which hinges in turn on the sign of $X'(m^*)$—that is, on whether realized begging increases or decreases if the parent marginally raises investment above the ESS level, m^*.

- If $X'(m^*)=0$, realized begging does not alter if the parent marginally raises or reduces investment about the ESS. This has the effect that the parental ESS, m^*, is identical to what would be the parental optimum, m_p, in the absence of any conflict. Simply put, if *Mechanism I* is inoperative, the parent plays its own optimum.

- If $X'(m^*) < 0$, so that realized begging decreases if the parent marginally increases investment from m^*, then the parent is coerced into investing more than its own optimum. The negotiations lead either to some form of offspring-wins or to a compromise solution.
- And finally, if $X'(m^*) > 0$, so that realized begging increases if the parent marginally raises investment above m^*, then we obtain a paradoxical result: the parent is somehow constrained to give less than its own optimum.

The initial assumption, and the most comprehensively analyzed of these possibilities, is the second one, which can be developed a bit more by applying an explicit function to X. Parker & Macnair (1979) used a simple one:

$$X = x^* \left[\frac{m^*}{m} \right] \tag{17}$$

which has the desired property that realized begging increases when $m < m^*$ and decreases when $m > m^*$. Then around the ESS, where $x = x^*$; we obtain

$$X'(m^*) = - \frac{x^*}{m^*} \tag{18}$$

The *Supply Function* (Mechanism II), which specifies how a change in offspring begging might alter parental investment, can be treated similarly. This time we imagine a long-term or *strategic* change caused by a mutation that shifts the offspring from its ESS baseline value, x^*, and explore how that deflects the parental response from m^* to a *realized* level we call μ. Once again, "strategy" is used to represent something that changes only in an evolutionary sense, while the term "realized" behavior is used to connote the inevitable, proximate consequence of the first party's change on the response by the second party.

This can be modeled for either interbrood types of conflict—wherein a current offspring's selfishness may erode the parent's capacity for future investment—or intrabrood conflict. For brevity we address only the latter here, since it is the kind of sibling competition treated earlier (but see Parker & Macnair 1979, Parker 1985, Mock & Parker 1997). If we imagine the parent to fix the total investment per brood at M, a total of M/m^* offspring will be produced at the parent's ESS. The payoff for a mutant offspring is

$$W_o(x, m^*) = \left[\frac{M}{m} \right] f(m) S(x)$$

and applying equation (15b) gives

$$-S'(x^*) = \mu'(x^*) \, S(x^*) \left[\frac{f'(\mu)}{f(\mu)} \right] \tag{19}$$

We now need to know how x affects μ. It seems likely that $\mu'(x)$ will be positive: More investment is allocated if more food is given. One possibility

(Parker & Macnair 1979) is to assume that parents allocate on the basis of relative begging across the brood, following what has been termed "mean-matching" (a mutant offspring obtains a share of resources that is proportional to how its begging compares with that of the whole brood's average). That is, in a two-chick brood we have

$$\mu = m^* \left[\frac{x}{0.5\ (x+x^*)} \right]$$ (20)

and

$$\mu'(x^*) = \frac{m^*}{2x^*}$$ (21)

Taking stock at this point, we now have general expressions for the parent's ESS [equation (16)] and the offspring's ESS [equation (19)], neither of which specify any specific formulations for *Mechanisms I* and *II*. If we bring in equation (18) (Parker & Macnair's formulation for *Mechanism I*) and equation (21) (their *Mechanism II*) for purposes of fleshing out the final result, we get the following two-part ESS:

When in the role of parent, play

$$f'(m^*) = \alpha \frac{f(m^*)}{m^*}$$ (22a)

When in the role of offspring, play

$$-S'(x^*) = \beta \frac{S(x^*)}{x^*}$$ (22b)

where α and β are positive constants whose values depend on whether the conflict under consideration is intrabrood or interbrood. As we are considering only the former in this discussion, $\alpha = 2/3$ and $\beta = 1/3$.

7.4 Testing Model Predictions

We close with a few thoughts on model testing, since it seems likely that most readers will consider themselves to be empiricists primarily. One of the values of modeling, of course, is that counterintuitive predictions are sometimes generated by the process. And we have tried to suggest a few points where these sibling rivalry and parent–offspring conflict models might be tested. But as guides for empirical work, we must also mention some caveats that may not be immediately apparent to first-time users of models as guides for empirical work. This might be communicated most clearly by walking through a study and contemplating how one should interpret possible results.

Suppose, for example, that you wish to test the prediction that increases in the competitive weighting (signal effectiveness) between an *A*-chick and its *B* sibling ought to be accompanied by increased disparities in the begging effort they expend. You measure the begging levels of *A* and *B* when their size difference has been experimentally increased (by swapping hatchlings among nests) and compare the results with an appropriate control (similarly handled nonsiblings that differ in age and size by the degree typically found in nature). Now, in Scenario One, imagine that your results turn out to support the null: No significant difference is detected in the relative begging of *A* and *B* across treatments. We fear the temptation here is simply to conclude that the model is inappropriate (its assumptions are incorrect for the biological situation); after all, you set out to test an explicit prediction from the model and your results came out the other way. The more interesting question, though, is why *A*-chicks failed to trim begging effort when their size advantage (and presumably their signal effectiveness) was enhanced. There are several possibilities (including mundane empirical problems like small sample size, lack of appropriate operational definitions of "begging" and so on), but we focus on two that relate intimately to model testing. First, both the benefit and cost functions in the model define relationships that, to the modeler, seem plausible (and perhaps, secondarily, are mathematically tractable). That does not guarantee, however, that the explicit functions chosen to represent the relationships between begging and food obtained, or between begging and effort, will apply to every system. Consequently, a "good" empirical test of a model includes a careful assessment of how realistic the benefit and cost functions are for the system in question. Either or both may need to be modified if they prove to be statistically poor predictors of what happens. Another way of saying this is that just because you have employed some fancy-looking models does not mean you no longer need common sense.

Second, there are sometimes assumptions involved in deriving the model's solution that need to be checked thoroughly for each individual case. In the begging model, for instance, energetic costs of begging were assumed to rise linearly at equal rates for *A* and *B* chicks; if this does not hold, then the predictions change. Thus the assumption of equal cost functions should be viewed merely as a "first hunch," which may not apply in all cases and which, ideally, should be verified by the empiricist. In a similar vein, critics of modeling sometimes point to the fact that modelers lay out a series of equations and, if embarrassed by subsequent facts, simply alter the models. The ease with which this can sometimes be done appears to be highly vexatious to nonmodelers (see Sigmund 1993, p. 47), but what alternative is there? An obdurate refusal to change one's argument is hardly a productive posture.

Finally, let us consider Scenario Two, in which you set out to test the prediction and found wildly positive support for it. Does this mean the system is now perfectly understood? Not likely, but it may mean that you are on the right track and that may improve your ability to make an even more insightful prediction as you proceed. One of the beauties of science is that the questions never really stop; but then, nobody ever said it was going to be easy.

ACKNOWLEDGMENTS   We thank the U.S. National Science Foundation for support (IBN-9408149) to the research programs of DWM and PLS and thank the U.K. Science and Engineering Research Council for support of GAP during the preparation of this chapter. Coral McAllister helped greatly with the figures. Our chapter also benefited from the tactful criticisms of H. Kern Reeve, David Haskell, and one anonymous reviewer. Finally, DWM thanks E. L. Charnov for having expressed the last nine words of the text after prefacing them with the admonition, "Stop whining. . . ."

Notes

1. $br - c > 0$ (where b is benefit to recipient's fitness, c is cost to donor's fitness, and r is the coefficient-of-relatedness between the two).
2. Just for the record, Wright's (1922) coefficient-of-relatedness is used in this context to estimate the probability $(0 \leq r \leq 1.0)$ that a rare mutant allele in one individual exists as a copy, identical-by-descent, in a second individual. In outbred diploids, each probability is bidirectional, but in haplodiploid taxa, it is asymmetrical between two siblings of opposite sexes. For certain plant tissues, calculating r can get very complicated (e.g., Haig 1987, Queller 1989).
3. The convention of specifying this as a *rare* mutant is to isolate the effects of kinship from other factors that might cause the allele to be present in a sibling's body. That is, if it is so rare as to be essentially unique, then the probability that a full sibling has an identical copy is almost exactly the 0.50 expected from having two parents in common.
4. This is a standard technique in optimality modeling, but we offer a brief explanation for readers new to these approaches. From basic calculus, it will be remembered that the first derivative of any curve is its slope (= "gradient"). Because this fitness function is parabolic, rising and then falling, we seek its highest point. That peak occurs at the point where the slope is zero. So this identifies the value of p where fitness is maximized. In many cases, one does not know the shape of the function being explored in advance, it is therefore customary to make sure that the second derivative is negative, indicating that the point identified is, in fact, a maximum and not a minimum (where, of course, the slope is also zero). For a short introduction to some basic optimality modeling techniques, including game-theoretic ones, see Parker and Maynard Smith (1990).
5. We capitalize the word Simple here to identifiy it as jargon. Some readers are infuriated by that term, since it seems to connote that any amount of labyrinthine mathematics built into the model is transparently obvious. And while we are trying to keep the math "simple" in the vernacular sense, the term Simple Optimality Model refers merely to the fact that there are not two or more coevolving parties and that this is not an evolutionary game (which would be considered a Competitive Optimality problem). Whether a given piece of math is easy to understand is a different matter.
6. There is, of course, no necessity for nervous systems to be involved in such a dynamic. For example, plant offspring may send chemical signals of need to the maternal sporophyte, which might or might not respond in ways that maximize offspring fitness. This is a useful thing to remember, lest the whole argument might seem to depend on particular proximate mechanisms.

References

Alexander, R. D. 1974. The evolution of social behavior. *Annu. Rev. Ecol. Syst.,* 5, 325–383.

Blick, J. E. 1977. Selection for traits which lower individual reproduction. *J. Theor. Biol.* 67, 597–601.

Brown, J. L. & Brown, E. R. 1981. Kin selection and individual selection in babblers. In *Natural Selection and Social Behavior,* R. D. Alexander & D. W. Tinkle, eds., pp. 244–256. New York: Chiron Press.

166   Douglas Mock, Geoffrey Parker, & P. L. Schwagmeyer

Bustamente, J., Cuervo, J. J. & Moreno J. 1992. The function of feeding chases in the chinstrap penguin *Pygoscelis antarctica. Anim. Behav.*, 44, 753–575.

Cramer, C. P. & Blass E. M. 1983. Mechanisms of control of milk intake in suckling rats. *Am. J. Physiol.*, 245, R154–R159.

Dawkins, R. 1976. *The Selfish Gene.* Oxford: Oxford University Press.

Dickins, D. W. & Clark, R. A. 1987. Games theory and siblicide in the kittiwake gull, *Rissa tridactyla. J. Theor. Biol.*, 125, 301–305.

Forbes, L. S. 1990. Insurance offspring and the evolution of avian clutch size. *J. Theor. Biol.*, 147, 345–359.

Forbes, L. S. 1993. Avian brood reduction and parent–offspring "conflict". *Am. Nat.*, 142, 82–117.

Forbes, L. S. & Ydenberg, R. C. 1992. Sibling rivalry in a variable environment. *Theor. Popul. Biol.*, 41, 335–360.

Fujioka, M. 1985. Food delivery and sibling competition in experimentally even-aged broods of the cattle egret. *Behav. Ecol. Sociobiol.*, 17, 67–74.

Godfray, H. C. J. 1991. Signalling of need between parents and offspring. *Nature*, 352, 328–330.

Godfray, H. C. J. 1995a. Signalling of need between parents and young: parent–offspring conflict and sibling rivalry. *Am. Nat.*, 146, 1–24.

Godfray, H. C. J. 1995b. Evolutionary theory of parent–offspring conflict. *Nature*, 376, 133–138.

Godfray, H. C. J. & Harper, A. B. 1990. The evolution of brood reduction by siblicide in birds. *J. Theor. Biol.*, 145, 163–175.

Godfray, H. C. J. & Parker, G. A. 1992. Sibling competition, parent–offspring conflict, and clutch size. *Anim. Behav.*, 43, 473–490.

Haig, D. 1987. Kin conflict in seed plants. *Trends Ecol. Evol.*, 2, 337–340.

Haig, D. 1990. Brood reduction and optimal parental investment when offspring differ in quality. *Am. Nat.*, 136, 550–566.

Hamilton, W. D. 1964. The genetical evolution of social behaviour. *J. Theor. Biol.*, 7, 1–52.

Harper, A. B. 1986. The evolution of begging: Sibling competition and parent–offspring conflict. *Am. Nat.*, 128, 99–114.

Haskell, D. 1994. Experimental evidence that nestling begging behaviour incurs a cost due to nest predation. *Proc. R. Soc. London B*, 257, 161–164.

Hussell, D. J. T. 1988. Supply and demand in tree swallow broods: A model of parent–offspring food provisioning interactions in birds. *Am. Nat.*, 131, 175–202.

Lack, D. 1947. The significance of clutch-size. Parts 1 and 2. *Ibis*, 89, 302–352.

Lack, D. 1954. *The Natural Regulation of Animal Numbers.* Oxford: Clarendon Press.

Lamey, T. C. 1990. Hatch asynchrony and brood reduction in penguins. In *Penguin Biology*, L. S. Davis & J. Darby, eds., pp. 399–417. New York: Academic Press.

Lamey, T. C. & Lamey, C. S. 1994. Hatch synchrony and bad food years. *Am. Nat.*, 143, 734–738.

Lamey, T. C. & Mock, D. W. 1991. Nonaggressive brood reduction in birds. *Acta XX Congr. Int. Ornithol.*, III, 1741–1751.

Macnair, M. & Parker, G. A. 1978. Models of parent–offspring conflict. II. Promiscuity. *Anim. Behav.*, 26, 111–122.

Macnair, M. & Parker, G. A. 1979. Models of parent-offspring conflict. III. Intra-brood conflict. *Anim. Behav.*, 27, 1202–1209.

McCarty, J. P. 1996. The energetic cost of begging in nestling passerines. *Auk*, 113, 178–188.

Mock, D. W. 1985. Siblicidal brood reduction: the prey-size hypothesis. *Am. Nat.*, 125, 327–343.

Mock, D. W. & Forbes, L. S. 1992. Parent-offspring conflict: A case of arrested development? *Trends Ecol. Evol.*, 7, 409–413.

Mock, D. W. & Forbes, L. S. 1994. Life-history consequences of avian brood reduction. *Auk,* 111, 115–123.

Mock, D. W. & Parker, G. A. 1997. *The Evolution of Sibling Rivalry.* Oxford: Oxford University Press.

Mock, D. W. & Ploger, B. J. 1987. Parental manipulation of optimal hatch asynchrony in cattle egrets: an experimental study. *Anim. Behav.*, 35, 150–160.

Mock, D. W., Lamey, T. C., Williams, C. F. & Pelletier, A. 1987a. Flexibility in the development of heron sibling aggression: An intraspecific test of the prey-size hypothesis. *Anim. Behav.*, 35, 1386–1393.

Mock, D. W., Lamey, T. C. & Ploger, B. J. 1987b. Proximate and ultimate roles of food amount in regulating egret sibling aggression. *Ecology,* 68, 1760–1772.

Mock, D. W., Schwagmeyer, P. L. & Parker, G. A. 1996. The model family. In *Permanent Partnerships in Birds, The Study of Monogamy*, J. M. Black, ed., pp. 52–69. Oxford: Oxford University Press.

Nilsson, J.-Å. & Svensson, M. 1993. Fledging in altricial birds: Parental manipulation or sibling competition? *Anim. Behav.*, 46, 379–386.

O'Connor, R. J. 1978. Brood reduction in birds: Selection for infanticide, fratricide, and suicide? *Anim. Behav.*, 26, 79–96.

Parker, G. A. 1985. Models of parent–offspring conflict. V. Effects of the behaviour of the two parents. *Anim. Behav.*, 33, 519–533.

Parker, G. A. & Macnair, M. 1978. Models of parent–offspring conflict. I. Monogamy. *Anim. Behav.*, 26, 97–111.

Parker, G. A. & Macnair, M. 1979. Models of parent–offspring conflict. IV. Suppression: Evolutionary retaliation by the parent. *Anim. Behav.*, 27, 1210–1235.

Parker, G. A. & Maynard Smith, J. 1990. Optimality theory in evolutionary biology. *Nature,* 348, 27–33.

Parker, G. A. & Sutherland, W. J. 1986. Ideal free distributions when individuals differ in competitive ability: Phenotype-limited ideal free models. *Anim. Behav.,* 34, 1222–1242.

Parker, G. A., Mock, D. W. & Lamey, T. C. 1989. How selfish should stronger sibs be? *Am. Nat.,* 133, 846–868.

Pijanowski, B. C. 1992. A revision of Lack's brood reduction hypothesis. *Am. Nat.,* 139, 1270–1292.

Ploger, B. J. & Mock, D. W. 1986. Role of sibling aggression in distribution of food to nestling cattle egrets (*Bubulcus ibis*). *Auk,* 103, 768–776.

Queller, D. C. 1989. Inclusive fitness in a nutshell. In *Oxford Surveys in Evolutionary Biology,* Vol. 6., P. H. Harvey & L. Partridge, eds., pp. 73–109. New York: Oxford University Press.

Sigmund, K. 1993. *Games of Life.* Oxford: Oxford University Press.

Stamps, J. & Metcalf, R. A. 1980. Parent–offspring conflict. In: *Sociobiology, Beyond Nature–Nurture,* G. A. Barlow & J. Silverberg, eds., pp. 598–618. Boulder, CO: Westview Press.

Stamps, J., Metcalf, R. A., & Krishnan, V. V. 1978. A genetic analysis of parent–offspring conflict. *Behav. Ecol. Sociobiol.,* 3, 369–392.

Trivers, R. L. 1972. Parental investment and sexual selection. In *Sexual Selection and the Descent of Man, 1871–1971,* B. Campbell, ed., pp. 136–279. Chicago: Aldine Atherton.

Trivers, R. L. 1974. Parent–offspring conflict. *Am. Zool.,* 14, 249–264.

van Heezik, Y. M. & Seddon, P. J. 1996. Scramble feeding in jackass penguins: Within-brood food distribution and the maintenance of sibling asymmetries. *Anim. Behav.,* 51, 1383–1390.

Wright, S. 1922. Coefficients of inbreeding and relationship. *Am. Nat.*, 56, 330–338.

MART R. GROSS
JOE REPKA

Game Theory and Inheritance in the Conditional Strategy

8.1 Introduction

Many populations contain more than one behavioral or life-history phenotype within a sex, such as sneakers and fighters in animal mating systems (Gross 1996). Maynard Smith (1982) introduced game theory and the concept of the evolutionarily stable strategy (ESS) in part to help explain the evolution of such alternative phenotypic tactics. He emphasized frequency-dependent selection, giving rise to alternative phenotypes with equal average fitnesses. He suggested that this could occur either through a mixed ESS in which each individual randomly plays one or both of the alternative tactics, such as fight with probability p and sneak with probability $1-p$, or through a genetically polymorphic evolutionarily stable state (ESSt) in which different individuals play different strategies within the population, such as a proportion p of individuals that are fighters and $1-p$ that are sneakers. Theoretical analyses of the genetically monomorphic mixed ESS and the genetically polymorphic ESSt became popular in the 1980s and remain so today. However, few examples of alternative phenotypes, which on close inspection are consistent with the conditions of the mixed ESS or ESSt, have been found in nature (Gross 1996).

New theoretical ground (Repka & Gross 1995, Gross 1996) and the lack of empirical support for the mixed ESS and ESSt suggest that we should shift the emphasis to the "conditional strategy." In the conditional strategy, a term coined by Dawkins (1980) and further defined by Gross (1996), an individual incorporates information about its ability to obtain fitness through alternative tactics and expresses the tactic which maximizes its fitness. Unlike alternative tactics in a mixed ESS, or alternative strategies in an ESSt, the alternative tactics in a conditional strategy do not result in equal average fitnesses among the different phenotypes within the population. Instead, tactic fitnesses in a conditional strategy are equal only at the ESS switchpoint between the tactics (Parker 1982, Charnov 1993, Repka & Gross 1995).

An important issue in the development of theory for the conditional strategy is the influence of heritability on evolutionary stability. In Maynard Smith's mixed ESS, individuals are typically treated as phenotypically and genetically similar, and therefore heritability is not a critical issue (Maynard Smith 1982). In Maynard Smith's ESSt, phenotypic differences are irrelevant and classical population genetics methods for studying frequency-dependent selection and genetic polymorphisms can be used to model the evolution of the alternative strategies (e.g., Maynard Smith 1989). In the conditional strategy, however, individuals are usually thought to differ in their phenotypic state or condition, and this difference influences the expression of their alternative tactics. Specifically, an individual's condition determines its status or relative competitive ability in the population and thus the fitnesses it can obtain from the alternative tactics (Gross 1996). One important source of variation in phenotypic condition is additive genetic variance resulting in heritability of the alternative tactics. Does this prevent the evolution of the conditional strategy?

In this chapter we address the issue of inheritance in the conditional strategy. We begin in Section 8.2 by reviewing the conditional strategy model presented by Gross (1996). This allows us to define our terms, and sets the stage for our study of inheritance. In Section 8.3, we extend the conditional strategy model by introducing inheritance. We model a situation where heritability through additive genetic variance (or its analog of environmental or cultural inheritance) influences the probability that offspring will adopt the same tactic as their father. We develop a set of conditions and formulas to show the relationships that exist among tactic fitnesses, tactic frequencies, and tactic inheritance in the conditional strategy. This leads to a new Inheritance Theorem for the conditional strategy in Section 8.4. The Inheritance Theorem defines how inheritance influences the shape of the conditional strategy, in terms of tactic fitnesses and frequencies. In Section 8.5 we graphically explore the Inheritance Theorem and demonstrate the important result that tactic inheritances, fitnesses, and frequencies together set the bounds on the conditional strategy. Various considerations about our model development are discussed in Section 8.6. In Section 8.7 we draw together the implications of the Inheritance Theorem for the study of animal behavior and argue that the inheritance of tactics in a conditional strategy is an important concept for understanding behavioral diversity. In Section 8.8 we summarize our study.

8.2 The Conditional Strategy

8.2.1 Defining Conditional Strategy and Alternative Tactics

We follow Gross's (1984, 1996) definition of strategy and tactic, and we define our notion of inheritance of alternative tactics within the framework outlined there. A *conditional strategy* is a genetically based program (decision rule) that results in the allocation of the somatic and reproductive effort of an organism (such as energy and development) among alternative phenotypes (tactics). A useful example is the allocation of reproductive effort into fighting versus sneaking. Much of the discussion in this chapter will be formulated in terms of the example of fighting versus sneaking. Of course, it applies to other situations as well. The conditional *strategy* operates through a mechanism (physiological, neurological, or developmental) that detects appropriate cues and puts the strategy's decision rule into effect; for example, to fight when larger than some switchpoint x and to sneak when smaller. Fighting and sneaking are the alternative *tactics* within the strategy, and they usually have associated behavioral, morphological, physiological, and life-history features by which they can be distinguished.

8.2.2 Model

Conditional strategy models have been developed in different contexts and different forms by many people (e.g., Ghiselin 1974; Charnov & Bull 1977; West-Eberhard 1979, 1989; Dawkins 1980; Maynard Smith 1982; Parker 1982, 1984; Warner 1988; Milinski & Parker 1991; Gross 1996). We follow here the conditional strategy model presented by Gross (1996) (Fig. 8.1). Individuals in the population vary in their status (e.g., relative size, condition, etc.) and thus in their relative competitive ability in using phenotypic tactics. Imagine two tactics, fight or sneak, for which status is determined by relative body size. In Fig. 8.1a, individuals vary in status from low to high, such that larger individuals are on the right of the graph and smaller on the left. The positive slopes of fitness with respect to status, for the fighting and sneaking tactics, indicate that the fitnesses of both tactics (in this example) are positively status-dependent. Where the two fitness functions intersect, the fitnesses from fighting and sneaking are equal, and this represents the ESS switchpoint s^* between the two tactics (Parker 1982, Repka & Gross 1995; also see Brown, this volume). Individuals greater than s^* in status should fight, and those less than s^* in status should sneak. Thus we have two phenotypes in the population, F (fighters) and S (sneakers), determined by the switchpoint s^*.

The population as a whole is divided into two groups according to their expressed tactic (Fig. 8.1b). A proportion p of the individuals are of tactic F, and a proportion $1-p$ are individuals of tactic S. In this case, individuals of tactic F are larger in body size than individuals of tactic S, since body size was the status cue used by the strategy.

Note that individuals of tactic F have higher average fitness than individuals of tactic S (superimposing the results of Fig. 8.1b onto Fig. 8.1a provides a means for locating the average fitnesses shown in Fig. 8.1a). Alternative tactics in a conditional strategy do not have equal average fitnesses within the population. Instead, the conditional strategy has an ESS switchpoint, and each individual expresses the tactic which maximizes its individual fitness. Adopting a sneaker tactic, even if it has less average fitness in the population, is evolutionarily stable if those individuals that become sneakers obtain higher fitness through sneaking than they can through fighting (Gross 1984). This difference in average tactic fitnesses, together with the fact that individuals are choosing their tactics based on their status, are two important features distinguishing a conditional strategy from a mixed ESS and ESSt.

The conditional strategy, therefore, has several important types of parameters. One is average fitnesses of the alternative tactics. A second is the frequencies of the alternative tactics in the population. The purpose of this chapter is to introduce a third type of parameter, namely, inheritance of the alternative tactics. If (a) status is heritable, perhaps because of additive genetic variance in the population for body

(a)

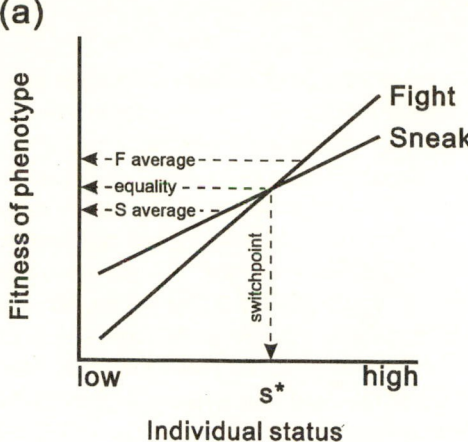

(b)

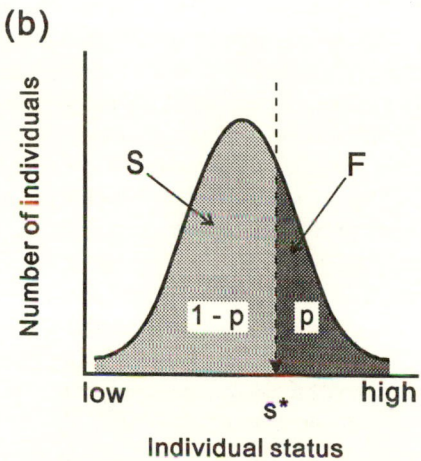

Figure 8.1. In a conditional strategy (Gross 1996), fitnesses of the alternative tactics vary with individual status, and the ESS switchpoint s* exists where the fitnesses of the alternatives are equal. (a) Individuals larger than s* should fight (F), smaller than s* should sneak (S). (b) This divides the population into two proportions, p being the fighters and $(1 - p)$ being the sneakers.

size, (b) individuals of tactic F overproduce F offspring and S individuals overproduce S offspring, relative to each other, and (c) individuals of tactic F produce, on average, more offspring relative to individuals of phenotype S, will the conditional strategy be stable? Specifically, is it possible to have a conditional strategy with inheritance of alternative tactics that differ in average fitnesses? This is the question we address in this study.

8.2.3 Inheritance

There are at least three types of inheritance associated with the conditional strategy in Fig. 8.1 (see also West-Eberhard 1992). First, the definition that the conditional strategy is a genetically based program implies that one or more genes underlie the decision process. It is generally presumed that all individuals within the population share the same conditional strategy and thus the same strategy gene(s). In other words, the population is genetically monomorphic for the decision mechanism and the switchpoint. However, in reality, complete monomorphism is unlikely to be achieved. For instance, the strategy's decision-making mechanism requires appropriate machinery, such as nerves, glands, and hormones. These proximate mechanisms will be coded genetically. Thus, there will be genetic variance in the switchpoint, due to background mutation across the gene loci coding for the proximate mechanisms. Furthermore, there will be movement of the fitness functions for F and S in Fig. 8.1a due to fluctuating or shifting environmental conditions that affect tactic fitnesses (e.g., predators, parasites, disease, food, temperature). In addition, Mendelian shuffling of alleles during reproduction will churn the genetic variance into many different combinations. Therefore, not all individuals in a real population would be expected to switch between fighting and sneaking at exactly the same status or size. Some may switch at sizes slightly above or below s^*.

The amount of variance around the ESS switchpoint will depend on many factors, including the number of loci involved in the proximate machinery, changes in the fitness functions (which move the ESS s^*), population size, generation time, and the overall mutation-selection balance. The conditional strategy will therefore show some heritability in the population for its switchpoint. A recent empirical example is given by Emlen (1996). The essential idea is that the alternative tactics are regulated by a single conditional strategy which has evolved because it dictates the expression of the tactics in a manner that maximizes the strategy's fitness, even if the biological reality includes some variance around the switchpoint.

A second form of inheritance emerges from the genes that underlie the proximate mechanisms that comprise the tactics themselves. For example, fighting and sneaking tactics may each have a set of genes that code for their phenotypes. If fighting involves antlers, then genes for antlers must exist, and if sneaking involves being cryptic, then genes for being cryptic must exist. The conditional strategy determines whether fighting or sneaking is expressed, and the genes for the appropriate tactic build the phenotype. Again, there may be variance among individuals in these genes, and therefore there will be heritability for the details of the alternative tactics. It is generally assumed, in conditional strategy models, that all individuals in the population share the same tactic phenotype and thus tactic genes. However, biological reality is that there will be genetic variance in tactic expression.

There is a third source of genetic variance. The conditional strategy evolves because individuals differ in their phenotypic state and the resulting status and ability to obtain fitness from a particular action (Fig. 8.1a). We suggest that this difference in status among individuals will often be due to additive genetic variance in the population. For example, at maturity, individuals in a population will be a variety of sizes (Fig. 8.1b) due in part to additive genetic variance in growth rate, which arises from the multitude of loci that underlie a complex trait such as body size. Body size is determined by a large number of genes, including those involved in foraging, metabolism, disease control, temperature tolerance, skeletal properties, and developmental timing. The alleles at these loci are subject to mutation-selection balance, shifting selection pressures, and Mendelian stirring. It is not surprising that in virtually all populations examined, biologists find heritability for body size (Falconer 1989). Therefore, if the conditional strategy dictates that larger individuals will fight and smaller individuals will sneak, the fighters will overproduce fighters and the sneakers will overproduce sneakers, among their offspring. It is this third source of genetic variance which is the primary topic of our chapter.

Although the conditional strategy is usually thought to be free of tactic inheritance, the very nature of the conditional strategy may, in fact, "shelter" inheritance. An alternative tactic often evolves because it provides fitness for a less competitive individual in the system. For instance, if competitively inferior individuals are sneakers, and competitive superiority is partly determined by genetic quality, then the alleles which reduce quality are not purged from the population at the same rate as in a nonconditional strategy (cf. Roff 1994). Therefore, contrary to general expectations, heritability for the alternative tactics within a conditional strategy may be quite common and strong. This inheritance of the alternative tactics has not previously been considered in modeling the conditional strategy.

In summary, in this study we use the term *inheritance* to refer to the probability that offspring will express the tactic of their fathers. This probability occurs through the inheritance of status (the cue used in the strategy's decision—for example, body size). We assume that the population is genetically monomorphic for the strategy's switchpoint, we ignore heritable variance in the tactic structures themselves, and we model how inheritance of the probability of expressing a tactic influences the conditional strategy.

8.3 A New Model

We model a population that has a conditional strategy with two male tactics, fighter (F) phenotypes, and sneaker (S) phenotypes (cf. Fig. 8.1). In this section we show how tactic inheritance from father to son, together with tactic frequency and tactic fitness, set bounds on the conditional strategy. In Section 8.4 we prove that the strategy has an equilibrium within these bounds.

Our model has been designed to (a) show the relationships among the parameters that comprise a conditional strategy and (b) test whether a conditional strategy with inheritance can have an equilibrium. The model can, of course, be extended further. For instance, our model is discrete—we treat the average individuals within the sneak and fight tactics—while the population is continuous. It is our impression that the conclusions of our model would not be altered in the continuous case. Our model is also not a formal genetic model. For instance, we do not assume any particular genetic mechanism underlying status and its inheritance within the population. We have not assumed any particular flow of genes among females and males when they mate, nor have we allowed for any particular interaction among genes, such as between the genes of females of low status with those of males of high status or between the genes for status and those for the strategy itself. We have instead modeled the population's genetic and mating structure quite simply, by defining inheritance in terms of the proportion of a progeny-type to come from each male tactic *on average*. This seems a rather robust approach, although it will be subject to factors that can affect averages. We believe that we have captured the basic aspects of inheritance through our definition, although a formal genetic model would be welcome.

8.3.1 Population and Strategy Parameters

We define the structure of the population in terms of its tactic frequencies, tactic fitnesses, and tactic inheritances. First, let the proportions of fighters F and sneakers S be p and $1-p$, respectively, with $0<p<1$ (both tactics are present). Second, let r_F be the number of offspring from F fathers which reach maturity and let r_S be the number of offspring from S fathers which reach maturity (subscripts refer to the father, not offspring). We use these "recruitment" values (r_F and r_S) as our measure of fitness. As required for a conditional strategy, both r_F and r_S are nonzero. Third, among the maturing offspring from F fathers, let i_F be the proportion that are F; and among the maturing offspring from S fathers, let i_S be the proportion that are F. Then a proportion $1-i_F$ of the offspring from F fathers are S and a proportion $1-i_S$ of the offspring from S fathers are S. We use these "inheritance" values (i_F and i_S) as our measure of heritability. For mathematical ease, we deal with the case where i_F and i_S are neither 0 nor 1; accordingly, both phenotypes produce both types of recruit and we investigate how a heritable bias in recruit type affects the conditional strategy.

Table 8.1 summarizes the three types of parameters in our model: tactic frequency p, recruitment or tactic fitness r, and tactic inheritance or heritability i. These three types together have five fundamental parameters, p, r_F, r_S, i_F, and i_S, the interrelationships of which define the population and the conditional strategy. The frequency of sneakers $(1-p)$ is not considered to be a fundamental parameter, since it is determined by the frequency of fighters p (knowing the frequency of either tactic determines the other). The model we develop is static; we assume that the five parameters are constant.

For mathematical convenience, so that we don't have to keep track of the total population size, we normalize so that the total population size at maturity is 1. Each F father has r_F offspring reaching maturity; since the proportion of F fathers in the population is p, the total number of offspring from F fathers which reach maturity is pr_F. Similarly, the total number of offspring from S fathers which reach maturity is $(1-p)r_S$. When we normalize the number of offspring reaching maturity within the population as a whole, we get the condition that

$$\textit{normalization condition: } pr_F+(1-p)r_S=1 \tag{1}$$

Note that condition (1) is a mathematical convenience; in particular, we do not restrict our model to a fixed population size across generations.

8.3.2 The Equilibrium Condition

To say that the strategy is at equilibrium means that the proportions of the two tactic phenotypes, F and S, remain constant across generations. Among the pr_F offspring

Table 8.1 The Three Types of Parameters and the Five Fundamental
Parameters That Define a Conditional Strategy with Two Tactics—For
Example, Fight and Sneak

Tactic	Frequency (p)	Recruitment (r)	Inheritance (i)
		Parameter Type	
Fight (F)	p	r_F	i_F
Sneak (S)	$(1-p)*$	r_S	i_S

*Not a fundamental parameter.

from F fathers, a proportion i_F are of type F. So F fathers contribute $pr_F i_F$ offspring of type F to the next generation. Similarly, S fathers contribute $(1-p)r_S i_S$ offspring of type F to the next generation. Within the population as a whole, the number of F offspring reaching maturity in the next generation is $pr_F i_F + (1-p)r_S i_S$. In a population at equilibrium, this must exactly replace the F individuals in the original population, of whom there are p. Therefore, the equilibrium condition is

$$equilibrium\ condition:\ pr_F i_F + (1-p)r_S i_S = p \tag{2}$$

Note that condition (2)—that the tactic proportions remain unchanged from one generation to the next—is the crux of our analysis. We assume that (2) holds and we then consider the consequences for tactic inheritance, recruitment, and frequency within the population.

8.3.3 Allowable Values for Recruitment, Inheritance and Frequency

We now show that the model parameters r, i, and p can only exist within certain restricted ranges as determined by equilibrium condition (2). First, we assume that F is the phenotype with higher fecundity; that is, $r_F > 1$ (the F phenotype produces to maturity more offspring than average). From normalization condition (1), it follows that the S phenotype must produce fewer offspring than average. Furthermore, we can see from (1) that pr_F must be less than 1 and thus $r_F < 1/p$. Therefore, the allowable values for recruitment r and frequency p are as follows:

$$recruitment\ and\ frequency\ restrictions:\ 0 < r_S < 1 < r_F < 1/p \tag{3}$$

Next, we assume that there is tactic inheritance, that is, $p < i_F$. This means that the F phenotype overproduces F offspring. From equilibrium condition (2), it follows that the S phenotype must underproduce F offspring. We can therefore write that in a population at equilibrium, the allowable values for inheritance i and frequency p are as follows:

$$inheritance\ and\ frequency\ restrictions:\ 0 < i_S < p < i_F < 1 \tag{4}$$

Finally, we consider the relationship among recruitment r, inheritance i, and frequency p. Since the total number of F offspring from an F father in one generation is $i_F r F$, and in a population at equilibrium this cannot exceed 1, then $i_F r_F < 1$, so $r_F < 1/i_F$ and $i_F < 1/r_F$. Combining these observations with restrictions (3) and (4), we find that r, i, and p are related by

$$1 < r_F < 1/i_F < 1/p \tag{5}$$

and

$$p < i_F < 1/r_F < 1 \tag{6}$$

Restriction (5) shows how the allowable values of the recruitment parameter r_F are restricted by the inheritance i_F, which is itself limited by frequency p. Specifically, the larger p is, the larger must be the value of i_F. Yet the larger the value of i_F, the narrower is the allowable range for r_F. Restriction (6) shows that parameter p and parameter r_F impose specific bounds on the value of the inheritance parameter i_F. In a population, a high fitness differential is incompatible with high inheritance. Specifically, the larger r_F is, the narrower is the allowable range for i_F. The allowable range for i_F also decreases with an increase in its phenotypic frequency p. A similar set of constraints can be found by deriving the limits for the parameters of phenotype S. The main point is that the three parameters, r, i, and p, constrain one another's allowable range within their own phenotypes. Thus, there are only certain allowable sets of parameter values, due to the conditions (1) and (2) and due to the inherent relationships among the parameters themselves. These relationships help to mathematically define the conditional strategy.

8.3.4 Relating Recruitment, Inheritance, and Frequency Across Phenotypes

A further mathematical feature of the conditional strategy is the existence of specific relationships that bind the parameters of the two alternative tactics. Specifically, the values of the parameters describing recruitment and inheritance for one tactic are related to the values for the other. From normalization condition (1) we find the following relationship:

$$recruitment\ across\ phenotypes:\ r_S = (1 - p r_F)\ /\ (1 - p) \tag{7}$$

Substituting (7) into equilibrium condition (2) gives

$$p r_F i_F + (1 - p r_F) i_S = p$$

Rearranging and solving for i_S, we find the relationship

$$inheritance\ across\ phenotypes:\ i_S = p(1 - r_F i_F)/(1 - p r_F) \tag{8}$$

It is of course possible to find analogous formulas expressing r_F and i_F in terms of r_S and i_S.

8.3.5 Other Relations

Here we present formulas which express each parameter in terms of the others. The formulas are all derived from previous formulas by simple algebraic manipulations. In general, any choice of three of the five parameters p, r_S, r_F, i_S and i_F will determine the remaining two, with the exception of the three parameters p, r_S, and r_F which, because they are already related by condition (1), do not contain enough information to determine i_S and i_F. Thus, one of the three parameters chosen from the set of five must be i_S or i_F.

The following formulas demonstrate the ability of our model to describe the conditional strategy. They also provide a useful tool for biologists studying the conditional strategy as discussed in Section 8.7.

Rearranging (1) to solve for p, we find

$$p = (1 - r_S)/(r_F - r_S) \tag{9}$$

Substituting (7) into (2) and rearranging to solve for p, we see that

$$p = i_S/(1 - r_F(i_F - i_S)) \tag{10}$$

Rearranging (1) to solve for r_F, we find

$$r_F = (1 - (1 - p)r_S)/p \tag{11}$$

Substituting (7) into (2) and rearranging to solve for i_F, we find

$$i_F = (p - (1 - pr_F)i_S)/pr_F \tag{12}$$

Substituting (7) into (2) gives $pr_F i_F + (1 - pr_F)i_S = p$, from which we find

$$r_F = (p - i_S)/(p(i_F - i_S)) \tag{13}$$

From (10) we find

$$p - pr_F (i_F - i_S) = i_S$$

Substituting for r_F from (11), we get

$$p - (1 - (1 - p)r_S)(i_F - i_S) = i_S, \quad \text{so } p(1 - r_S(i_F - i_S)) = i_S + i_F - i_S - r_S(i_F - i_S)$$

Solving for p, we find

$$p = (i_F - r_S(i_F - i_S))/(1 - r_S(i_F - i_S)) \tag{14}$$

Rearranging (14) to solve for r_S, we find

$$r_S = (i_F - p)/((1 - p)(i_F - i_S)) \tag{15}$$

Finally, substituting (11) into (12) gives

$$i_F = (p - (1 - p)r_S i_S)/(1 - (1 - p)r_S) \tag{16}$$

8.3.6 Model Summary

We have described in this section the necessary mathematical relationships to incorporate tactic inheritance into the conditional strategy (cf. Fig. 8.1). We have shown mathematically how tactic inheritance is related to tactic fitness and tactic frequency within the population. For convenience, Table 8.2 summarizes the principal conditions and formulas of our model. In the next section we introduce an Inheritance Theorem and use the relationships we have described in this section to prove that a conditional strategy can exist.

8.4 The Inheritance Theorem

The model developed in Section 8.3 allows us to address the question of inheritance of tactics in the conditional strategy. This leads to a new Inheritance Theorem.

INHERITANCE THEOREM   *A conditional strategy with heritable alternative tactics can be in equilibrium.*

Specifically, inheritance is one of three types of parameters which define the conditional strategy: tactic proportion p; tactic recruitment r_F, r_S; and tactic inheritance i_F, i_S. These five parameters interact subject to the conditions given in Table 8.3. When these conditions are met, there is a unique

Table 8.2 Summary of the Model

	Phenotypes (Tactics)	
	F (fighter)	S (sneaker)
Proportion (p) in population	p = proportion of fighter individuals $(0 < p < 1)$	$1 - p$ = proportion of sneaker individuals $(0 < 1 - p < 1)$
Inheritance (i) of F phenotype	i_F = proportion of offspring of F fathers that are F	i_S = proportion of offspring of S fathers that are F
Recruitment (r) to adulthood	r_F = average number of recruits from F fathers	r_S = average number of recruits from S fathers
Allowable values	$1 < r_F < 1/i_F < 1/p$ (5) $p < i_F < 1/r_F < 1$ (6)	$0 < i_S < p < i_F < 1$ (4) $0 < r_S < 1 < r_F < 1/p$ (3)
Relations across phenotypes	$r_F = (1 - (1-p)r_S)/p$ (11) $r_F = (p - i_S)/(p(i_F - i_S))$ (13) $i_F = (p - (1-p)r_S i_S)/(1 - (1-p)r_S)$ (16)	$r_S = (1 - pr_F)/(1-p)$ (7) $r_S = (i_F - p)/((1-p)(i_F - i_S))$ (15) $i_S = p(1 - r_F i_F)/(1 - pr_F)$ (8)

Table 8.3 Model Parameters, Allowable Conditions, and Solutions

Choice of Three Specified Parameters	Allowability Conditions	Equations to Solve for Remaining Two Parameters
1. p, r_F, i_F	$p < i_F < 1/r_F < 1$	(7), (8)
2. p, r_F, i_S	$0 < i_S < p < 1/r_F < 1$	(12), (7)
3. p, r_S, i_F	$0 < r_S < 1, 0 < p < 1,$ $p < i_F < p/(1-(1-p)r_S)$	(11), (8)
4. p, r_S, i_S	$0 < r_S < 1,$ $0 < i_S < p < 1$	(11), (12)
5. p, i_S, i_F	$0 < i_S < p < i_F < 1,$ $p - i_S > p(i_F - i_S)$	(13), (7)
6. r_F, r_S, i_F	$(1-r_S)/(r_F - r_S) < i_F$ $< 1/r_F < 1,$ $0 < r_S < 1$	(9), (8)
7. r_F, r_S, i_S	$0 < r_S < 1 < r_F,$ $0 < i_S <$ $(1-r_S)/(r_F - r_S)$	(9), (12)
8. r_F, i_F, i_S	$0 < i_S <$ $i_S/(1 - r_F(i_F - i_S))$ $< i_F < 1/r_F < 1$	(10), (7)
9. r_S, i_F, i_S	$0 < r_S < 1,$ $0 < i_S < i_F < 1$	(14), (11)

conditional strategy satisfying equilibrium condition (2) that the tactic proportions remain unchanged across generations.

PROOF OF THE INHERITANCE THEOREM   Table 8.3 lists all the possible choices of three parameters, displaying for each choice the allowability conditions that apply to them. The last column lists the formulas needed in each case to solve for the remaining two parameters. To prove the theorem, we show that the values resulting from the formulas in Table 8.3 satisfy the equilibrium condition (2), and moreover are allowable, meaning that they satisfy conditions (3) through (6). This proof is provided in Appendix 8.1.

A consequence of the Inheritance Theorem is that for any choice of three parameters satisfying the relevant conditions, solving for the remaining two will result in a set of values for all five parameters that is consistent with all the requirements of a conditional strategy.

8.5 Exploring the Conditions

In this section we graphically explore the structure of a conditional strategy with inheritance. We show the potential shape or bounds of the conditional strategy as determined by possible values of tactic inheritance, tactic fitness, and tactic frequency. These possible values are set by the conditions in Tables 8.2 and 8.3.

Figure 8.2 shows how the values of tactic inheritance i are related to those of tactic recruitment r, for specified values of tactic frequency p. The graphs show the possible

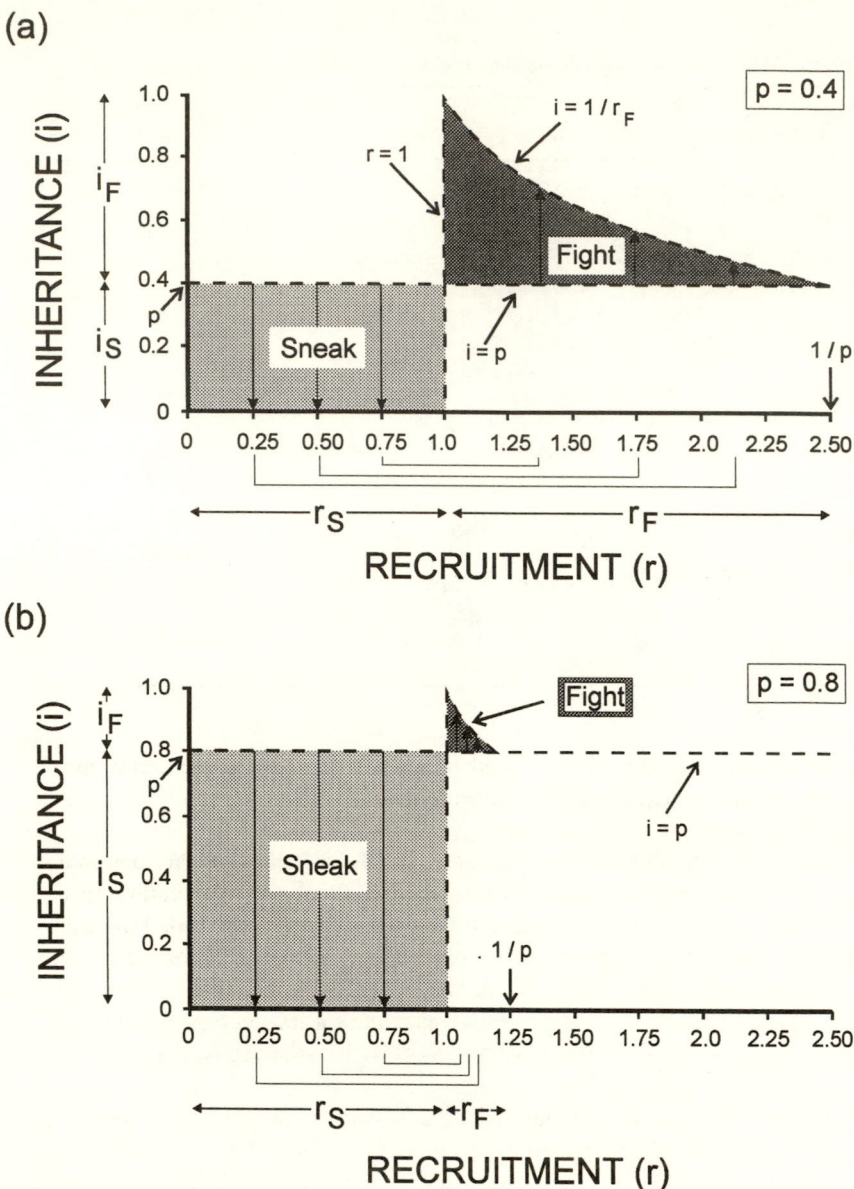

Figure 8.2. The structure of a conditional strategy with two tactics, fight (F) and sneak (S). The structure of the tactics is defined by five parameters of three types: tactic frequency (p), tactic recruitment (r), and tactic inheritance (i). The graphical representation is of the allowable relationship among the parameters, shown for two values of p, $p = 0.4$ (8.2a) and $p = 0.8$ (8.2b). The allowable values of r_F and i_F for tactic F are in the dark space, while the allowable values of r_S and i_S for tactic S are in the light space.

Equations (7) and (8) determine r_S and i_S. From (7) we also see that as r_F ranges from 1 up to $1/p$, r_S ranges backward from 1 down to 0 in the same proportion. The brackets at the bottom of each graph link corresponding values of r_F and r_S.

For a given value of r_F, i_F can range from p up to $1/r_F$. As it does this, (8) shows values for the parameters, given the constraints that exist both within and between the tactics of a conditional strategy in equilibrium. In Fig. 8.2a, the dark shaded interior of the F tactic is its allowable space, and the light shaded interior of the S tactic is its allowable space, when the F tactic has a frequency of $p = 0.40$. Any possible value in the F tactic space can be matched with a value in the corresponding S tactic space to result in a conditional strategy. The inheritance i_F can have a wide range of values when r_F is small, but the range of possible values for i_F falls rapidly with increasing r_F. For instance, when r_F is near 1, i_F can range in value from nearly 0.40 (p) to about 1.0 ($1/r_F$), but when r_F is large, such as 2.0, the allowable range for i_F is small, $0.4 < i_F < 0.5$. This is because the high productivity of tactic F would result in an overproduction of F in the next generation if inheritance was high. It would be impossible for an "underproduction" of F offspring by the S tactic to compensate for the overproduction of F by the F tactic, if the inheritance of F offspring from the F tactic exceeded 0.5.

Now consider the relationship among the parameters in tactic S to those in tactic F. Because the total population size is normalized to be 1, increasing values of r_F are only possible with decreasing values of r_S. For each value of r_S, there is a range of possible values for i_S; the actual value of i_S will be determined by the value of i_F for which it must compensate.

Thus, the possible values of r_F, i_F, r_S, and i_S depend on each other and are circumscribed as shown in Fig. 8.2. Both the within-tactic and between-tactic parameter relationships will determine the final values of the conditional strategy; that is, the location within the shaded regions at which the inheritance and recruitment parameters, and thus the tactics, will be balanced.

Finally, consider the influence of tactic frequency p on the allowable inheritance and recruitment values (see Fig. 8.2.b, where $p = 0.8$). When the F tactic is quite common (i.e., p is large), the allowable ranges for the values of i_F and r_F become very small. This is because the F tactic has a large total effect due to its high frequency in the population. In contrast, the allowable ranges for the parameters i_S and r_S for the rare S tactic become quite large. As the graph shows, a small change in i_F or r_F can be offset only by a large change in i_S or r_S. Thus, Fig. 8.2 demonstrates through numerical example that each type of parameter—tactic fitness r, tactic inheritance i, and tactic frequency p— imposes substantial bounds on the values of the other parameters and thus on the final structure of the conditional strategy.

8.6 Modeling Considerations

Although our model analyzes fitness using the recruitment (r) of progeny into the next generation, the existence of inheritance (i) introduces an additional consideration

---

that i_S ranges down from p to 0, as shown by the arrowheads. The further i_F is above p, the further i_S must be below p to compensate. If i_F and i_S both equal p, there is no heritability and the production of offspring types is random within each tactic.

With an increase in p from 0.4 (Fig. 8.2a) to 0.8 (Fig. 8.2b), the allowable range in values for the F tactic decreases. The narrowed range in F corresponds to a wide allowable range in S. Thus, a small change in r_F or i_F is mirrored by a large change in r_S or i_S.

for the calculation of fitness beyond a single generation. Consider, for instance, that an individual of the F tactic will not only produce more recruits into the next generation ($r_F > r_S$), but because of inheritance ($i_F > p$) a disproportionate number of these recruits will also be of the F tactic and will produce more recruits into their next generation. An individual of the F tactic, therefore, not only produces more recruits into the next generation, but also produces more grand-recruits, and so on. Inheritance causes the single-generation fitness advantage of the F tactic to compound. Conversely, an individual of the S tactic has a compounding fitness disadvantage. Although this compounding of fitness is an important aspect of interpreting the relative fitnesses of alternative tactics in a conditional strategy, it does not affect the parameter values modeled here and thus we leave its consideration for future work.

In developing our model, we have used r_F and r_S to represent the numbers of offspring reaching maturity, or recruitment, into the adult stage. It is also possible to express these quantities as the product of the number of births and their survivorship. For instance, it might be that the number of births is equal between F and S tactics, but that the survivorship to maturity of their progeny differs. It turns out that this does not affect our analysis, but it may be of interest to biologists to pursue such calculations in a particular system.

Another natural direction would be to build a model that includes status as an explicit variable and therefore attempt to locate the specific status at which the switchpoint resides. This could lead to further explorations of the conditional strategy, including its progression, its stability, and its sensitivity.

Our model has been developed under the assumption that $i_F > p$; that is, the F tactic produces more F recruits among its offspring than the S tactic. Other inheritance schemes are certainly possible, but they would not affect the conclusions and this seems to be the most natural case.

We have treated the additive variance in status as due to classical additive genetic variance. We also note, however, that the inheritance in our model is not restricted to genetics: cultural or environmentally induced inheritance, such as each tactic resulting in different nursery locations with different growth rates, will have similar effects. Thus, the conclusions of our model apply to heritabilities which are genetic, cultural, and environmental in origin.

8.7 Discussion

Game theory in animal behavior has largely overlooked important biological processes such as inheritance and phenotype development [see discussions by Austad (1984) and by Caro & Bateson (1986); also see Hammerstein and Gomulkiewicz, both in this volume]. Moreover, the focus on the mixed ESS and the ESSt has generally ignored variance in the phenotype. Selection arising from phenotypic variance gives rise to the conditional strategy and its ESS s^*, perhaps the most relevant biological application of game theory for understanding behavioral diversity (Gross 1996). We have shown that it is possible to incorporate biological processes such as inheritance into an analysis of the conditional strategy and that the incorporation enriches our understanding of how animal behaviors may evolve.

The legacy of game theory modeling without genetics gives the general impression that the conditional strategy has no heritable variance. Thus, when inheritance of alternative phenotypes is found, the phenotypes are usually interpreted in the context of an ESSt (e.g., Shuster & Wade 1991, Lank et al. 1995) rather than a conditional strategy. In our view, the complexity of the conditional strategy ensures an increased likelihood that an offspring expresses the tactic of its father—that is, heritability of its expression—and thus many of the proposed ESSt examples may in fact be conditional strategies. One important source of inheritance is additive genetic variance in an individual's status relative to the switchpoint, as discussed here. The inheritance of status is itself a form of "noise" in the system. However, this noise is a biological property that, because it generates variance in the phenotype, is a foundation for a conditional strategy to evolve upon. Our model shows, for a two-state situation, that in the presence of tactic inheritance, a conditional strategy can be in equilibrium.

Our model allows the biologist to make precise predictions about tactic frequency p, recruitment r, and inheritance i. Our model shows how the five parameters that define the tactics of a conditional strategy are related to each other and, through this relationship, define the shape of the conditional strategy. For instance, for any fixed frequency of the alternative tactics in the population, the greater the recruitment differential, the smaller must be the heritability of the favored tactic (Fig. 8.2). On the other hand, if the average recruitment of the tactics is similar, then a wide range of theoretically possible inheritances exists for the tactics. If p is large, it will be difficult to detect significant inheritance of the fight tactic among offspring from F fathers, but the inheritance of the sneak tactic among offspring from S fathers can be high. Conversely, if p is small, it could be relatively easy to find inheritance of the fight tactic among offspring from F fathers, while inheritance of the fight tactic from S fathers will be low. Our analysis therefore helps to define the influence of inheritance on the expression of the alternative tactics in a conditional strategy. More specifically, knowing any three of the five parameters (one parameter must be inheritance, either i_F or i_S), the other two parameters can be derived, reducing measurement work for the biologist.

As an example of how our model can be applied to an actual biological situation, consider a case of alternative male mating tactics with inheritance. In certain mites, some males develop into fighters while others develop into nonfighters, which we will call sneakers. An interesting study by Radwan (1995) reported that in *Rhizoglyphus robini*, 76.3% of the male progeny of fighter males mature into fighters, while only 35.1% of the male progeny of sneaker males mature into the fighter phenotype, a statistically significant bias in production of fighter offspring. He also reports that 66.9% of males in the population are of the fighter phenotype. Knowing these three parameters—i_F, i_S, and p—allows us to answer two important questions about the mite system with our conditional strategy model: (1) Does the significant inheritance of alternative tactics preclude the existence of a conditional strategy in the mite population? (2) What are the fitnesses of the alternative male phenotypes in the mite population? To answer the first question, we note that the information available satisfies the allowability condition in Table 8.2, namely, condition (4). Thus, the significant inheritance of the alternative tactics in the mite system is allowable within a conditional strategy. Although the significant heritability of the alternative phenotypes would appear to suggest the possibility of a genetic polymorphism and an ESSt for these mites, our analysis shows that the mite system could just as well have evolved as a conditional strategy with an ESS switchpoint s^*.

To answer the second question, we extract from Table 8.2 the formulas for r_F and r_S. Substituting, we find that $r_F = 1.15$ and $r_S = 0.69$. This shows that the fighter phenotype has considerably greater recruitment into the next generation than does the sneaker phenotype $((1.15 - 0.69)/0.69 = 67\%$ higher recruitment) (we note that it is possible to calculate the fitness compounding due to inheritance, and if this is done, the compounded fitness of fighters is 1.23 and the compounded fitness of sneakers is 0.55, more than a twofold difference). Assuming that the mite population is in equilibrium, and that the mite sample is an accurate description of the population, then our calculation of unequal fitnesses shows that the two morphs are unlikely to coexist as a genetic polymorphism.

Finally, our analysis of a conditional strategy helps to explain why, for this mite system, the proportion of fighter males increases when food resources, and thus male body size, are experimentally increased (Radwan 1995).

8.8 Summary

Many alternative phenotypes in the behavior and life history of organisms are alternative tactics in a conditional strategy. Classic game-theoretic modeling (e.g., Maynard Smith 1982) has not provided a sufficient framework for understanding the evolution of alternative tactics because it has generally ignored inheritance and phenotypic variance. Gross (1996) has recently modeled the conditional strategy in terms of two types of parameters: (a) the status of an individual determines the fitnesses of alternative tactics and (b) the frequencies of the tactics in the population affect their fitnesses. Repka & Gross (1995) showed that the status and frequency fitness functions will result in a stable switchpoint or ESS s^* for the conditional strategy. In this chapter we now demonstrate how inheritance of the alternative tactics affects the conditional strategy (Fig. 8.1).

Our model provides a new Inheritance Theorem for the conditional strategy. This theorem specifies the conditions that are necessary for the conditional strategy to be at equilibrium when the alternative tactics are heritable—that is, when the tactic adopted by an offspring is correlated to the tactic adopted by its father. We show that a conditional strategy can persist at equilibrium under a wide range of possible inheritance values (Tables 8.2 and 8.3). Moreover, we show mathematically how tactic inheritance, tactic fitness, and tactic frequency will together determine the bounds of the conditional strategy. An increase in tactic inheritance, for example, decreases the potential difference in recruitment among the tactics. The tactics within a conditional strategy are therefore circumscribed by relationships that exist among tactic inheritance, recruitment, and frequency. We illustrate this graphically in Fig. 8.2.

It is traditional for game-theoretic analyses to ignore inheritance of alternative phenotypes (e.g., mixed ESS) or to treat alternative phenotypes as "like begets like" (e.g., ESSt). However, inheritance of alternative tactics is likely a widespread property of nature and is a natural expectation of a conditional strategy, and its analysis can tell us interesting things about how biological systems operate. Biologists can use our formulas to derive information about several interesting properties of their systems without having to measure each independently. We calculate, for instance, the recruitment for a mite system with two alternative tactics, fight and sneak, given only inheritance and frequency data (Radwan 1995). We suggest that the mite system may be stable as a conditional strategy, despite the high inheritance of its alternative tactics. This conclusion differs from that suggested by classical perspectives of game-theoretic modeling.

ACKNOWLEDGMENTS   This chapter grew from a question about stability with inheritance raised by Curtis Eaton (Department of Economics, Simon Fraser University) at the August 1995 Game Theory Conference in Waterloo, Canada. Dr. Eaton suggested a way for us to think about the answer and we appreciate his insight.

For suggestions and help we thank Luca Cargnelli, Lee Dugatkin, Doug Emlen, David Houle, Bryan Neff, Jacek Radwan, Kern Reeve, Peter Taylor, and Franyo Weissing. Drs. Taylor and Weissing provided valuable suggestions on our modeling technique, and Dr. Radwan generously shared his mite data.

This study was supported by research grants from the Natural Sciences and Engineering Research Council of Canada to the authors.

References

Austad, S. N. 1984. A classification of alternative reproductive behaviors and methods for field-testing ESS models. *Am. Zool.,* 24, 309–319.

Caro, T. M. & Bateson, P. 1986. Organization and ontogeny of alternative tactics. *Anim. Behav.,* 34, 1483–1499.

Charnov, E. L. 1993. *Life History Invariants: Some Explanations of Symmetry in Evolutionary Ecology.* New York: Oxford University Press.

Charnov, E. L. & Bull, J. J. 1977. When is sex environmentally determined? *Nature,* 266, 828–830.

Dawkins, R. 1980. Good strategy or evolutionarily stable strategy? In *Sociobiology: Beyond Nature/Nurture,* G. W. Barlow & J. Silverberg, eds., pp. 331–367. Boulder, CO: Westview Press.

Emlen, D. J. 1996. Artificial selection on horn length-body size allometry in the horned beetle *Onthophagus acuminatus* (Coleoptera: Scarabaeidae). *Evolution,* 50, 1219–1230.

Falconer, D. S. 1981. *An Introduction to Quantitative Genetics.* New York: Longman House.

Ghiselin, M. T. 1974. *The Economy of Nature and the Evolution of Sex.* Berkeley: University of California Press.

Gross, M. R. 1984. Sunfish, salmon, and the evolution of alternative reproductive strategies and tactics in fishes. In *Fish Reproduction: Strategies and Tactics,* R. Wootton & G. Potts eds., pp. 55–75. London: Academic Press.

Gross, M. R. 1996. Alternative reproductive strategies and tactics: Diversity within sexes. *Trends Ecol. Evol.,* 11, 92–98.

Lank, D. B., Smith, C. M., Hannotte, O., Burke, T., & Cooke, F. 1995. Genetic polymorphism for alternative mating behavior in lekking male ruff, *Philomachus pugnax. Nature,* 378, 59–62.

Maynard Smith, J. 1982. *Evolution and the Theory of Games.* Cambridge: Cambridge University Press.

Maynard Smith, J. 1989. *Evolutionary Genetics*. Oxford: Oxford University Press.

Milinski, M. & Parker, G. A. 1991. Competition for resources. In *Behavioural Ecology: An Evolutionary Approach*, J. R. Krebs & N. B. Davies, eds., 3rd ed. pp. 137–168. Oxford: Blackwell Scientific Publications.

Parker, G. A. 1982. Phenotype-limited evolutionarily stable strategies. In Current *Problems in Sociobiology*, King's College Sociobiology Group, ed., pp. 173–201. New York: Cambridge University Press.

Parker, G. A. 1984. Evolutionarily stable strategies. In *Behavioral ecology: An evolutionary approach*, J. R. Krebs & N. B. Davies, eds., 3rd ed. pp. 30–61. Oxford: Blackwell Scientific Publications.

Radwan, J. 1995. Male morph determination in two species of acarid mites. *Heredity*, 74, 669–673.

Repka, J. & Gross, M. R. 1995. The evolutionarily stable strategy under individual condition and tactic frequency. *J. Theor. Biol.*, 176, 27–31.

Roff, D. A. 1994. Evolution of dimorphic traits: Effect of directional selection on heritability. *Heredity*, 72, 36–41.

Shuster, S. M. & Wade, M. J. 1991. Equal mating success among male reproductive strategies in a marine isopod. *Nature*, 350, 608–610.

Warner, R. R. 1988. Sex change and the size-advantage model. *Trends Ecol. Evol.*, 3, 133–136.

West-Eberhard, M. J. 1979. Sexual selection, social competition, and evolution. *Proc. Am. Philos. Soc.*, 123, 222–234.

West-Eberhard, M. J. 1989. Phenotypic plasticity and the origins of diversity. *Annu. Rev. Ecol. Syst.*, 20, 249–278.

West-Eberhard, M. J. 1992. Behavior and evolution. In *Molds, Molecules and Metazoa: Growing Points in Evolutionary Biology*, P. R. Grant & H. S. Horn, eds., pp. 57–75. Princeton, NJ: Princeton University Press.

Appendix 8.1 Proof of the Inheritance Theorem

Since the equations in the third column of Table 8.3 are derived from equilibrium condition (2), it is evident that the resulting values must satisfy (2).

The remainder of this proof is devoted to showing that the resulting values are allowable, namely, that they satisfy conditions (3) through (6).

The condition $1 < r_F < 1/p$ from (5) is equivalent to $p < pr_F < 1$. This, in turn, is equivalent to $1 - p > 1 - pr_F > 0$, or $0 < (1 - pr_F)/(1 - p) < 1$. This means that r_S as given by (7) satisfies $0 < r_S < 1$, showing that r_S satisfies (3). This means that the condition $1 < r_F < 1/p$ on r_F is equivalent to the condition (3), $0 < r_S < 1$, on r_S.

Similarly, the condition $p < i_F < 1/r_F$ is equivalent to $pr_F < r_F i_F < 1$, or $1 - pr_F > 1 - r_F i_F > 0$. This is equivalent to $0 < (1 - r_F i_F)/(1 - pr_F) < 1$, which says that $i_S = p(1 - r_F i_F)/(1 - pr_F)$ satisfies $0 < i_S < p$.

These equivalences prove that in cases 1–4 in Table 8.3, when the equations listed in the third column are used to solve for the remaining two parameters, the resulting values are allowable.

Equation (9) says $p = (1 - r_S)/(r_F - r_S)$. If $0 < r_S < 1$, then the resulting p satisfies $0 < p < 1$. This and the above remarks about the conditions on i_S and i_F are enough to handle cases 6 and 7.

For 8, we use (10) to find p, noting that the condition given in Table 8.3 implies that $i_S < p < i_F$. Then r_S is given by (7) and its allowability follows as before.

For case 5, we note that $p < i_F$ implies $pi_F - i_F i_S < pi_F - pi_S$, which shows that $i_F < p(i_F - i_S)/(p - i_S) = 1/r_F$. The second condition given in Table 8.3 for case 5 implies that $1/r_F < 1$. The allowability of r_S then follows as above.

For case 9 we note that $(1 - i_S)r_S < 1$, so $(1 - i_S)r_S(i_F - i_S) < i_F - i_S$. This shows $i_S - i_S r_S(i_F - i_S) < i_F - r_S(i_F - i_S)$, so $i_S < (i_F - r_S(i_F - i_S))/(1 - r_S(i_F - i_S)) = p$. Similarly, $i_F < 1$, so $i_F - r_S(i_F - i_S) < i_F - i_F r_S(i_F - i_S)$, so $p = (i_F - r_S(i_F - i_S))/(1 - r_S(i_F - i_S)) < i_F$.

Finally, since $i_F < 1$, we have $i_S < i_S/i_F$, so $1 - r_S(i_F - i_S) - r_S + r_S i_F < 1 - r_S + r_S(i_S/i_F)$. This implies that $1 - r_S(1 - i_F)/(1 - r_S(i_F - i_S)) < (i_F - r_S(i_F - i_S))/(i_F(1 - r_S(i_F - i_S)))$, which amounts to $1 - (1-p)r_S < p/i_F$, or $(1 - (1-p)r_S)/p < 1/i_F$. This last inequality says $r_F < 1/i_F$, the last condition needed for case 9.

This completes the proof of the Inheritance Theorem.

JOEL S. BROWN

Game Theory and Habitat Selection

9.1 Introduction

Evolution by natural selection comes in three flavors: density-independent, density-dependent, and frequency-dependent. Density-independent selection means that the fitness consequences of an organism's heritable traits remain uninfluenced by the population. In response to density-independent selection, natural selection produces adaptations maximizing population growth rates (Wright 1931, 1960). Density-dependent selection means that population size does influence the fitness consequences of an organism's traits. Density-dependent selection produces adaptations that maximize the population's size (Wright 1960, Roughgarden 1976). Frequency-dependent selection means that the fitness consequences of an individual's traits are influenced by others' traits and the frequency of particular traits within the population. Frequency-dependent selection produces adaptations, but these adaptations neither maximize population growth rates nor maximize sizes (Vincent & Brown 1984; Metz et al. 1992). Such adaptations can be evolutionarily stable and are called ESSs (evolutionarily stable strategies). Frequency-dependence creates the need for evolutionary game theory (see Hammerstein, this volume). Habitat selection, the study of how organisms assess and respond to habitat heterogeneity, is frequency-dependent; the evolutionary ecology of habitat selection is an evolutionary game.

9.1.1 Scope of the Chapter

There are a number of excellent reviews of theories and empirical studies of habitat selection (Rosenzweig 1985, 1987a, 1991; Kacelnik et al. 1992; Kennedy & Gray 1993; Morris 1994). Instead of taking on the Herculean task of improving upon them, I shall take advantage of their groundwork to focus on habitat selection as a game theoretic process. How does one set up habitat selection as an evolutionary game? How does one solve for the ESSs? And how does one interpret results and translate the models into predictions?

In evolutionary game theory, the organisms are the players, their heritable phenotypes are strategies drawn from some evolutionarily feasible set, and the payoff to an individual represents the fitness consequence to an individual of possessing a particular strategy within a particular setting that includes the strategies and densities of others (Vincent & Brown 1988, Mitchell and Valone 1990). Insofar as population densities influence an individual's fitness, natural selection is density-dependent. Insofar as the frequencies of strategies among others influences an individual's fitness, selection is frequency-dependent (Brown & Vincent 1987a).

In habitat selection, the heritable phenotype often involves a behavior of biasing effort toward an advantageous subset or mix of temporal or spatial habitats. The behavior requires the ability to assess and respond to heterogeneity. The adaptation (subject to costs and constraints) requires assessing accurately and responding appropriately.

Throughout, I consider one or several species that exploit an environment that is spatially heterogeneous with respect to resource abundances, predation risk, and/or physical properties that influence harvest rates, foraging efficiencies, or predation. Depending upon the degree of heterogeneity, a given habitat type may be fragmented into one, several, or many patches. The organisms in this environment seek to harvest resources from the patches. By harvesting the patches, some or all of the resources may be used up, but the patch and its habitat association remain. For example, during a flowering cycle, the flowers of a plant may represent food patches to bees and hummingbirds (Pyke 1981, 1982). The nectarivores harvest nectar or pollen from the flower, and the species of flower may represent its habitat type. In the case of flowers, the distribution of "patches" of a given habitat tends to be contagious, because a single plant may contain numerous flowers (Feinsinger et al. 1991) and a single plant may occur in either a mixed species or single species stand of flowers (Milchtaich 1996). Other examples of habitats include the bush and open microhabitats of seed-eating desert rodents (Rosenzweig & Winakur 1969, Brown & Lieberman 1973), upper versus lower leaf surfaces for insect gleaning warblers (also, height in tree or radial distance from tree trunk), different fruiting shrubs or trees for frugivorous birds (Sallabanks 1993, Whelan & Willson 1994), height in the water column for crustacean zooplankton, different limnetic and benthic habitats of fish and invertebrates, and various tidal zones for crustaceans, starfish, limpets, fish, and mollusks (e.g., Schmitt 1982).

Let the foragers both respond to and influence the distribution and abundance of resources among patches of the various habitat types. Upon encountering a patch, the forager can harvest resources from it or reject the opportunity and move on. In this way, a forager can choose its degree of selectivity; that is, it can either (a) harvest resources selectively from patches of just one habitat type or (b) behave opportunistically and harvest resources from all encountered patches (Rosenzweig 1981). For instance, a warbler may elect to be selective and only search for insects on the undersides of leaves or it may be opportunistic and search the entire leaf for food (Whelan 1989). The densities and behaviors (selective versus opportunistic) of the foragers shape the abundance of resources among patches and habitats. In general, increasing the density of foragers will decrease resource abundances, and increasing a population's selectivity toward a particular habitat will depress resource abundances within the favored habitats and increase resources in other habitats. For instance, increasing the number of lobsters and octopus harvesting bivalves and gastropods from shallow cobble flats and lower intertidal reefs should depress the overall abundance of prey. If the predators shift their effort toward the cobble and away from the reef, this should depress prey in the cobble and increase prey abundances on the reef (adapted from Schmitt 1987).

The game of habitat selection that will form the basis of what follows includes a heterogeneous environment composed of patches of different habitat types. The habitat selectors harvest resources from these patches, and their behaviors and densities influence the distribution and abundance of resources, which, in turn, determines the optimal decisions of a given individual. I will develop and expand on only a few models of habitat selection. These models will provide continuity as we explore a variety of ecological and evolutionary scenarios, and they will illustrate the mathematical tools required to elucidate the ecological and evolutionary outcomes.

I will begin with cost-free habitat selection as proposed by Fretwell and Lucas (1970) for one species and expanded to two species by Rosenzweig (1981). In determining the ESS behavior for single- and two-species systems, the development will touch upon concepts such as the ideal free distribution, resource matching rule (Parker 1978, Fagan 1987, Morris 1994), isodars (Morris 1988), isolegs (Rosenzweig 1981), and the ghost of competition past (Connell 1980, Rosenzweig 1981, Brown & Rosenzweig 1986). This scenario will be extended to include predation risk and its consequences for the ESS of the single- and two-species systems. Finally, we will consider a scenario in which the degree of habitat fragmentation into patches can vary from fine-grained (costly habitat selection) to coarse-grained (cost-free habitat selection), and we will consider the evolution of additional fixed morphological and/ or physiological traits that influence the habitat selector's aptitudes among the different habitat types (Rosenzweig 1987b). In this case, the ESS will include the coadaptation between the behavioral (opportunistic versus selective) trait and the fixed trait (generalist versus specialist). Instead of imposing the number of species on the system, the diversity of species will emerge as the ESS (Brown 1990, Brown & Vincent 1992).

9.2 Cost-free Habitat Selection in a Single Species

9.2.1 A Simple Example

Consider a "coarse-grained" environment divided into two habitats. In such an environment, habitat selection is "cost-free," because the fragments or patches of a habitat type are sufficiently large or contiguous that an individual spends negligible search effort seeking new patches of the habitat. Let the fitness of an individual be determined solely by the rate at which it harvests resources from one or the other habitats. Let this rate of resource harvest, H, be influenced by the habitat type, the number of individuals, and the distribution of those individuals:

$$H_i = \frac{R_i\{1 - \exp(-a_i N_i)\}}{N_i} \tag{1}$$

where $i = 1,2$ represents the two habitat types, R_i is the productivity in habitat i, a_i is the individual's harvest probability in i, and N_i is the number of individuals in i. Assume that all individuals have the same a_i.

In this model, individuals within a habitat compete exploitatively for a stream of resources that flow by at rate R_i. Increasing the number of individuals within a habitat has two effects. The first is to increase the fraction of resources harvested, the numerator of equation (1). The second is to reduce the rate of harvest by each individual, the denominator of equation (1). Because the model assumes that each individual within the habitat shares equally in the harvest, the addition of another individual increases somewhat the collective harvest, at the expense of each individual's harvest. At very large and very small population sizes, the model has the following properties:

$$\text{as } N_i \to \infty, \qquad H_i \to R_i/N_i \to 0$$

$$\text{as } N_i \to 0, \qquad H_i \to a_i R_i$$

(2)

At low numbers of foragers, the individual's harvest rate is limited by its ability to encounter the available resource pool or stream (same as patch use models with at most a single forager per patch). At high numbers of foragers, essentially all of the resources are harvested and divided among the foragers (same as resource matching models; Parker 1978, Kennedy & Gray 1993, Morris 1994). The model probably best applies to systems where resource productivity occurs as a pulse (e.g., nectar, seed rain, and seasonal flushes of insects) or as a steady stream (aggregations of filter feeders).

We now need a function that determines the expected payoff or per capita growth rate of an arbitrary individual possessing an arbitrary strategy. The resulting function is the fitness-generating function, G (Vincent & Brown 1984, 1988; Brown & Vincent 1987b). Equation (1) provides the fitness generating function of the present model. The harvest rate of an individual is influenced by its choice of habitat and the habitat choices of others. If behaving sensibly, the individual should try to maximize its harvest rate:

$$G = \max\{H_1, H_2\}$$

(3)

9.2.2 Solving for the ESS

We have all the pieces for a simple game-theoretic model of habitat selection: players, strategies, and payoffs. The players represent the population of habitat selectors, N. The strategy set includes the two pure strategies of Inhabit habitat 1 and Inhabit habitat 2. Payoffs to the strategies are given by equation (1) for $i = 1$, 2. Also, the objective of the habitat selectors is to maximize their own payoff.

In solving for the ESS, let habitat 1 be preferred in the sense that $a_1 R_1 > a_2 R_2$. Under this assumption, there exists a critical value of the population's size, N', such that

$$H_1(N') = a_2 R_2$$

(4)

For population sizes below N', the pure strategy Inhabit 1 comprises the ESS (Fig. 9.1). Above N', the ESS has a mixture of the two pure strategies; and the number of individuals using each strategy must satisfy

$$H_1(N_1) = H_2(N_2) \tag{5}$$

which gives conditions for an ideal free distribution (Fretwell & Lucas 1970).

Population size represents a bifurcation parameter which determines when the ESS changes from a single strategy to two strategies. Above N', the ESS contains both strategies, but the mix of these strategies in the population continues to be influenced by total N. The isodar (Morris 1988, 1992), all combinations of N_1 and N_2 satisfying equation (5), gives the distribution of individuals among habitats at the ESS as N changes (Fig. 9.2). For this model, the isodar is nonlinear (Morris 1994), and the distribution of individuals among habitats that equalizes fitness does not conform to the resource-matching rule of $R_1/N_2 = R_1/N_2$ (Parker 1978, Kennedy & Gray 1993). Relative to the resource matching rule, individuals overutilize the more productive habitat, or the habitat with the higher encounter probability on resources.

9.2.2.1 A Comment on Pure Versus Mixed Strategies

The above analysis only permitted two strategies: Inhabit 1 or Inhabit 2. But, if individuals can exchange habitats at no expense, then the strategy set might be thought of as including a continuum of mixed strategies in which the strategy $q \in [0, 1]$ represents the fraction of time or effort devoted to habitat 1. In game theory, and particularly in matrix games, the distinction between a mix of individuals playing pure strategies (Inhabit 1 or Inhabit 2) and a population of individuals using a mixed strategy (q) has important consequences both for the interpretation of the game and for the evolutionary stability of the ESS (for detailed discussions see Taylor & Jonker 1978; Hines 1980, 1987; Zeeman 1981; Vincent & Brown 1984, 1988).

As a mixed strategy ESS, q^* gives the fraction of time each individual spends in each habitat so as to equalize harvest rates among habitats. Such an ESS is resistant to invasion by any single alternative strategy because a single invading strategy would skew the distribution of individuals among habitats away from the ESS. However, p^* can be invaded by two or more strategies if the strategies lie on either side of p^*. In fact, when multiple mutant strategies can occur, any combination of mixed and pure strategies that straddles p^* can persist in the population (Vincent & Brown 1984). In the present game, an ESS that is resistant to invasion by any number or combination of rare, alternative strategies occurs either by including some additional benefit to experiencing both habitats (see Section 9.4) or by including a cost to moving back and forth between habitats (the mixed strategy ESS vanishes in favor of the mix of pure strategies).

9.2.2.2 Alternative Solution Concepts: Centrally Planned Distribution

An ESS is optimal in the sense that each individual maximizes its fitness given the abiotic and biotic circumstances. Like the Nash (1951) equilibrium of classic game

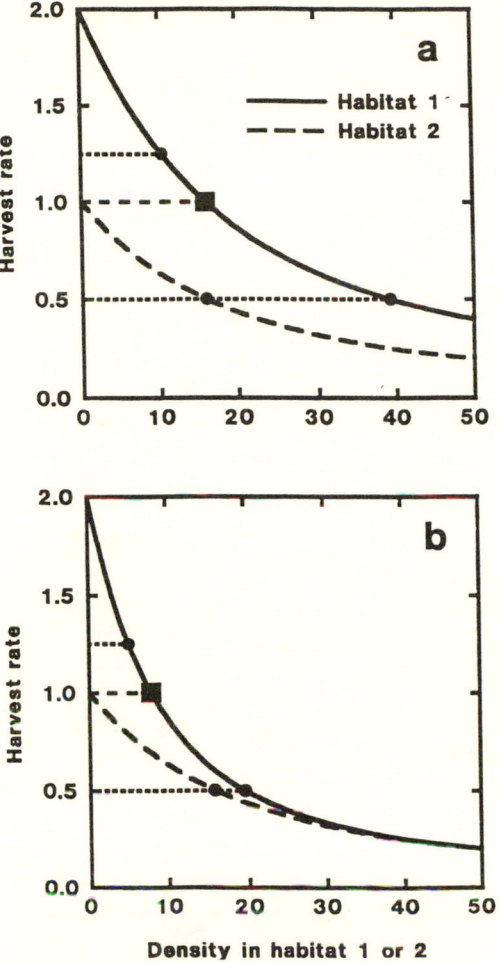

Figure 9.1. Relationship between harvest rate and density of foragers. Habitat 1 is preferred because of (a) a higher productivity $(R_1 > R_1)$, or (b) ease of encountering resources $(a_1 > a_2)$. The square (horizontal dashed line) indicates the threshold density of individuals in habitat 1, at which individuals should begin using the less preferred habitat. The circles (horizontal dotted lines) indicate equilibrium population distributions among habitats when foraging costs are high (upper line) and low (lower line), respectively. When costs are high, only the preferred habitat is profitable, and the ESS consists of all individuals inhabiting 1. When costs are low, the ESS contains a mixture of inhabit 1 and inhabit 2. The following parameter values were used: (a) $R_1 = 20$, $R_2 = 10$, $a_1 = a_2 = 0.1$; (b) $R_1 = R_2 = 10$, $a_1 = 0.2$, $a_2 = 0.1$

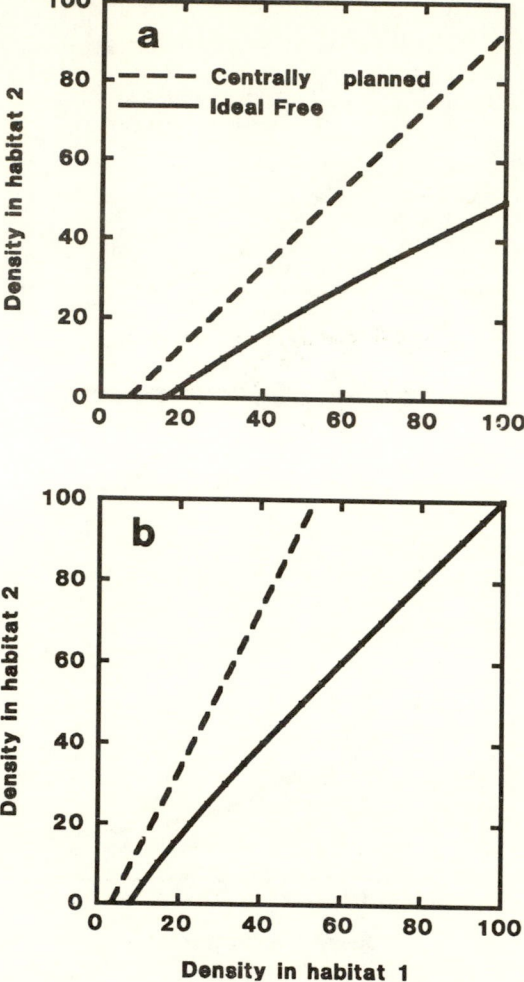

Figure 9.2. The isodars for the habitat selection scenario shown in Fig. 9.1 where (a) habitat 1 is more productive than habitat 2, and (b) habitat 1 offers the higher encounter probability on resources. The isodar under the ideal free distribution (solid lines) gives all combinations of habitat-specific population densities such that the per capita harvest rate within each habitat is the same. This is the ESS when individuals do not share their harvests. The dashed line represents the centrally planned distribution, where the collective harvest rate is maximized. This is the ESS when individuals share their harvest as subunits of an integrated colony or plant. In both (a) and (b), the centrally planned distribution results in a heavier use of the less preferred habitat than the ideal free distribution.

theory, no individual can benefit from a unilateral change in strategy (see Auslander et al. 1978; Vincent & Brown 1984). However, frequency-dependent selection and ESSs in particular do not necessarily or ordinarily result in combinations of strategies among individuals that are pareto optimal—that is, solutions that would benefit everyone and harm no one. Such pareto solutions require cooperative, coordinated, or collective changes in strategies among individuals (Moody et al. 1996). In the present model, such pareto points are evolutionarily unstable and highly invadable by cheaters that deviate from the collective bargain. However, a solution that maximizes a collective measure of fitness may result from individual selection when the distribution of "individuals" among habitats, N_1 and N_2, represents efforts by a "central planner" such as some social insects and modular growth in plants (Sachs et al. 1993), or, equivalently, individuals with strongly overlapping genetic interests (i.e., kin selection).

For an ant colony, N_1 and N_2 may be the distribution of workers among the two habitats, and for a plant, N_1 and N_2 may be root growth in two adjacent habitats accessible to the root system of the same plant (Gersani & Sachs 1992). For such organisms where individual harvests are shared with a single colony or plant, equation (3) may not provide an appropriate measure of the organism's objective. Under centrally planned habitat selection, the appropriate fitness function for the example of this section is

$$G = R_1\{1 - \exp(-a_1 N_1)\} + R_2\{1 - \mathrm{Exp}(-a_2 N_2)\} \tag{6}$$

subject to the constraint that $N_1 + N_2 = N$. (Allowing the plant or colony to select the optimal value for N provides an interesting and additional dimension to the question).

The following optimal centrally planned habitat distribution results, after substituting the constraint for N_2, taking the derivative of equation (6) with respect to N_1, and setting the derivative equal to zero:

$$N_2 = (1/a_2)\ln(a_2 R_2/a_1 R_1) + (a_1 N_1/a_2) \tag{7}$$

The isodar represented by equation (7) yields a very different allocation of effort or individuals among habitats than the isodar for the ideal free distribution of equation (5) (see Fig. 9.2; see Moody et al. 1996 for a similar example). Relative to the centrally planned distribution, the ideal free distribution over-utilizes the more productive habitat, or the habitat with the higher encounter probability on resources. The predictions of a centrally planned distribution could be tested by comparing solitary versus group foraging species (solitary versus social bees), or by contrasting the distribution of workers or effort among habitats when a single colony or plant has sole use of the habitats (centrally planned) versus multiple colonies or plants sharing the same habitats (closer to an ideal free distribution).

9.3 Two-Species Density-Dependent Habitat Selection

Two-species density-dependent habitat selection has been modeled in a number of works (Rosenzweig 1981, 1991; Brown & Rosenzweig 1986; Morris 1988, 1994).

Empirical tests and applications include hummingbirds (Pimm et al. 1985, Rosenzweig 1986), two species of gerbil inhabiting the Negev Desert (Abramsky et al. 1990, 1991; Ovadia and Abramsky, 1995), several North American rodents (Morris 1989a,b), and fish (Rodriguez 1995).

9.3.1 Adding a Second Species to the Simple Example

The previous section considered the ideal free distribution and density-dependent habitat selection as a symmetric game (see Hammerstein 1981, Maynard Smith 1982) in the sense that players were completely interchangeable in terms of strategies and the consequences of using particular strategies. Furthermore, individuals were evolutionarily identical (*sensu* Brown & Vincent 1987b) in that they possessed the same strategy set and fitness-generating function. Rosenzweig's (1981) extension of the ideal free distribution considers two species that are not evolutionarily identical. The individuals of both species possess the same strategy set of choosing how to allocate effort among two habitats. But, members of different species experience different fitness consequences of using a particular behavioral strategy. Each species has a distinct fitness-generating function.

Consider a two-species extension of the model presented in equation (1):

$$H_{ij}(N_{i1}, N_{i2}) = \frac{a_{ij}R_i\{1 - \exp - (a_{i1}N_{i1} + a_{i2}N_{i2})\}}{a_{i1}N_{i1} + a_{i2}N_{i2}} \tag{8}$$

where the subscripts refer to habitat i and species j, respectively. The collective harvest within a habitat is now determined by the combined efforts of species 1 and 2 weighted by their species-specific and habitat-specific harvest probabilities, a_{ij}. The collective harvest is then divided among the individuals within a habitat according to the individuals' harvest probability (in the numerator) and the weighted average of others' harvest probabilities (in the denominator).

In this example, species differ in their habitat-specific harvest probabilities. There is a tradeoff among the species if each species possesses a habitat in which it has the higher harvest rate—for instance, if $a_{11} > a_{12}$ and $a_{22} > a_{21}$. Under such a tradeoff, the two species, at very low population sizes, prefer the same habitat if each has its higher encounter probability in the same habitat; shared preferences (*sensu* Rosenzweig 1987a) occur when $a_{1j} > a_{2j}$. Distinct preferences occur when each species has its higher harvest probability in a different habitat; $a_{11} > a_{21}$ and $a_{22} > a_{12}$.

The fitness of an individual, G, is influenced by its choice of habitat and the habitat choices of others. If behaving sensibly, the individual should choose among habitats so as to maximize its harvest rate:

$$Gj = \max\{H_{1j}, H_{2j}\} \tag{9}$$

where we now have a fitness generating function for each species $j = 1, 2$.

9.3.1.1 Solving for the ESS

Potentially, the ESS can include strategies from both within (as in the previous section) and between the species (Brown & Vincent 1992). The conditions for species 1 or 2 to be selective on a particular habitat include

$$H_{i1}(N_{i1}, N_{i2}) > H_{k1}(0, N_{k2})$$

$$H_{i2}(N_{i1,} N_{i2}) > H_{k2}(N_{k1}, 0)$$

(10)

for habitats $i \neq k$. The decision by the individuals of a species to be selective on one habitat or to be opportunistic and distribute themselves among both depends upon the habitat selection behavior of the other species, as well as the inherent characteristics of each habitat.

When condition (10) does not hold for a species within either habitat, then the optimal behavior among the individuals of a species includes using both habitats in accord with an ideal free distribution:

$$H_{1j}(N_{11}, N_{12}) = H_{2j}(N_{21}, N_{22})$$

(11)

where j refers to species 1 or 2.

We can consider four candidate ESS solutions formed by all combinations of species 1 behaving selectively or opportunistically and species 2 behaving selectively or opportunistically. The candidate ESS of each species behaving selectively can be obtained when condition (10) can be satisfied simultaneously for both species. If the species have distinct preferences, then this ESS has both species selectively utilizing a different habitat. If the species have shared preferences, then the ESS may have both species selectively using either the same or different habitats depending upon the species' aptitudes and their population sizes (see Fig. 9.3). This condition occurs most easily for the present model when population sizes of the two species are similar.

The candidate solution of species 1 behaving selectively and species 2 behaving opportunistically is an ESS when condition (10) for species 1 is satisfied simultaneously with condition (11) for species 2. Similarly, an ESS of species 1 behaving opportunistically and species 2 behaving selectively requires simultaneously satisfying conditions (11) and (10) for species 1 and 2, respectively. This outcome becomes likely under lopsided population sizes. The fourth candidate solution of both species using both habitats is not possible under the assumption that species 1 and 2 differ in at least one of their harvest probabilities: $a_{11} \neq a_{12}$ and/or $a_{21} \neq a_{22}$. In this case, it is not possible to satisfy equation (11) simultaneously for both species.

The total population sizes of species 1 and 2 determine the number and distribution of strategies at the ESS. The state space of total population sizes ($N_{12} + N_{22}$ versus $N_{11} + N_{21}$) can be divided into three or four regions, depending upon whether preferences are distinct or shared, respectively (Fig. 9.3; also see Rosenzweig 1987a, 1991). The regions represent ESSs where (1) both species possess a single pure strategy of inhabiting just one or the other of the habitats (region B in Fig. 9.3), (2) species 1 possesses a mixture of pure strategies of inhabit 1 and inhabit 2, and species 2 possesses a single strategy of selectively inhabiting just one of the habitats (region

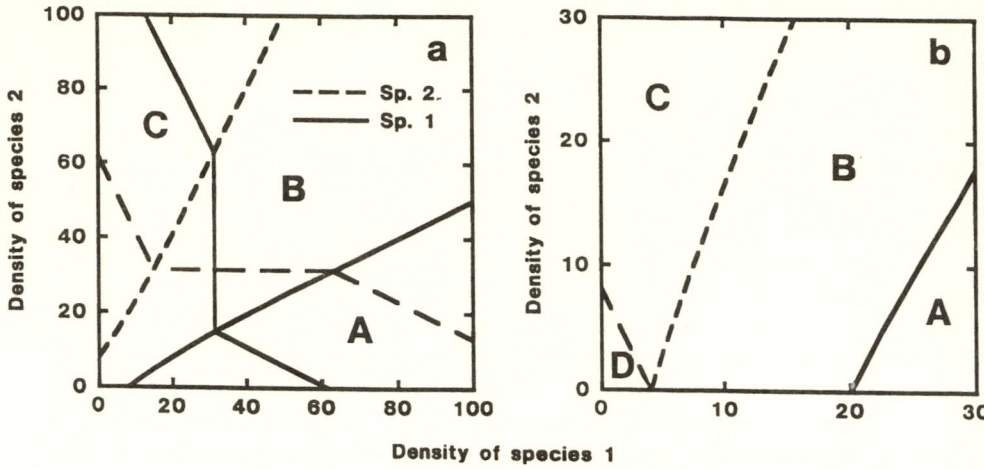

Figure 9.3. Isolegs and isoclines for (a) distinct and (b) shared preference two- species density-dependent habitat selection (see figures in Rosenzweig 1981, 1985, 1987). The positively sloped lines (solid for species 1 and dashed for species 2) separate the combinations of species densities that generate different behavioral ESSs. The behavioral ESSs include (A) species 1 inhabits both habitats and species 2 inhabits 2; (B) species 1 inhabits 1 and species 2 inhabits 2; (C) species 1 inhabits 1 and species 2 inhabits both habitats; and (D) species 1 inhabits 1 and species 2 inhabits 1. In (a) the zero growth isoclines (solid line for species 1 and dashed line for species 2) are also shown. When habitat selection is cost-free, the ghost of competition past (the equilibrium point in region C) is the two-species ESS under both evolutionary and ecological stability. This is true for both shared and distinct preferences; (b) would generate a similar set of isoclines to (a). In (a) species 1 prefers 1 and species 2 prefers 2: $R_1 = R_2 = 10$, $a_{11} = a_{22} = 0.2$, $a_{21} = a_{12} = 0.1$. In (b) both species prefer habitat 1, but species 2 is more generalist in its encounter rate than species 1: $R_1 = R_2 = 10$, $a_{11} = 0.5$, $a_{12} = 0.4$, $a_{21} = 0.1$, and $a_{22} = 0.2$, where the first subscript refers to habitat and the second refers to species.

A of Fig. 9.3), and (3) species 2 possesses a mixture of pure strategies and species 1 possesses a single pure strategy (region C of Fig 9.3). Isolegs (Rosenzweig 1981), combinations of species population sizes such that condition (10) is satisfied with equality, mark the boundaries among these different ESS outcomes. Each species has its own isoleg. A species' isoleg marks the boundary between an ESS possessing a single behavioral strategy (selectively Inhabit 1 or Inhabit 2) and an ESS possessing a mixture of the two behavioral strategies (Inhabit 1 and Inhabit 2).

9.2.3 Ecological Dimension

Models of habitat selection have both an evolutionary and ecological dimension. As the evolutionary dimension, individuals can choose behaviors so as to maximize fitness. As an ecological dimension, these decisions have fitness consequences that determine whether the individuals possessing a particular behavioral strategy increase or decrease in numbers. In a model that has both of these dimensions, the ESS must be evolutionarily stable in the sense that rare alternative strategies cannot invade and the ESS must be ecologically stable in the sense that the constituent species and strategies can persist together through time at positive population sizes (Vincent & Brown 1987, 1988). Ecological stability requires either population dynamics that tend toward stable equilibria or nonequilibrium dynamics that are bounded away from zero for any of the species or strategies (Vincent & Brown 1987, Kisidi & Meszena 1993, Abrams & Matsuda 1996, Diekmann et al. 1995).

The requirement of ecological stability can further reduce the range of ESS outcomes. In our example, we can introduce ecological dynamics by assuming that the individuals possess a subsistence level of harvest, c, such that when the rate of harvest is greater than, less than, or equal to c, the strategy's per capita growth rate is positive, negative, or zero, respectively. If we assume equilibrial population dynamics, then we need only specify that per capita growth rate increases with a strategy's harvest rate. The subsistence level of harvest, c, now becomes the bifurcation parameter that determines the number of strategies at the ESS. Consider just a single species. At very large values of c, the species cannot persist within the environment ($c > a_i R_i$ for habitats $i = 1$, 2). At smaller values of c, the preferred habitat, say habitat 1, becomes profitable and the ESS includes the strategy of inhabit 1 ($a_1 R_1 > c > a_2 R_2$). At still smaller values of c, both habitats become profitable and the ESS contains both behavioral strategies ($a_i R_i > c$ for all i). The numbers of individuals within each habitat is determined by the subsistence harvest rate (see Fig. 9.1).

Similarly, ascribing a subsistence harvest rate, c_j, to each species in the two-species example influences the ESS. The combined effects of foraging costs and the optimal behavioral strategies determines the isoclines in the state space of species population sizes (Fig. 9.3). In the present example, the ecological dimension precludes all ESSs except for the one where the two species selectively inhabit separate habitats (even when both habitats can be profitable to both species: $a_{ij} R_{ij} > c_j$ for all i and j). To have a solution where both species inhabit the same habitat at the ESS requires

$$H_{ij}(N_{i1}, N_{i2}) = c_j$$

$$H_{i1} = a_{i1} H_{i2} / a_{i2}$$

But, these equations cannot be satisfied simultaneously with just the two population sizes, N_{i1} and N_{i2}, except as a singularity. In fact, whichever species has the higher value for the ratio of harvest probability and subsistence harvest rate will exclude the other species from the habitat. For coexistence,

$$a_{11}/c_1 > a_{12}/c_2 \quad \text{and} \quad a_{22}/c_2 > a_{21}/c_1 \tag{12}$$

which corresponds to an ESS where species 1 only inhabits 1 and species 2 only inhabits 2 (Fig. 9.3). The above result, first noted and modeled by Rosenzweig (1981), has been widely found in models of exploitative competition between two species in an environment where habitat selection is cost-free (Brew 1982, Brown & Rosenzweig 1986, Parker & Sutherland 1986, Vincent et al. 1996). Whichever species is the most efficient drives the resource of a habitat to a level that excludes less efficient species (R^* rule of Tilman 1980, 1982). The outcome includes either (a) the competitive exclusion of one species by another or (b) species coexistence under the "ghost of competition past" (Connell 1980), where each species restricts itself to inhabiting exclusive habitats. This narrow range of outcomes can be broken by either (a) increasing the number of inputs into fitness (e.g., food and safety—the topic of the next section) or (b) rendering the environment less coarse-grained and increasing the costliness of habitat selection (i.e., breaking habitats into smaller and interspersed fragments—the topic of the last model of this chapter).

9.4   Habitat Selection in Response to Food and Safety

Most feeding animals experience spatial variability in food and safety (see Lima & Dill 1990). The interplay between food and safety tends to generate environments in which risky habitats offer higher feeding rates, while safe habitats offer fewer feeding opportunities. This occurs because foragers generally exploit safe habitats more thoroughly and demand lower harvest rates than from risky habitats (Sih 1980, Werner et al. 1983, Gilliam & Fraser 1987, Brown 1988). Frequent examples involve both terrestrial and aquatic animals feeding near and away from protective cover (Grubb & Greenwald 1982, Kotler 1984, Fraser & Gilliam 1987, Brown & Alkon 1990, Persson & Eklov 1995). Holt (1984, 1987) and Moody et al. (1996) provide models of density-dependent habitat selection under predation risk.

9.4.1 Extending the Simple Model to Include Predation Risk

I will maintain the assumption of cost-free habitat selection in an environment consisting of two coarse-grained habitats. Also, I will begin with a single species. While in a habitat, an individual harvests resources and incurs a risk of mortality by predation. As before, the individual's harvest rate in a habitat declines with the level of activity from other individuals in that habitat. For simplicity, let predation risk be independent of the activity of individuals within a habitat [van Balaan & Sabelis (1993) provide a predator–prey foraging game in a patchy environment]. I will modify the fitness function by assuming that an individual must survive T units of time before realizing any fitness rewards from its feeding. If an individual dies between reproduction events, it realizes no fitness gains from resources harvested since last reproduction. Finite growth is the product of fitness gains in the absence of predation, F, and the probability of surviving predation to realize fitness, p (see Abrams 1991, Brown 1992):

$$G(q, \mathbf{q}, N) = p(q)F(q, \mathbf{q}, N) \tag{13}$$

where $q \in [0, 1]$ is the fraction of time that the individual spends in habitat 1, $\mathbf{q} \in [0, 1]$ is the population's average time spent in habitat 1, and N is population size. If μ_i is the predation risk while feeding in habitat i, then the probability of surviving the time interval is

$$p(q) = \exp\{-T[\mu_1 q + \mu_2(1 - q)]\} \tag{14}$$

and let F be a function of the amount of resources harvested, e, where

$$e(q, \mathbf{q}, N) = T[qH_1 + (1-q)H_2] \qquad (15)$$

and H_1 and H_2 are decreasing functions of $\mathbf{q}N$ and $(1-\mathbf{q})N$, respectively.

The ESS will consist of one or several strategies that must maximize fitness. For ecological stability, the ESS strategies must have frequencies and equilibrium population sizes such that each strategy yields a fitness of 1: $pF = 1$. (Alternatively, factors independent of habitat selection may maintain a constant population size, N^*, in which case the optimal habitat selection still involves maximizing G, subject to $N = N^*$.)

9.4.1.1 Can the Pure Strategies Be an ESS?

Start with an ideal free distribution of individuals among habitats, the two pure strategies of either inhabit 1 or inhabit 2, and equilibrium population sizes $F(TH_1)e^{-T\mu_1} = F(TH_2)e^{-T\mu_2} = 1$. For purposes of discussion, let habitat 1 be the riskier habitat, which means that at equilibrium the individuals inhabiting 1 have the lower probability of surviving predation ($\mu_1 > \mu_2$) and the higher harvest rate ($H_1 > H_2$). To see whether the two pure strategies can simultaneously maximize fitness and be the ESS, we first evaluate the effect of an individual unilaterally changing q on its fitness:

$$\frac{\delta G}{\delta q} = pT\left[\frac{\delta F}{\delta e}(H_1 - H_2) - F(\mu_1 - \mu_2)\right] \qquad (16)$$

For the two pure strategies to comprise the ESS, we require the following condition:

$$\left.\frac{\delta G}{\delta q}\right|_{q=\mathbf{q}=1,\, N_1^*} \geq 0 \geq \left.\frac{\delta G}{\delta q}\right|_{q=\mathbf{q}=0,\, N_2^*} \qquad (17)$$

But, if the habitats differ in predation risk, the following always holds:

$$\left.\frac{\delta G}{\delta q}\right|_{q=\mathbf{q}=0,\, N_2^*} \geq 0 \geq \left.\frac{\delta G}{\delta q}\right|_{q=\mathbf{q}=1,\, N_1^*}$$

and the two pure strategies cannot be the ESS because each can be invaded by any strategy $q \in (0, 1)$. The two pure strategies at equilibrium population sizes are actually the worst strategies to use. The advantage of using both habitats accrues from the complementarity of food and safety. The marginal values of food and safety, respectively, are

$$\delta G/\delta e = p(\delta F/\delta e)$$

$$\delta G/\delta p = F$$

The animal that inhabits the safe habitat will have a higher marginal value of food and lower marginal value of safety than the individual that inhabits the risky habitat. The grass is always greener in the others' habitat. The risky habitat looks greener to the safe habitat denizen, because it offers what the denizen craves: high feeding rates. The safe habitat looks greener to the risky habitat denizen, because it offers what the denizen craves: safety. When habitat selection is cost-free and habitats vary in predation risk, a mixed strategy can always invade an equilibrium mix of pure strategies.

9.4.1.2 The ESS Under Food and Safety

This model has a mixed strategy ESS, q^*. The first-order necessary conditions for ecological and evolutionary stability are

$$\left.\frac{\delta G}{\delta q}\right|_{q=q=q^*,\ N^*} = 0 \rightarrow p(\delta F/\delta e) = (\mu_1 - \mu_2)/(H_1 - H_2)$$

$$\left. pF \right|_{q=q=q^*,\ N^*} = 1$$

At the ESS, the risky habitat offers a higher feeding rate and the individuals balance their use of each habitat so as to find the optimal compromise between food and safety. Adding predation risk to models of cost-free habitat selection creates two striking changes in the ESS. When habitats offer the same perfectly substitutable resource (e.g., energy), the ESS consists of a mixture of two pure behavioral strategies; and at the ESS, individuals distribute themselves among habitats according to an ideal free distribution. Under predation risk, the ESS consists of a mixed strategy and individuals no longer balance their activity among habitats so as to equalize average fitness returns.

The differences have to do with the structure of the fitness generating function, G. In the absence of predation risk, G results from a linear averaging of time spent within each habitat. In such models, the ESS results in an environment in which average fitness returns from each activity must be equal (Bishop & Cannings 1976) and the individual's fitness becomes independent of its own strategy (matrix games with mixed strategies provide a bilinear subset of this kind of fitness-generating function). Under predation risk, G is a multiplicative and nonlinear function of the individual's mixed strategy. At the ESS, the individual's strategy continues to influence its fitness, and equalizing the marginal fitness returns from using each habitat does not necessarily result in equalizing average fitness returns.

9.4.1.3 Isodars: Distribution of Individuals
Among Habitats

In the absence of predation risk, the isodar only intercepts the origin if harvest rates in the virgin habitats are equal: $H_1(0) = H_2(0)$ (for the worked example, this meant $a_1R_1 = a_2R_2$). Otherwise, individuals will first selectively occupy the habitat with the highest virgin harvest rate and then spill into the other habitat as the rate declines in the occupied habitat. Adding predation risk greatly increases the likelihood that the isoleg will intercept the origin (Fig. 9.4). Let habitat 1 be the riskier. The isodar will intercept the origin under the following conditions:

$$\frac{F}{\delta F/\delta e}\bigg|_{q=q=1,\,N=0} > \frac{[H_1(0)-H_2(0)]}{\mu 1-\mu 2} > \frac{F}{\delta F/\delta e}\bigg|_{q=q=0,\,N=0} \qquad (18)$$

where the above expression was found by invoking expression (17) for $N=0$.

When the isodar intercepts the origin, the habitat selectors do not possess a preferred habitat; instead, the habitats are viewed collectively as contributing to the optimal balance of food and safety. An extreme case of this occurs when one habitat is a risky feeding site and the other is a completely safe refuge that offers no feeding opportunities (Gilliam & Fraser 1987). For the isodar to intercept the origin, the riskier habitat must offer a higher virgin harvest rate than the safe habitat, otherwise the isodar intercepts the axis of the safer habitat. Similarly, for a sufficiently high virgin harvest rate in the riskier habitat or sufficiently small differences in predation risk among habitats, foragers will begin by selectively using the risky habitat and the isodar will intercept the axis of the risky habitat.

If habitat 1 is riskier, then the isodar lies above that under no predation risk (Fig. 9.4). As population size increases, fitness in the absence of predation declines and the marginal value of energy increases or remains constant. Hence, as N increases, the marginal value of safety declines and the marginal value of food increases, and the population should demand a smaller harvest rate premium in the riskier habitat (Houston et al. 1993, Brown 1992, Moody et al. 1996). Hence, the difference between the isodars (predation risk versus no predation risk) is largest at low population sizes, and at very high population sizes the two isodars converge.

9.4.2 Isolegs: Two-Species Density-Dependent Habitat Selection Under Predation

When exploitatively competing for substitutable resources, the isolegs allow for three regions: both species selectively using the same habitat, both species selectively using exclusive habitats, and one species using both habitats while the other uses just one. The ESS only allows for the ghost of competition past in which each species, at equilibrium, selectively uses the habitat within which it has, relative to the other species, the highest foraging efficiency. Predation risk introduces new possibilities. The configuration of isolegs may include a region within which individuals of both species use both habitats (Fig. 9.5). The ESS may, in addition to the ghost of competition past, include both species using both habitats or one species using both habitats while the other selectively uses just one.

9.4.2.1 Solving for the ESS with Two Species

The model for the two-species system includes two fitness-generating functions, one for each group of evolutionarily identical individuals. The fitness of an individual spending a particular fraction of time within each habitat, $q \in [0, 1]$, is influenced by the average strategy of each species, q_j, and the population sizes of the two species, N_j:

$$Gj = p_j(q)F_j(q,\, \mathbf{q}_1,\, \mathbf{q}_2,\, N_1,\, N_2) \qquad (19)$$

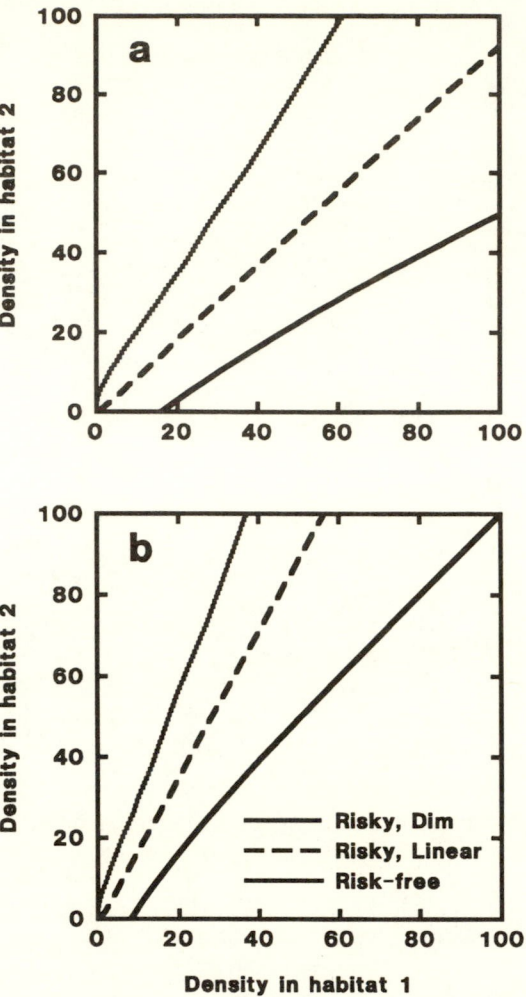

Figure 9.4. ESS distributions of individuals among habitats in the absence (solid line) and presence of predation risk (dashed and dotted lines) for the scenarios where (a) habitat 1 is riskier and has higher productivity, and (b) habitat 1 is riskier and offers a higher encounter rate on resources. In the presence of predation risk, the ESS does not consist of a mix of inhabit 1 and inhabit 2 (solid line = isodars from Fig. 9.2), but consists of individuals using a mixed strategy of allocating some time to each habitat. Under predation risk, individuals bias their behavior away from the riskier habitat and the bias becomes even more extreme when there are diminishing returns to fitness from resource harvest (dotted line) versus constant returns (solid line). The parameter values are the same as those in Fig. 9.1 with the addition of predation risk ($\mu_1 = 0.8$, $\mu_2 = 0.2$). For this illustration, fitness either increased linearly (dashed line) or as the square root (dotted line) of resource harvest.

for $j = 1, 2$. Notice how each species shares the same strategy set, q, but individuals of each species may experience different survival and harvest consequences of using a particular value of q.

At the ESS, both species must be able to coexist at positive population sizes ($N_j^* > 0$, where $p_j F_j = 1$), and each species' ESS, q_j^*, must maximize fitness: $Gj(q_j^*, q_1^*, q_2^*, N_1^*, N_2^*) > Gj(q, q_1^*, q_2^*, N_1^*, N_2^*)$ for $j = 1, 2$, and for all $q \in [0, 1]$. For each species, one of three necessary conditions must be satisfied at the ESS:

$$\delta G_j / \delta q \bigg|_{q = q_j^* = 0, \, q_k^*, \, N_1^*, \, N_2^*} \leq 0 \qquad (20a)$$

$$\delta G_j / \delta q \bigg|_{q = q_j^* = 1, \, q_k^*, \, N_1^*, \, N_2^*} \geq 0 \qquad (20b)$$

$$\delta G_j / \delta q \bigg|_{q = q_j^* \in (0, \, 1), \, q_k^*, \, N_1^*, \, N_2^*} = 0 \qquad (20c)$$

where $j, k = 1, 2$ and $j \neq k$.

In evaluating the possible ESSs, I assume that both habitats are profitable to a species in the sense that, in the absence of the other species, individuals of the remaining species would use both habitats. There are three permissible combinations of necessary conditions (20a–c). First, if condition (20a) and condition (20b) are satisfied for species 1 and 2, respectively, then the ESS consists of the ghost of competition past. This outcome likely occurs if there is a tradeoff among the two species in their perceptions of which is the riskier habitat. In the example, the ghost of competition past results when the two species are identical in all respects except for perceptions of predation risk: $\mu_{11} \sim \mu_{22} < \mu_{12} \sim \mu_{21}$, $a_{11} \sim a_{12} \sim a_{21} \sim a_{22}$, and $R_1 \sim R_2$. As a consequence of the other species depressing resources in its safer habitat, each species perceives relatively similar feeding opportunities across habitats and, hence, gains no advantage from using its riskier habitat (e.g., Schmitt 1982).

Second, if condition (20c) holds for both species, then at the ESS, both species use both habitats (Fig. 9.5). This outcome likely occurs if species differ in their perceptions of safe and risky habitats, and if each species has a higher foraging efficiency in its riskier habitat. In the example, this ESS results when $\mu_{11} \sim \mu_{22} < \mu_{12} \sim \mu_{21}$, $a_{11} \sim a_{22} < a_{12} \sim a_{21}$, and $R_1 \sim R_2$. A kind of resource partitioning takes place within each habitat. Species 1 uses habitat 2 as a source of food and habitat 1 as a source of safety, and vice versa for species 2 and its use of habitats. Species 1 depresses feeding opportunities most severely in the habitat in which species 2 derives benefits other than feeding. The most extreme case of this occurs as a_{11} and a_{22} approach zero, at which point the two species no longer are competitors. Third, if condition (20a) or (20b) holds for one species and condition (20c) holds for the second, then the ESS comprises one species selectively using just one habitat, $q_j^* = 0$ or 1, and the other species using both habitats, $q^* \in (0, 1)$. This ESS likely occurs when there is a tradeoff among species in foraging efficiency and predation risk. One species is the more efficient forager of the two in both habitats, while the other species has a lower risk of predation than the first in both habitats: $\mu_{i1} > \mu_{i2}$, $a_{i1} > a_{i2}$, $\mu_{1j} > \mu_{2j}$, $a_{1j} \sim a_{2j}$, and $R_1 = R_2$. By itself, species 1 creates a steep gradient in

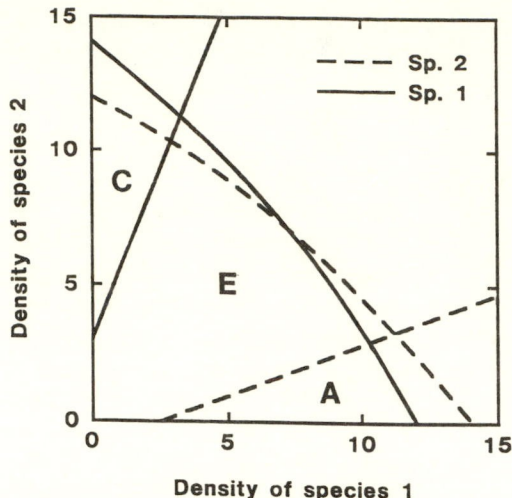

Figure 9.5. Isolegs and isoclines for habitat selection under food and safety. Individuals of species 1 use both habitats below their isoleg and selectively use habitat 1 above. Individuals of species 2 use both habitats above their isoleg and selectively use habitat 2 below. There are three regions of behavioral ESSs for the two species. The behavioral ESSs include (A) individuals of species 1 use a mix of both habitats and species 2 inhabits 2; (C) species 1 inhabits 1 and individuals of species 2 use a mix of both habitats; and (E) individuals of both species use a mix of both habitats. The following parameter values were used: $R_1 = R_2 = 10$, $a_{11} = a_{22} = 0.1$, $a_{21} = a_{12} = 0.2$, $\mu_{11} = \mu_{22} = 0.1$, $\mu_{21} = \mu_{12} = 1.0$, $T = 1$, and $c = 0$.

feeding opportunities between the safe and risky habitats, while species 2 creates a shallower gradient. In this way, species 2 removes feeding opportunities from the risky habitat which discourages species 1 from even using the risky habitat; the ESS for species 1 involves selectively using the safe habitat. Species 1, while removing feeding opportunities from the safe habitat, does not remove the opportunity for species 2 to seek safety. Thus, so long as the risky habitat is substantially risky for both species, then the ESS for species 2 involves its use of both habitats. If, however, species 2 experiences very low predation risk, μ_{i2} very small for $i = 1$, 2, then the ESS returns to the ghost of competition past.

The analysis of this section could be extended and generalized to consider any two resources whose availability varies somewhat independently among habitats and whose contributions to fitness are complementary (McNamara & Houston 1990, Messier et al. 1990). Or, the two habitats may contain entirely different resources that vary somewhat in their composition of two complementary nutrients. In either case, individuals should not distribute themselves among habitats in accord with an ideal free distribution, and the ESS under two-species density-dependent habitat selection can exhibit a variety of configurations beyond the ghost of competition past.

9.5 Costly Habitat Selection

Consider an environment in which the two habitat types are broken into patches of insufficient size or productivity to support an individual. A forager must roam from patch to patch, harvesting resources from profitable habitats and rejecting the opportunity to harvest unprofitable ones. Let the forager's search for patches be random in that it does not know the habitat type of the next encountered patch. Upon encountering a patch, the forager knows its type and the average resource abundance for patches of the habitat type. Likely systems include microhabitats (near and away from cover—for example, desert rodents: Rosenzweig & Winakur 1969, Brown & Lieberman 1973), foliage height diversity for birds (MacArthur 1972), and various leaf and other plant surfaces to herbivorous insects.

The forager engages in two activities. The first involves searching for habitat patches where a_1 and a_2 are the encounter rates on patches of habitat 1 and 2, respectively. The second involves harvesting the resources of a patch where h_1 and h_2 are the handling times on the two habitats, respectively. Let the amount of food harvested from a patch be the product of the forager's harvest ability, u_1 and u_2, and the average resource abundance of patches of the particular type, S_1 and S_2. This gives the following form for the forager's harvest rate, H (food per unit time; Holling 1965, Rosenzweig 1987b, Brown 1990, Kunin & Iwasa 1996):

$$H = \frac{q_1 a_1 u_1 S_1 + q_2 a_2 u_2 S_2}{1 + q_1 a_1 h_1 + q_2 a_2 h_2} \tag{21}$$

where q_1 and q_2 are the forager's probabilities of accepting for harvest patches of habitat 1 and 2, respectively. The probabilities of harvesting patches of the two habitat types represent the foragers' habitat selection behavior. The model becomes a game when dynamics are specified for resource abundances, S_1 and S_2, and the number of foragers. For simplicity, assume that R_1 and R_2 are the renewal rates of resources into habitats 1 and 2, respectively, and that these renewal rates are independent of resource standing crops. Also, assume that c gives the subsistence rate of harvest for the foragers, such that when harvest rates are greater than, less than, or equal to this subsistence level the population size of the foragers is growing, declining, or remaining constant, respectively. Hence, resource renewal supports the following equilibrium population size:

$$N^* = (R_1 + R_2)/c \tag{22}$$

and resource dynamics are given by

$$\frac{\delta S_i}{\delta t} = R_i - \frac{N^* q_i a_i u_i S_i}{1 + q_1 a_1 h_1 + q_2 a_2 h_2} \tag{23}$$

where $i = 1$, 2 and q_i represents the population's average acceptance rate of patches of habitat i. Setting this expression equal to zero and substituting equation (22) for N^* determines the equilibrium abundance of resources among patches of a given habitat type:

$$Si^*(q_1, q_2) = \frac{cR_i(1 + q_1 a_1 h_1 + q_2 a_2 h_2)}{q_i a_i u_i (R_1 + R_2)} \tag{24}$$

Substituting the equilibrium abundance of resources into the forager's harvest rate establishes the evolutionary game. The forager's harvest rate is influenced by its use of habitat patches, q_1 and q_2, and the abundance of resources which are influenced by the strategies of others, q_1 and q_1. The equilibrium abundance of resources among habitats has a number of ecological properties, and these properties are crucial because they will determine the ESS values for habitat utilization. In particular, any factor that reduces a forager's preference for a habitat type may reduce the ESS utilization of that habitat type. Preference for patches of a habitat type can be defined as the rate of reward from handling a patch of type i: $u_i S_i / h_i$.

Habitat preferences have the following ecological properties: (1) Increasing the handling time on patches of a habitat type will decrease the forager's preference for that habitat type and increase its preference for patches of the other habitat, (2) increasing the productivity of a habitat will increase preference for that habitat and decrease preference for the other habitat (apparent competition, Holt 1977), (3) increasing the forager's ability on a habitat will leave unchanged its preference for both habitats, and (4) increasing the forager's encounter rate on a habitat will decrease its preference for that habitat and increase its preference for the other habitat. In addition to their effects on preferences, encounter rates determine the costliness of habitat selection in this game. Very low encounter rates correspond to a highly fragmented, fine-grained habitat, while very high encounter rates correspond to a coarse-grained environment (Levins 1968). As the encounter rates become very large, this model converges on cost-free habitat selection. Costliness of habitat selection pertains to the time cost of searching for patches of a particular habitat type. Under a very high encounter rate, it takes little search time to remain exclusively within a given habitat type.

9.5.1 ESS Under Costly Habitat Selection

The game of habitat selection in this section is similar to bilinear matrix games, in that the payoff to the individual is linear in its strategy and linear in the average strategy of others. In this way, it has a similar structure and ESS to the game of cost-free habitat selection. This game differs in that the forager possesses two independent behavioral strategies pertaining to its acceptance of habitat 1 and 2, respectively. In the model of cost-free habitat selection, the forager had a single strategy pertaining to the fraction of time spent within each habitat. The ESS takes one of two forms. Either all individuals use all encountered patches of both habitat types, $q_1^* = q_2^* = 1$, or the ESS contains a mixture of two strategies that include individuals using all encountered patches of both habitats and individuals that selectively use all encountered patches of one habitat type while rejecting all patches of the other type.

The latter ESS is likely under lopsided habitat-specific productivities, in which case the behaviorally selective individuals only use the most productive habitat (Brown 1990).

9.6 The Evolution of Habitat Selectors

The behavior of habitat selection directs and is directed by the evolution of those morphological and physiological traits determining an individual's habitat-specific aptitudes. Individuals that selectively use just one habitat among several are under strong selection to evolve specialized morphologies and physiologies for that habitat. In this way, selective behavior toward habitats can select for niche conservatism (Holt & Gaines 1992). In this section, I follow Rosenzweig's (1981, 1987b) lead. Behaviors exist on a continuum from selective (using just one or several habitats, while rejecting the opportunity to use others) to opportunistic (using all habitats indiscriminately). Also, fixed morphological traits pertaining to habitat-specific aptitudes exist on a continuum from specialist (extremely apt on only one or a small subset of habitats and extremely poor at utilizing the rest) to generalist (moderately apt at utilizing all or most of the habitats). Insofar as an individual's aptitudes (specialist versus generalist) determine its optimal use of habitats and its use of habitats determines selection on its fixed aptitudes, we can expect to see (a) a coadaptation within individuals between behavioral and fixed traits relevant to habitat selection and (b) coevolution among species or populations that possess different strategies (behavioral and morphological).

We can extend the behavioral model of the previous section to include a fixed evolutionary trait or strategy, u_1 and u_2, that influences the efficiency with which an individual can extract resources from patches of the different habitats. Since natural selection favors those strategy values that simultaneously increase efficiency on all habitat types, we restrict our interest to the strategy set that represents a tradeoff between habitat-specific efficiencies. To evolve greater aptitude on one habitat necessarily means reduced aptitude on the other (the active edge of the fitness set; see Levins 1962).

The harvest rate of an individual is now determined by its behavioral strategies, q_1 and q_2, its fixed morphological strategies, u_1 and u_2, and the distribution and abundance of resources among patches of the two habitat types. The average resource abundance within patches of each habitat type is determined by the numbers of foragers and their respective behavioral and morphological strategies. As a model of coevolution and diversification of habitat selectors, different behavioral strategies may be thought of as phenotypic plasticity within individuals, while differences in morphology might define different species. Competitive speciation (Rosenzweig 1978) provides a mechanism for promoting sympatric speciation within evolutionary games. For the actual mathematics and analyses for finding and characterizing the ESSs of the present game, I refer the interested reader to Rosenzweig (1987b), Brown (1990, 1996), and Kunin and Iwasa (1996). The following subsections describe the types of ESSs that emerge when the environment has either two or three habitats.

9.6.1 ESSs in a Two-Habitat Environment

Costly habitat selection can lead to a mixture of behaviors in the ESS. For instance, the ESS may contain a mixture of individuals who forage opportunistically ($q_1 = q_2 = 1$) and individuals who harvest selectively from patches of just one habitat type ($q_1 = 1$ and $q_2 = 0$, for instance). The behaviorally different individuals should experience very different selection on their morphological strategies. When foraging opportunistically, selection favors generalist morphological strategies that represent a compromise between habitat-specific efficiencies and the opportunist's experience with each habitat. When foraging selectively, selection favors the extreme specialist strategy on the selected habitat at the expense of any aptitude on the rejected habitat. There should be a coadaptation between an individual's behavioral strategy and its morphological strategies. Individuals with different behaviors should speciate and diverge morphologically.

And indeed, when the behavioral ESS of the previous section includes a mix of two different behavioral strategies, the morphological ESS will include two species with different and coevolved values for their morphological strategies. When there are two habitats, three types of ESSs are possible. Under a very coarse-grained environment (small values for $a_1 \sim a_2$), the ESS includes a single generalist species (intermediate values for u_1 and u_2) behaving opportunistically ($q_1 = q_2 = 1$). Under a fine-grained environment (large values of $a_1 \sim a_2$), the ESS results in the ghost of competition past and contains the two extreme specialist species, each behaving selectively toward its respective habitat type. Under either lopsided habitat-specific encounter rates ($a_1 > a_2$) or lopsided productivities ($S_1 > S_2$), the ESS results in nested niches (Hutchinson 1958, Schoener 1974) and contains two species: (1) an extreme specialist species behaving selectively toward the less encountered habitat or the more productive habitat and (2) a generalist species behaving opportunistically (Brown 1990).

9.6.2 ESS in a Three-Habitat Environment

The three-habitat extension of equation (21) gives rise to seven possible behavioral strategies within the ESS. These include the opportunist, the three behaviors of foraging selectively on just one of the three habitats, and the three behaviors of foraging selectively on two of the three habitats. Under coadapted behaviors and morphologies, an opportunistic behavior gives rise to the most generalist species, and the one-habitat selectors give rise to the extreme specialist species. With three habitats, the number of possible ESSs increases from three to ten (see Table 9.1).

The outcomes include one one-species community, four two-species communities, and five three-species communities. Three of the communities exhibit some form of the ghost of competition past, with two or three species exhibiting no niche overlap. Five of the communities exhibit a nesting of niches, where one species uses the same and a larger range of habitats than another, more specialized species. As before, a very course-grained environment yields an ESS with a single generalist species behaving opportunistically, and a very fine-grained environment has an ESS with three extreme specialist species foraging selectively on their respective habitats.

The two-species communities include three organizations: the ghost of competition past (a one-habitat selector and the nonoverlapping two-habitat selector), nested

Table 9.1 The Effect of Habitat Diversity, Costliness of Habitat Selection, Evolution of Morphological Coadaptations, and Number of Species on the ESS*

Environmental Circumstances				
Number of Habitats	Costliness of Habitat Selection	Morphological Coadaptation	Number of Species	Number of ESSs and Their Disposition
2	Cost-free	No	1	Mixture of two pure strategies of Inhabit Habitat 1 and Inhabit Habitat 2
2	Cost-free	No	2	Ghost of Competition Past: Species 1 uses strategy of Inhabit Habitat 1 and Species 2 uses strategy of Inhabit Habitat 2
2	Cost-free and habitats vary in food and predation risk	No	1	Single mixed strategy where each individual spends time in each habitat
2	Cost-free and habitats vary in food and predation risk	No	2	Three possible ESSs: (1) Species 1 inhabits 1, Species 2 inhabits 2 (2) Species 1 uses a mix of both habitats, Species 2 inhabits 2 (3) Both species use a mix of both habitats
2	Costly	No	1	Two possible ESSs: (1) All individuals use both habitats (2) Mixture of two strategies: some individuals use both habitats, some individuals use just habitat 1
3	Costly	Yes	Up to 3 emerges as property of the ESS	*Ten possible ESSs:* (1) O; (2) O & S3; (3) O & S23; (4) O, S23 & S3; (5) O, S2 & S3; (6) S13 & S23; (7) S1, S12 & S13; (8) S1 & S23; (9) S13, S2 & S3; (10) S1, S2 & S3 where O = an opportunistic species that uses all three habitats, S12 = species using habitats 1 & 2, and S1 = a selective species that only uses habitat 1

*Environmental circumstances influence the numbers of strategies in an ESS, the types of strategies, and the number of different ESSs that can occur.

niches (an opportunist species with a one- or two-habitat selector), and centrifugal community organization (two different two-habitat selectors). Under centrifugal organization (Rosenzweig & Abramsky 1986), two species each utilize two of three habitats. The two competitors share one habitat in common, and then each possesses a habitat free from its competitor. The three species communities exhibit the ghost of competition past (three one-habitat selectors), nested niches (an opportunist, a two-habitat selector, and a one-habitat selector sharing a habitat in common with the two-habitat selector), and combinations of different community organizations.

One such community combines centrifugal organization with nested niches; another combines nested niches with the ghost of competition past. This outcome is consistent with empirical evidence that several mechanisms of coexistence and community organization combine to promote diversity (e.g., desert rodents; see Brown 1989).

Three general results regarding the coevolution of community organization emerge among the ESSs:

1. Increasing the grain size of the environment encourages the ghost of competition past among species.
2. Increasing the encounter rate with just one habitat encourages nested niches among species.
3. Increasing the productivity of just one habitat encourages centrifugal community organization.

9.7 A Note on Evolutionary Equilibria

Throughout this chapter, I have assumed that ESSs describe the evolutionary and ecological outcome of habitat selection. While an ESS, once established, is stable to invasion by rare alternative strategies (Maynard Smith & Price 1973), it may not be attainable through the ecological or evolutionary dynamics of the system. Game theorists continue to discover a range of evolutionary outcomes that are ESSes.

The evolutionary dynamic has the strategy or strategies evolving up the slope of the frequency-dependent adaptive landscape (evolutionary change is in the direction of and proportional to the magnitude of the fitness gradient; see Brown & Vincent 1987a, Taper & Case 1992, Abrams et al. 1993a, Vincent et al. 1993). The following outcomes often depend upon the speed of evolution along the adaptive landscape or the starting number of species. For instance, the evolutionary dynamics may be nonequilibrial with each species continually coevolutionarily chasing the other (Marrow et al. 1992, Rand et al. 1994, Diekmann et al. 1995). The evolutionary dynamics may not converge on the ESS (Eshel 1983, Kisidi & Meszena 1994). The species, by occurring on the same sides of a valley in the adaptive landscape, may evolve in a direction that results in their convergence and that places both of them far from the actual ESS. The single strategy of a single species may evolve to an evolutionarily stable minimum (*sensu* Abrams et al. 1993b; e.g., Brown & Pavlovic 1992), in which case a mechanism such as competitive speciation (Rosenzweig 1978; e.g., Feder et al. 1988) may be required to produce the two or more species comprising a multi-strategy ESS. Finally, ESS learning rules (Harley 1981, 1987) may facilitate or impede (Frischknecht 1996) a population's progress toward an ESS distribution of individuals among habitats.

For the moment, the ESS seems to be the most likely, consistent, and applicable concept for modeling (a) the distribution of individuals among habitats (Milinski 1984) and (b) the coevolution of habitat selectors. However, as other solution concepts for evolutionary games become better understood, habitat selection should provide an ideal phenomena for integrating, testing, and applying new solution concepts.

9.8 Conclusions

Habitat selection spans and integrates behavioral, populational, community-level, and evolutionary phenomena. At the level of the individual, habitat selection integrates behavioral decisions with often diverse inputs into fitness such as food, safety, and breeding. At the population level, habitat selection can determine the distribution of a species in time and space (MacArthur & Pianka 1966, Holt 1985). At the community level, habitat selection influences species coexistence and community organization (Rosenzweig 1981, Werner 1992). As a product of evolution, habitat selection manifests the coadaptation of traits within individuals and the coevolution of traits among species. This richness of phenomena becomes mirrored in the appropriate evolutionary games for modeling habitat selection.

Single species, cost-free, habitat selection for a substitutable resource encompasses much of present empirical research into how groups of feeding animals distribute themselves among food sources, patches, or habitats (e.g., Tyler & Gilliam 1995). As a game, the individual's best choice of habitats depends upon how others select habitats. The payoff to the individual is generally the sum of expected rewards from each habitat weighted by the fraction of time that the individual devotes to each habitat. The linear relationship between payoff and strategy makes this game similar to the payoff function of a player choosing a mixed strategy in a 2×2 matrix game.

For this reason, the ESS of density-dependent habitat selection involves individuals choosing among habitats so as to equalize the fitness rewards from exploiting each of the habitats (Bishop & Cannings 1976). This general result, embodied in the ideal free distribution, no longer holds when the game is asymmetric, as in the case of interference competition, despotic distributions, and source-sink distributions (Pulliam 1988). Asymmetries can take the form of priority effects (owner versus intruder games: Maynard Smith 1982, Parker 1983), competitive differences among individuals within the same species (e.g., resource-holding power: Hammerstein 1981, Maynard Smith 1982), and competitive differences among species (Rosenzweig 1981). This latter case leads to interspecific density-dependent habitat selection.

Interspecific density-dependent habitat selection extends the behavior of individuals to include community-level phenomena such as interspecific competition, mechanisms of coexistence, and community organization. Adding a second species to the ESS of the above scenario requires that the ESS include both evolutionary stability and ecological stability, in the sense that each species must be able to persist together at positive population sizes. The ESS analysis requires two, instead of one, fitness generating functions; and conditions for evolutionary and ecological stability must be satisfied simultaneously for each fitness function. Before imposing ecological stability, the ESS can consist of (1) each species selectively using separate habitats, (2) each species selectively using the same habitat (shared preference habitat selection, Rosenzweig 1987a), or (3) one species selectively using a single habitat, while the other species contains a mixture of the two behavioral strategies of select habitat 1 and select habitat 2. When ecological stability is imposed, then the ESS with both species present can only exhibit the ghost of competition past, where each species selectively uses an exclusive habitat (Table 9.1).

Relaxing the assumption that the two habitats offer substitutable resources results in a fitness-generating function that is nonlinear in the individual's behavioral strategy. The combined inputs of food and safety for foragers exploiting safe and risky habitats provides such an example (Gilliam & Fraser 1987; Brown 1988, 1992). Unlike the ESS mix of strategies found under substitutable resources, the ESS for a single species can be a mixed strategy of each individual allocating some effort to each habitat. In this way, the payoff to an individual using the ESS mix of strategies is greater than that of individuals using pure strategies from the mix. In fact, in the case of two habitats that differ in predation risk, the ESS will always include individuals using a mixed strategy (Table 9.1). Because a mixed strategy becomes optimal under food and safety, an ideal free distribution does not apply to habitat selection for two complementary inputs into fitness (Moody et al. 1996).

Adding a second species to habitat selection under food and safety adds a second nonlinear fitness function. The conditions for ecological and evolutionary stability permit three ESS outcomes (Table 9.1). The first results in the ghost of competition past, despite the nonlinear fitness functions. The second includes one species selectively using its safer habitat and the other species using a mixed strategy that includes using both habitats. The third ESS outcome has both species using mixed strategies.

Making habitat selection costly can generate nonlinear fitness functions (Brown & Rosenzweig 1986) and produce ESSs that include mixed strategies. But, even if the fitness function remains linear, as in the example with the Holling's (1965) disc equation, the ESS can take new forms from that seen previously. The reason: Under cost-free habitat selection, there can only be a single mixed strategy describing proportional effort devoted to each habitat; under costly habitat selection, the forager has a vector-valued strategy describing the probability of rejecting or accepting patches of each habitat. The vector-valued strategy has a separate and independent element for each habitat type. Because of the linear form of the fitness function, the ESS for each element takes on extreme values (either always accept or always reject). In the example of this chapter, the ESS could include a mix of opportunistic individuals (use all encountered patches regardless of habitat type) and selective individuals (use only the patches of one habitat type) (Table 9.1). Because the fitness of an opportunistic forager combines its experience with each habitat type, the conditions of an ideal free distribution do not apply to either the distribution of foragers or the fitness rewards from patches of each habitat.

Habitat selection becomes a model of coadaptation and coevolution when the experiences of individuals with each habitat (consequence of the behavior of habitat selection) provides the context for natural selection to drive the evolution of additional fixed traits that determine an individual's aptitude in each habitat. For example, in the previous case, those individuals behaving opportunistically should be under selection to evolve a somewhat generalist set of aptitudes, while the behaviorally selective individuals are under strong directional selection to become extreme habitat specialists. In this way, the fitness-generating function now includes both behavioral and morphological strategies. Also, if different morphologies become analogous to different species, the ESS can either promote or inhibit diversity, and the evolutionary dynamics can become a source of competitive speciation (Rosenzweig 1978). With three habitats, the ESS can include up to three species that exhibit a wide variety of different community organizations (ghost of competition past, nested niches, centrifugal organization). The patchiness of the environment and the relative productivities of each habitat are bifurcation parameters that govern the number of species (= morphological strategies) at the ESS (Table 9.1).

The game theory of habitat selection seems to successfully mirror the patterns and complexities of nature (Rosenzweig 1991). Simple models of habitat selection can exhibit a complete set of outcomes ranging from the optimal behaviors of individuals to their population, community, and evolutionary consequences. Natural selection probably occurs most often and interestingly in a frequency-dependent context. Within such a context, natural selection can influence behaviors, coadapted traits, coevolution, and adaptive speciation. As an evolutionary game, habitat selection resides firmly within this rich and exciting context.

ACKNOWLEDGMENTS   I thank Lee Dugatkin and Kern Reeve for their patience, dedication, and talents on behalf of this volume. I am grateful for stimulating discussions over many years with Burt Kotler and Zvika Abramsky regarding many of the topics of the chapter. I owe credit to Bill Mitchell for his comraderie that steered me into the Optimization Research Program (Mitchell & Valone 1990) within which I believe evolutionary game theory resides. Also, much credit is given to Tom Vincent as my game theory mentor and to Michael Rosenzweig as my mentor in habitat selection.

References

Abrams, P. A. 1991. Life history and the relationship between food availability and foraging effort. *Ecology,* 72, 1242–1252.

Abrams, P. A., Harada, Y. & Matsuda, H. 1993a. On the relationship between quantitative genetics and ESS models. *Evolution,* 47, 982–985.

Abrams, P. A., Matsuda, H. & Harada, Y. 1993b. Evolutionarily unstable fitness maxima and stable fitness minima of continuous traits. *Evol. Ecol.,* 7, 465–487.

Abrams, P. A. & Matsuda, H. 1996. Fitness minimization and dynamics instability as a consequence of predator prey coevolution. *Evol. Ecol.,* 10, 167–186.

Abramsky, Z., Rosenzweig, M. L., Pinshow, B., Brown, J. S., Kotler, B. P. & Mitchell, W. A. 1990. Habitat selection: An experimental field test with two gerbil species. *Ecology,* 71, 2358–2369.

Abramsky, Z., Rosenzweig, M. L. & Pinshow, B. 1991. The shape of a gerbil isocline: an experimental field study using principles of optimal habitat selection. *Ecology,* 72, 329–340.

Auslander, D., Guckenheimer, J. & Oster, G. 1978. Random evolutionarily stable strategies. *Theor. Pop. Biol.,* 13, 276–293.

Bishop, D. T. & Cannings, C. 1976. Models of animal conflict. *Adv. Appl. Prob., 8,* 616–621.

Brew, J. S. 1982. Niche shift and the minimization of competition. *Theor. Pop. Biol.,* 22, 367–381.

Brown, J. H. & Lieberman, G. 1973. Resource utilization and coexistence of seed-eating rodents in sand dune habitats. *Ecology,* 54, 788–797.

Brown, J. S. 1988. Patch use as an indicator or habitat preference, predation risk, and competition. *Behav. Ecol. Sociobiol.,* 22, 37–47.

Brown, J. S. 1989. Desert rodent community structure: A test of four mechanisms of coexistence. *Ecol. Monogr.,* 20, 1–20.

Brown, J. S. 1990. Habitat selection as an evolutionary game. *Evolution,* 44, 732–746.

Brown, J. S. 1992. Patch use under predation risk: I. Models and predictions. *Ann. Zool. Fenn.,* 29, 301–309.

Brown, J. S. 1996. Coevolution of community organization in three habitats. *Oikos,* 75, 193–206.

Brown, J. S. & Alkon, P. A. 1990. Testing values of crested porcupine habitats by experimental food patches. *Oecologia,* 83, 512–518.

Brown, J. S. & Pavlovic, N. B. 1992. Evolution in heterogeneous environments: Effects of migration on habitat specialization. *Evol. Ecol.,* 6, 360–382.

Brown, J. S. & Rosenzweig, M. L. 1986. Habitat selection in slowly regenerating environments. *J. Theor. Biol.,* 123, 151–171.

Brown, J. S. & Vincent, T. L. 1987a. Coevolution as an evolutionary game. *Evolution,* 41, 66–79.

Brown. J. S. & Vincent, T. L. 1987b. A theory for the evolutionary game. *Theor. Pop. Biol.,* 31, 140–166.

Brown, J. S. & Vincent, T. L. 1992. Organization of predator–prey communities as an evolutionary game. *Evolution,* 46, 1269–1283.

Connell, J. H. 1980. Diversity and the coevolution of competitors, or the ghost of competition past. *Oikos,* 35, 131–138.

Diekmann, U., Marrow, P. & Law, R. 1995. Evolutionary cycling in predator–prey interactions: Population dynamics and the Red Queen. *J. Theor. Biol.,* 176, 91–102.

Eshel, I. 1983. Evolutionary and continuous stability. *J. Theor. Biol.,* 103, 99–111.

Fagan, R. 1987. A generalized habitat matching rule. *Evol. Ecol.,* 1, 5–10.

Feder, J. L., Chilcote, C. A. & Bush, G. L. 1988. Genetic differentiation and sympatric host races of the apple maggot fly, *Rhagoletis pomonella.*, Nature, 336, 61–64.

Feinsinger, P., Tiebout, H. M., III & Young, B. E. 1991. Do tropical bird pollinated plants exhibit density-dependent interactions? Field experiments. *Ecology,* 72, 1953–1963.

Fraser, D. F. & Gilliam, J. F. 1987. Feeding under predation hazard: Response of the guppy and Hart's rivulus from sites with contrasting predation hazard. *Behav. Ecol. Sociobiol.,* 21, 203–209.

Fretwell, S. D. & Lucas, H. L., Jr. 1970. On territorial behavior and other factors influencing habitat distribution in birds. I. Theoretical development. *Acta Biotheor.,* 19, 16–36.

Frischknecht, M. 1996. Predators choosing between patches with standing crop: the influence of switching rules and input types. *Behav. Ecol. Sociobiol.,* 38, 159–166.

Gersani, M. & Sachs, T. 1992. Development correlations between roots in heterogeneous environments. *Plant, Cell Environ.* 15, 463–469.

Gilliam, J. F. & Fraser, D. F. 1987. Habitat selection under predation hazard: A test of a model with foraging minnows. *Ecology,* 68, 1856–1862.

Grubb, T. C. & Greenwald, L. 1982. Sparrows and a brushpile: Foraging responses to different combinations of predation risk and energy cost. *Anim. Behav.,* 30, 637–640.

Hammerstein, P. 1981. The role of asymmetries in animal contests. *Anim. Behav.,* 29, 193–205.

Harley, C. B. 1981. Learning the evolutionarily stable strategy. *J. Theor. Biol.,* 89, 611–633.

Harley, C. B. 1987. Learning rules, optimal behaviour, and evolutionary stability. *J. Theor. Biol.,* 127, 377–379.

Hines, W. G. S. 1980. Three characterizations of population strategy stability. *J. Appl. Prob.,* 17, 333–340.

Hines, W. G. S. 1987. Evolutionary stable strategies: A review of basic theory. *Theor. Pop. Biol.,* 31, 195–272.

Holling, C. S. 1965. The functional response of predators to prey density and its role in mimicry and population regulation. *Mem. Entom. Soc. Canada,* 45, 1–60.

Holt, R. D. 1977. Predation, apparent competition and the structure of prey communities. *Theor. Pop. Biol.,* 12, 197–229.

Holt, R. D. 1984. Spatial heterogeneity, indirect interactions, and the coexistence of prey species. *Am. Nat.,* 124, 377–406.

Holt, R. D. 1985. Population dynamics in two-patch environments: Some anomalous consequences of an optimal habitat distribution. *Theor. Pop. Biol.,* 28, 181–208.

Holt, R. D. 1987. Prey communities in patchy environments. *Oikos,* 50, 276–290.

Holt, R. D. & Gaines, M. S. 1992. Analysis of adaptations in heterogeneous landscapes: Implications for the evolution of fundamental niches. *Evol. Ecol.,* 6, 433–447.

Houston, A. I., McNamara, J. M. & Hutchinson, J. M. C. 1993. General results concerning the trade-off between gaining energy and avoiding predation. *Philos. Trans. R. Soc. London B,* 341, 375–397.

Hutchinson, G. E. 1958. Concluding remarks. *Cold Spring Harbor Symp. Quant. Biol.,* 22, 415–427.

Kacelnik, A., Krebs, J. R. & Bernstein, C. 1992. The ideal free distribution and predator-prey populations. *Trends Ecol. Evol.,* 7, 50–55.

Kennedy, M. & Gray, R. D. 1993. Can ecological theory predict the distribution of foraging animals? A critical analysis of experiments on the ideal free distribution. *Oikos,* 68, 158–166.

Kisidi, E. & Meszena, G. 1993. Density-dependent life history evolution in a fluctuating environment. In *Adaptation in Stochastic Environments,* J. Yoshimura & C. W. Clark, eds. *Lect. Notes Biomath.,* 98, 26–62.

Kisidi, E. & Meszena, G. 1994. Life histories with lottery competition in a stochastic environment: An ESS that does not win. *Theor. Pop. Biol.,* 47, 191–211.

Kotler, B. P. 1984. Predation risk and the structure of desert rodent communities. *Ecology,* 65, 689–701.

Kunin, W. & Iwasa, Y. 1996. Pollinator foraging strategies in mixed floral arrays: Density effects and floral constancy. *Theor. Pop. Biol.,* 49, 232–263.

Levins, R. 1962. Theory of fitness in a heterogeneous environment: I. The fitness set and adaptive function. *Am. Nat.,* 96, 361–373.

Levins, R. 1968. *Evolution in Changing Environments.* Princeton, NJ: Princeton University Press.

Lima, S. L. & Dill, L. M. 1990. Behavioral decisions made under the risk of predation: Review and prospectus. *Can. J. Zool.,* 68, 619–640.

MacArthur, R. 1972. *Geographical Ecology.* Princeton, NJ: Princeton University Press.

MacArthur, R. & Pianka, E. 1966. On optimal use of a patchy environment. *Am. Nat.,* 100, 603–609.

Marrow, P., Law, R. & Cannings, C. 1992. The coevolution of population interactions: ESSs and Red Queen dynamics. *Proc. R. Soc. London B,* 250, 133–141.

Maynard-Smith, J. 1982. *Evolution and the Theory of Games.* Cambridge: Cambridge University Press.

Maynard Smith, J. & Price, G. R. 1973. The logic of animal conflict. *Nature,* 246, 15–18.

McNamara, J. M. & Houston, A. I. 1990. State-dependent ideal free distribution. *Evol. Ecol.,* 4, 298–311.

Messier, F., Virgl, J. A. & Marinelli, L. 1990. Density-dependent habitat selection in muskrats: A test of the ideal free distribution model. *Oecologia,* 84, 380–385.

Metz, J. A. J., Nisbet, R. M. & Geritz, S. A. H. 1992. How should we define 'fitness' for general ecological scenarios? *Trends Ecol. Evol.,* 7, 198–202.

Milchtaich, I. 1996. Congestion models of competition. *Am. Nat.,* 147, 760–783.

Milinski, M. 1984. Competitive resource sharing: An experimental test of a learning rule for ESSs. *Anim. Behav.,* 32, 233–242.

Mitchell, W. A. & Valone, T. J. 1990. The optimization research program: Studying adaptations by their function. *Q. Rev. Biol.,* 65, 43–52.

Moody, A. L., Houston, A. I. & McNamara, J. M. 1996. Ideal free distributions under predation risk. *Behav. Ecol. Sociobiol.,* 38: 131–143.

Morris, D. W. 1988. Habitat-dependent population regulation and community structure. *Evol. Ecol.,* 2, 253–269.

Morris, D. W. 1989a. Habitat-dependent estimates of competitive ability. *Oikos,* 59, 111–120.

Morris, D. W. 1989b. Density-dependent habitat selection: Testing the theory with fitness data. *Evol. Ecol.,* 3, 80–94.

Morris, D. W. 1992. Scales and costs of habitat selection in heterogeneous landscapes. *Evol. Ecol.,* 6, 412–432.

Morris, D. W. 1994. Habitat matching: Alternatives and implications to populations and communities. *Evol. Ecol.,* 4, 387–406.

Nash, J. 1951. Non-cooperative games. *Annals of Mathematics,* 54, 286–295.

Ovadia, O. & Abramsky, Z. 1995. Density-dependent habitat selection: Evaluation of the isodar method. *Oikos,* 73, 86–94.

Parker, G. A. 1978. Searching for mates. In *Behavioral Ecology: An Evolutionary Approach,* first edition, J. R. Krebs & N. B. Davies, eds., pp. 214–244. Oxford: Blackwell Scientific Publications.

Parker, G. A. 1983. Arms race in evolution—An ESS to the opponent-independent costs game. *J. Theor. Biol.,* 101, 619–648.

Parker, G. A. & Sutherland, W. J. 1986. Ideal free distributions when individuals differ in competitive abilities: Phenotype-limited ideal free models. *Anim. Behav.,* 34, 1222–1242.

Persson, L. & Eklov, P. 1995. Prey refuges affecting interactions between piscivorous perch and juvenile perch and roach. *Ecology,* 76, 70–81.

Pimm, S. L., Rosenzweig, M. L. & Mitchell, W. 1985. Competition and food selection: Field tests of a theory. *Ecology,* 66, 798–807.

Pulliam, H. R. 1988. Sources, sinks, and population regulation. *Am. Nat.,* 132, 652–661.

Pyke, G. H. 1981. Optimal foraging in hummingbirds: Rule for movement between inflorescences. *Anim. Behav.,* 29, 889–896.

Pyke, G. H. 1982. Foraging in bumblebees: Rule of departure from inflorescence. *Can. J. Zool.,* 60, 417–428.

Rand, D. A., Wilson, H. B. & McGlade, J. M. 1994. Dynamics and evolution: evolutionarily stable attractors, invasion exponents and phenotype dynamics. *Philos. Trans. R. Soc. B,* 343, 261–283.

Rodriguez, M. A. 1995. Habitat-specific estimates of competition in stream salmonids: A field test of the isodar model of habitat selection. *Evol. Ecol.,* 9, 169–184.

Rosenzweig, M. L. 1978. Competitive speciation. *Biol. J. Linn. Soc.,* 10, 275–289.

Rosenzweig, M. L. 1981. A theory of habitat selection. *Ecology,* 62, 327–335.

Rosenzweig, M. L. 1985. Some theoretical aspects of habitat selection. In *Habitat Selection in Birds,* M. L. Cody, ed., pp. 517–540. New York: Academic Press.

Rosenzweig, M. L. 1986. Hummingbird isolegs in an experimental system. *Behav. Ecol. Sociobiol.,* 19, 313–322.

Rosenzweig, M. L. 1987a. Community organization from the point of view of habitat selectors. In *Organization of Communities: Past and Present,* J. H. R. Gee & P. S. Giller, eds., pp. 469–490. Oxford: Blackwell Scientific Publications.

Rosenzweig, M. L. 1987b. Habitat selection as a source of biological diversity. *Evol. Ecol.,* 1, 315–330.

Rosenzweig, M. L. 1991. Habitat selection and population interactions. *Am. Nat.,* 137, S5–S28.

Rosenzweig, M. L. & Abramsky, Z. 1986. Centrifugal community structure. *Oikos,* 46, 339–348.

Rosenzweig, M. L. & Winakur, J. 1969. Population ecology of desert rodent communities: habitat and environmental complexity. *Ecology,* 50, 558–572.

Roughgarden, J. 1976. Resource-partitioning among competing species—A coevolutionary approach. *Theor. Pop. Biol.,*9, 388–424.

Sachs, T., Novoplansky, A. & Cohen, D. 1993. Plants as competing populations of redundant organs. *Plant, Cell and Environment,* 16, 765–770.

Sallabanks, R. 1993. Hierarchical mechanisms of fruit selection by an avian frugivore. *Ecology,* 74, 1326–1336.

Schmitt, R. J. 1982. Consequences of dissimilar defenses against predation in a subtidal marine community. *Ecology,* 63, 1588–1601.

Schmitt, R. J. 1987. Indirect interactions between prey: Apparent competition, predator aggregation, and habitat segregation. *Ecology,* 68, 1887–1897.

Schoener, T. W. 1974. Resource partitioning in ecological communities. *Science,* 185, 27–39.

Sih, A. 1980. Optimal behavior: Can foragers balance two conflicting demands? *Science,* 210, 1041–1043.

Taper, M. & Case, T. J. 1992. Models of character displacement and the theoretical robustness of taxon cycles. *Evolution,* 46, 317–333.

Taylor, P. D. & Jonker, L. B. 1978. Evolutionary stable strategies and game dynamics. *Math. Biosci.,* 40, 145–156.

Tilman, D. 1980. Resources: A graphical–mechanistic approach to competition and predation. *Am. Nat.,* 116, 362–393.

Tilman, D. 1982. *Resource Competition and Community Structure.* Princeton, NJ: Princeton University Press.

Tyler, J. A. & Gilliam, J. F. 1995. Ideal free distribution of stream fish: A model and test with minnows, *Rhinicthys atratulus. Ecology,* 76, 580–592.

van Balaan, M. & Sabelis, M.W. 1993. Coevolution of patch strategies of predator and prey and the consequences for ecological stability. *Am. Nat.,* 142, 646–670.

Vincent, T. L. & Brown, J. S. 1984. Stability in an evolutionary game. *Theor. Pop. Biol.,* 26, 408–427.

Vincent, T. L. & Brown, J. S. 1987. Evolution of non-equilibrium dynamics. *Mathematical Modelling,* 8, 766–771.

Vincent, T. L. & Brown, J. S. 1988. The evolution of ESS theory. *Annu. Rev. Ecol. Syst.,* 19, 423–443.

Vincent, T. L., Cohen, Y. & Brown, J. S. 1993. Evolution via strategy dynamics. *Theor. Pop. Biol.,* 44, 149–176.

Vincent, T. L. S., Scheel, D., Brown, J. S. & Vincent, T. L. 1996. Tradeoffs and coexistence in consumer-resource models: It all depends on what and where you eat. *Am. Nat.,* 148, 1038–1058.

Werner, E. E. 1992. Individual behavior and higher-order species interactions. *Am. Nat.,* 140, S5–S32.

Werner, E. E., Gilliam, J. F., Hall, D. J. & Mittlebach, G. G. 1983. An experimental test of the effects of predation risk on habitat use in fish. *Ecology,* 64, 1540–1548.

Whelan, C. J. 1989. Avian foliage structure preferences for foraging and the effect of prey biomass. *Anim. Behav.,* 38, 839–846.

Whelan, C. J. & Willson, M. F. 1994. Fruit choice in migratory North American birds: Field and aviary experiments. *Oikos,* 71, 137–151.

Wright, S. 1931. Evolution in Mendelian populations. *Genetics,* 16, 97–159.

Wright, S. 1960. Physiological genetics, ecology of populations, and natural selection. In *The Evolution of Life,* S. Tax, ed., pp 429–475. Chicago: University of Chicago Press.

Zeeman, E. C. 1981. Dynamics of the evolution of animal conflicts. *J. Theor. Biol.,* 89, 249–270.

ANDREW SIH

Game Theory and Predator–Prey Response Races

10.1 Introduction

A key issue in ecology is the study of animal habitat or patch use. Why are animals where they are? Why do they go where they go? In the past three decades, behavioral ecologists have focused on the effects of foraging, competition, and predation risk on habitat use. Optimality theory and its cousin, game theory, have provided conceptual frameworks guiding work in this field (Stephens & Krebs 1986, Mangel & Clark 1988, Milinski & Parker 1991; Brown, this volume).

In the absence of predation risk, individual foragers often show patch use patterns that are consistent with the goal of maximizing rates of net energy intake (Stephens & Krebs 1986; Brown, this volume). In the absence of competition, energy maximizing behaviors can be assessed without considering strategies shown by other foragers. Competition and predation risk, however, clearly influence patterns of patch use. Because the presence of competitors generally causes a reduction in individual feeding rates (Hassell 1978, Schoener 1983), the value of a given patch for an individual forager depends on the patch use of its competitors. When the value of each behavioral option (here, time spent foraging in each patch) depends on decisions made by other individuals, the appropriate conceptual framework is game theory (Maynard Smith 1982). Ideal free distribution (IFD) theory uses game theory to predict patch use patterns in a world with competition for resources (Fretwell 1972, Milinski & Parker 1991, Kacelnik et al. 1992).

Predation risk also causes shifts in patch use (Sih 1987, Lima & Dill 1990). Numerous studies suggest that in the presence of predation risk, foragers show patterns of patch use that reflect a balance between the conflicting demands of foraging and avoiding predators (Sih 1980, Werner et al. 1983, Gilliam & Fraser 1987, Abrahams & Dill 1989). Most of these studies, however, do not account explicitly for competition among foragers; that is, only a few studies have looked at IFD under predation risk (but see Abrahams & Dill 1989, McNamara & Houston 1990).

Incorporating competition and predation risk represents a significant step forward in our conceptual framework for understanding animal distributions. This chapter focuses on another key aspect of reality that is missing from most extant studies of predator–prey patch use: the possibility that predators and prey show simultaneous, adaptive responses to each other. While it seems obvious that in many situations, predators and prey each respond to the other, to date, almost all empirical and theoretical studies on the effects of predation risk on prey patch use treat predation risk as fixed in space. Typically, the assumption is that one patch is dangerous (usually, the one with more resources for prey), while another patch is safe. Clearly, this assumption is too simplistic if predator patch use responds to prey patch use and vice versa. In that case, we have what Sih (1984) referred to as a predator–prey behavioral response race. Predators attempt to aggregate in patches where prey are more available. Prey avoid areas with more predators. Prey also tend to go where their own resources are more abundant, and both predators and prey respond to competition within their own trophic level. The result is a set of simultaneous games between predators and prey, among predators and among prey.

The focus of this chapter is on simultaneous predator and prey ideal free distributions in a three-trophic-level system. At the "double IFD" (i.e., where both predators and prey are following IFD), what are the relationships between the spatial distributions of predators, prey, and resources? Do predators aggregate where there are more prey? Do prey aggregate where their resources are more abundant? Do predators aggregate where resources for prey are more abundant? These questions have been addressed by a few recent models (Schwinning & Rosenzweig 1990, van Baalen & Sabelis 1992, Hugie & Dill 1994, also see Brown, this volume). Here, I discuss and extend these extant models.

10.2 A Brief History of Ideal Free Distribution Theory

Ideal free distributions have been reviewed in detail elsewhere (Milinski & Parker 1991, Kacelnik et al. 1992). Here, I provide a brief overview to ensure that readers are familiar with some basic concepts and terminology.

Picture a simple scenario with two patches (A and B) and two trophic levels—prey that consume resources (I call the consumers "prey" because I will later add predators). N_a and N_b are prey densities in patches A and B respectively, and R_a and R_b are resource availabilities in the two patches. Resource availabilities do not respond to prey patch use; that is, resources do not respond behaviorally to prey. The focal question is, Given a resource ratio (R_a/R_b), how should prey distribute themselves between the two patches? What is the ideal free prey ratio (N_a/N_b)?

Given some simplifying assumptions (that are discussed below), at the IFD, prey should have equal feeding rates in both patches. The logic is that if one patch is better than the other (i.e., prey have higher feeding rates in that patch), then prey should move from the poorer patch into the better patch, thus increasing competition in the better patch until it is no longer better than the other patch. At the IFD, prey should have equal feeding rates in all patches, so that no prey can benefit from switching patches.

In the simplest version of IFD theory, prey feeding rates are linearly related to resource availability and inversely related to prey density in a given patch; that is, feeding rates in the two patches are qR_a/N_a and qR_b/Nb, where q is the proportion of resources consumed per unit time by a prey individual in the absence of competition. (Given the simplifying assumption that q is the same in all patches, the q's cancel; thus in subsequent analyses, I leave out q.) At the IFD these feeding rates should be equal. With a simple rearrangement, it emerges that at the IFD, $N_a/N_b = R_a/R_b$. The prediction is thus that prey should "match" resources—that is, that the ratio of prey densities in the two patches should be equal to the ratio of inherent resource availabilities in the two patches.

Kennedy & Gray (1993) reviewed over 50 tests of the "matching" prediction and found that animals sometimes match, occasionally "overmatch" (i.e., $N_a/N_b > R_a/R_b$), and often "undermatch" ($N_a/N_b < R_a/R_b$) their resources. Modifications of the simple theory outlined above attempt to explain discrepancies from matching by adding various aspects of reality. (1) *Nonomniscient consumers:* Simple theory assumes that consumers have and optimally utilize perfect knowledge of a static resource distribution. Modified theory accounts for imperfect assessments of resource availability (Abrahams 1986) and the need to learn about shifting resource distributions (Bernstein 1988). (2) *Unequal competitors:* Simple theory assumes that all competitors have identical feeding rates within a given patch. More recent work acknowledges that foragers vary in their competitive abilities (Parker & Sutherland 1986, Houston & McNamara 1988). (3) *Travel costs:* Most IFD models assume that consumers choose patches sequentially and then do not move, or that subsequent movements have no time or energy costs. In reality, movements between patches must have costs (Bernstein 1988, Kennedy & Gray 1993). Here, I discuss two other modifications in some detail: "nonideal competition" and predation risk.

As noted above, simple IFD theory assumes that prey feeding rates in each patch i are R_i/N_i. I refer to this as "ideal competition." It might occur if resources become available at a constant, continuous rate, all resources are consumed as they become available, and all resources are shared equally among consumers. This scenario, however, assumes an unrealistically intense level of competition among prey. It assumes that if a solitary prey individual has a feeding rate of R, the presence of a single competitor reduces that feeding rate by 50%. This is a stronger reduction than is typically observed with real exploitative competitors in either laboratory or field situations (Hassell 1978, Schoener 1983). This scenario also assumes that the total feeding rate of all prey is constant (and equal to R) regardless of whether a patch has one consumer or one million consumers. This assumption is clearly unrealistic.

To allow for more realistic competitive scenarios, following Sutherland (1983), I draw from the literature on mutual interference among consumers (Hassell & Varley 1969) to express consumer feeding rates as R/N^x, where x is a competition coefficient. If $x = 0$, then consumers do not compete; that is, consumer feeding rate is R regardless of local consumer density. If $x = 1$, then consumers show "ideal competition" as defined above. Real competitors almost always have weaker effects on each other than ideal competition; that is, $0 < x < 1$. Although the term mutual interference often implies aggression between consumers (Hassell 1978), the above mathematical formulation has no behavioral implications. It is merely a simple way of expressing variable intensities of competition.

The expression R/N^x has two potentially undesirable properties. First, when $N < 1$, then increasing x increases prey feeding rate, which goes against the notion that x is a measure of competition among prey. Thus the following analyses define a unit of area such that prey densities are greater than one. Also, if the average prey individual's feeding rate is R/N^x, then if $x<1$, the total prey population's feeding rate ($= RN^{1-x}$) shows no asymptote with increasing prey density. That is, if $x<1$, then increases in prey population size are always associated with an increase in total prey population feeding rate. While this is reasonable for realistic prey densities, it obviously will not hold for infinite (or unrealistically high) prey densities.

If consumer feeding rates in each patch are R/N^x, then at the IFD (i.e., setting feeding rates equal in the two patches) we have

$$N_a/N_b = (R_a/R_b)^{1/x} \tag{1}$$

If $x = 1$, then consumers should match resources. If $0 < x < 1$, then consumers should overmatch resources. For example, if the resource ratio is 2 (patch A is twice as good as patch B) and $x = 0.5$, then at the IFD the consumer ratio should be 4 (patch A contains four times as many consumers as patch B). Weaker competition among consumers (i.e., smaller x) should result in greater overmatching of resources by consumers. This makes sense. Competition keeps consumers from all foraging in the patch that is inherently better (higher R). If competition is weaker (x is smaller), this allows consumers to aggregate more heavily in the patch with higher R. At the extreme, if $x = 0$ (i.e., consumers do not compete), then all consumers should be in the patch with more resources. That is, if one patch is better than the other, and the presence of other consumers has no effect on individual feeding rates, then all consumers should feed in the better patch.

In a three-trophic-level scenario, equation (1) is useful for expressing consumption rates of both predators and prey. Later, I will use x as the competition coefficient for prey and m as the competition coefficient for predators.

10.3 Predation Risk

In a three-trophic-level world, prey (i.e., the middle trophic level) must balance feeding demands and the need to avoid predators. Gilliam and Fraser (1987) showed that, given a set of simplifying assumptions (see their article for discussion of these assumptions), prey optimally balance these conflicting demands by minimizing the ratio u/f or, alternatively, by maximizing f/u, where f and u are the feeding rate and mortality risk for individual prey. In theory, f/u could be prey density-independent. That would be the case, for example, if prey do not compete with each other (i.e., individual prey feeding rates do not depend on prey density) and predation rates are density-independent (e.g., if predators show a linear functional response and no aggregative response). If f/u is prey density-independent, then the optimal patch choice for prey does not depend on patch choices made by other prey. All prey should feed in the patch with higher f/u (Gilliam & Fraser 1987).

In nature, however, feeding and mortality rates probably both usually depend on prey density within a patch. As noted in the previous section, if prey compete with each other, then increased prey density in a patch results in reduced individual feeding rates in that patch. Per capita predation risk should also depend on prey density if predators show nonlinear functional responses (because either predator foraging or prey defense behavior is prey density-dependent) or predators exhibit a tendency to aggregate in patches with more prey (Hassell 1978). As discussed in the next section, it is possible for f/u to increase with increasing prey density (i.e., for prey to enhance each other's fitness); however, in most situations considered in this chapter, f/u decreases with increasing prey density.

10.4 Three Trophic-Level Ideal Free Distributions

For the remainder of this chapter, I examine the situation where predators eat prey and prey consume resources. Predators do not consume resources. For example, we might think of carnivores, herbivores, and plants. P is predator density and N and R are prey density and resource availability, respectively. For simplicity, I again consider a situation with two patches, A and B, where resource availability is not influenced by prey or predator patch use and resource availability is higher in patch A ($R_a/R_b > 1$). In the carnivore–herbivore–plant scenario, resource availability is net plant productivity which is assumed to be influenced primarily by nutrient availability rather than herbivory. The goal is to solve for the simultaneous IFD for both predators and prey. That is, if predators tend to go where prey are more abundant, but prey avoid predators while also responding to their resource distribution, and both predators and prey respond to competition within their trophic levels, what sorts of spatial distributions of predators and prey do we expect to find?

To solve for the simultaneous ideal free distribution, I use the "equal fitness in both patches" criterion; that is, I look for the distribution of predators and prey that simultaneously yields equal feeding rates (F) for predators in both patches, as well as equal feeding rate/predation risk ratios (f/u) for prey in both patches. This situation is a simultaneous IFD if F and f/u both show negative frequency dependence at the equal fitness point for both predators and prey; that is, if F decreases with predator density in a patch and f/u decreases with prey density in a patch. Predator feeding rates always decrease with predator density, provided that predators compete for food.

Prey fitness is negatively frequency dependent if $(f/u)' = d(f/u)/dN < 0$. Assuming that $f' < 0$ (i.e., prey compete for resources), then this occurs if $-f'/f > u'/u$, where f' and u' are df/dN and du/dN respectively. In other words, prey fitness decreases with increasing prey density if the proportional decrease in individual prey feeding rate (with increasing prey density) is greater than the proportional increase in individual prey safety due to increasing prey density. In many situations, increasing prey density results in increased risk for individual prey (e.g., when the predator's functional response is accelerating or roughly linear, and predators show a tendency to aggregate in areas with more prey). In these situations, increasing prey density in a patch results in both reduced prey feeding rate and increased risk for prey; that is, prey fitness clearly declines with increasing prey density.

Even if one of the above assumptions about predator behavior is violated, prey fitness is usually negatively frequency-dependent. For example, if $f = R/N$ and $u = c(N)P$ (where $c(N)$ is the proportion of prey killed per predator per unit time), then f/u ($= R/(c(N)NP)$) decreases with prey density as long as either (a) individual predators increase their feeding rate when more prey are available (i.e., the functional response, $c(N)N$ is positive) or (b) predators show any tendency to aggregate in patches with more prey. The former is almost always true, and the latter is often true (Hassell 1978).

There are scenarios in which prey fitness is positively frequency-dependent (e.g., no competition among prey, a type 2 predator functional response, strong competition among predators, low overall predator density, and little or no predator aggregation). The probability of that occurring in an "ideal free world" is reduced by the fact that at the equal fitness point for both predators and prey, predators usually aggregate strongly in patches with more prey (see below). It is important to note that nonlinear fitness functions can sometimes yield solutions that violate the "equal fitness" solution criterion (Brown, this volume), but this will not be true for the models considered here. Analytical solutions and simulations suggest that in the context of double IFD, the "equal fitness" criterion virtually always identifies an ESS (also see Hugie & Dill 1994).

Below, I first solve for the double IFD in a very simple model and then investigate how the characteristics of the double IFD depend on the intensity of prey competition, the intensity of competition among predators, the predator's functional response, and the existence of refuges.

10.4.1 Two Simple Three-Trophic-Level Models

First, consider the situation where prey show "ideal" competition (i.e., $x = 1, f = R/N$), and the two patches do not differ in inherent safety (i.e., neither patch is a refuge from predators). For predators, simple models often assume either that predation rates are prey-dependent (e.g., $F = cN$, where c is the proportion of prey killed per unit time by a solitary predator) or ratio-dependent (i.e., dependent on the ratio of prey density to predator density, $F = cN/P$; see Arditi et al. 1991). Simple prey-dependence essentially assumes that predators do not compete with each other, while simple ratio-dependence assumes that predators show "ideal" competition. In reality, the degree of predator competition usually falls between these two extremes (Hassell 1978).

If predation rate is prey-dependent, then predators have equal feeding rates in the two patches if $cN_a = cN_b$. Since the c's cancel, at the ESS we have $N_a = N_b$. Prey have equal f/u in the two patches if $(R_a/N_a)/(cP_a) = (R_b/N_b)/(cP_b)$. Since the c's cancel and $N_a = N_b$, with a bit of re-arrangement, at the ESS, $P_a/P_b = R_a/R_b$. In words, the predictions are that: (1) despite spatial variation in resource availability, prey should be uniformly distributed; and (2) predators should match resources. I refer to the latter as a "leapfrog effect" since the distribution of predators is predicted to match not the distribution of prey (that they eat), but instead the distribution of resources (that predators do not consume).

This solution is an ESS even though predator feeding rates do not depend directly on predator density. If prey are more abundant in either patch, then since predators do not compete, all predators should go to the patch with more prey. This favors prey returning to a uniform distribution. If predators overmatch resources (overaggregate in patch A), then prey should shift out of patch A, which should favor predators moving out of patch A. The opposite occurs if predators undermatch resources. The result is an ESS produced by indirect feedback through effects of predator density on prey movement and vice versa.

If predation rates are ratio-dependent, then for predator feeding rates in the two patches to be equal, we need: $cN_a/P_a = cN_b/P_b$, or $P_a/P_b = N_a/N_b$. That is, at the double IFD, predators should match prey. From the prey view, $f/u =$ (individual prey feeding rate)/((individual predator feeding rate)(predator density)/(prey density)), or $(R/N)/((cN/P)(P)/N)$, which reduces to R/cN. At the double IFD, $R_a/cN_a = R_b/cN_b$, or re-arranging, $N_a/N_b = R_a/R_b$. Thus, with simple ratio-dependent predation, at the double IFD, both predators and prey should match resources. This is an ESS because both predator and prey fitnesses are negatively frequency-dependent.

These simple models set the tone for predictions that are generated by a more complicated, more realistic model. That is, in a three-trophic-level system, at the double IFD, predators should tend to aggregate in patches with more resources even though they do not consume those resources, while prey distributions could vary between matching resources (if predators compete heavily) to being uniformly distributed (if predators do not compete). In most conditions, prey do not aggregate with resources as strongly as predators do, because prey must balance the conflicting demands of feeding and avoiding predators. For example, in a carnivore–herbivore–plant system, the prediction is that carnivores should aggregate in areas with high net primary productivity (NPP), while herbivores should be relatively uniformly distributed.

10.4.2 A More Realistic Predator–Prey Game

Now, let us add the following aspects of reality into the model: (1) nonlinear predator functional responses ($F = c(N)N$, where c varies with N); (2) variable prey competition (i.e., $f = R/N^x$; $x =$ prey competition coefficient), and (3) variable predator competition ($F = c(N)N/P^m$; $m =$ predator competition coefficient). Algebraic rearrangements of the equations for f/u and F show that at the double IFD, prey and predator ratios in the two patches are

$$\frac{N_a}{N_b} = \left[\left(\frac{R_a}{R_b} \right) \left(\frac{c(N_b)}{c(N_a)} \right)^{1/m} \right]^{\frac{m}{m(x-1)+1}} \tag{2}$$

$$\frac{P_a}{P_b} = \left[\left(\frac{R_a}{R_b} \right) \left(\frac{c(N_a)}{c(N_b)} \right)^{1-x} \right]^{\frac{1}{m(x-1)+1}} \tag{3}$$

Equations (2) and (3) predict that at the ESS, in most situations, both predators and prey should tend to be more abundant in patches with a higher resource availability (i.e., in patch A, if $R_a > R_b$). The distributions of predators and prey depend, however, not only on the resource ratio (R_a/R_b), but also on prey and predator competition coefficients (m and x) and on the nonlinearity of the functional response.

Examination of equations (2) and (3) shows that nonlinear predator functional responses have opposite effects on predator and prey distributions. To see this, focus on the predator attack ratios: $c(N_a)/c(N_b)$ and $c(N_b)/c(N_a)$. If, for example, predators have a type 2 functional response (e.g., when predators satiate at high prey densities), then assuming that $N_a > N_b$, a decelerating (type 2) functional response means that $c(N_a) < c(N_b)$, or $c(N_a)/c(N_b) < 1$ and $c(N_b)/c(N_a) > 1$. From the predator view, a mechanism that produces a type 2 functional response decreases the value of patches with high prey density (relative to a linear functional response). As a result, the degree of predator aggregation in the richer patch should decrease (see equation (3)). In turn, this allows prey to aggregate more heavily in the patch with more resources (see equation (2)). Although an increase in prey numbers in the richer resource patch should tend to attract predators back into that patch, at the ESS, a type 2 functional response tends to decrease predator aggregation and increase prey aggregation in the richer patch. Conversely, in the accelerating region of a type 3 functional response (where if $N_a > N_b$, $c(N_a) > c(N_b)$), the nonlinearity generates an increase in predator aggregation and a decrease in prey aggregation in the richer resource patch.

Effects of the intensity of competition among prey (as measured by x) and among predators (as measured by m) are more complex. To illustrate these effects, consider the situation where predators have a linear functional response. The $c(N)$ terms drop out of equations 2 and 3. Both predator and prey ratios are then functions of the resource ratio raised to an exponent that I refer to as a z-score. If $z = 1$, then predators or prey match resources; $z > 1$ represents overmatching of resources, $0 < z < 1$ indicates undermatching, but still a tendency to be more abundant in patches with more resources, while $z < 0$ indicates a preference for the patch with lower resource availability.

First note that rearrangement of equations (2) and (3) shows that at the double IFD, predator and prey distributions are related by the simple functions:

$$(N_a/N_b) = (P_a/P_b)^m \tag{4}$$

$$(P_a/P_b) = (N_a/N_b)^{1/m} \tag{5}$$

If predators do not compete ($m = 0$), then prey should be uniformly distributed and predators should match resources (see equation (3)). If $0 < m < 1$, then predators should overmatch prey. Increasing competition among predators reduces the degree of predator overmatching of prey. These are the usual predictions of IFD theory that accounts for varying levels of competition among consumers (Sutherland 1983).

Figure 10.1 shows z-scores for the tendency for prey to match resources. Prey avoid predators in the sense that prey utilization of the richer resource patch is reduced by the presence of predators in the system. For example, if prey show ideal competition ($x = 1$), then in the absence of predators, prey should match resources, whereas in the presence of predators, prey should undermatch resources, as long as predators do not compete too heavily [if $x = 1$, then at the ESS we have $N_a/N_b = (R_a/R_b)^m$]. In another sense, however, if both predators and prey are free to choose patches, then prey cannot avoid predators; that is, at the double IFD, if patches do not differ in refuge availability, then prey should almost always be more abundant in patches with more predators. Put another way, if patches do not differ in inherent safety, then in most circumstances, predators should win the "behavioral response race" between predators and prey (Sih 1984). The underlying reason for this is that while predators are "free" to follow the distribution of prey, prey avoidance of predators is constrained by the conflicting demands of feeding and avoiding predators. As a result, at the double IFD, both predators (e.g., carnivores) and prey (e.g., herbivores) tend to aggregate in patches with more resources (i.e., higher net primary productivity). The only exception (again, given that neither patch is inherently a refuge) is when predators do not compete with each other ($m = 0$). As shown earlier, in that case, predators should match resources while prey should be uniformly distributed.

The strength of prey aggregation in patches with more resources depends on prey and predator competition coefficients (Fig. 10.1). As noted above, if prey compete strongly (e.g., $x = 1$), then in a three-trophic-level IFD, prey should generally undermatch their resources ($z < 1$). This occurs because the combination of strong competition among prey and the presence of predators in the richer patch reduces the value of that patch (relative to a situation where predators are absent and prey do not compete heavily). A reduction in competition among prey (reduced x) increases the value of the richer patch and causes an increase in prey aggregation in the patch with more resources. An increase in competition among predators (increased m) decreases predation rates and thus also allows for an increase in prey aggregation in the richer resource patch.

Perhaps the most surprising predictions to emerge from this model are those addressing predator aggregation in patches with more resources that they do not feed on (Fig. 10.2). Given the simplifying assumptions of no differences between patches in refuge availability and linear functional responses, predators should always match or overmatch resources; for example, carnivores should aggregate heavily in patches with higher net plant productivity. The rationale behind this is that predators should follow prey, and despite predation risk, prey should tend to be more abundant in richer resource patches. Interestingly, at the double IFD, predators should aggregate in high resource patches more strongly than prey do. That occurs because predators

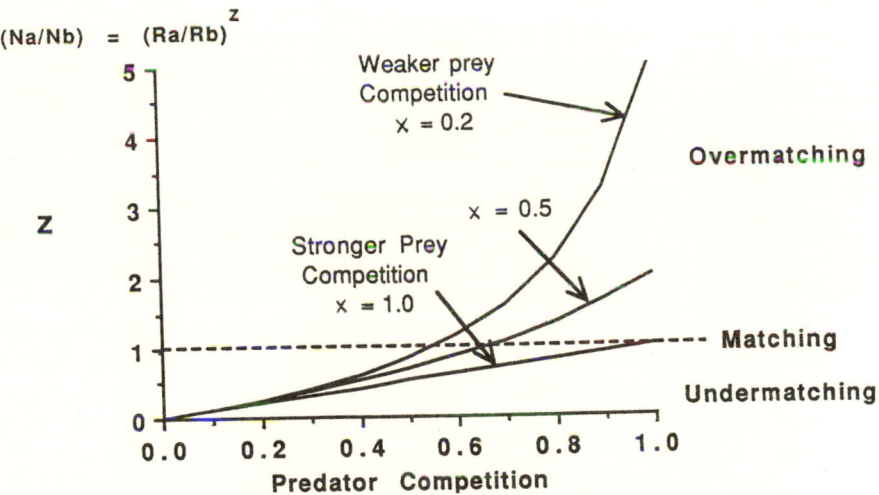

Figure 10.1. Predictions on prey patch use at the double ideal free distribution as a function of the resource distribution. Shown are exponents (z-scores) for the predicted relationships between the resource ratio (R_a/R_b) and the prey distributional ratio (N_a/N_b) across two patches. If $z = 1$, then prey match resources; $z > 1$ indicates overmatching, while $z < 1$ indicates undermatching. z-scores depend on the magnitude of per capita predator competition (m) and prey competition (x).

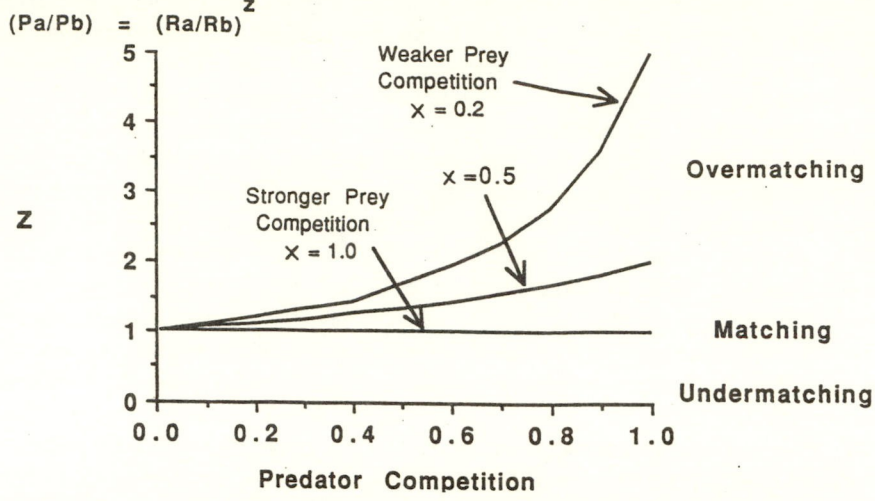

Figure 10.2. Predictions on predator patch use at the double ideal free distribution as a function of the resource distribution. Shown are exponents (z-scores) for the predicted relationship between the resource ratio (R_a/R_b) and the predator distributional ratio (P_a/P_b) across two patches. If $z = 1$, then predators match resources; $z > 1$ indicates overmatching, while $z < 1$ indicates undermatching. z-scores depend on the magnitude of per capita predator competition (m) and prey competition (x).

tend to overmatch prey [as long as $m < 1$; see equation (5)], while predation risk often keeps prey from overmatching on resources (Fig. 10.1).

Stronger prey competition reduces predator overmatching on resources. This occurs because stronger competition among prey reduces the value of high resource patches to prey, and thus causes prey to aggregate less heavily in these patches. In turn, predators aggregate less heavily in high resource patches.

Finally, at the double IFD, stronger competition among predators tends to increase the tendency for predators to aggregate in high resource patches. This prediction seems counterintuitive. If predators compete more heavily, one might predict that they should avoid each other more. In a three-trophic-level ideal free system, however, when predators compete more heavily, this makes them less dangerous to prey. Prey thus tend to aggregate more strongly in the richer patch (i.e., prey show less avoidance of predators), and this draws more predators into that patch (despite the increased per capita competition among predators).

10.4.3 Prey Refuges

In most natural situations, patches differ in per predator predation risk; that is, some patches are refuges for prey. For example, in aquatic systems, prey are often safer in vegetated areas or in shallow water (Werner et al. 1983, Power 1987, Sih et al. 1992). To examine the effects of prey refuges, consider the simple situation where predators have a linear functional response, and both predators and prey show ideal competition. Predator feeding rate in patch A is cN_a/P_a, while in patch B it is $k(cN_b/P_b)$, where k is the refuge effect. If $k<1$, this indicates lower predator feeding success in patch B; that is, patch B is a refuge for prey. Total risk is not necessarily lower in patch B; total risk depends on both k and the predator ratio, P_a/P_b.

Not surprisingly, the addition of refuge in the poorer resource patch tends to decrease prey aggregation in the high resource patch. In the absence of refuges, if both prey and predators show ideal competition, then at the double IFD, both prey and predators should match resources. With refuges, at the double IFD, $N_a/N_b = k(R_a/R_b)$. If the low resource patch is a refuge ($k<<1$), then prey should undermatch resources. If the refuge effect is strong ($k<1$, so that $kR_a/R_b<1$), then prey should aggregate in the safer patch, despite lower resource availability in that patch. Interestingly, under these simple conditions, the predator distribution (P_a/P_b) should not be influenced by the existence of refuge; predators should match resources. This result is due to the fact that at the double IFD, the decrease in predator feeding efficiency in the refuge patch is exactly offset by an increase in prey numbers in that patch.

Double IFDs become quite complex in situations with: (1) differences among patches in refuge availability, (2) variable competition among predators and among prey, and (3) nonlinear functional responses. These complexities will be considered in a later article (Sih, in preparation).

10.4.4 Summary of Predictions of the Three Trophic-Level Ideal Free Model

1. Prey should aggregate in patches with more resources. This is not surprising.
2. Predators should generally overmatch prey. This seems reasonable, though we know there are exceptions; many of the exceptions, however, involve two-trophic-level systems with immobile prey (Kennedy & Gray 1993). It should be interesting to test this prediction for three-trophic-level systems with predators feeding on mobile prey.
3. Predators should also aggregate in patches with more resources, even though they do not feed on those resources. Indeed, predators should aggregate on resources more strongly than prey do. The latter is a novel prediction that needs testing.
4. Stronger competition among prey should result in less aggregation of both prey and predators in high resource patches. This prediction is also not unexpected.
5. Stronger competition among predators should result in greater aggregation of both predators and prey in high resource patches. This is a counterintuitive prediction, particularly for predators.
6. If one patch is a refuge (i.e., is relatively safe), then prey should increase use of that patch. If the refuge effect is strong, prey should aggregate in the safe patch even if it has lower resource availability. Even if prey are primarily in refuge, predators should still be more abundant outside of refuge.

10.5. Discussion

Below, I discuss the following three topics: (1) other models of multi-trophic-level ideal free distributions; (2) relevant data, or the lack of them; and (3) suggestions for future theoretical and empirical study.

10.5.1 Other Models of Multi-Trophic-Level Ideal Free Distributions

Sih (1984) discussed the conflicting effects of prey and predator patch choice on the resulting codistributions of predators and prey. Without using an explicit model, Sih (1984) suggested that if prey are immobile and refuges are absent, then predators should aggregate in areas with more prey; that is, predators should win the "behavioral response race." However, if prey are mobile and refuges exist, then prey avoidance of predators should override the tendency for predators to aggregate in areas with more prey. That is, prey should aggregate in refuges, but predators should not.

The model presented here suggests that, at the double IFD, the former prediction should hold even if prey are mobile, provided that the resource distribution is static. The resource distribution essentially provides a spatial anchor to the system. Even though prey avoid predators, because prey must also gather resources, in the absence of refuge, both prey and predators should aggregate in the patch with more resources. The double IFD model also corroborates the latter prediction, provided that the refuge effect is strong ($kR_a/R_b < 1$). If, however, the refuge effect is weak ($kR_a/R_b > 1$), then even with refuges present, predators and prey should both aggregate outside of refuge (i.e., in the richer patch).

Motivated by Sih (1982, 1984), Schwinning and Rosenzweig (1990) modeled a system where all three trophic levels are free to move (i.e., even resources can redistribute themselves). They found that under many conditions, distributions oscillated, rather than settling on a stable IFD. Their model differed, however, from both the present model and two other models discussed below in two fundamental ways. First, their model was a computer simulation with discrete time steps, rather than an analytical model. It is well known that the inherent time lag present in discrete time simulations tends to generate oscillations. In addition, rather than solve for an ESS, Schwinning and Rosenzweig (1990) approximated fitness maximization by assuming that the proportion of animals moving between patches is proportional to the difference in fitness between the patches. While this is a reasonable assumption, it can generate overshoots that produce oscillations that do not converge on an ESS. Their specific predictions about effects of refuges and competition among resources are difficult to compare to the present model, because they allowed all three trophic levels to move.

In contrast, van Baalen and Sabelis (1992) solved for the double IFD in a system where predators and prey move, but resources are static. That is, their model resembled the one presented in this chapter. They found that at the double IFD, predators should match resources (as measured by prey instantaneous rate of increase, r, in the different patches), while prey should undermatch resources. These predictions hinge on their assumption that predators exhibit weak competition, while prey do not compete with each other at all ($x=0$). van Baalen and Sabelis (1992) investigated the ecological stability arising from the predicted double IFD. Further investigation of the effects of a broader range of double IFD scenarios on predator–prey population dynamics should prove insightful.

The model that most resembled the present one is the study by Hugie and Dill (1994). They focused on the interacting effects of the relative inherent safety of prey in two patches (the risk ratio; in my terms, k) and relative resource availability (the productivity ratio; in my terms, R_a/R_b). They also included metabolic costs that are independent of feeding, a factor which I did not consider. Their model, however, only considered the situation where prey exhibit ideal competition. Their article stated several predictions that were corroborated by the present model. For example, they also predicted that (1) predators should generally aggregate in patches with more resources, (2) prey distributions should respond to the inherent riskiness of the habitat, and (3) if predators do not compete, then prey should be uniformly distributed, while predators should match resources.

More interestingly, our articles provided complementary insights on some issues. For example, they showed that (1) if predators do not compete, then the prey ratio should match the inherent risk ratio (in my terms, $N_a/N_b=k$; that is, their model predicted that prey should not respond to the resource ratio), while predators should match resources discounted by prey metabolic costs, and (2) if predators compete, then predators and prey alike should respond in a complex fashion to both the resource ratio and the inherent risk ratio. My model generated the complementary prediction that when both predators and prey show ideal competition, predators should match resources, while the prey distribution should be a simple product of the risk ratio and the productivity ratio. An interesting extension would involve exploration of the effects of relative risk and resource availability on the double IFD in situations where neither prey nor predators exhibit ideal competition.

Hugie and Dill (1994) also predicted that the addition of a handling time for predators (thus producing a type 2 functional response using Holling's disc equation) should have no effect on prey or predator distributions. My model suggests that this finding only holds given their assumption that prey show ideal competition [$x=1$; see my equation (3)]. If $x<1$, then the shape of the functional response should influence both predator and prey distributions.

Most interestingly, the present model and that of Hugie and Dill (1994) generated opposite predictions with regard to the effects of the intensity of predator competition on predator aggregation in high resource patches. Their model predicted that increased predator competition should result in reduced predator aggregation in the high resource patch. In contrast, my model generated the counterintuitive prediction that increased predator competition should often result in increased predator aggregation in the high resource patch. These opposing predictions can apparently be explained by the different scenarios considered by the two models. Whereas Hugie and Dill's (1994) model incorporated metabolic costs for prey, while assuming ideal prey competition, my model ignored metabolic costs, but considered nonideal prey competition. In the situation where our models overlapped in their scenarios (i.e., no metabolic costs, ideal prey competition), both models predict that at the double IFD, predators should match resources regardless of the intensity of predator competition. The overall effect of predator competition on predator aggregation in a three-trophic IFD world presumably depends on the relative importance of metabolic costs for prey versus nonideal prey competition.

Hugie and Dill (1994) looked at metabolic costs. A cost not considered by previous models is prey background mortality (i.e., mortality outside of predation). If both predators and prey display ideal competition, then algebraic manipulations show at the double IFD, $N_a/N_b = (R_a/R_b)(ck + d_b)/(c + d_a)$ and $P_a/P_b = N_a/(kN_b)$, where d_a and d_b are prey death rates (in patches a and b, respectively), not including predation. If background death rates are patch-independent, then higher background death rates result in greater prey aggregation in the high resource patch. The rationale for this prediction is as follows. Prey should maximize f/u, where u includes both predation and background mortality. If background mortality is high and patch-independent, then this reduces the effect of spatial variation in predation risk on the overall ratio of feeding rates to mortality rates. Prey patch choice should then depend primarily on spatial variation in f; that is, prey should tend to match resources. Of course, if prey background death rates are higher in one patch than the other, then this should cause prey to shift out of the patch with higher background death rates.

10.5.2 Relevant Data

Dozens of experimental studies have shown that predators tend to forage in areas with more prey (Stephens & Krebs 1986). Conversely, numerous experiments show that prey avoid areas with higher predation risk (Sih 1987, Lima & Dill 1990, Sih et al. 1992); in particular, some studies suggest that prey can adaptively balance the conflicting demands of feeding and avoiding predators (Sih 1980, 1982; Gilliam & Fraser 1987, Abrahams & Dill 1989). Most studies examining effects of predation risk on prey patch use, however, use constrained predators. That is, a common experimental design uses predator-specific screening to keep predators on one side of an arena, while prey are allowed to move freely between the sides of the arena. Some experiments allowed both predators and prey to move freely (e.g., Savino & Stein 1989, Kotler et al. 1991); however, these studies generally have not presented analyses on the codistribution of predators and prey. Only two studies, to my knowledge, have explicitly examined the predator–prey behavioral response race (Sih 1984, Formanowicz & Bobka 1989). Clearly, given that in nature predators and prey are often both free to choose patches, more experiments are needed to test the predictions of three-trophic-level IFD models.

Field surveys of predator and prey codistributions yield some relevant, but not ideal, data. Numerous studies suggest that predators tend to aggregate in areas with more prey, though not as strongly as one might expect. For example, two reviews (Stiling 1987, Walde & Murdoch 1988) emphasized that although some studies show spatial density-dependence in parasitoid attack rates on hosts (higher per capita attack rates in patches with more hosts), many studies show density-independence, or inverse density-dependence. Note that while these studies include data on the spatial pattern of attacks, they do not directly address the spatial distribution of parasitoids per se. Parasitoids can aggregate spatially, but produce density-independent attack rates if, for example, individual parasitoids have type 2 functional responses.

Field studies point out the importance of spatial scale in evaluating the codistributions of predators and prey. Stiling's (1987) review, for example, showed that aggregated attacks were more likely to occur if a patch was a whole plant or several plants (i.e., an area on the order of 0.1–10 m^2 in size). Rose and Leggett (1990) used simulations and data from fish in the open ocean to reveal the effects of scale on predator–prey codistributions. They found that predator and prey distributions were strongly positively related (as predicted by ideal free models) if the sampling unit was larger than the size of both a prey refuge and a single aggregation of predators. Smaller sampling units tended to result in weaker spatial correlations between predators and prey. For example, multiple samples taken from one aggregation of predators would likely quantify a relatively uniform high density of predators that is unrelated to fine-scale variation in prey density. At the extreme, if a sampling unit is so small that it can only include one individual, then predator and prey distributions must be negatively correlated. Future investigators working on three-trophic-level IFD should take care to choose the appropriate spatial scale for their studies.

The field surveys described above considered only two trophic levels. More relevant data come from community studies that address correlated changes in the relative abundances of three trophic levels. Some studies suggest that increases in habitat plant productivity are associated with an increase in carnivore numbers, but little or no change in herbivore numbers (Oksanen et al. 1992). This fits the prediction of the simple prey-dependent double IFD model presented here and elsewhere (van Baalen & Sabelis 1992, Hugie & Dill 1994). Other studies found that increased plant productivity correlated with an increase in both herbivore and carnivore densities (see references in Arditi et al. 1991). This pattern is predicted by the ratio-dependent IFD model and by the more complex three-trophic-level IFD model discussed here.

These multi-trophic-level field patterns, however, are usually thought to be due to trophic dynamics (e.g., predation mortality per se) rather than behavioral dynamics (i.e., patch choice). Indeed these field patterns play a central part in the debate on the relative value of prey-dependent versus ratio-dependent predator–prey trophic models in community ecology (Arditi et al. 1991, Abrams 1994). Interestingly, the trophic models generate predictions that run parallel to those generated by the ideal free models discussed here. For example, prey-dependent predator–prey trophic models (that have no behavioral component) predict that an increase in habitat productivity should result in an increase in predator numbers, but not prey numbers, while ratio-dependent trophic models predict positive correlations between productivity, prey, and predator densities (compare these to the predictions in this article's section subtitled *Two simple three-trophic-level models*). These parallel predictions emerge because both types of models solve for equilibria governed by the interplay of predation rates and prey feeding rates. While in many cases, it is clear that patch choice could not explain the observed patterns (e.g., the studies compare plankton communities in spatially separated lakes), in other situations the relative roles of birth/death rates (trophic) versus immigration/emigration rates (patch choice) in determining spatial patterns needs further investigation (also see Sih & Wooster 1994).

Finally, the most intriguing three-trophic-level studies might be those that suggest that predators or parasitoids find herbivorous prey by searching for the prey's host plants or by aggregating in areas with more host plants (Monteith 1958, Read et al. 1970, Vinson 1985, Thomas 1989). The effects of this behavioral mechanism on overall three-trophic-level spatial distributions, however, are yet to be determined.

10.5.3 Suggestions for Future Study

One main conclusion that emerges from the brief data survey is that very few experimental studies include relevant data to test three-trophic-level IFD models. These models can be tested experimentally at three levels. At the most fundamental level, an experiment should examine predator–prey patch choices in situations that allow both predators and prey the freedom to make patch choices. At a deeper level, the spatial distribution of resources (R_a/R_b) can be manipulated to see how predators and prey alter their distributions in response to varying resource ratios. Finally, manipulations of refuge availability and conditions that alter competition coefficients (e.g., via manipulations of resource throughflow) can be done to test the effects of these factors on prey and predator responses to variations in resource ratios.

With regard to theory, the existing models of three-trophic-level IFD have only scratched the surface of this field. Extensions of these models that could prove insightful include: (1) using more mechanistic competition and predator–prey models; (2) using dynamic programming to account for explicit state variables, time constraints, and nonlinear fitness functions; (3) incorporating more realistic refuges, travel costs, lack of information and learning, and variation among individuals in both competitive ability and antipredator ability—these elements can be included for both prey and predators; (4) examining effects of ideal free behaviors on three-trophic-level community dynamics—this requires models that explicitly link behavior and population dynamics; and (5) developing models of multispecies ideal free distributions.

ACKNOWLEDGMENTS   This work benefited from comments made by Alisdair Houston, Alex Kacelnik, John Krebs, and Jon Wright following a seminar at Oxford University in 1990, from suggestions from numerous people after the 1995 Game Theory workshop in that hot spot of behavioral ecology, Lincoln, Nebraska, from highly critical and useful comments supplied by Larry Dill and Don Hugie, and from ideal feedback from Loric Sih and Marie-Sylvie Baltus-Sih. This work was supported by grants from the National Science Foundation and from the NSF/Kentucky/EPSCoR program.

References

Abrahams, M. V. 1986. Patch choice under perceptual constraints: A cause for departure from an ideal free distribution. *Behav. Ecol. Sociobiol.,* 19, 409–415.

Abrahams, M. V. & Dill, L. M. 1989. A determination of the energetic equivalence of the risk of predation. *Ecology,* 70, 999–1007.

Abrams, P. A. 1994. The fallacies of "ratio-dependent" predation. *Ecology,* 75, 1842–1850.

Arditi, R., Ginzburg, L. R. & Akçakaya, H. R. 1991. Variation in plankton densities among lakes: A case for ratio-dependent predation models. *Am. Nat.,* 138, 1287–1296.

Bernstein, C. 1988. Individual decisions and the distribution of predators in a patchy environment. *J. Anim. Ecol.,* 57, 1007–1026.

Formanowicz, D. R. & Bobka, M. S. 1989. Predation risk and microhabitat preference: an experimental study of the behavioural responses of prey and predator. *Am. Midl. Nat.,* 21, 379–386.

Fretwell, S. D. 1972. *Populations in a Seasonal Environment.* Princeton, NJ: Princeton University Press.

Gilliam, J. F. & Fraser, D. F. 1987. Habitat selection under predation hazard: A test of a model with foraging minnows. *Ecology,* 68, 1856–1862.

Hassell, M. P. 1978. *The Dynamics of Arthropod Predator–Prey Systems.* Princeton, NJ: Princeton University Press.

Hassell, M. P. & Varley, G. C. 1969. New inductive population model for insect parasites and its bearing on population control. *Nature,* 223, 1133–1136.

Houston, A. I. & McNamara, J. M. 1988. The ideal free distribution when competitive abilities differ: an approach based on statistical mechanics. *Anim. Behav.,* 36, 166–174.

Hugie, D. M & Dill, L. M. 1994. Fish and game: A game theoretic approach to habitat selection by predators and prey. *J. Fish Biol.,* 45A, 151–169.

Kacelnik, A., Krebs, J. R. & Bernstein, C. 1992. The ideal free distribution and predator-prey populations. *Trends Ecol. Evol.,* 7, 50–55.

Kennedy, M. & Gray, R. D. 1993. Can ecological theory predict the distribution of foraging animals? A critical analysis of experiments on the ideal free distribution. *Oikos,* 68, 158–166.

Kotler, B. P., Brown, J. S. & Hasson, O. 1991. Factors affecting gerbil foraging behavior and rates of owl predation. *Ecology,* 72, 2249–2260.

Lima, S. L. & Dill, L. M. 1990. Behavioral decisions made under the risk of predation: A review and prospectus. *Can. J. Zool.,* 68, 619–640.

Mangel, M. & Clark, C. W. 1988. *Dynamic Modeling in Behavioral Ecology.* Princeton, NJ: Princeton University Press.

Maynard Smith, J. 1982. *Evolution and the Theory of Games.* Cambridge: Cambridge University Press.

McNamara, J. M. & Houston, A. I. 1990. State-dependent ideal free distributions. *Evol. Ecol.,* 4, 298–311.

Milinski, M. & Parker, G. A. 1991. Competition for resources. In *Behavioural Ecology: An Evolutionary Approach,* J. R. Krebs & N. B. Davies, eds., pp. 137–168. Oxford: Blackwell Scientific Publications.

Monteith, L. G. 1958. Influence of food plant of host on attractiveness of the host to tachinid parasites with notes on preimaginal conditioning. *Can. Entomol.,* 90, 478–482.

Oksanen, L., Moen, J. & Lundberg, P. A. 1992. The time-scale problem in exploiter–victim models: Does the solution lie in ratio-dependent exploitation? *Am. Nat.,* 140, 938–960.

Parker, G. A. & Sutherland, W. J. 1986. Ideal free distributions when individuals differ in competitive ability: Phenotype-limited ideal free models. *Anim. Behav.,* 34, 1222–1242.

Power, M. E. 1987. Predator avoidance by grazing fishes in temperate and tropical streams: Importance of stream depth and prey size. In *Predation: Direct and Indirect Impacts on Aquatic Communities* W. C. Kerfoot & A. Sih, eds., pp. 333–351. Hanover, NH: University Press of New England.

Read, D. P., Feeny, P. & Root, R. B. 1970. Habitat selection by the aphid parasite *Diaeretiella rapae. Can. Entomol.,* 102, 1567–1578.

Rose, G. A. & Leggett, W. C. 1990. The importance of scale to predator–prey spatial correlations: An example of Atlantic fishes. *Ecology,* 71, 33–43.

Savino, J. F. & Stein, R. A. 1989. Behavioral interactions between fish predators and their prey: Effects of plant density. *Anim. Behav.,* 37, 311–321.

Schoener, T. W. 1983. Field experiments on interspecific competition. *Am. Nat.,* 122, 240–285.

Schwinning, S. & Rosenzweig, M. L. 1990. Periodic oscillations in an ideal free predator–prey distribution. *Oikos,* 59, 85–91.

Sih, A. 1980. Optimal behavior: Can foragers balance two conflicting demands? *Science,* 210, 1041–1043.

Sih, A. 1982. Foraging strategies and the avoidance of predation by an aquatic insect, *Notonecta hoffmani. Ecology,* 63, 786–796.

Sih, A. 1984. The behavioral response race between predator and prey. *Am. Nat.*, 123, 143–150.

Sih, A. 1987. Predator and prey lifestyles: An evolutionary and ecological overview. In *Predation: Direct and Indirect Impacts on Aquatic Communities*, W. C. Kerfoot & A. Sih, eds., pp. 203–224. Hanover, NH: University Press of New England.

Sih, A., Kats, L. B. & Moore, R. D. 1992. Effects of predatory sunfish on the density, drift and refuge use of stream salamander larvae. *Ecology*, 73, 1418–1430.

Sih, A. & Wooster, D. E. 1994. Prey behavior, prey dispersal, and predator impacts on stream prey. *Ecology*, 75, 1199–1207.

Stephens, D. W. & Krebs, J. R. 1986. *Foraging Theory*. Princeton, NJ: Princeton University Press.

Stiling, P. D. 1987. The frequency of density-dependence in insect host–parasitoid systems. *Ecology*, 68, 844–856.

Sutherland, W. J. 1983. Aggregation and the 'ideal free' distribution. *J. Anim. Ecol.*, 52, 821–828.

Thomas, C. D. 1989. Predator–herbivore interactions and the escape of isolated plants from phytophagous insects. *Oikos*, 55, 291–298.

van Baalen, M. & Sabelis, M. W. 1992. Coevolution of patch selection strategies of predator and prey and the consequences for ecological stability. *Am. Nat.*, 142, 646–670.

Vinson, S. B. 1985. The behavior of parasitoids. In *Comprehensive Insect Physiology, Biochemistry, and Pharmacology*, G. A. Kerkut & L. I. Gilberg, eds., pp. 417–469. Oxford: Pergamon Press.

Walde, S. J. & Murdoch, W. W. 1988. Spatial density-dependence in parasitoids. *Annu. Rev. Entomol.*, 33, 441–466.

Werner, E. E., Gilliam, J. F., Hall, D. J. & Mittelbach, G. G. 1983. An experimental test of the effects of predation risk on habitat use. *Ecology*, 64, 1540–1548.

DAVID W. STEPHENS
KEVIN C. CLEMENTS

Game Theory and Learning

II.1 Introduction: Mechanisms of Equilibrium Seeking?

The basic idea of applied game theory is the Nash equilibrium together with Maynard Smith's subsidiary idea of the evolutionarily stable state. We say that two players have adopted Nash equilibria if each is playing a strategy that is the best reply to the other's strategy. These mutual-best-replies are *equilibria* in the sense that a player deviating from this strategy will do worse, and so we might expect that economic forces will *punish* the deviator and bring the system back into equilibrium.

The empirical validity of game theory hinges on the existence of *some* mechanism or mechanisms that return players to equilibrium after a deviation or perturbation. (We defer, for the moment, the problem of finding the equilibrium in the first place.) Most students of evolutionary game theory follow Maynard Smith (1982) in thinking of these "restoring forces" as evolutionary and genetic: Suppose an allele a codes for Nash equilibrium strategy A, then in a population dominated by a some deviant a' will be selected against by definition (where, conveniently, we're imagining a population of sexual haploids). Of course, fundamentally the "restoring" force we're interested in must be, at some level, an evolutionary force.

Consider for a moment the range of behavioral games: animals bluffing and escalating over a resource, cooperating to obtain food, selecting an intensity of territorial defense, and so on. These games are probably played many times during an individual's lifetime, and it seems unlikely that the economic details of such games have been fixed on any plausible evolutionary time scale; indeed the features of many games probably change several times within an individual's lifetime. We would be quite surprised to discover that the mechanisms that enforce strategic equilibria in these games are solely genetic. Such purely genetic mechanisms could not respond to changes in the structure of games that occur within an individual's lifetime. It seems reasonable to suppose, therefore, that behavioral (nongenetic) mechanisms for "restoring equilibria" should exist. Behavioral mechanisms are not only the only way to respond to games that change within lifetimes, but they offer two other intriguing possibilities (Stephens 1991). First, a single behavioral mechanism guided by economic principles might offer a single mechanism of equilibrium maintenance for many different games [Harley (1981) seemed to have this possibility in mind when he suggested his "relative payoff sum rule" for learning ESSs]; and second, a behavioral mechanism might be a straightforward extension of well-documented nongame mechanisms. For example, a "best reply" might be enforced in the same way that feeding animals track the best way to feed in a changing environment.

II.2 The Law of Effect

Where might we look for behavioral mechanisms to enforce strategic equilibria? If we are thinking about behavioral change guided by "economic" forces, then we are in the realm of operant conditioning. The most basic idea in operant conditioning is the "law of effect" originally formulated by E. L. Thorndike (1911): "Of several responses made to the same situation those which are accompanied or closely followed by satisfaction . . . will be more firmly connected with the situation . . .; those accompanied . . . by discomfort will have their connection with the situation weakened." In a nutshell, Thorndike argued that responses associated with *reward* would increase in frequency, and responses associated with *punishment* would decrease in frequency. This straightforward and uncontroversial claim actually says rather little about animal behavior. For example, it doesn't specify which consequences are rewarding or punishing. Indeed, some critics view it as circular: Rewards are things that increase a response's frequency, and so on. (Staddon 1983). Nonetheless, the law of effect provides a useful organizing framework for much of operant psychology, which one can view as the study of this effect, in the sense that operant psychologists seek refinements of the law of effect in terms of the economic and psychophysical properties of stimuli. It is now clear, for example, that Thorndike overemphasized the importance of the immediacy of consequences. The work of Rescorla and others (e.g., Rescorla & Wagner 1972) shows that a "predictive" link between action and consequence (called *contingency* in psychological terminology) is also necessary for conditioning to occur.

In this chapter, we begin an exploration of the relationship between the law of effect and game theoretic equilibria. It would seem to be simple. Surely, Nash had something like the law of effect in mind when he formulated his idea of equilibria: The punishment of doing less well by deviating is supposed to return a player to his equilibrium strategy. The outstanding question is whether a game theorist's concept of "doing less well" is meaningfully punishing to a real animal. For example, there is a stark contrast between this "Nashian" view of punishment and the "typical" psychological view. In the Nash view, a player who has been receiving (for example) five units of food by playing its putative equilibrium tactic is punished by receiving only three units when it deviates. Psychological discussions of the law of effect, however, typically emphasize the view that punishing and rewarding consequences are qualitatively different: Some food is rewarding, no food is punishing; electric shock, blasts of hot air, and extremely loud noises are punishing.

II.3 Crime and Punishment: The Law of Effect and the Iterated Prisoner's Dilemma

We focus on the well-studied Iterated Prisoner's Dilemma (IPD; see also Dugatkin, this volume). We will investigate how differing "standards" of reward and punishment influence the extent of cooperation in the IPD. The Prisoner's Dilemma is a two-player symmetric game typified by the game matrix:

$$
\begin{array}{c}
\quad\quad C \quad\quad D \\
\begin{array}{c} C \\ D \end{array}
\left[
\begin{array}{cc}
R=3 & S=0 \\
T=5 & P=1
\end{array}
\right]
\end{array}
$$

The entries in the matrix represent the payoff received by the "row player" based on its action and the action of its opponent, the column player: If the row player chooses C and the column player chooses D, then the row player receives S. The numerical values (5, 3, 1, 0) are provided for concreteness, and a Prisoner's Dilemma exists whenever $T>R>P>S$ and $R>(T+P)/2$. The game is symmetric because both players experience the same game matrix; that is, if the row player gets T, the column player must get S, and so forth. The action C is cooperative in the dictionary sense of "joint action for mutual benefit," because at least one player does less well if either deviates from mutual C. The D option is usually called "defection" or cheating.

For a single play, defection is the only Nash equilibrium, because defection pays better regardless of what your opponent chooses. Axelrod and Hamilton (1981) argued that mutual cooperation could correspond to a Nash equilibrium if (a) players used a "reciprocating strategy" called tit for tat (abbreviated TFT, and defined as cooperate on the the first move and copy your opponent's moves from then on) and (b) the game was played repeatedly, say $z+1$ times. In this case, we can imagine a modified game matrix:

$$
\begin{array}{c}
\quad\quad\quad TFT \quad\quad\quad All\text{-}D \\
\begin{array}{c} TFT \\ All\text{-}D \end{array}
\left[
\begin{array}{cc}
R+zR & S+zP \\
T+zP & P+zP
\end{array}
\right]
\end{array}
$$

Each entry is now an equation in the slope-intercept form of a straight line in the "repetition" variable z. One can now see that All-D is a Nash equilibrium, since $P+zP>S+zP$ for all z; and that TFT can be a Nash equilibrium for large z, because although $T+zP$ has a higher intercept, $R+zR$ has a higher slope. We remark that a seldom-stated assumption of this analysis is that payoffs can be combined by addition. The analysis shows that for sufficient repetition the IPD game has (at least) two Nash equilibria, a cooperative equilibrium and noncooperative one. A question that arises, therefore, is whether the law of effect favors one equilibrium over another.

11.3.1 Pavlov

Recently, Nowak and Sigmund (1993) have advocated a strategy called Pavlov. They present simulation results suggesting that Pavlov is superior to TFT in some situations (but see Stephens et al. 1995), and they claim that Pavlov is psychologically realistic because its can be viewed as an implementation of the law of effect. A Pavlov strategist repeats its own behavior after receiving a payoff of R or T, and it does the opposite of its most recent choice after receiving a payoff of P or S. Hence, it is consistent with the law of effect in the sense that the "reward" of the two larger payoffs (T and R) leads to a repetition of earlier behavior, and the "punishment" of the two lower payoffs (P and S) leads to a change. Of course, there is no guarantee that the law of effect will work this way. Real animals may not categorize rewards and punishments in this way; moreover the law of effect states only that there will be a *tendency* to repeat rewarded actions, not that a rewarded action will necessarily be immediately repeated. Finally, we remark that the name Pavlov is historical non-sense; this is like calling Einstein's model of special relativity "Newtonian" because Newton is the only physicist's name you can remember.

II.4 Modeling the Law of Effect

Students of mathematical psychology have advocated a variety of models of learning. Of these, the most widely used is the linear operator family of models originally proposed by Bush and Mosteller (1951, 1955). A concrete example illustrates the central ideas of this approach. Suppose that a rat is being trained in a T maze. On the right is food, and on the left is nothing. Initially, we characterize the rat's behavior by the complementary probabilities p_r, the probability of a right turn, and p_l, the proba-bility of a left turn. Now suppose that on the first trial, the rat turns right and is rewarded. Guided by the law of effect, we suppose that this should increase the probability of subsequent right-hand turns. Specifically, we suppose that

$$p'_r = (1 - \beta)p_r + \beta\gamma$$
$$= p_r + \beta(\gamma - p_r) \tag{1}$$

where the prime symbol means "next" (hence p' is the next p-value). The first version of the equation shows that the next p_r value is a weighted average of the present value and γ, while the second version shows that the change in p_r is a proportion β of the distance between γ and the present value of p_r. The parameter β can, therefore, be thought of as a measure of the rate of learning, and the parameter γ represents the direction of learning. Usually, γ equals either zero or one. If $\gamma = 1$ the process mod-elled by eqn (1) represents *acquisition* of the right turning behavior, as we'd expect if right-turning was rewarded; and if $\gamma = 0$, then we have *extinction* of right-turning, as we'd expect if right-turning was punished.

A full model for a our T maze would be

$$\text{If right, } p'_r = (1 - \beta)p_r + \beta \tag{2}$$

$$\text{If left, } p'_l = (1 - \beta)p_l \tag{3}$$

assuming that right turns are rewarded and left turns are punished, and that the learn-ing rate β is the same in both cases. Now recalling that $p_r + p_l = 1$, we rewrite the second equation to find

$$\text{If right, } p'_r = (1 - \beta)p_{r} + \beta \tag{4}$$

$$\text{If left, } p'_r = (1 - \beta)p_r + \beta \tag{5}$$

So, we'd expect steady acquisition of right-turning as the rat experiences this schedule of reward and punishment. Of course, this model is absurdly simple; we would seldom expect the same equation (or operator) to apply regardless of outcome. How might we study the evolution of p_r in a more complicated situation?

Consider a set of probabilities of turning right $\{p_1, p_2, p_3, \ldots\}$, and a corresponding list of the probabilities that each of these will apply, say $\{\pi_1, \pi_2, \pi_3, \ldots\}$, so $\pi_i = \Pr(p_r = p_i)$. The expected value is

$$\bar{p} = \sum \pi_i p_i$$

Now if $p_r = p_i$, then the linear operator model specifies that the next value will be

$$(1 - \beta)p_i + \beta\gamma$$

but since $p_r = p_i$ with probability π_i, we can write the expected value in the next trial, say $\bar{p}'$, by

$$\bar{p}' = \sum \pi_i[(1 - \beta)p_i + \beta\gamma]$$

which reduces to

$$\bar{p}' = (1 - \beta)\bar{p} + \beta\gamma$$

that is, the linear operator applies to the mean, in the same way that it applies to the individual probabilities.

To recap, the linear operator models offer a crude guide to the time course of learning, in which the parameter β measures the speed of learning (if $\beta = 1$, then p moves to γ in a single step; although if $\beta = 0$, experience has no effect on p), and the parameter γ measures the direction of learning ($\gamma = 1$ implies acquisition, and $\gamma = 0$ implies extinction). It is often convenient to study the expected probabilities associated with linear operator models.

II.5 Linear Operator Learning in the IPD

The ideas of reward and punishment enter these models via the parameter γ: A rewarding consequence increments the probability of the associated action toward $\gamma = 1$, while a punishing consequence decrements the probability toward $\gamma = 0$. If we are to apply these ideas to the the four outcomes of the IPD (i.e., the payoffs T, R, P, S), then we must somehow decide which is rewarding and which is punishing. We begin by supposing that there exists a *standard* s_0 such that an outcome X is rewarding if $X > s_0$, and punishing otherwise. Hence, if action A implies consequence

X and the current probability of action A is p_A, then after the animal experiences an (A, X) action–consequence pair, this probability becomes

$$p'_A = (1 - \beta)p_A + \beta H(X - s_0) \tag{6}$$

where $H(X - s_0)$ is the Heaviside unit step function,

$$H(x) = \begin{cases} 0, & x < 0 \\ 1, & x \geq 0 \end{cases}$$

We remark that when we consider two mutually exclusive actions such as A with consequence X and $\bar{A}$ (read "not A") with consequence Y, then if (A, X) occurs, equation (6) applies; but if $(\bar{A}, Y)$ occurs, then we have

$$p'_{\bar{A}} = (1 - \beta)p_{\bar{A}} + \beta H(Y - s_0)$$

and since $p_{\bar{A}} = 1 - p_A$, we have

$$p'_A = (1 - \beta)p_A + \beta[1 - H(Y - s_0)]$$

Our full model for a pair of mutually exclusive actions, A and $\bar{A}$, is

$$p'_A = \begin{cases} (1 - \beta)p_A + \beta H(X - s_0) & \text{if } (A, X) \text{ occurs} \\ (1 - \beta)p_A + \beta[1 - H(Y - s_0)] & \text{if } (\bar{A}, Y) \text{ occurs} \end{cases}$$

Up to now, we have supposed that the standard s_0 is a "given," specified by something external to the model. This need not be the case; one can imagine a more complex model that incorporates a dynamic equation for s_0, so that the "standard" of reward and punishment is itself determined by experienced consequences. Although we will consider this possibility later, for now we restrict our attention to the idea of an absolute, externally determined standard.

It is now straightforward to write down a "law of effect" model for the Prisoner's Dilemma. Suppose that the row player cooperates with probability p and the column player cooperates with probability q. Then we can write the equations shown in Table 11.1 (note that the upper equation within each cell applies to the row player, and the lower equation applies to the column player). We have supposed, for simplicity, that both players adopt the same standard s_0 and the same learning rates β (in traditional applications of the linear operator models the learning rates are often allowed to depend on the outcome—for example, β_l for a left turn, β_r for a right turn). Since a PD implies the ordering $T > R > P > S$, there are five cases:

1. $S > s_0$, all payoffs are rewarding.
2. $P > s_0 > S$, only S is punishing.
3. $R > s_0 > P$, only P and S are punishing.
4. $T > s_0 > R$, R, P and S are punishing, only T is rewarding.
5. $s_0 > T$, all payoffs are punishing.

Table II.I Table of Dynamic Equations

		C q	D $1-q$
C	p	$p' = (1-\beta)\,p + \beta H(R - s_0)$ $q' = (1-\beta)q + \beta H(R - s_0)$	$p' = (1-\beta)p + \beta H(S - s_0)$ $q' = (1-\beta)q + \beta[1 - H(T - s_0)]$
D	$1-p$	$p' = (1-\beta)p + \beta[1 - H(T - s_0)]$ $q' = (1-\beta)q + \beta H(S - s_0)$	$p' = (1-\beta)p + \beta[1 - H(P - s_0)]$ $q' = (1-\beta)q + \beta[1 - H(P - s_0)]$

We proceed to study these five cases analytically and numerically. The numerical study of this system is straightforward. One simply runs a large number of Monte Carlo style simulations of the system and examines the resulting average p and q values. The analytical approach is more complex. Imagine that at the ith play of the game the "real" p and q are realizations of corresponding random variables P and Q. From Table 11.1 it is straightforward to write an equation for expected value of the random value P in the next trial, *given* that particular values of p and q apply in the current trial, in symbols:

$$
\begin{aligned}
E(P'|P=p,\,Q=q) = {} & pq\{(1-\beta)p + \beta H(R - s_0)\} \\
& + p(1-q)\{(1-\beta)p + \beta H(S - s_0)\} \\
& + (1-p)q\{(1-\beta)p + \beta[1 - H(T - s_0)\} \\
& + (1-p)(1-q)\{(1-\beta)p + \beta[1 - H(P - s_0)\}
\end{aligned}
$$

where the terms in curly braces correspond to p' entries of Table 11.1. Simplifying, we find

$$
\begin{aligned}
E(P'|P=p,\,Q=q) = {} & (1-\beta)p + \beta\{1 - H(P - s_0) \\
& + p[-1 + H(P - s_0) + H(S - s_0)] \\
& + q[-H(T - s_0) + H(P - s_0)] \\
& + pq[H(T - s_0) + H(R - s_0) - H(P - s_0) - H(S - s_0)]\}
\end{aligned}
$$

similarly for Q we find:

$$
\begin{aligned}
E(Q'|P=p,\,Q=q) = {} & (1-\beta)q + \beta\{1 - H(P - s_0) \\
& + p[-H(T - s_0) + H(P - s_0)] \\
& + q[-1 + H(P - s_0) + H(S - s_0)] \\
& + pq[H(T - s_0)p + H(R - s_0) - H(P - s_0) - H(S - s_0)]\}
\end{aligned}
$$

Next we'd like to find the unconditional expectations of P' and Q'. We do this by taking the expected values of the left-hand sides of the two expressions above:

$$
\begin{aligned}
E(P') = {} & (1-\beta)E(P) + \beta\{1 - H(P - s_0) \\
& + E(P)[-1 + H(P - s_0) + H(S - s_0)] \\
& + E(Q)[-H(T - s_0) + H(P - s_0)] \\
& + E(PQ)[H(T - s_0) + H(R - s_0) - H(P - s_0) - H(S - s_0)]\} \quad (7)
\end{aligned}
$$

$$
\begin{aligned}
E(Q') = (1-\beta)E(Q) + \beta\{1 &- H(P-s_0) \\
&+ E(P)[-H(T-s_0) + H(P-s_0)] \\
&+ E(Q)[-1 + H(P-s_0) + H(S-s_0)] \\
&+ E(PQ)[H(T-s_0) + H(R-s_0) - H(P-s_0) - H(S-s_0)]\}
\end{aligned}
\tag{8}
$$

Now these would be fairly elementary difference equations, except for the terms involving the expected value of the product $E(PQ)$. Students of statistics will recall that $E(PQ)$ only equals $E(P)\,E(Q)$ when P and Q are independent, uncorrelated random variables. It is clear, however, that in general, P and Q will not be independent. Indeed, numerical results suggest that p and q often converge, because in most cases the same difference equation applies to both p and q. This means that, typically, p and q step toward the same γ value (0 or 1), so if p is far from γ and q is close, then the linear operator will move p a large step toward γ, while q will take a small step; this process pushes p and q closer together.

To (partially) overcome this problem, we consider a system of five difference equations. In addition to equations for $E(P)$ and $E(Q)$, we find equations for $E(P^2)$ and $E(Q^2)$ (measures of variability) and $E(PQ)$ (a measure of covariance). Unfortunately, higher-order terms such as $E(P^2Q)$ sometimes occur in these equations; when this happens we eliminate these terms by expanding the equation (for conditional expectation) in a multivariable Taylor Series about $p=E(P)$ and $q=E(Q)$. Once a system of five difference equations is in hand, our analysis follows convention: We solve for fixed points [set $E(P')=E(P)$, $E(Q')=E(Q)$, $E(P^{2'})=E(P^2)$ $E(Q^{2'})=E(Q^2)$, and $E(PQ')=E(PQ)$ and solve for the vector $(E(P),\,E(Q),\,E(P^2),\,E(Q^2),$ and $E(PQ))$]. We then solve for the system's eigenvalues in the neighborhood of the fixed point; for a discrete time system, fixed points in which all eigenvalues have absolute value less than one are said to be linearly stable.

11.5.1 Cases 1 and 5

We remark that in two cases, this approximation is unnecessary. If the coefficient of $E(PQ)$ is zero in equations (7) and (8), then we need only study a system of two equations. Hence, in case 1, when all payoffs are rewarding (all the $H(\ )$ functions become 1), equations (7) (8) become

$$
E(P') = E(P)
$$
$$
E(Q') = E(Q)
$$

a system in which all $(E(P),\,E(Q))$ are neutrally stable fixed points. In case 5, when all payoffs are punishing [all the $H(\ )$ functions are zero], equations (7) and (8) become

$$
E(P') = (1-2\beta)E(P) + \beta
$$
$$
E(Q') = (1-2\beta)E(Q) + \beta
$$

a system with a unique fixed point at $E(P)=E(Q)=1/2$ that is linearly stable for the plausible range of β values: $(1>\beta>0)$.

11.5.2 Case 2. Only S Punishing

In this case we have

$$
\begin{aligned}
E(P') &= (1-\beta)E(P) + \beta E(PQ) \\
E(Q') &= (1-\beta)E(Q) + \beta E(PQ) \\
E(P^{2'}) &\approx \beta(1-\beta)[4E(PQ)E(P) - 4E(Q)E(P)^2 + 2E(P^2)E(Q) \\
&\quad + (1-\beta)^2 E(P^2) + \beta^2 E(PQ) \\
E(Q^{2'}) &\approx \beta(1-\beta)[4E(PQ)E(Q) - 4E(Q)^2 + 2E(Q^2)E(P)] \\
&\quad + (1-\beta)^2 E(Q^2) + \beta^2 + \beta^2 E(PQ) \\
E(PQ') &\approx \beta(1-\beta)[E(Q^2)E(P) + 2E(PQ)E(P) - 2E(Q)^2 E(P) - 2E(Q)E(P)^2 \\
&\quad + E(P^2)E(Q) + 2E(PQ)E(Q)] \\
&\quad + (\beta^2 + (1-\beta)^2)E(PQ)
\end{aligned}
$$

Our analysis proceeds by solving for fixed points of this system—that is, setting $E(P') = E(P)$, $E(Q') = E(Q)$, and so on, and solving for $E(P)$, $E(Q)$, $E(P^2)$, $E(Q^2)$, $E(PQ)$. We find three such points:

$$
E(P) = E(Q) = E(P^2) = E(Q^2) = E(PQ) = 0
$$

corresponding to mutual defection;

$$
E(P) = E(Q) = E(P^2) = E(Q^2) = E(PQ) = \tfrac{1}{2}
$$

corresponding to "random" choice of cooperation and defection; and

$$
E(P) = E(Q) = E(P^2) = E(Q^2) = E(PQ) = 1
$$

corresponding to mutual cooperation. Next, we linearize the system in the neighborhood of each of these fixed points and calculate the eigenvalues of the linearized system.

1. Analysis of the "all defection" fixed point shows two repeated eigenvalues $1 - \beta$, $(1-\beta)^2$ (both of multiplicity two), and a fifth eigenvalue $\beta^2 + (1-\beta)^2$. All these eigenvalues are clearly less than one for $0 < \beta < 1$. We conclude, therefore, that all defection is a linearly stable fixed point when S is punishing.
2. Analysis of the "random choice" fixed point shows that one eigenvalue $1 + \beta(1 - \beta)$ exceeds one for $\beta \in (0, 1)$, so this fixed point is linearly unstable.
3. Analysis of the mutual cooperation fixed point shows three eigenvalues that are clearly less than one: $1 - \beta$, $(1-\beta)^2$, and $1 - \beta^2$. The remaining two eigenvalues are the conjugate pair $-2\beta^2 + \tfrac{3}{2}\beta + 1 \pm \tfrac{1}{2}\beta\sqrt{1 - 16\beta(1-\beta)}$. Numerical analysis shows that the absolute value of these eigenvalues exceed one whenever $\beta < .8228$. We conclude that mutual cooperation is unstable when β is less than about 0.82, but stable for larger β values. This is the first hint of a theme that emerges throughout our analysis: Higher learning rates (β's) favor cooperation.

When $\beta > 0.82$, there are two possible stable fixed points corresponding to mutual defection and mutual cooperation. Numerical analyses suggest that the mutual defection fixed point may be more "attractive" than the mutual cooperation fixed point. Moreover, measured values of β (primarily from rats) are very low, typically less than 0.1. Learning rates might, of course, vary dramatically for different taxa and for different types of learning problems.

11.5.3 Case 3. S and P Punishing

In this case we have the system

$$
\begin{aligned}
E(P') &= (1 - 2\beta)E(P) + \beta(1 - E(Q)) + 2\beta E(PQ) \\
E(Q') &= (1 - 2\beta)E(Q) + \beta(1 - E(P)) + 2\beta E(PQ) \\
E(P^{2'}) &\approx \beta(1 - \beta)[-8E(Q)E(P)^2 - 8E(PQ)E(P) + 3E(P) + 4E(P^2)E(Q)] \\
&\quad - \beta E(P) - \beta^2 E(Q) + (1 - \beta)(1 - 3\beta)E(P^2) \\
&\quad - 2\beta(-2\beta)E(PQ) + \beta^2 \\
E(Q^{2'}) &\approx \beta(1 - \beta)[-8E(P)E(Q)^2 + 4E(Q^2)E(P) - 8E(PQ)E(Q) + 3E(Q)] \\
&\quad - \beta^2 E(P) + -\beta E(Q) + (1 - 3\beta)(1 - \beta)E(Q^2) - 2\beta(1 - 2\beta)E(PQ) + \beta^2] \\
E(PQ') &\approx \beta(1 - \beta)[-4E(Q)E(P)^2 - 4E(Q)^2 E(P) + 2E(Q^2)E(P) - 4E(PQ)E(P) \\
&\quad + 2E(P^2)E(Q) - 4E(PQ)E(Q) - E(P^2) - E(Q^2)] \\
&\quad + (1 - 4\beta + 5\beta^2)E(PQ) + \beta^2 + \beta(1 - 2\beta)E(P) + \beta(1 - 2\beta)E(Q)
\end{aligned}
$$

This system has three fixed points:

$$
E(P) = E(Q) = E(P^2) = E(Q^2) = E(PQ) = 1
$$

corresponding to mutual cooperation, and two fixed points of the form

$$
E(P) = \alpha, \qquad E(Q) = \alpha, \qquad E(P^2) = E(Q^2) = E(PQ) = \tfrac{3}{2}\,\alpha - \tfrac{1}{2}
$$

where α may be either of the two roots of

$$
-16(1 - \beta)Z^2 + 20(1 - \beta)Z - 6 + 5\beta \tag{9}
$$

These fixed points correspond to intermediate (strictly between 0 and 1) levels of cooperation, since roots of equation (9) are

$$
\frac{5}{8} \pm \frac{1}{8}\sqrt{\frac{1 - 5\beta}{1 - \beta}}
$$

1. The mutual cooperation fixed point has associated eigenvalues $1 - \beta^2$, $1 - \beta$, and $(1 - \beta)^2$ and the conjugate pair

$$
\frac{(1 - \beta)(5\beta + 2) \pm \sqrt{(1 - 25\beta)(1 - \beta)}}{2}
$$

The first three eigenvalues are clearly less than one. The members of the conjugate pair are typically complex (when $\beta > 1/25$), and numerical analysis shows that they lie within the unit circle when $\beta > 0.7913$. We conclude that mutual cooperation is a linearly stable fixed point only for $\beta > 0.7913$. Again, we see that high learning rates favor mutual cooperation.

2. The intermediate fixed points are only real when $\beta < 1/5$. The analysis is simplified (although still messier than one would like) by writing the $E(P)$ and $E(Q)$ fixed values in the form

$$\frac{5}{8} \pm \frac{1}{8}\delta$$

where $\beta = (1 - \delta^2)/(5 - \delta^2)$; hence δ takes values in the range of 0 (when $\beta = 1/5$) to 1 (when $\beta = 0$), so that $0 < \delta < 1$ corresponds to the entire range of real-valued fixed points. An analysis of eigenvalues shows that $E(P) = E(Q) = \frac{5}{8} + \frac{1}{8}\delta$ is linearly unstable and that $E(P) = E(Q) = \frac{5}{8} - \frac{1}{8}\delta$ is linearly stable.

Figure 11.1 shows both analytical and numerical results for this case. When the learning rate β is less than $1/5$, then the expected level of cooperation increases gradually with increasing β from $1/2$ to $5/8$. When the learning rate exceeds 0.79, we expect 100% cooperation. Our analytical results say nothing about intermediate learning rates, (i.e., $1/5 < \beta < 0.79$); however, Monte Carlo simulations suggest a smooth sigmoid transition between the two analytically tractable cases.

11.5.4 Case 4. *S*, *P* and *R* Punishing

In this case we have the system

$$E(P') = E(P)(1 - 2\beta) + \beta(1 - E(Q)) + \beta E(PQ)$$
$$E(Q') = E(Q)(1 - 2\beta) + \beta(1 - E(P)) + \beta E(PQ)$$
$$\begin{aligned} E(P^{2\prime}) &\approx \beta(1 - \beta)[-4E(Q)E(P)^2 + 4E(PQ)E(P) + 2E(P) \\ &\quad + 2E(P^2)E(Q) + 2E(PQ)] \\ &\quad + (1 - 3\beta)(1 - \beta)E(P^2) - \beta^2(E(P) - E(PQ) + E(Q)) + \beta^2 \end{aligned}$$
$$\begin{aligned} E(Q^{2\prime}) &\approx \beta(1 - B)[-4E(Q^2)E(P) + 2E(Q^2)E(P) + 4E(PQ)E(Q) \\ &\quad + 2E(Q) - 2E(PQ)] \\ &\quad + (1 - 3\beta)(1 - \beta)E(Q) + B^2(-E)(P + E(PQ) - E(Q)) + \beta^2 \end{aligned}$$
$$\begin{aligned} E(PQ') &\approx \beta(1 - B)[-2E(Q)E(P)^2 - 2E(P)E(Q)^2 + E(Q^2)E(P) \\ &\quad + 2E(PQ)E(P) + E(P^2)E(Q) + 2E(PQ)E(Q) + E(Q) - E(Q^2) - E(P^2)] \\ &\quad + (1 - 3\beta)(1 - \beta)E(PQ) + \beta^2(-E(P) + E(PQ) - E(Q)) + \beta^2 \end{aligned}$$

The fixed points of this system are

$$E(Q) = E(P) = \alpha$$

$$E(Q^2) = E(P^2) = E(PQ) = 3\alpha - 1$$

where α is any of the roots of

$$- 4(1-\beta)z^3 + 18(1-\beta)z^2 - (22-20\beta)z - 5\beta + 6 \qquad (10)$$

Further analysis shows that only the smallest of these roots lies in the interval 0 to 1. Hence there is only one feasible fixed point for this case. The value of this fixed point is a relatively complicated function of β, ranging from $\frac{3}{2}-\frac{\sqrt{5}}{2} \approx 0.38$ (when $\beta=0$) to ½ when $\beta=1$. Although it is rather messy, it's possible to calculate (numerically) the system's five eigenvalues in the neighborhood of this fixed point as functions of β. Plots of the absolute value of the eigenvalues versus β show that all five are typically less than one; hence we conclude that the minimum root of equation (10) is a linearly stable fixed point. Figure 11.2 shows both the analytical predictions and the results of analogous Monte Carlo simulations. We predict that in situations where players view only the T payoff as rewarding, there will be low levels of cooperation ranging from approximately 0.4 to 0.5. We note that the probability of cooperation is again expected to increase with the learning rate, even though the effect is less striking in this case.

Figure 11.3 summarizes these results, by showing the output from two Monte Carlo simulations in which the standard s_0 was varied. The figure shows that the highest levels of cooperation are expected when the S and P payoffs are punishing, and the lowest levels are expected when only S is punishing. The figure also shows generally higher levels of cooperation when the learning rate, β, is higher.

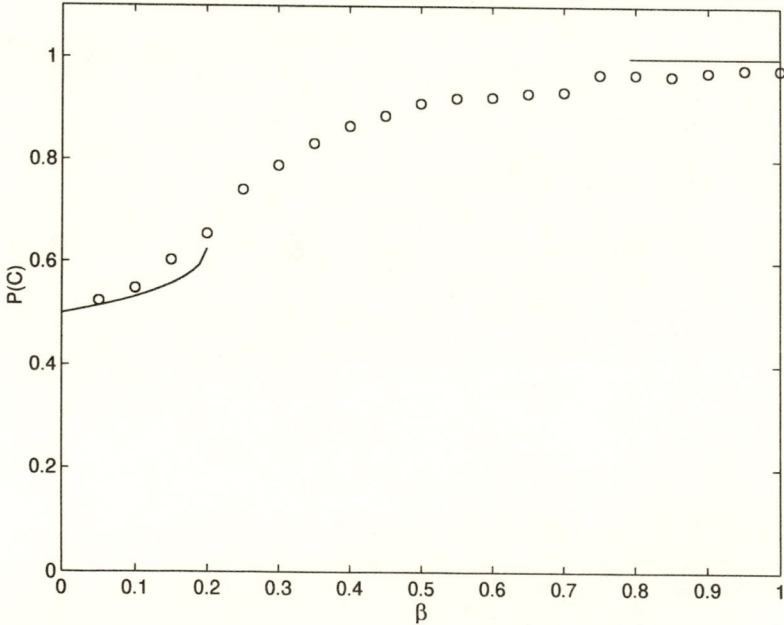

Figure 11.1. Results for case 3, S and P punishing. The solid curves show the stable fixed points predicted analytically, and the dotted line shows the results of Monte Carlo simulations of the system.

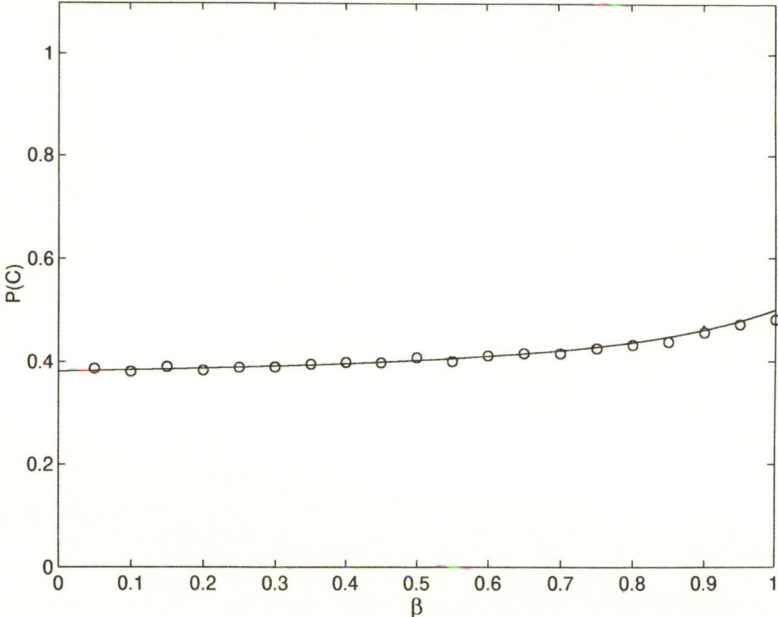

Figure II.2. Results for case 4, *S, P* and *R* punishing. The solid curves show
the stable fixed points predicted analytically, and the dotted line shows the results of Monte Carlo simulations of the system. In this case, the coincidence
between analytical and simulation results is remarkable.

These results raise several issues. First, all five cases and the entire range of
learning rates $(1 > \beta > 0)$ describe instances of the law of effect applied to an iterated
Prisoner's Dilemma. Nowak and Sigmund's "Pavlov" strategy corresponds to the special case where only S and P are punishing and $\beta = 1$. We see, contrary to the impression left by Nowak and Sigmund's (1993) discussion, that there is no necessary connection between the law of effect and cooperation in an IPD: The law of effect may
lead to defection or to cooperation, or to something in between. Second, one wonders
when animals might categorize consequences as "absolutely" rewarding or punishing.
Two possibilities are shown in the game matrices below:

$$
\begin{array}{c}
\quad C \qquad\qquad\qquad D \\
\begin{array}{c} C \\ D \end{array}
\left[\begin{array}{cc}
3 \text{ units of food} & 10 \text{ seconds of shock} \\
5 \text{ units of food} & 1 \text{ second of shock}
\end{array}\right]
\end{array}
\qquad
\begin{array}{c}
\quad C \qquad\qquad\qquad D \\
\begin{array}{c} C \\ D \end{array}
\left[\begin{array}{cc}
1 \text{ offspring} & .01 \text{ Probability of Survival} \\
5 \text{ offspring} & .5 \text{ Probability of Survival}
\end{array}\right]
\end{array}
$$

In both cases, we could probably agree that a "sensible" player should rank the
payoffs as required for a Prisoner's Dilemma (i.e., 5 units of food are better than 3,
and food without shock is better than shock, while a shorter shock is better than a
longer one). In both cases, however, the punishing consequences are qualitatively
different from the rewarding consequences; so that it would be quite impossible to
add 5 units of food to 1 second of shock as conventional analyses suggest. Hence,
while our law-of-effect model predicts the highest levels of cooperation in games like

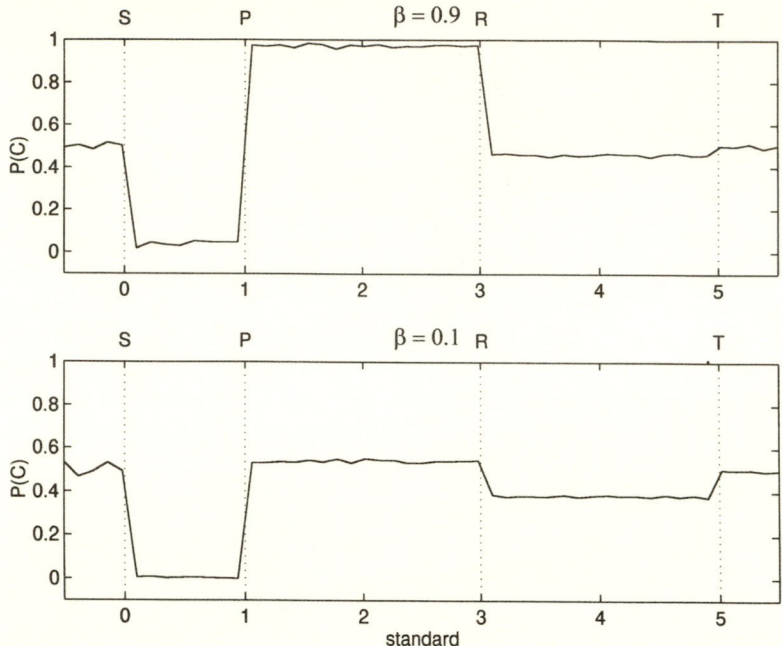

Figure II.3. Numerical results for a series of Monte Carlo simulations in which the standard s_0 was varied from -0.5 to 5.5 at two different learning rates, $\beta = 0.9$ and $\beta = 0.1$. The range of "standards" covers each of the five cases discussed in the text; for example, the figure shows that case 3, S and P punishing, produced the highest rates of cooperation.

these (where the S and P consequences are absolutely punishing), current models of cooperation cannot be applied to these situations because payoffs cannot be added.

Finally, we remark that there is a body of experimental evidence that is, crudely, in agreement with our predictions. Colman (1982) reports that human experiments show two trends: One striking trend is "the DD lock-in effect" in which human subjects play long strings of joint defection. For example, in a very early study Scodel et al. (1959) show the DD lock-in effect with the game matrix

$$
\begin{array}{c}
 \quad C \qquad D \\
\begin{array}{c} C \\ D \end{array}
\begin{bmatrix} R=3 & S=0 \\ T=5 & P=1 \end{bmatrix}
\end{array}
$$

where the payoffs were pennies. [A similar study using feeding bluejays playing for food pellets (Clements & Stephens 1995), using the same matrix, also showed the DD lock-in effect.] If, as in many psychological experiments, we were to view the zero outcome as absolutely punishing, then we might interpret these results as consistent with the current model. Colman also reports that higher levels of cooperation (about 60%) have been observed in a sequence of studies following the procedures of Rapoport & Chammah (1965) that use game matrices like

$$\begin{array}{cc} & \begin{array}{cc} C & \qquad D \end{array} \\ \begin{array}{c} C \\ D \end{array} & \left[\begin{array}{cc} R=5 & S=-10 \\ T=10 & P=-4 \end{array}\right] \end{array}$$

where the payoffs are points that can be exchanged for cash at some later time. Again, this seems consistent with our model, in that the S and P consequences are qualitatively distinct (i.e., they are losses) from the T and R consequences. Indeed, the idea that humans treat losses and gains as qualitatively distinct entities is one of the cornerstones of Kahneman & Tversky's empirically successful prospect theory of human decision making (1979).

If we agree that positive rewards (food or money) are rewarding and nonpositive "rewards" are punishing, then our "law-of-effect" model is crudely consistent with the pattern of results seen in the human and animal experimental PD literature. Specifically, matrices like

$$\begin{array}{cc} & \begin{array}{cc} C & \qquad D \end{array} \\ \begin{array}{c} C \\ D \end{array} & \left[\begin{array}{cc} R=+ & S=- \\ T=+ & P=+ \end{array}\right] \end{array}$$

favor defection (usually "DD lock-in,"), and matrices like

$$\begin{array}{cc} & \begin{array}{cc} C & \qquad D \end{array} \\ \begin{array}{c} C \\ D \end{array} & \left[\begin{array}{cc} R=+ & S=- \\ T=+ & P=- \end{array}\right] \end{array}$$

favor cooperation (usually $P(C) \approx .60$).

It is clear however, that this agreement is at best "crude." To see how these predictions fail, consider the following results from our laboratory. Using procedures outlined by Clements and Stephens (1995), we have tested the behavior of blue jays (*Cyanocitta cristata*) in a range of game matrices. In our procedures, stable mutual cooperation is created by presenting the birds with a C-dominating (mutualism) matrix, and then the stability of mutual C is tested by switching to a test matrix. Figure 11.4 shows the time course of mutual cooperation in tests of the matrices shown in Table 11.2. In addition, Table 11.2 shows statistical measures of the results. The matrix $\left[\begin{smallmatrix} 3 & 0 \\ 5 & 1 \end{smallmatrix}\right]$ was originally tested because it is the single most widely given example of a Prisoner's Dilemma. Coincidentally, the zero in the S payoff makes this an "S punishing" matrix in the context of our law-of-effect model; and, as predicted, we see convincing DD lock-in. The reader may recall that Axelrod and Hamilton (1981) claimed that cooperative equilibria were possible only when the probably of repetition exceeded critical level $\hat{w}$ that depends on the elements of the game matrix. The critical value for test matrix $\left[\begin{smallmatrix} 5 & 1 \\ 5 & 1 \end{smallmatrix}\right]$ is $\hat{w}=0$ (i.e., cooperation should be sustained without any repetition!), and the critical value for test matrix $\left[\begin{smallmatrix} 3 & 1 \\ 5 & 3 \end{smallmatrix}\right]$ is $\hat{w}=1$ (i.e., no amount of repetition can sustain cooperation because $w<1$). Neither of these test matrices contain a zero or negative value, and so our current interpretation of the "absolute standard" of reward and punishment offers no mechanism to distinguish between them. Yet, we see a clear difference between $\begin{bmatrix} 5 & 1 \\ 5 & 1 \end{bmatrix}$ and $\begin{bmatrix} 3 & 1 \\ 5 & 3 \end{bmatrix}$: Blue jays defect more and reach their asymptotic defection rate more quickly in the $\begin{bmatrix} 3 & 1 \\ 5 & 3 \end{bmatrix}$ matrix (Table 11.2). This suggests that we need something more than the simple "$+/-$" standard discussed earlier. On the positive side, there is evidence that the zero ($S = 0$) in the standard PD matrix, $\begin{bmatrix} 3 & 0 \\ 5 & 1 \end{bmatrix}$, is important; because although its predicted $\hat{w} = 2/3$ value is intermediate, it produced the lowest level of cooperation of the three matrices.

11.6 Dynamic Standards

One possible explanation for these empirical results is that our "standard" s_0 of reward and punishment can vary with experience. To investigate this possibility, imagine that an animal experiences a stream of outcomes whose magnitudes can be characterized by a sequence of random variables: $X_1, X_2, X_3, \ldots$ and that the "standard" at time i can be expressed as a weighted mean of the most recent outcome X_i and the previous standard:

$$s_{i+1} = \begin{cases} (1 - \alpha)X_i + \alpha s_i, & i > 0 \\ X_0, & i = 0 \end{cases}$$

This implies a "geometric" weighting of current and past experience: When $\alpha = 0$, only the most recent outcome affects the standard; however, as α approaches one, the decision-maker can be thought of as using an increasingly long time horizon to establish its standard. We analyzed this possibility by performing Monte Carlo simulations of two players using this geometrically-weighted standard in the classical IPD matrix $\begin{bmatrix} 3 & 0 \\ 5 & 1 \end{bmatrix}$. The results (Fig. 11.5) show that giving a higher weighting to past experience (higher α) increases the likelihood of cooperation, as do higher learning rates (higher β as we found earlier). There is a straightforward and compelling connection between this qualitative result, and two equilibria of the IPD. When only recent experience determines the standard, then players seek out the single play equilibrium (mutual defection) as we would expect; however, when experience over the long term influences the standard, then players tend toward the repeated-play "cooperative" equilibria. Interestingly, this result is reached not via economic considerations [as, for example, it was by Axelrod & Hamilton (1981)], but by a consideration of the moment-to-moment behavioral dynamics of the law of effect.

Despite this intriguing parallel, we must account for the preponderance of defection in the experimental literature. The present model suggests that either small learning rates or short-term standards might account for this trend. Psychological evidence suggests that both might occur. Reported learning rates for Norway rats are typically less than 0.1 (Coombs et al. 1970). Moreover, there is a body of psychological evidence suggesting that animals focus on recent experience in deciding which outcomes represent improvements and which do not. For example, Staddon (1983) characterizes the behavior of pigeons as "hill-climbing" or momentary-maximizing in that they

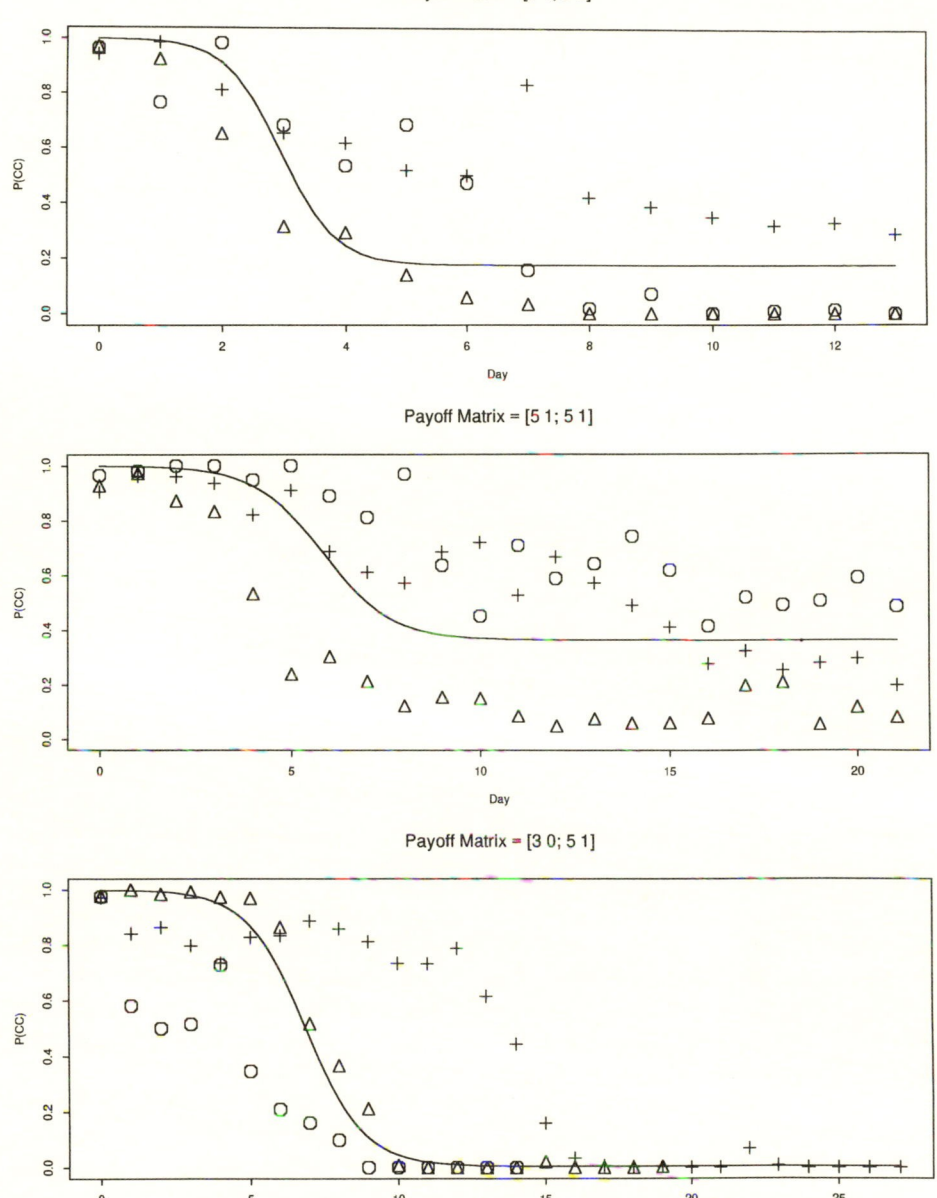

Figure 11.4. Daily frequencies of mutual cooperation *(P(CC))* in three different test matrices (we use the notation *[R S; TP]* in the figure headings). The lower panel shows previously reported data (Clements & Stephens 1995). A distinct symbol (○, +, or △) denotes data from different pairs of birds. The solid curves show an averaged fit to the differential equation

$$\frac{dp}{dt} = r(b - x)(1 - x), \; x(0) \approx 1,$$

where *r* is a measure of "decay rate" and *b* is a measure of asymptotic value of *P(CC)*. Table 11.2 shows the fitted parameters.

Table 11.2 Parameters Measuring the Decay of Mutual Cooperation in Three
Experimental Game Matrices

Matrix	Pair ID	r (1/days)	b	T_{50} (days)
$\begin{bmatrix} 3 & 1 \\ 5 & 3 \end{bmatrix}$				
	Pair 1	1.28	0.019	5.48
	Pair 2	2.93	0.055	2.47
	Pair 3	4.09	0.450	2.55
	Means	2.76	0.175	3.5
$\begin{bmatrix} 5 & 1 \\ 5 & 1 \end{bmatrix}$				
	Pair 1	1.69	0.552	8.06
	Pair 2	1.97	0.123	3.92
	Pair 3	1.55	0.417	7.04
	Means	1.74	0.364	5.84
$\begin{bmatrix} 3 & 0 \\ 5 & 1 \end{bmatrix}$				
	Pair A	1.61	0.040	4.44
	Pair B	0.928	−0.007	7.40
	Pair C	0.519	−0.022	13.06
	Means	1.01	0.0037	8.3

appear to choose options that follow the steepest gradient of reward in the short-
term. [Vaughan and Herrnstein's (1984) idea of "melioration" is similar, if less well
articulated.]

Although this point of view can account for the preponderance of defection in
game matrices like $\begin{bmatrix} 3 & 0 \\ 5 & 1 \end{bmatrix}$ and $\begin{bmatrix} 3 & 1 \\ 5 & 3 \end{bmatrix}$, it can't account for elevated levels of cooperation
in matrices like $\begin{bmatrix} 5 & -10 \\ 10 & -4 \end{bmatrix}$ as studied by Rapoport and Chammah (1965). In this "dy-
namically adjusting standard" model, low learning rates and an emphasis on recent
experience predict defection in *all* PDs, because this behavior tracks the single play
equilibrium which is always mutual defection. To account for all the evidence, we
probably need a model that somehow incorporates dynamically changing standards
and absolute standards: For example, we need a model in which a gain is considered
rewarding if it's greater than the previous gain, but a loss is punishing even if a
larger loss was experienced previously.

11.7 Discussion

Ours is not the first attempt to consider learning in the Prisoner's Dilemma. Rapoport
and Chammah (1965) made extensive use the of Bush and Mosteller family of models to analyze the results of their experiments. Their use of linear operator models,
however, does not lend itself to generalization. They simply fitted the linear operator
models to their results. By considering models with 16–256 fitted parameters, they
were able (not surprisingly!) to find satisfactory fits to their data. In contrast, our
approach has been to severely restrict the number of free parameters, and to try to
formulate generalizations about the effects of parameters like the "standard" s_0 and

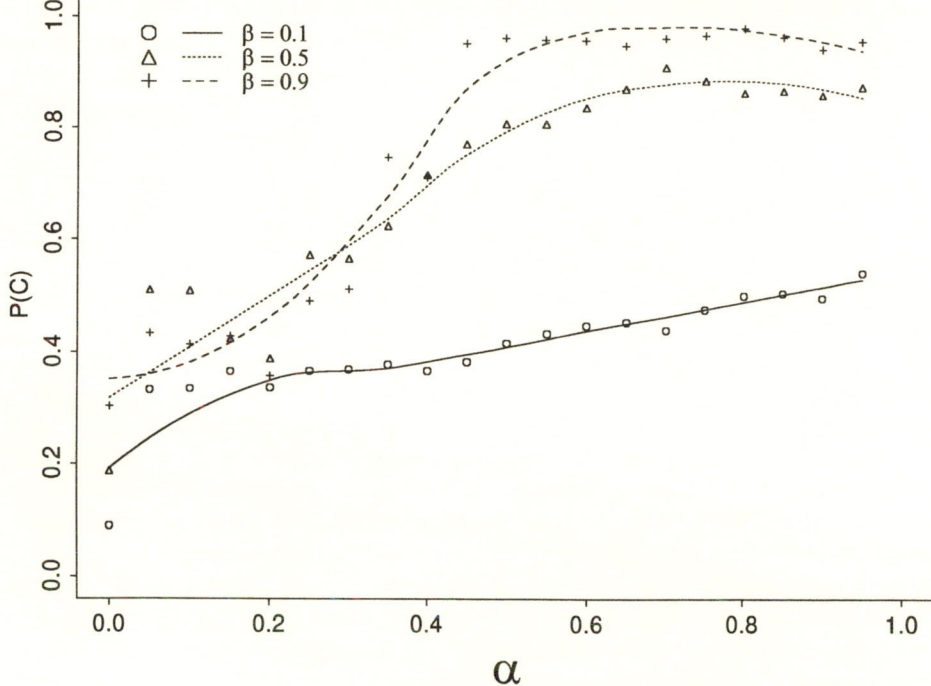

Figure 11.5. Results of Monte Carlo simulations in which the standard s_0 changes dynamically according to the outcomes experienced by the players. The weighting given to past experience α and the learning rate β were varied systematically. The figure shows that increases in α and β increase the probability of cooperation. The curves are fits to the data using the "loess" regression technique (locally linear smooth curves) advocated by Cleveland (1993).

the learning rate β. We make two comments about the style of models we have adopted. First, a reviewer has asked that we speculate about the effect of allowing different β values to apply in different situations. We believe that there will be no "general" effect of such a change, other than the obvious one of allowing a "fit" to more situations. However, these additional parameters buy us a better "fit" at the expense of analytical clarity. We believe that this exercise should wait until we have some empirical guidance about which outcomes should have different β values associated with them. Second, mathematical psychologists have developed several other learning models; we have studied the linear operator models because of their analytical simplicity. Indeed, Harley's (1981) relative payoff-sum model is a learning model originally proposed by Duncan Luce to correct some deficiencies in the linear operator models. We refer the interested reader to Luce et al.'s (1963) seminal *Handbook of Mathematical Psychology* for a treatment of this and many other behavioral issues that are relevant to game theory.

Kraines and Kraines (1989) proposed a "law-of-effect" model that is easily analyzed numerically, but without the history of psychological justification of the Bush and Mosteller models. In the Kraines and Kraines model, n units of reward shift the probability of the corresponding action p, up by amount nx within the constraints 0

$\le p \le 1$ [i.e., n units of reward shifts p to $\min(1, p+nx)$], similarly, n units of punishment shift the probability down by nx units [i.e., to $\max(0, p-nx)$]. Moreover, Kraines and Kraines restricted their analysis to $x = \frac{1}{10}$ and to the Rapoport-and-Chammah-style matrix

$$
\begin{array}{cc}
 & \begin{array}{cc} C & \qquad D \end{array} \\
\begin{array}{c} C \\ D \end{array} &
\begin{bmatrix} R=1 & S=-2 \\ T=2 & P=-1 \end{bmatrix}
\end{array}
$$

and they explicitly assumed that the negative payoffs are punishing while the positive payoffs are rewarding. In light of our analysis showing that the S and P punishing case greatly favors cooperation, it is hardly remarkable that their "Pavlov" generally converges on cooperation. Nowak and Sigmund's (1993) analysis follows Kraines and Kraines, except that their "Pavlov" is an extreme variant of the original with $x = 1$, so that an act followed by punishment is never repeated, and an act followed by reward is always repeated. Nowak and Sigmund, however, do not restrict themselves to the $S < P \le 0$ case; and it is unclear why they believe that these two consequences are universally punishing. Our models show that deciding which consequences are punishing and which are rewarding is a critical issue.

Our model suggests that games in which the S and P consequences are (a) unambiguously and universally bad and (b) *qualitatively* distinct from the T and R consequences will lead to the highest levels of cooperation. That is, matrices like

$$
\begin{array}{cc}
 & \begin{array}{cc} C & \qquad\qquad\qquad\qquad D \end{array} \\
\begin{array}{c} C \\ D \end{array} &
\begin{bmatrix} R \text{ is something good, but not quite } T & S \text{ is something terrible} \\ T \text{ is something good} & P \text{ something terrible, but not quite } S \end{bmatrix}
\end{array}
$$

are the PD-like situations in which some cooperation is the most likely. Are these games really Prisoner's Dilemmas? The answer seems to be "maybe." The consequences can probably be ranked in the sense that T is preferred to R is preferred to P is preferred to S, but the condition $R > (T+S)/2$ is nonsense (at least until the payoffs are somehow transformed into a common currency). The analysis of repeated play is greatly complicated because we probably cannot add up the payoffs, as in the classical analysis of Axelrod and Hamilton (1981, and all subsequent analyses we are aware of). Of course, games like this are much less enigmatic than ordinary PDs, simply because some cooperation is required if "terrible" consequences are to be avoided. Yet, such games still present an intriguing social problem: Avoidance of the terrible is solely in the hands of your opponent, and we must collude if we are to avoid the terrible thing.

Our analysis suggests several directions for future study. As argued in the preceding paragraphs, PD-like games with more than one type of consequence should be analyzed further: Do the classical results about repetition and reciprocity still apply in such games? In this chapter we have analyzed game-theoretic situations from a largely nongame-theoretic perspective. A more traditional game-theoretic analysis may provide valuable insights. Is there an equilibria standard s_0? (Or, an equilibrium learning rate β?) We might speculate that in brief or heavily discounted IPDs, equilibrium standards between S and P will arise; while in long-term interaction equilibrium standards between *P* and *R* might enhance the likelihood of cooperation. Another possibility is to (a) consider the pair (s, β) to be a "strategy" and ask how such strategies fare against TFT and (b) consider the menagerie of champions and patsies that typifies much of the theoretical IPD literature.

II.8 Summary and Conclusions

The implications of the law of effect for animal behavior in repeated Prisoner's Dilemmas depends critically on one's assumptions about how the law of effect operates. Specifically, the predicted behavior is extremely sensitive to (1) assumptions about which outcomes are rewarding and which are punishing—if only *S* is punishing then mutual defection is strongly favored, yet the most favorable case for cooperation occurs when only *S* and *P* are punishing; (2) assumptions about the rate of learning—conservative, slow learning organisms favor defection while organisms that respond quickly to experience should favor cooperation; and (3) assumptions about how experiences affect the "standard" separating reward from punishment—when only recent experience determines the standard, defection is favored; however, when animals use a longer sequence of outcomes to determine their "standard," cooperation is favored.

References

Axelrod, R. & Hamilton, W. 1981. The evolution of cooperation. *Science,* 211, 1390–1396.

Bush, R. R. & Mosteller, F. 1951. A mathematical model for simple learning. *Psychol. Rev.,* 58, 313–323.

Bush, R. R. & Mosteller, F. 1955. *Stochastic Models for Learning.* New York: Wiley.

Clements, K. C. & Stephens, D. W. 1995. Testing models of non-kin cooperation: mutualism and the prisoner's dilemma. *Anim. Behav.,* 50, 527–535.

Cleveland, W. S. 1993. *Visualizing Data.* Summit, NJ: Hobart Press.

Colman, A. M. 1982. *Game Theory and Experimental Games: The Study of Strategic Interaction.* Oxford: Pergamon Press.

Coombs, C. H., Dawes, R. M. & Tversky, A. 1970. *Mathematical Psychology: An Elementary Introduction.* Englewood Cliffs, NJ: Prentice-Hall.

Harley, C. B. 1981. Learning the evolutionarily stable strategy. *J. Theor. Biol.,* 89, 611–633.

Kahneman, D. & Tversky, A. 1979. Prospect theory: An analysis of decision under risk. *Econometrica,* 47, 263–291.

Kraines, D. & Kraines, V. 1989. Pavlov and the prisoner's dilemma. *Theory and Decision,* 26, 47–79.

Luce, R. D., R. R. Bush & E. Galanter 1963. *Handbook of Mathematical Psychology.*, Vol. 1. New York: Wiley.

Maynard Smith, J. 1982. *Evolution and the Theory of Games.* Cambridge: Cambridge University Press.

Nowak, M. & Sigmund, K. 1993. A strategy of win–stay, lose–shift that outperforms tit-for-tat in the prisoner's dilemma. *Nature,* 364, 56–58.

Rapoport, A. & Chammah, A. M. 1965. *Prisoner's Dilemma: A Study in Conflict and Cooperation.* Ann Arbor, MI: University of Michigan Press.

Rescorla, R. A. & Wagner, A. R. 1972. A theory of pavlovian conditioning: Variations in the effectiveness of reinforcement and non-reinforcement. In *Classical Conditioning II.* A. Black & W. R. Prokasy, eds.. New York.: Appleton-Century-Crofts.

Scodel, A. J., Minas, S., Ratoosh, P. & Lipetz, M. 1959. Some descriptive aspects of two-person non-zero-sum games. *J. Conflict. Res.,* 3, 114–119.

Staddon, J. E. R. 1983. *Adaptive Behavior and Learning.* New York: Cambridge University Press.

Stephens, D. W. 1991. Change, regularity and value in the evolution of animal learning. *Behav. Ecol.,* 2, 77–89.

Stephens, D. W., Nishimura, K. & Toyer, K. B. 1995. Error and discounting in the iterated prisoner's dilemma. *J. Theor. Biol.,* 176, 457–469.

Thorndike, E. L. 1911. *Animal Intelligence.* New York: Hafner Publishing Co. (reprinted in 1965).

Vaughan, W. Jr., & Herrnstein, R. J. 1984. Stability, melioration and natural selection. In *Advances in behavioral economics, Vol. 1,* L. Green & J. Kagel, eds. New York: Ablex.

DAVID SLOAN WILSON

Game Theory and Human Behavior

12.1 Introduction

Game theory has long been used by economists, psychologists, and other social scientists to predict the behavior of people in a variety of situations. More recently, evolutionary biologists have used game theory to predict the behavior of nonhuman species. It is safe to say that evolutionary game theory has transformed the study of animal behavior, although theory has so far outpaced empirical studies.

Evolutionary approaches to human behavior are not new, but they have recently gathered momentum and show signs of being accepted by the human sciences. As might be expected, evolutionary predictions about human behavior are often framed in the language of evolutionary game theory. Are these predictions really new, or do they merely restate the predictions of traditional game theory? What can evolutionary game theory say about human nature that its much larger and older parent tradition cannot?

In traditional game theory, strategies are assumed to be adopted by rational choice. In evolutionary game theory, strategies are assumed to simply exist in the population and to compete with each other in Darwinian fashion. As a result, the strategies that emerge from evolutionary game theory maximize the relative fitness of individuals in the population. Traditional game theory can make no such claim, because the utilities that are assumed to be maximized by rational choice are not defined.

It has often been said that evolutionary game theory enjoys an advantage over its parent discipline precisely because it can say something about the utilities that individuals strive to maximize. In my opinion, this distinction is overstated. In the first place, evolutionary game theory models are not about the maximization of fitness. They are about cooperating, fighting over resources, being altruistic, or any number of other proximate activities that can be plugged into the model by assuming a direct relationship between the activity and biological fitness. Thus, evolutionary game theory has the same flexibility as traditional game theory in choosing its utilities, merely by assuming (usually without data) that a proximate utility leads to the ultimate utility of biological fitness. In the second place, the phrase "compete with each other in Darwinian fashion" is often interpreted quite loosely. It *can* mean that individuals who employ the most successful strategies have the most offspring, who resemble their parents, causing the best strategies to increase in frequency in the next generation. However, it can also mean that individuals who employ the most successful strategies are imitated by others, causing the best strategies to spread by a social learning process. These two sets of assumptions lead to equivalent results only if individuals are programmed to imitate behaviors that maximize their biological fitness. If the learning rules deviate from fitness-maximizing criteria, strategies will spread in a "Darwinian fashion" (loosely interpreted) but the utilities that they maximize will not necessarily correspond to Darwinian fitness.

In making these comments, I am not denying the relevance of evolutionary theory to human behavior. It is just that the relationship between human behavior and biological fitness is complex, as most human evolutionary biologists are happy to concede (e.g., Barkow et al. 1992; Betzig et al. 1988). Evolutionary game theory would be in trouble if it actually required strong assumptions about the maximization of biological fitness. The fact that the phrase "compete with each other in a Darwinian fashion" can be interpreted loosely is usually regarded as a strength rather than a weakness. Nevertheless, if evolutionary game theory doesn't make strong assumptions about biological fitness, what does it say about human nature that was not forthcoming from traditional game theory?

Other technical differences exist between evolutionary and traditional game theory, such as the difference between an evolutionarily stable state and a Nash equilibrium. However, there is a larger and more fundamental difference that needs to be considered in addition to these technical differences. Evolutionary biology and the human social sciences have very different historical roots and preconceptions that influence the kinds of questions that are asked and are reflected in the use of game theory as an analytical tool. In short, traditional game theory *can* generate many of the same insights as evolutionary game theory; it merely *hasn't*. I will illustrate this point with an example in which evolutionary game theory has yielded insights about human behavior that were not forthcoming from either traditional game theory or other branches of the human social sciences. Then I will show how future developments in evolutionary game theory might account for some aspects of human behavior that are often thought to defy any kind of evolutionary explanation.

12.2 Human Populations as a Multistrategy Community

One of the most important insights to emerge from evolutionary game theory is that natural selection often favors a diversity of adaptive strategies within a single population. For example, many species consist not only of males and females, but also a number of distinct male forms that are adapted to fertilize females in different ways. Some defend territories, others attempt to intercept females on their way to the territories, still others mimic females to gain access to territories and mate with real females, and so on (Gross 1996; Gross & Repka, this volume). As a second example, many species of fish consist of a range of forms that are adapted to forage in different ways. Some swim through the open water feeding on zooplankton, others search along the bottom feeding on snails, and so on (Robinson & Wilson 1994). The morphological and behavioral differences among these intraspecific forms are sometimes so great that they were originally mistaken for different species. Adaptive phenotypic diversity can be maintained by environmental heterogeneity or by frequency-dependent forces that cause the fitness of a particular form to decline when it becomes common. The proximate mechanisms that cause adaptive phenotypic diversity include genetic polymorphisms, developmental plasticity, or a mixture of both (Wilson 1994).

The idea that competition forces individuals to perform different activities to make a living dates back to the earliest economists (e.g., Smith 1776), who profoundly influenced Darwin's theory of natural selection. However, it is not a major theme that emerges from traditional game theory, nor has it been generalized beyond the narrow sphere of economics to other aspects of human behavior. Although many exceptions can be found in its vast literature (e.g., Cohen & Malachek 1988), traditional game theory has not led to a view of human populations as a multistrategy community in which phenotypic diversity is maintained by environmental heterogeneity and frequency-dependent forces. For that matter, neither have the fields of psychology, anthropology, or sociology. Thus, traditional game theory in particular and the human social sciences in general *could* have arrived at this vision of human behavioral diversity; they simply *didn't*.

Cooperation provides an excellent example of how evolutionary game theory can deliver insights on one of the most venerable subjects in traditional game theory and the human social sciences. Cooperation can succeed as an adaptive strategy to the extent that cooperators interact with each other and avoid exploitation. Exploiters can succeed to the extent that they can prey upon cooperators and avoid retaliation (see Dugatkin, this volume). Although the simplest game theory models predict that one or the other strategy will evolve to fixation (e.g., Axelrod & Hamilton 1981), more sophisticated models predict a mixture of both strategies, maintained by environmental heterogeneity and frequency-dependent forces (e.g., Boyd & Lorberbaum 1987; Dugatkin 1990, 1992; Dugatkin & Wilson 1991; Farrell & Ware 1989; Feldman & Thomas 1987; Frank 1988; Hirshleifer 1987; Hirshleifer & Coll 1988; Peck and Feldman 1986; Peck 1990, 1992, 1993). For example, if exploitation is favored in short relationships without the likelihood of repeated interactions and cooperation is favored by long relationships, both strategies should be expected in populations that experience both short and long relationships. Individuals should be able to facultatively switch strategies to some extent, but we might also expect a degree of specialization, with some individuals seeking out short-term exploitative relationships and others seeking out long-term cooperative relationships. We can even imagine an intraspecific coevolutionary process, similar to interspecific coevolution between predators and their prey, in which exploiters evolve a diversity of ways to gain access to cooperators, who in turn evolve a diversity of ways to protect themselves. In short, there is every reason to expect a single population to evolve into a multi-strategy community with respect to cooperation and exploitation.

The eternal conflict between cooperators and exploiters is as likely to exist in humans as in other species. Strangely, however, traditional game theory and the human sciences have not converged on the multistrategy vision outlined above. I speak with some authority on this subject because I have recently reviewed the social psychology literature on Machiavellianism (Wilson et al. 1996; see Mealey 1995 for a review of the related subject of sociopathy from an evolutionary perspective). Christie and Geis (1968, 1970) were the first psychologists to study the ability to manipulate others as an important personality trait. They developed a questionnaire based on the writings of Niccolo Machiavelli, whose name has come to symbolize manipulative strategies of social conduct. Subjects who take the questionnaire are assigned a score based on their agreement with such questions as "Never tell anyone the real reason you did something unless it is useful to do so." Christie, Geis, and their colleagues showed that high and low scorers on the test, referred to as "high-Machs" and "low-Machs" respectively, differ in many other aspects of their behavior, from vocational choice to success at games that involve forming alliances. The literature on Machiavellianism in social psychology now includes over 300 papers.

The Machiavellianism literature shows beyond doubt that people differ in their tendency to manipulate others for personal gain, often at the expense of the other person. However, this literature has not even remotely converged on the multistrategy framework that emerges from evolutionary game theory. A few articles are influenced by traditional game theory, but even the most basic questions, such as the effects of repeated interactions on the tendency to exploit others, have not been addressed. In fact, interest in the entire subject of Machiavellianism has waned among social psychologists, with the number of publications per annum peaking in 1982 (psychology is such a large field that 300 articles is a small literature!). As with so many other subjects in psychology, Machiavellianism was popular for a brief period and then faded into obscurity. Recent textbooks either do not discuss Machiavellianism at all or provide a short paragraph that reads like an obituary—a description of something that happened in the history of psychology, unconnected to any ongoing conceptual theme. The entire subject of cooperation and exploitation as an intraspecific predator–prey relationship is not recognized as an important issue.

Even though the Machiavellianism literature is disappointing from the conceptual standpoint, it provides a data base for testing evolutionary hypotheses. For example, Harrell and Hartnagel (1976) gave high- and low-Machs an opportunity to steal in a worker–supervisor situation. In one treatment the supervisor (a confederate of the experiment) made it clear that he thought the subject would steal and monitored the subject's behavior periodically during the session. In another treatment the supervisor was more trusting and announced that he did not need to monitor the behavior of the subject. The majority of all subjects stole from the distrustful supervisor (95% of high-Machs stole an average of 81¢, 86% of low-Machs stole an average of 92¢; the differences between high- and low-Machs were not statistically significant). However, high-Machs were much more likely to steal from the trusting supervisor and also stole greater amounts than low-Machs. Specifically, 81% of the high-Machs stole an average of 101¢, whereas 24% of the low-Machs stole an average of 25¢ (both of these differences were highly statistically significant). Furthermore, high- and low-Mach's stole in different ways from the distrustful supervisor. Low-Machs were more righteous about their behavior, in some cases stealing openly and challenging the distrustful supervisor to "do something about it." This experiment can be nicely interpreted in game theoretic terms. Low-Machs seemed to be guided by a "tit-for-tat" strategy in which the distrustfulness of the supervisor was perceived as an act of defection that calls for overt retaliation. High-Machs seem to be guided by a "defect" strategy that allows exploitation as a first-strike option.

As another example, Shultz (1993) studied the sales performance of stock brokers from companies that differed in their organizational structure. One was a highly structured, rule-bound corporation that allowed little room for improvisation. Employees were required to abide by a two-volume sales manual and were assigned potential clients, making it virtually impossible to manipulate transactions to affect commissions. The other corporation was loosely structured and encouraged wheeling and dealing. Employees were provided with a brief "suggestion pamphlet" rather than a sales manual and their pool of clients was unlimited, providing ample opportunities to manipulate commissions. Shultz gave the Mach test to employees of both companies and split the distribution of Mach scores at the median to define "high-Mach" and "low-Mach" categories. In the loosely structured corporation, high-Machs had more clients and earned twice as much in commissions than low-Machs. The reverse was true in the tightly structured corporation, with low-Machs earning more than high-Machs. This and other studies leave no doubt that the Mach test is measuring an important axis of human behavioral variation with real-world consequences. High-Machs perform well in some social environments and low-Machs perform well in others. Perhaps this kind of heterogeneous social environment promotes a mix of social strategies coexisting in the general population.

Analyzing the past literature provides intriguing hints that Machiavellianism can be understood in game-theoretic terms (Wilson et al. 1996). Of course, it would be even better to design empirical studies with evolutionary game theory in mind. This enterprise is only beginning, but already has produced results that were not forthcoming from the previous literature, as illustrated by the following examples.

The questions on the Mach test ask how the subject is likely to behave toward all people (e.g., "Never tell anyone the real reason you did something unless it is useful to do so"). However, one of the most elementary predictions of evolutionary theory is that social conduct should depend on one's partner. Individuals should be less manipulative toward genetic relatives and reciprocators, more manipulative toward strangers, and so on. Barber (1994) and Barber and Raffield (1997) tested some of these predictions simply by altering the Mach test to refer to specific classes of people. Barber showed that subjects are less manipulative toward family members and friends than toward people in general. However, there were no differences between the categories of "friends" and "family members," nor among finer degrees of friendship or genetic relatedness. Barber and Raffield had subjects complete the Mach test in reference to individuals of the same vs. the opposite sex. When the Mach test refers to people in general, the average female score was usually lower than the average male score. However, when the test was made sex-specific, the average degree of Machiavellianism was ranked (from low to high) females interacting with females < males interacting with males < males interacting with females < females interacting with males. In other words, women were the *most* manipulative sex when it came to interacting with members of the opposite sex!

Another basic prediction that emerges from evolutionary game theory is that exploiters should be avoided in most social interactions. However, the Machiavelli literature shows quite clearly that high-Machs are socially attractive, at least over the short term (Bochner et al. 1975, Cherulnik et al. 1981, Christie & Geis 1970, Geis & Levy 1970, Okanes & Stinson 1974). Cherulnik et al. reported that high-Machs were perceived to be more "charming" and "intelligent" than low-Machs, despite the fact that Machiavellianism does not correlate with any measure of general intelligence (reviewed by Wilson et al. 1996). In their earlier review of the literature, Christie and Geis concluded that "high-Machs are preferred as partners, chosen and identified as leaders, judged as more persuasive, and appear to direct the tone and content of interaction—and usually the outcome" (1970, p. 313). Indeed, Christie and Geis themselves admitted to a "perverse admiration for high-Machs" (p. 339).

If high-Machs are exploiters, the best way to interpret their social attractiveness is as a form of impression management that allows them to bypass the defenses of cooperators. However, it is also possible that high-Machs are genuinely attractive as social partners and that the game-theoretic interpretation is on the wrong track. A more subtle prediction is that high-Machs might be desirable social partners *despite* the fact that they are exploitative. For example, it might be advantageous to be in the same group as a high-Mach who is using his or her talents to exploit another group. We might therefore expect high-Machs to be attractive social partners in some contexts but not others.

Near et al. (ms.) attempted to test some of these predictions with a projective test that bypasses impression management skills. A variety of studies have shown that story writing engages a more intimate level of personality than face-to-face interactions. We therefore asked subjects who took the Mach test to write a story in which the main character (referred to as "I") is washed up on a desert island with two other individuals of the same sex. Stories by high- and low-Mach authors were then read by another set of subjects, who completed the Mach test as they thought the main character of each story would fill it out. The readers also evaluated the main character's personality and attractiveness as a social partner in a variety of relationships.

The stories revealed aspects of Machiavellianism that are not apparent in face-to-face interactions. A typical quote from a low-Mach male author was "We are all together in this plight. . . . We realize that we must all cooperate, and John, Peter and I decide to equally distribute the limited supplies." Similarly, a low-Mach female author wrote "Mary, Jane and I seem to be getting along pretty well. . . . It's funny how we immediately began to trust each other." In contrast, a high-mach male author wrote "I didn't particularly care for John and Peter, and I suspected that there were going to be problems real soon. . . . They are two and I am one. . . . I hope that I can get rid of the human threat soon." A female high-Mach author wrote "Mary and Jane are cold bitches who constantly complain . . . when I got really hungry I wondered how I could cook them with the limited cooking equipment we had." This is the range of phenotypic variation (at the fantasy level) that exists in an average class of American undergraduate students!

The Mach score of the main characters, as perceived by the readers, correlated with the actual Mach score of the authors. Thus, at least some personality characteristics that are measured by the Mach test are faithfully represented in the stories. Although high-Machs are socially attractive in short-term face-to-face interactions, the main characters of their stories were rated as more selfish, uncaring, judgmental, overbearing, untrustworthy, aggressive, undependable, and suspicious than the main characters of low-Mach authors. The main characters of high-Mach authors were rejected as social partners for relationships that were vulnerable to exploitation (e.g., sharing an apartment) but were accepted for relationships that involved working as a group to manipulate others (members of a debating team). In short, the projective test suggests that high-Machs are employing an exploitative strategy of social conduct that they attempt to conceal in face-to-face interactions. When their impression management skills are bypassed, high-Machs can appear attractive or unattractive, depending on the social context.

These examples of empirical studies in humans that were motivated by evolutionary game theory only scratch the surface of a very large subject. Many other predictions emerge from a view of exploitation and cooperation as a community of social strategies that play off against each other in a heterogeneous environment (reviewed by Mealey 1995; Wilson et al. 1996). These predictions may or may not be confirmed, but the fact that the multistrategy view *generates* so many testable hypotheses is impressive by itself. The multistrategy view *could* have emerged from traditional game theory or other branches of the human social sciences, but it *didn't*. As a result, the entire subject has become moribund, at least within the branches of the human social sciences that I have explored. Evolutionary game theory can revitalize the subject. However, the novelty of evolutionary game theory must be appreciated not only at the level of technical details but also at the level of bedrock assumptions that have divided the study of humans and nonhuman species for centuries.

My own excursions into other subjects reveal a similar state of affairs (e.g., Wilson et al. 1994 for shyness and boldness, Wilson 1997 for human decision making). In fact, I will venture the following prediction: Take *any* subject that is relevant to human behavior, and study it in the way that a behavioral ecologist or an evolutionary game theorist would study the subject in nonhuman species, and that approach will be largely new from the standpoint of the human social sciences.

12.3 Social Norms, Nonadaptive Behavioral Diversity, and Ultrasociality

For the rest of this chapter I will speculate on future developments in evolutionary game theory, based largely on the work of Boyd and Richerson (1985, 1990, 1992). Consider the following broad topics:

1. Evolutionary game theory, as currently understood.

2. Social norms, or the use of rewards and punishments to promote certain behaviors. It is obvious that social norms have a potent influence on human behavior (e.g., Alexander 1987, Trivers 1971), but they do not yet play a large role in evolutionary game theory (but see Axelrod 1986, Hirshleifer & Rasmusen 1989).

3. Nonadaptive behavioral diversity. Human behavior is highly variable in ways that often seem to defy functional explanation. Cultural anthropologists such as Geertz (1983) and others who are wary of adaptationism often say that biology sets broad limits on how people behave, but cannot explain the bulk of behavioral diversity that exists within those limits.

4. Ultrasociality. In some respects, human groups seem to rival social insect colonies and clonal organisms in their functional organization, yet the population structure of human groups does not seem conducive to this kind of ultrasociality. Most evolutionary game theorists think that cooperation should be restricted to genetic relatives and small numbers of reciprocating partners. Alexander (1987) has attempted to develop a concept of "indirect reciprocity" that accounts for larger scale cooperation, but initial efforts to model indirect reciprocity have encountered difficulties (e.g., Boyd & Richerson 1988, 1989). Thus, evolutionary game theory cannot yet explain human ultrasociality.

No one doubts the importance of social norms and it should be relatively easy to incorporate them into evolutionary game theory. By contrast, critics and advocates of evolution alike often regard nonadaptive behavioral diversity and ultrasociality as outside the orbit of evolutionary explanation. The point I want to make is that, when powerful social norms are incorporated into evolutionary game theory, nonadaptive behavioral diversity and ultrasociality emerge as a natural consequence.

The following account is based on the group selection approach to evolutionary game theory (Sober & Wilson 1997, Wilson & Sober 1994). Consider a behavior that, by itself, would be defined as strongly altruistic. This means that individuals who express the behavior increase the fitness of their group but nevertheless decline in frequency within their group. Even though the behavior is disfavored within groups, it can still evolve if there is a population of groups that vary in the frequency of altruistic behaviors. In this case, the frequency of the behavior in the global population is influenced by the differential contribution of groups, in addition to the differential contribution of individuals within groups. For the extreme case of groups that consist entirely of altruists or nonaltruists, it is obvious that the altruistic behavior will evolve. For less extreme variation, the outcome will depend on the relative intensity of selection within and among groups.

When groups are formed by asexual reproduction of a single individual, genetic variation within groups is eliminated (except by mutation) and variation between groups is maximized. It is therefore not surprising that coral colonies and other clonal organisms act like "superorganisms." In some species of social insects, groups are founded by a single diploid female carrying the sperm of a single haploid male. This population structure creates a large amount of variation among groups, although it does not eliminate variation within groups. Members of social insects colonies are therefore expected to be largely, but not entirely, altruistic. More recently, it has been discovered that some social insect colonies are founded by multiple queens or queens who have mated with multiple males. We might expect altruism and group-level functional organization to be less common in these species, a point that I will return to below.

The population structure of human groups is very different than clonal organisms and social insect colonies. If modern hunter–gatherer societies can be used as a model of human social evolution, most groups consist of a mix of genetic relatives and nonrelatives. This means that genetic variation among groups will be above random, but not nearly as extreme as for social insects and clonal organisms. Therefore, we should not expect highly altruistic behaviors that extend to all members of such groups to automatically evolve, as they do for clonal organisms and social insect colonies.

Against this background, we can now consider the evolution of social norms. Let x be the original behavior that would be highly altruistic if performed voluntarily. Let y be a reward or a punishment that causes another individual to perform x. The evolution of y can be studied in exactly the same way as the evolution of x. By causing another individual to perform x, the individual who performs y indirectly increases the fitness of the entire group. At the same time, y is likely to require at least some time, energy, or risk for the individual who performs it. Behavior y is therefore disfavored within groups and requires a population structure to evolve, just like behavior x. Economists call this a second-order public goods problem; any behavior that promotes a public good is itself a public good (Heckathorn 1990, 1993).

Although behaviors x and y are both disfavored within groups and require group selection to evolve, there is an important difference between them. The activities that are required to transform a social group into a functional unit often involve a substantial cost for the individuals who perform them. The costly nature of these activities is imposed by the external environment. It is just a fact of life that resource acquisition, defense, aggression, and so on, on behalf of the group requires time, energy, and risk on the part of individuals. That is why extreme variation among groups is required for such behaviors to evolve by themselves. Causing others to perform these behaviors also requires time, energy, and risk, but these costs are not necessarily large. In fact, it is often possible for individuals to greatly increase (reward) or decrease (punish) the fitness of other individuals in their group at trivial cost to themselves. If y is only slightly deleterious or even neutral within groups, then minor (even random) variation among groups is sufficient for them to evolve by group selection. In short, the x,y combination can evolve in population structures that would not be sufficient for x to evolve by itself. Sober and Wilson (1997) call this *the amplification of altruism*.

Before applying these ideas to human behavior, it is interesting to revisit the social insects. As mentioned above, genetic variation among social insect colonies is sometimes not as extreme as originally thought because the colonies are founded by more than one female and/or females mate with more than one male. If altruism and group-level functional organization were based entirely on how genetic variation is partitioned within and among groups, we might expect these colonies to be less functionally integrated than species in which colonies are founded by a single female mated by a single male. In general, this prediction has *not* been confirmed. Honeybee queens usually mate with many males, yet the functional organization of bee hives remains truly superorganismic (Seeley 1995), in part because of social norms that alter the costs and benefits of other behaviors. For example, a gene that causes honeybee workers to lay unfertilized eggs (that develop into males) would be favored by within-hive selection, even if it disrupted the functional organization of the hive. A gene that causes workers to refrain from laying eggs therefore counts as altruistic and requires substantial variation among groups to evolve. Despite an extensive search, egg laying in honeybee workers has been observed only rarely, in part because the egg layers are immediately attacked by other workers. In addition to "lay eggs" versus "refrain from laying eggs," we therefore have another set of behaviors to consider: "attack workers who lay eggs" versus "don't attack workers who lay eggs." The population structure of honeybee colonies is sufficient for "attack/refrain" to evolve as a package, even though it is not sufficient for "refrain" to evolve by itself.

More generally, extreme genetic variation among groups is not sufficient to explain ultrasociality in honeybees and other social insects. The amplification of altruism by rewards and punishments is also required (Ratnieks 1988, Ratnieks & Visscher 1989).

So far, I have suggested that social norms can promote the evolution of behaviors that benefit whole groups and would be considered highly altruistic if they were performed voluntarily. It is also likely that social norms promote behavioral diversity per se. Game theory models have already shown that social interactions can result in multiple stable equilibria. Because the fitness of each strategy depends on the other strategies that it interacts with, there are often majority effects in which a strategy can persist when it interacts with its own type but cannot invade a population consisting of other types. Powerful social norms vastly increase the potential for multiple stable equilibria. In fact, Boyd and Richerson (1992) have shown that *any* behavior can become an "evolutionarily stable strategy" if the following conditions are met: (1) The norms that reinforce the behavior are sufficiently common, (2) the rewards and punishments are sufficiently strong compared to the costs and benefits that are naturally associated with the behavior, (3) the costs of imposing the social norms are sufficiently small, and (4) individuals are punished for failing to enforce the norms, in addition to failing to abide by the norms. The behavior that is promoted could be altruistic, but it could also be selfish or just plain stupid. The details of the behaviors that are promoted simply become irrelevant if they are overwhelmed by the rewards and punishments imposed by the social norms. As the title of Boyd and Richerson's article puts it, "Punishment allows the evolution of cooperation (or anything else) in sizable groups."

The idea that rewards and punishments can make anything advantageous is deeply familiar, but it creates a crisis when it is formally incorporated into evolutionary game theory. If *any* behavior can become an evolutionarily stable strategy, how can we possibly predict how animals behave? It is humbling to contemplate that this crisis might be fully warranted and might not have a solution. Critics of adaptationism have long emphasized the unpredictable nature of evolution and the diversity of behavior that defies simple functional explanations. Perhaps they are right and the reason that human behavior is so exceptionally diverse is because powerful rewards and punishments have opened a Pandora's box in which anything can prevail when sanctified as a social convention. If so, then the seemingly opposing camps of evolutionary game theory and anti-adaptationism suddenly become joined.

Although powerful social norms can turn any behavior into an evolutionarily stable strategy within groups, the group-level consequences can still be subject to natural selection. Consider a large number of social groups that vary in the behaviors that are promoted by social norms. By definition, each set of social conventions is internally stable and will resist change. However, some social conventions may be more functional than others at the group level, persisting longer and contributing differentially to the formation of new groups. The end result could be a subset of social norms that is favored by *both* within- and between-group selection. This scenario of "group selection among alternative ESS's" (Boyd & Richerson 1990) may be far more important than the evolution of strong altruism, which is evolutionarily unstable within groups and requires a constant process of strong group selection for its maintenance.

12.4 A Survey of Social Norms and Their Consequences Across World Cultures

I have attempted to paint a picture in which groups of unrelated individuals function as adaptive units and many specific behaviors make no adaptive sense apart from the social norms that promote them. This picture is usually associated with critics of adaptationism, yet it emerges from evolutionary game theory—a major tool in the adaptationist's toolkit—when powerful rewards and punishments that can be imposed at low cost are considered.

This leaves us with a set of empirical questions. How important are social norms in humans and other species? How is it possible for individuals to greatly increase (reward) or decrease (punish) the fitness of others in their social group at trivial cost to themselves? What is the process by which the costs and benefits of a behavior are modified by rewards and punishments? Can powerful social norms replace extreme genetic variation among groups as a mechanism for the evolution of ultrasociality? Are humans different from other species in their ability to apply and enforce social norms? What is the evidence that human social groups function as adaptive units? Is human ultrasociality a recent cultural invention or did it originate sufficiently early to influence genetic evolution?

As a first step toward answering these questions, Elliott Sober and I have conducted a survey of social norms in 25 cultures that were selected randomly from the hundreds of cultures included in the Human Relations Area Files (HRAF; Sober and Wilson 1997). The HRAF is an anthropological data base that is designed to facilitate cross-cultural studies. The information for each culture consists of ethnographies that have been read, coded, and indexed according to a large number of categories, one of which is "norms" (code #183). By looking up code #183 for a given culture, one can quickly obtain a sample of what has been written about social norms, which can range from brief anecdotes to extended discussions. It is important to stress that the HRAF is by no means an exhaustive data base and has all of the biases of the original accounts.

Statements about human nature are often supported with anecdotes from one or a few cultures, which can be highly biased. The way to avoid this problem is to select a random sample of world cultures, as we have done in our survey. The next task is to convert the verbal accounts of behavior into a quantitative form amenable to statistical analysis. A number of methods exist in the human social sciences for doing this (e.g., Tetlock et al. 1992), which ultimately will allow us to frame and test specific hypotheses. However, the purpose of this chapter is merely to provide an intuitive picture of social norms and their consequences in cultures around the world. As we shall see, this picture stands in stark contrast to the current game-theoretic image of individuals as free agents who can choose among many alternative strategies to maximize their individual fitness.

12.4.1 The Influence of Social Norms on Human Behavior

The degree of social control that takes place in most traditional societies, including hunter–gatherer societies that serve as a model for human evolution, is difficult for many of us to imagine. Among the Bhil (Asia), "Any infringement of the socially accepted way or value of life may be a crime . . . , however small it may be. . . . They have a large body of civil laws, a system of rights and obligations in all spheres of life, traditional, social and religious, which are fulfilled very scrupulously" (Naik 1956, p 223). For the Gilyak (Russia), "All more or less important acts of social life, even including sacrificing one's life in a battle of vengeance for one's clansman, are categorical imperatives of a religious world-outlook which neither allow hesitation or require compulsion" (Shternberg 1933, p166). For the Apaches (North America), "In a culture where practically all the customs, even those concerned with the daily round of life, are validated by the blessing and approval of some supernatural, any deviation from, freedom with, or levity regarding the mores smacks of profanity" (Hoijer & Opler, 1938, pp. 215–216). For the Lesu (Oceania), "To be gossiped about in a derogatory manner, to have it said . . . that one has infringed even a minor aspect of the social code, is to bring disgrace" (Powdermaker 1933, p.323). For the Mbuti (Africa), " . . . even the most insignificant and routine action in the daily life of the family is potentially of major concern to the band as a whole. . . . It is important that there should be a pattern of behavior that is generally accepted, and which covers every conceivable activity" (Turnbull 1965, p118). An ethnographer of the Papago indians (North America) summed up the general dynamic of social control in small tribal societies: "Public opinion censures those who deviate from accepted standards of conduct. In any community so small that all the members and their affairs are known to one another, this is a powerful force. Among the Papago there are almost no conventionalized variations from the normal behavior pattern; the guiding principles apply to everyone. No man can ignore them because of his wealth, position as village leader, or special skill. . . . The facts that failure to perform in a socially approved manner will inevitably become common knowledge and that general censure is sure to follow constitute a powerful deterrent to breaking the mores" (Joseph et al. 1949, p 166).

12.4.2 Social Norms Can Be Imposed at Low Cost to the Enforcers

The following examples illustrate how low-cost social norms can override even the strongest biological urges (Shternberg 1933, p. 184):

> During my residence of many years among the Gilyak, despite careful questioning, I heard of only two or three instances of clear violation of the prohibitive norms. The most outstanding of these instances took place in the settlement of Tamlevo, where a young Gilyak, after the death of his father, lived for some time with his young stepmother, purchased by his father shortly before his death. This incident shocked all Sakhalin, and he was spoken of as some kind of monster. Another commonly known incident involved the young Gilyak, Pavlinka, who married a woman from the clan of his ymg:i, i.e., from the clan that took its wives from Pavlinka's clan. But Pavlinka was a considerably Russified Gilyak, who had served in the police service and regarded the customs of his people superciliously. Another Russified Gilyak, Allykh, from the settlement of Tamlevo, after the death of one of his younger tuvn, compelled the gathering of clansmen which was deciding, as was customary,

to whom the widow of the deceased should pass, to award her to him, although, as an aki (elder brother), had no rights whatever to this. But these cases are the exception and evoked an energetic reaction from the community.

In the first two cases the violators had to go into voluntary exile, i.e. settle outside the settlement and lead a lonely existence, with all the deprivations of clan blessings associated with ostracism. But, we repeat, these were quite exceptional cases bound up with psyches changed under the influence of an alien culture.

In all three of these cases, the social norms appear designed to control reproduction within the group. From the evolutionary perspective, it is perfectly reasonable for a man to want to mate with a young woman close to his own age, purchased by his father shortly before his death, or a woman who happens to belong to the wrong clan, or a woman who was formerly married to his younger brother. Yet the benefits associated with these behaviors are overwhelmed by costs imposed by the group. The marvelous phrase "had to go into voluntary exile" illustrates the low cost of the norms for those who impose them. Enforcers of the social norm do not have to fight the deviant or otherwise spend much time, energy or risk. They merely have to decide that the deviant must go into exile and the deed is done. The balance of power so obviously favors the group over any particular individual that an actual contest does not take place.

It is notable that two of the three cases involved individuals who became deviant because of contact with another culture with different social norms. Evidently, the perfectly reasonable impulses expressed by the deviants are usually so thoroughly suppressed within the culture that they don't even surface as behaviors. According to the same ethnographer (Shternberg 1933, p. 184):

> Ordinarily the very idea of sexual connection with persons of the forbidden categories evokes an instinctive disgust. In the rare instances where feelings of love arise between such persons, the Gilyak regard it as the inspiration of an evil spirit, as a phenomenon unnatural not only in men, but in beasts. We have seen that in such instances they even slay a fornicating dog. The attitude toward people is entirely the same. Ordinarily lovers in the forbidden categories slay themselves by mutual agreement or under the direct urging of their relatives. In one last song of such an unhappy pair, the woman sings of how her elder sister called her a "bitch" for her love for her uncle, and called the latter a "devil," and how all—her mother, father, and sisters—urged upon her: "slay thyself, slay!" Incidentally, the object of her criminal passion, her uncle, could be of her age, could grow up far apart from her, and the love between the criminal pair might seem perfectly natural in our eyes.

Notice that the social norms have overridden not only the strongest sexual instincts, but also the strongest nepotistic instincts, causing parents and siblings to urge the death of a close genetic relative. Perhaps they are maximizing their inclusive fitness by salvaging the reputation of their family, but this only illustrates how completely inclusive fitness can be controlled by the group.

Another, less extreme example of low-cost social norms comes from the Lesu (Powdermaker 1933, p. 323):

> There is much talk in the village because Tsengali's pig has broken into Murri's garden and eaten much taro. Murri displays no particular anger, and appears undisturbed, but Tsengali is very much annoyed because of all the talk that the incident has occasioned. So he announces that he is going to Kabil, where his brother lives, to get a pig and give it to Murri to stop the talk. But Murri tells him that this would be foolish, "to eat a pig for nothing," and that Tsengali should not give him the pig. Instead, Murri declares that the incident is ended, and that there should be no more talk. The affair is ended. It is interesting to note that in this incident it was the transgressor who was annoyed because of the blow to his prestige and not the offended man who has suffered the loss of taro.

What is the cost of this kind of social control, that exerts such a powerful effect on members of small face-to-face groups? The person who was wronged did nothing except to forgive the transgressor and refuse payment. The people who talked would have talked about something else. The prestige that the transgressor was so anxious to recover is like a magical substance that can be given and taken away at will. It is possible that humans exceed most other species in the ability of groups to impose strong social norms on their members at minimal cost to the enforcers.

12.4.3 Social Norms Are Not All-Powerful

Despite the influence of social norms, many of the ethnographers in our survey also appreciate the potential for behaviors that deviate from the norms and often benefit individuals at the expense of others within their social group. For the Apaches, "despite the kindly interest of the supernaturals, the beneficial influence of ceremony and tradition, and the virtuous professions of most individuals, the Apache is faced with a world in which sorcery, deceit, ingratitude, and misconduct are not uncommon occurrences" (Hoijer & Opler 1938, p. 215). Among the Mbuti, "When the hunt returns to camp there is immediate excitement as those who stayed behind crowd around for tales of all that happened and maybe for a few tidbits of raw meat. In the confusion, men and women alike, but particularly women, may be seen furtively concealing some of their spoils under the leaves of their roofs, or in empty pots nearby. For although there will have been some sharing on the scene, there is always more back in the camp, and family loyalty is not that subject to band loyalty that there is no cheating" (Turnbull 1965, p 120). In Somoa (Oceania), "the talking chiefs whose duty it is to act as custodians of the political arrangements, are open to bribery and manipulation. The holders of smaller titles who wish to advance their position are ready and willing to bribe" (Mead 1930, p 21). Among the Tallensi (Africa), "the natives' keen sense of the importance of social obligations hides a tendency to aggressive self-assertion. . . . Firstly, they say, unscrupulous people never hesitate to break a customary rule if it suits their purpose" (Fortes 1945, p 9). Among the Toba (South America), one individual's "superior access to food arises through rupturing the norms of the system, through uninhibited demands and through the exercise of emotional coercion, by screaming" (Henry 1951, p 218). Thus, social norms are partially but not completely, successful at imposing a sanctioned set of behaviors on the group. The conflict between sanctioned and unsanctioned behavior is well described by an observer of the Kpelle (Africa): "There are two broad avenues to these goals, hard work and efficient management of one's resources and a reputation for fairness in dealing with others, or one can use sorcery, witchcraft, thievery and exploit one's advantages over others. The latter course is expedient and dangerous, but most ambitious individuals use a combination of sanctioned and unsanctioned means to achieve power. Finally, overambition is checked through various forces of retribution. There are the moot and town-chief's courts which penalize the overly-ambitious through fines and public ridicule. There is the power of the secret societies and Zos (medicine-men) to exact swift and often deadly punishment. Lastly, there is the force of public opinion vented through gossip and other forms of harassment to keep an individual in check" (Lancy 1975, p 29).

12.4.4 Social Norms and Cultural Diversity

What are the actual behaviors that are promoted by social norms? To a great extent, the answer to this question depends on the culture that is being examined. Among the Fellahin (Middle East), "Members of each sex dress more or less alike, and the observing of this convention is a very important factor in social equality. Their maxim in this connection is 'Eat what you yourself like, but dress according to what others like' " (Ammar 1954, p. 40). Yet in Somoa, "The dresses and adornments assumed for dancing or similar entertainments have little ceremonial or traditional significance; they are for decorative purposes only and to lend an air of festivity to the proceedings (Grattan 1948, p. 117). There is therefore no restriction on new ideas, and anything fresh that is likely to look well is eagerly adopted and often makes its way to adjoining villages and districts." For the Amish (North America), "the marriage norm is not love, but respect" (Hostetler 1980, p. 156). Yet among the Paez (South America), a wife "will laboriously make the multicolored keutand yahas which she will give as tokens of love to her husband" (Bernal-Villa 1953, p. 188). The Nootkan (North America) personality is described as "nonaggressive, rather amiable, disliking and disapproving violence in conflict situations, with a deep interest in that type of ceremony that was essentially a theatrical performance, and a keen and lively sense of humor" (Drucker 1951, p. 456). In contrast, the Amhara (Middle East) "considers a pitiless regime of fasting to be the only way he can keep his hostile impulses subdued, and believes that children must not be spared the rod lest they be rude and aggressive" (Levine 1965, p. 85). Social norms sometimes appear to prohibit behaviors that appear manifestly useful. For example, "A number of other, more specific, norms have had the effect of discouraging inventiveness among the Amhara. Experimentation with matter was inhibited by the disdain for puttering about with one's hands—doing anything, that is, similar to the activities of the socially dejected artisans and slaves. Hence the peasant retains the same rudimentary tools for wresting a subsistence from nature that he has used for millennia, and searches about the woods for a properly shaped piece of wood rather than improve his art of carpentry" (Levine 1965, p. 87). This contrasts with many other cultures in our sample, in which crafts are highly developed and innovation is encouraged within bounds.

Behavioral diversity is the hallmark of our species and is amply represented in our random sample of 25 cultures from around the world. The fact of diversity is obvious but the causes of diversity are not. Some of it can probably be explained in narrowly functional terms, but functionalism seems inadequate to explain all of it. Assuming that these descriptions are accurate, is it really functional for the Nootkans but not the Amhara to have a sense of humor, for the Paez but not the Amish to express affection in marriage, for the Samoans but not the Fellahin to have a sense of fashion? The seemingly nonfunctional nature of human behavioral diversity is one of the main reasons that many people remain skeptical about evolutionary approaches to human behavior. Unfortunately, the critics cannot explain the behavioral diversity themselves, beyond vague appeals to "culture." When strong rewards and punishments that can be imposed at low cost are incorporated into evolutionary game theory, the concept of behaviors that are nonfunctional and even dysfunctional outside of the context of the social norms becomes quite reasonable. The effect of social norms on the evolution of arbitrary behaviors is much like the effect of female preference on the evolution of arbitrary ornaments in males, such as the peacock's tail. Not only does this unite the seemingly opposed adaptationist and nonadaptationist camps, but it provides an explanation of behavioral diversity that is more specific than vague appeals to culture. If we could eliminate the ability to impose powerful social norms at low cost, but retain all other aspects of human cultural processes, we might witness a dramatic collapse of behavioral diversity.

12.4.5 Social Norms and Ultrasociality

Despite the variation among cultures that I have emphasized above, which does not necessarily require functional explanation, there is one sense in which the 25 cultures in the survey are not highly variable. Many social norms in most cultures appear designed to forge groups of individuals into functionally organized units. This conclusion emerges so strongly from the ethnographies and seems so embedded in the minds of the people themselves that I feel confident that it reflects the true nature of the societies and not a massive bias on the part of the ethnographers. In culture after culture, individuals are expected to avoid conflict and practice benevolence and generosity toward all members of a socially defined group, which usually includes individuals who are genealogically unrelated or only weakly related to each other. For the Gilyak (Shternberg 1933, p. 115–116):

> The basic axiom of everyone is that all his existence and welfare are completely in the hands of the gods, in particular the clan gods, who shower their beneficence not on one but on all. Any attempt to monopolize the gifts of the gods must inevitably incur just punishment by the common benefactors of the clan.

For the Amhara (Levine 1965, p. 83):

> Loyalty is proclaimed all around. Conviviality is the norm among peers, though the authoritarian character of the Amhara family inhibits camaraderie between those of greatly differing ages. Unlimited succor in time of sickness and death and profuse commensality in happier hours are important values to the Amhara peasant and ones about which he is self-conscious and articulate.

For the Apache (Basehart 1974, p. 139):

> . . . the extended family was not a self-sufficient traditional unit, even though this was possible in theory. The family group ordinarily formed part of a larger encampment, the members of which linked together by ties of kinship, friendship, and propinquity. Within the camp, the norms requiring the sharing of food were so pronounced that the entire community could be considered a single production–distribution–consumption unit.

For the Navaho (North America) (Shepardson 1963, p. 48):

> . . . the validation of 'imperative coordination' . . . lay in the fact that the actions of the members of the society were oriented to a normative order, to accepted values and beliefs, and to the correctness of certain sanctions for inducing conformity. . . . There was agreement on certain patterns of cooperation within groups, structured with great flexibility around kinship and affinal ties, for traditional subsistence, co-residence, sexual satisfaction . . . of hard work, of reciprocity, of generosity. Disputes should be settled through compromise and arbitration. Force should be used only against witches and aliens. Conformity should be secured through respect, praise, cooperation. Deviance should be punished through disrespect, ridicule and withdrawal of cooperation.

For the Toba (= Pilaga) (Henry 1951, p. 218):

> A primary function of a traditional system like that of the Pilaga is to convert the product of the individual into a social form. The individual's catch of fish or load of forest fruit must be given a social meaning, and must be transmuted from private into public property.

For the Yap (Oceania) (Schneider 1957, p. 798):

> This image of the relationship between moral norms and the acts of the living is congruent with the organization of the lineage. It is, after all, the fundamental social unit in which solidarity and unity are the cardinal conditions for its maintenance in that form. That it ought never to be rent by conflict must be balanced against the human beings of which it is composed. Yaps recognize the gap between what people ought to do and the persistent tendency to do wrong. Where unity and solidarity are the cardinal conditions of existence, as well as clearly expressed values, the problem is to limit wrongs to a minimum, not to compound them.

These passages suggest that human ultrasociality is not a recent invention of modern societies. Most small face-to-face groups in tribal societies function as highly integrated units, even when their members are not genealogically closely related. If anything, traditional societies may be better organized at the group level than modern societies, in which individual mobility makes the monitoring of behavior and imposition of social norms difficult. Boehm (1993, 1996, 1997) and Knauft (1991) have reached similar conclusions for hunter–gatherer societies, which are almost invariably highly egalitarian. This image of human society is very different than the image that emerges from current evolutionary game theory, in which individuals are regarded as free to behave in any way that maximizes their inclusive fitness and group-level functional organization plays almost no role at all.

12.5 Summary

In the first part of this chapter, I attempted to show that current evolutionary game theory has important implications for the study of human behavior. These implications are due less to technical differences between evolutionary and traditional game theory than to foundational differences between evolutionary biology and the human sciences, which are reflected in the use of game theory as a formal theoretical tool. There is a great need to import evolutionary thinking into the human social sciences. The many subdisciplines of economics, psychology, anthropology, and sociology simply do not approach the subject of human behavior in the same way that a behavioral ecologist routinely approaches the study of behavior in nonhuman species. This does not mean that the human sciences are worthless. Indeed, I have reviewed the literature sufficiently for three separate subjects (Machiavellianism, shyness/boldness, and decision making; see above-cited references) to know that the human social sciences are a gold mine of empirical information and methodology. What is lacking is a general conceptual framework for thinking about all aspects of human behavior. In the absence of such a framework, the study of human behavior is like a random walk through a very large parameter space; some interesting regions of the space are discovered, but it would be far better to have a map that tells us where to look. With the map, we can find regions of the parameter space that have received insufficient attention and in some cases are virtually unexplored. We also discover connections among regions of the parameter space that previously were studied in isolation. Evolutionary approaches to human behavior provoked hostility and resistance during the 1970s, but the intellectual climate has changed dramatically since then. It is safe to say that the integration of evolutionary biology and the human sciences has begun, with new insights emerging almost daily.

In the second part of this chapter, I suggested that future developments in evolutionary game theory may explain aspects of human behavior that critics and advocates alike regard as outside the orbit of evolutionary explanation. My suggestion is based not on vague optimism, but on a specific analysis of rewards and punishments, which almost everyone would agree are important determinants of behavior in humans and many nonhuman species. Therefore, in addition to importing current evolutionary thinking into the human sciences, there is a great need for current evolutionary thinking to expand its own horizons. Group-level functional organization and nonfunctional behavioral diversity are not heretical concepts, but predictions that emerge from evolutionary game theory under certain conditions that are plausible for humans and many other species. Furthermore, our survey of social norms and other surveys of hunter–gatherer societies provide empirical support for the concept of human social groups as adaptive units, even when their members are genealogically unrelated. It would be hard to imagine more exciting prospects for the future study of evolutionary game theory and human behavior.

ACKNOWLEDGMENTS   I thank C. Boehm, R. Boyd, A. B. Clark, L. A. Dugatkin, J. Hirshleifer, B. Knauft, R. R. Miller, D. Near, H. K. Reeve, P. J. Richerson, B. Smuts, E. Sober, Binghamton's Ecology, Evolution and Behavior Group, and many other colleagues for stimulating discussions.

References

Alexander, R. D. 1987. *The Biology of Moral Systems.* New York: Aldine de Gruyter.

Ammar, H. 1954. *Growing Up in an Egyptian Village: Silaw, Province of Aswan.* London: Routledge and Kegan Paul.

Axelrod, R. 1986. The evolution of norms. *Am. Polit. Sci. Rev.,* 80, 1095–1111.

Axlerod, R. & Hamilton, W. D. 1981. The evolution of cooperation. *Science,* 211, 1390–1396.

Barber, N. 1994. Selfishness and altruism: Effect of relatedness of target person on Machiavellian and helping attitudes. *Psychol. Rep.,* 75, 403–422.

Barber, N. & Raffield, in press. The battle of the sexes and the evolution of social manipulativeness.

Barkow, J. H., Cosmides, L. & Tooby, J. 1992. *The Adapted Mind: Evolutionary Psychology and the Generation of Culture.* Oxford: Oxford University Press

Basehart, H. W. 1974. *Mescalero Apache Subsistence Patterns and Socio-political Organization. Apache Indians.* New York: Garland Publishing.

Bernal-Villa, S. 1953. Aspects of Paez culture. The fiesta of San Juan in Calderas, Tierradentro. *Rev. Colomb. Antropol.,* 1, 177–221.

Betzig, L., Borgerhoff Mulder, M. & Turke, P., eds. 1988. *Human Reproductive Behavior: A Darwinian Perspective.* New York: Cambridge University Press,

Block, J. 1978. The Q-sort method. . Palo Alto, CA: Consulting psychologists press.

Bochner, A. P., di Salvo, V. & Jonas, T. 1975. A computer-assisted analysis of small group process: An investigation of two Machiavellian groups. *Small Group Behav.,* 6, 187–203.

Boehm, C. 1993. Egalitarian behavior and reverse dominance hierarchy. *Curr. Anthropol.,* 34, 227–254.

Boehm, C. 1996. Emergency decisions, cultural selection mechanics, and group selection. *Curr. Anthropol.,* 37, 763–793.

Boehm, C. 1997. Egalitarian behavior and the evolution of political intelligence. In R. W. Byrne & A. Whiten, eds., *Machiavellian Intelligence, II,* in press. Cambridge: Cambridge University.

Boyd, R. & Lorberbaum, J. 1987. No pure strategy is evolutionarily stable in the repeated Prisoner's Dilemma game. *Nature,* 327, 58–59.

Boyd, R. & Richerson, P. J. 1985. Culture and the Evolutionary Process. Chicago: University of Chicago Press.

Boyd, R. & Richerson, P. J. 1988. The evolution of reciprocity in sizable groups. *J. Theor. Biol.,* 132, 337–356.

Boyd, R. & Richerson, P. J. 1989. The evolution of indirect reciprocity. *Soc. Networks,* 11, 213–236.

Boyd, R. & Richerson, P. 1990. Group selection among alternative evolutionarily stable strategies. *J. Theor. Biol.,* 145, 331–342.

Boyd, R. & Richerson, P. J. 1992. Punishment allows the evolution of cooperation (or anything else) in sizable groups. *Ethol. Sociobiol.,* 13, 171–195.

Byrne, R. W., & Whiten, A. 1988. Machiavellian Intelligence: The Evolution of Intellect in Monkeys Apes and Humans. Oxford: Claredon Press,

Cherulnik, P. D., Way, J. H., Ames, S. & Hutto, D. B. 1981. Impressions of high and low machiavellian men. *J. Pers.,* 49, 388–400.

Christie, R. & Geis, F. 1968. Some consequences of taking Machiavelli seriously. In E. F. Borgotta & W. W. Lambert eds., *Handbook of Personality Theory and Research*. Chicago: Rand McNally.

Christie, R. & Geis, F. 1970. *Studies in Machiavellianism*. New York: Academic Press.

Cohen, J. & Malachek, R. 1988. A general theory of expropriative crime. *Am. J. Sociol.,* 94, 465–501.

Drucker, P. 1951. *The Northern and Central Nootkan Tribes*. Washington D.C.: Government Printing Office.

Dugatkin, L. A. 1990. *N*-person games and the evolution of cooperation: A model based on predator inspection behavior in fish. *J. Theor. Biol.,* 142, 123–135.

Dugatkin, L. A. 1993. The evolution of the 'con artist'. *Ethol. Sociobiol.,* 13, 161–169.

Dugatkin, L. A. & Wilson, D. S. 1991. Rover: A strategy for exploiting cooperators in a patchy environment. *Am. Nat.,* 138, 687–701.

Farrell, J. & Ware, R. 1989. Evolutionary stability in the repeated Prisoner's Dilemma. *Theor. Popul. Biol.,* 36, 161–168.

Feldman, M. & Thomas, E. 1987. Behavior-dependent contexts for repeated plays of the Prisoner's Dilemma. *J. Theor. Biol.,* 128, 297–315.

Fortes, M. 1945. *The Dynamics of Clanship Among the Tallensi; Being the First Part of an Analysis of the Social Structure of a Trans-Volta Tribe*. London: Oxford University Press for the International African Institute.

Frank, R. H. 1988. *Passions within Reason*. New York: W. W. Norton.

Geertz, C. 1983. *Local Knowledge: Further Essays in Interpretive Anthropology*. New York: Basic Books.

Geis, F. & Levy, M. 1970. The eye of the beholder. In R. Christie & F. Geis, eds., *Studies in Machiavellianism*. New York: Academic Press.

Grattan, F. J. H. 1948. *An Introduction to Samoan Custom*. Apia, Western Samoa: Samoa Printing and Publishing Co.

Gross, M. R. 1996. Alternative reproductive strategies and tactics: diversity within sexes. *Trends Ecol. Evol.,* 11, 92–98.

Harrell, W. A. & Hartnagel, T. 1976. The impact of Machiavellianism and the trustfulness of the victim on laboratory theft. *Sociometry,* 39, 157–165.

Heckathorn, D. D. 1990. Collective sanctions and compliance norms: A formal theory of group-mediated social control. *Am. Soc. Rev.,* 55, 366–385.

Heckathorn, D. D. 1993. Collective action and group heterogeneity: Voluntary provision vs. selective incentives. *Am. Soc. Rev.,* 58, 329–350.

Henry, J. 1951. The economics of Pilaga food distribution. *Am. Anthropol.* 53, 187–219.

Hirshleifer, D. & Rasmusen, E. 1989. Cooperation in a repeated prisoner's dilemma with ostracism. *J. of Trad. Behav. Org.,* 12, 87–106.

Hirshleifer, J. 1987. On the emotions as guarantors of threats and promises. In J. Dupre, ed., *The Latest on the Best: Essays on Evolution and Optimality,* pp. 307–326. Cambridge, MA: MIT Press.

Hirshleifer, J. & Coll, J. C. M. 1988. What strategies can support the evolutionary emergence of cooperation? *J. Conflict Resolut.,* 32, 367–398.

Hoijer, H. & Opler, M. E. 1938. *Chiricahua and Mescalero Apache Texts, by Harry Hoijer with Ethnological Notes by Morris Edward Opler*. Chicago: University of Chicago Press.

Hostetler, J. A. 1980. *Amish Society,* 3rd ed. Baltimore: John Hopkins University Press.

Joseph, A., Spicer, R. B. & Chesky, J. 1949. The desert people: A Study of the Papago Indians. Chicago: Chicago University Press.

Knauft, B. M. 1991. Violence and sociality in human evolution. *Curr. Anthropol.,* 32, 391–428.

Lamphere, L. 1977. To run after them: cultural and social bases of cooperation in a Navajo community. Tucson, AZ: University of Arizona Press.

Lancy, D. F. 1975 Work, Play and Learning in a Kpelle Town. Ph.D. thesis, University of Pittsburgh.

Levine, D. N. 1965. *Wax and Gold; Tradition and Innovation in Ethiopian Culture.* Chicago: Chicago University Press.

Mead, M. 1930. *Social Organization of Manua.* Honolulu: Pernice P. Bishop Museum.

Mealey, L. 1995. The sociobiology of sociopathy. *Behav. Brain Sci.,* 18, 523–599.

Naik, T. B. 1956. *The Bhils; a Study.* Delhi: Bharatiya Adimjati Sevak Sangh.

Near, D., Wilson, D. S. & Miller, R. R. Manuscript. Exploitative and Cooperative strategies of social conduct: An approach from evolutionary game theory.

Okanes, M. M. & Stinson, J. E. 1974. Machiavellianism and emergent leadership in a management simulation. *Psychol. Rep.,* 35, 255–259.

Peck, J. R. 1990. The evolution of outsider exclusion. *J. Theor. Biol.,* 142, 565–571.

Peck, J. R. 1992. Group selection, individual selection, and the evolution of genetic drift. *J. Theor. Biol.,* 159, 163–187.

Peck, J. R. 1993. Friendship and the evolution of cooperation. *J. Theor. Biol.,* 162, 195–228.

Peck, J. & Feldman, M. 1986. The evolution of helping behavior in large, randomly mixed populations. *Am. Nat.,* 127, 209–221.

Powdermaker, H. 1933. *Life in Lesu: The Study of a Melanesian Society in New Ireland.* Foreword by Dr. Clark Wissler. New York: Norton.

Ratnieks, F. L. 1988. Reproductive harmony via mutual policing by workers in eusocial Hymenoptera. *Am. Nat.,* 132, 217–236.

Ratnieks, F. L. & Visscher, P. K. 1989. Worker policing in the honeybee. *Nature,* 342, 796–797.

Robinson, B. W. & Wilson, D. S. 1994. Character displacement and character release in fish: a neglected literature. *Am. Nat.,* 144, 596–627.

Schneider, D. M. 1957. Political organization, supernatural sanctions and the punishment for incest on Yap. *Am. Anthropol.,* 59, 791–800.

Seeley, T. 1995. *The Wisdom of the Hive.* Cambridge, MA: Harvard University Press.

Shepardson, M. T. 1963. *Navajo Ways in Government: A Study in Political Process.* Menasha, WI: American Anthropological Association.

Shepardson, M.T., & Hammond, B. 1970. The Navaho mountain community: social organization and kinship terminology. Berkeley, CA: University of California Press.

Shternberg, L. I. 1933. *The Gilyak, Orochi, Goldi, Negidal, Ainu; Articles and Materials.* Khabarovsk: Dal'giz.

Shultz, J. S. 1993. Situational and dispositional predictions of performance: A test of the hypothesized Macchiavellianism X structure interaction among sales persons. *J. Appl. Soc. Psychol.,* 23, 478–498.

Smith, A. 1776. *Wealth of Nations,* 1937 edition. New York: Random House.

Sober, E., & Wilson, D. S. 1997. *Unto Others: The Evolution of Altruism.* Cambridge, Mass: Harvard University Press.

Tetlock, P. E., Peterson, R. S., McGuire, C., Chang, S., & Feld, P. 1992. Assessing political groups dynamics: A test of the groupthink model. *J. Pers. Soc. Psychol.,* 63, 403–425.

Trivers, R. L. 1971. The evolution of reciprocal altruism. *Q. Rev. Biol.,* 46, 35–57.

Turnbull, C. M. 1965. *The Mbuti Pygmies: An Ethnographic Survey.* New York: American Museum of Natural History.

Wilson, D. S. 1994. Adaptive genetic variation and human evolutionary psychology. *Ethology and Sociobiology,* 15:219–235.

Wilson, D. S. 1997. Incorporating group selection into the adaptationist program: A case study involving human decision making. In J. Simpson & D. Kendricks, eds.), *Evolutionary social psychology.* New York: Erlbaum.

Wilson, D. S., Clark, A. B., Coleman, K. & Dearstyne, T. 1994. Shyness and boldness in humans and other animals. *Trends Ecol. Evol.,* 9, 442–446.

Wilson, D. S., Near, D. & Miller, R. R. 1996. Machiavellianism: A synthesis of the evolutionary and psychological literatures. *Psychol. Bull.,* 119, 285–299.

Wilson, D. S. & Sober, E. 1994. Re-introducing group selection to the human behavioral sciences. *Behav. Brain Sci.,* 17, 585–654.

RICHARD GOMULKIEWICZ

Game Theory, Optimization, and Quantitative Genetics

13.1 Introduction

Game theory, optimization, and quantitative genetics are among the most frequently used theoretical approaches to study evolution by natural selection. Over the last few years, the three methods have been carefully compared and contrasted (Pease & Bull 1988, Charnov 1989, Charlesworth 1990, Iwasa et al. 1991, Mangel 1992, Taper & Case 1992, Abrams et al. 1993a,b). This chapter will summarize these comparisons, describing how the approaches are used to study and predict evolutionary dynamics and equilibria for traits that evolve by natural selection. Because all three theoretical approaches consider the evolutionary roles of adaptation and constraint, a general strategy will be proposed at the end of this chapter that an empiricist might wish to follow when assessing the relative importance of adaptation and constraint in the evolution of behavioral traits in natural populations.

Another goal of this chapter is to consider how game theory, optimization, and quantitative genetic approaches apply to the evolution of complex characters such as behavior. To this end, it will be helpful to introduce some terminology and notation that will be used throughout. A complex character can often be thought of as a collection of component traits or a set of measurements. For example, an individual's foraging behavior might consist of a number of basic elements (such as searching, handling, consuming, and resting). Measurements of foraging behavior might then consist of a set of durations of each element. Mating calls are another example of a complex behavioral character for which the component traits of interest might include a call's duration, energy, frequency, and so on. In this chapter, a column vector $z = (z_1, z_2, \ldots, z_k)^{\mathrm{T}}$ will be used to denote a set of k measurements that together describe a complex character with k components. (The superscript "T" means vector transpose.) For instance, if z is a mating call, the vector components $z_1, z_2, z_3, \ldots$ might be, respectively, measures of call duration, energy, frequency, and so on. The discussion below can be extended to characters with an infinite number of component traits (such as the set of potential sprint speeds that a lizard has over a range of thermal environments), but this will not be done here [see Kirkpatrick & Heckman (1989) and Kirkpatrick et al. (1990) for background].

The central aim of this chapter is to clarify when optimization, game theory, and quantitative-genetics approaches will lead to similar or different conclusions about adaptation given the same basic information on fitness and constraints. Comparisons will therefore be limited to conditions under which the approaches are equally applicable and might be expected to give comparable results. To begin, the next section will discuss how these methods are used to study the evolutionary dynamics of behavioral characters subject to natural selection.

13.2 Evolutionary Dynamics

Optimization methods were designed expressly to analyze evolutionary equilibria and thus cannot be used to study the dynamics of adaptation. Game theory and quantitative genetics approaches, however, can be applied for just such a purpose. This section will compare the assumptions and methods of game theory and quantitative genetics that are used in the study of evolutionary dynamics of a character's mean. To clarify the comparison, only continuous characters or strategies will be considered in this chapter.

Consider a continuous character (or strategy) z that evolves by natural selection. Assume that generations are discrete and nonoverlapping and that before selection the phenotypic distribution of z is described by the probability density function $f(z)$. Let $w(z)$ be the fitness of phenotype z, which may depend on the distribution of z in the population. After selection but before reproduction, the distribution of phenotypes is

$$f^*(z) = \frac{w(z)f(z)}{\bar{w}} \tag{1}$$

where $\bar{w}$ is the population's mean fitness:

$$\bar{w} = \int w(z)f(z) \, dz \tag{2}$$

(Integration here and below is assumed to be taken over all feasible values of z.)

By combining equation (1) with an appropriate description of the inheritance of z, evolutionary (i.e., between-generation) changes in the phenotypic distribution can be computed, at least in principle. Determining the between-generation change in the complete distribution is, however, usually challenging, even when approximate methods are used. Fortunately, it is often useful for many purposes to study the simpler problem of how the mean phenotype, $\bar{z}$, evolves, where

$$\bar{z} = \int zf(z) \, dz \tag{3}$$

For this reason—and to greatly simplify the math—this chapter will focus on evolutionary questions involving a population's mean phenotype. Evolutionary forces such as genetic drift and mutation are assumed to be negligible.

13.2.1 Standard Game Theory Approach

Standard evolutionary game theory assumes that phenotypes are asexually inherited (Maynard Smith 1982) or have an autosomal one-locus haploid genetic basis (Moore & Boake 1994). These assumptions are mathematically, if not biologically, equivalent. If the resemblance between parental and offspring phenotypes is perfect, then the offspring mean in the next generation, $\bar{z}'$, will be exactly the same as the mean, $\bar{z}^*$, of the selected parents. That is, $\bar{z}' = \bar{z}^* = \int z f^*(z)\, dz$, where $f^*(z)$ is the postselection distribution defined in equation (1). With such perfect asexual inheritance, the between-generation change in the population mean phenotype, $\Delta \bar{z} \equiv \bar{z}' - \bar{z}$, is simply

$$\Delta \bar{z} = s \qquad (4)$$

where the *selection differential,* $s = \bar{z}^* - \bar{z}$, measures within-generation changes in the population mean due to selection. A convenient way to rewrite equation (4) for a complex character, like behavior, is

$$\Delta \bar{z} = P\beta \qquad (5)$$

where P is the phenotypic covariance matrix for the components of z and $\beta = P^{-1}s$ is the *selection gradient* (Lande 1979). If the resemblance between a parent and its asexually produced offspring is not perfect, but the regression of offspring phenotype on parental genotype is linear, then the evolutionary dynamics of the population mean phenotype can be described by

$$\Delta \bar{z} = G_T \beta \qquad (6)$$

where G_T is the total genetic covariance matrix and β is the same selection gradient as in equation (5).

Each element of the selection gradient, $\beta = (\beta_1, \ldots, \beta_k)^T$, describes the force of linear selection acting directly on the mean of a particular trait component, holding other components constant (Lande & Arnold 1983, Brodie et al. 1995). By comparison, the components of the selection differential, $s = (s_1, \ldots, s_k)^T$, confound effects of direct selection on a trait and selection on correlated traits (Lande and Arnold 1983).

If fitness is frequency-independent (i.e., does not depend on the distribution of phenotypes), the selection gradient β has the biologically interesting property that it indicates the direction of evolution that would produce the steepest increase in population mean fitness (Lande and Arnold 1983). However, equations (5) and (6) show that whether parent and offspring phenotypes match perfectly or not, the evolutionary response to selection will tend to deviate from the direction of most rapid increase in mean fitness, β (see Fig. 13.1). Such adaptive "inefficiency" could be due to insufficient genetic variance for, or strong genetic correlations between, the traits being selected (as reflected in the covariance matrix P or G_T). This interpretation of β can break down if fitness is frequency-dependent, since even the most efficient evolutionary response (i.e., evolution in the direction of β) may reduce mean fitness in the next generation. Still, $\Delta\bar{z}$ will generally differ from β.

13.2.2 Quantitative Genetics Approach

The usual quantitative genetics approach used to study evolution assumes a sexually reproducing population in which genetic variation and covariation of traits are affected by many loci of small phenotypic effect (Bulmer 1985, Falconer 1989; other genetic models could also be used but will not be considered here). Under these assumptions, it can be shown (e.g., Lande 1979) that the evolutionary response to selection of the mean phenotype is

$$\Delta\bar{z} = G\beta \tag{7}$$

where G is the *additive-genetic* (for brevity, "genetic") covariance matrix and β is the selection gradient defined above. As with the asexual models, equation (7) shows that the evolutionary response to selection will generally differ from β (see Fig. 13.1).

Equation (7) does not require that G be constant to be valid. In fact, if G is changed by selection, equation (7) will still correctly describe evolutionary (between-generation) change in $\bar{z}$ provided the regression of offspring on parental phenotypes is linear (Bulmer 1985, p. 145; but see Hastings 1990, Nagylaki 1992). This implies that equation (7) is accurate for at least a single generation (see Grant & Grant 1995 for an empirical demonstration). Turelli and Barton (1994) have shown theoretically that G may be nearly constant over several generations for a broad range of selection strengths. Moreover, assuming that G is constant in equation (7) over several generations may give a reasonably accurate approximation to the evolution of $\bar{z}$, even if G actually changes between generations due to conventional evolutionary forces. This is because the mean often evolves much faster than the genetic variance (Barton & Turelli 1987).

It is reasonable to expect that the accuracy of such an approximation will break down after some period of time; however, it is an open question as to what the length of that period will be (Turelli 1988). Empirical results suggest that G (or its general matrix structure) may often be stable over fairly long evolutionary time scales (e.g., Lofsvold 1986, Kohn & Atchley 1988, Wilkinson et al. 1990, Arnold 1992). In any event, there is no reason why evolutionary changes in G could not be incorporated into equation (7). In fact, there are a number of ways this could be done; for example, one could update estimates of G every few generations (in an empirical application) or model the evolution of G using, say, an extension of Bulmer's infinitesimal model (Bulmer 1971, 1985). Regardless of how one handles the evolution of G, the critical point is that the constancy of genetic variances and covariances need not be an assumption underlying quantitative-genetic models of evolution by selection of mean phenotypes. Of course, the period over which individual fitnesses remain constant is

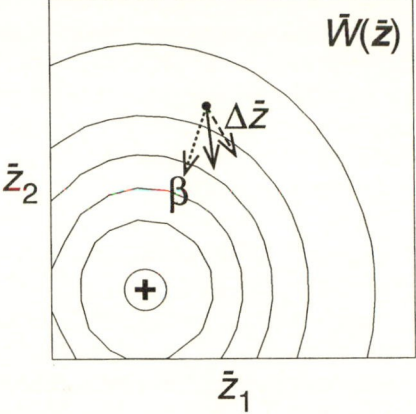

Figure 13.1. Evolutionary responses to selection in the mean of a two-component character, $\bar{z} = (\bar{z}_1, \bar{z}_2)$. Closed curves indicate mean phenotypes with the same population mean fitness, i.e., contours of $\bar{w}$. The plus sign shows the location of the mean phenotype with maximal mean fitness. The common base of the three arrows lies at a population's initial mean phenotype. Between-generation changes in the mean phenotype, $\Delta\bar{z}$, under perfect asexual inheritance and sexual inheritance are shown, respectively, by the solid and dashed arrows. The dotted arrow is the direction β favored by selection.

an equally important consideration when using any of the above models to draw long-term evolutionary inferences.

13.2.3 Comparing Evolutionary Dynamics

How do the above game theory and quantitative genetics models of evolution compare? The approaches are similar in that they use the selection gradient β to quantify the within-generation effects of selection on the mean phenotype. Another shared feature is that evolution generally does not proceed in the direction favored by selection (as indicated by β), even when parent and offspring resemble one another perfectly [equation (5)]. However, for a given selection regime and pattern of phenotypic/genotypic variances and covariances, evolution of the mean phenotype should proceed in a direction most similar to β with perfect asexual inheritance and least similar to β with sexual inheritance (see Fig. 13.1). This is because evolutionary constraints that are apparent at the phenotypic or total genetic level (P or G_T) must also occur at the additive-genetic level (G), but not necessarily vice versa (Pease and Bull 1988; see below).

Essentially, the only difference between game-theoretic and quantitative-genetic models for evolutionary dynamics of the mean phenotype is in how within-generation effects are assumed to be transmitted across generations. So provided that the basis of trait inheritance is understood, there is no actual distinction between game-theoretic and quantitative-genetic descriptions of the evolutionary dynamics of $\bar{z}$ under natural selection. It turns out, however, that equilibrium predictions of the approaches can differ widely, as will be discussed in the next section.

13.3 Evolutionary Equilibria

Optimization, game theory, and quantitative genetics offer different ways to predict evolutionary equilibria of continuous characters under selection. Game-theoretic approaches are appropriate when fitness is frequency-dependent (i.e., when individual fitness depends on the distribution of phenotypes), while optimization methods are appropriate when fitnesses are frequency-independent. Quantitative genetic approaches can be used to analyze equilibria for both types of fitness. The next two sections compare these approaches for frequency-independent and, then, frequency-dependent fitness. The dynamic stability of equilibria will not be considered here; see Abrams et al. (1993b) for an interesting discussion.

For simplicity, assume that the distribution of phenotypes, $f(z)$, is normal with mean $\bar{z} = (\bar{z}_1, \ldots, \bar{z}_k)^T$ and covariance matrix P. This condition is commonly satisfied in natural populations when traits are measured on appropriate scales (see, e.g., Falconer 1989). If the fitness function, $w(z)$, is differentiable with respect to the components of $\bar{z}$, then

$$\nabla_{\bar{z}} \bar{w} = \int w(z) \nabla_{\bar{z}} f(z) \; dz + \int f(z) \nabla_{\bar{z}} w(z) \; dz = \bar{w} P^{-1} s + \overline{\nabla_{\bar{z}} w} \qquad (8)$$

where $\nabla_{\bar{z}} = (\partial/\partial \bar{z}_1, \partial/\partial \bar{z}_2, \ldots, \partial/\partial \bar{z}_k)^T$ is the gradient operator with respect to components of $\bar{z}$, and $\overline{\nabla_{\bar{z}} w} = \int f(z) \nabla_{\bar{z}} w(z) \; dz$ is the mean gradient of individual fitness. Since $\beta = P^{-1} s$, equation (8) can be rearranged to express the selection gradient in terms of population mean fitness and individual fitness as

$$\beta = \frac{\nabla_{\bar{z}} \bar{w} - \overline{\nabla_{\bar{z}} w}}{\bar{w}} \qquad (9)$$

For a simple character ($k = 1$), equation (9) reduces to $\beta = (d\bar{w}/d\bar{z} - \int \partial w/\partial \bar{z} f(z) \; dz)/\bar{w}$, an expression first given by Lande (1976). If fitness is frequency-independent, the term $\overline{\nabla_{\bar{z}} w}$ vanishes because $\nabla_{\bar{z}} w(z) = 0$ for every z; then equation (9) reduces to the well-known equation $\beta = (\nabla_{\bar{z}} \bar{w})/\bar{w} = \nabla_{\bar{z}} \ln \bar{w}$ (Lande 1979). If fitness is frequency-dependent, $\overline{\nabla_{\bar{z}} w}$ may or may not be zero, depending on the form of w.

13.3.1 Frequency-Independent Fitness

When fitness is frequency-independent, optimization approaches assume individual fitness is maximized at an evolutionary equilibrium, possibly subject to phenotypic

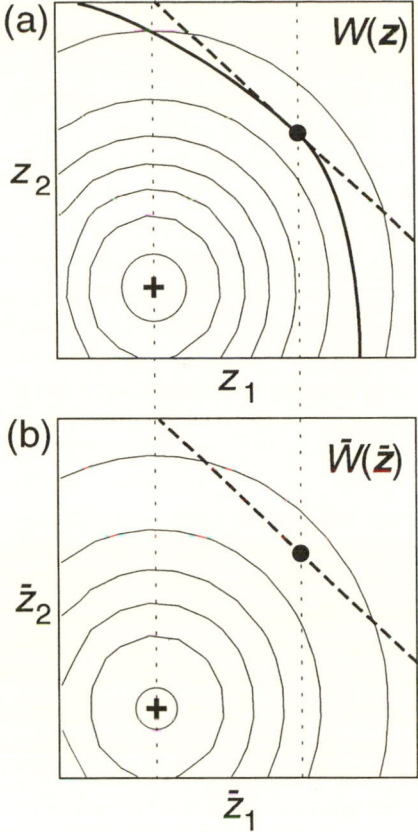

Figure 13.2. Optimization and quantitative genetics analyses of evolutionary equilibria for a two-component character. (a) Thin lines are contours for individual fitness, w, as a function of the character components z_1 and z_2. The plus sign indicates the phenotype with highest individual fitness, i.e., the global optimum. The thick curve shows a hypothetical constraint function, which determines the possible values of z_1 and z_2. The filled circle shows the location of the optimal phenotype, given these constraints. (b) Contours for mean fitness, $\bar{w}$, based on the individual fitness function shown in (a). Scales for $\bar{z}_1$ and $\bar{z}_2$ are the same as for z_1 and z_2 above. The fixed fitness difference between contours in (b) is the same as in (a), so the topography of $\bar{w}$ is less rugged than w. The plus sign indicates the mean phenotype associated with highest mean fitness, i.e., the global optimum. The dashed line represents the evolutionarily accessible directions given the constraint in (a); this line is also drawn in (a). The filled circle is the constrained optimum. The position of the constrained (unconstrained) optimum in (a) is similar to the corresponding optimum in (b).

constraints (reviewed in Parker & Maynard Smith 1990). That is, the predicted equilibrium phenotype maximizes $w(z)$, perhaps subject to satisfying a set of constraints. For example, if $w(z)$ were smooth and there were no constraints on z, then the optimal phenotype $\hat{z}$ would be a solution of the equation

$$\nabla_z w(z) = 0 \qquad (10)$$

where $\nabla_z = (\partial/\partial z_1, \partial/\partial z_2, \ldots, \partial/\partial z_k)^T$ is the gradient with respect to components of z. Figure 13.2a illustrates this approach when individual fitness depends on a character with two trait components, $z = (z_1, z_2)$, such as a mating call characterized by its duration (z_1) and intensity (z_2). Without constraints, fitness is globally maximized at an evolutionary equilibrium (indicated by the plus sign), whereas with constraints, fitness is maximized at equilibrium (filled circle) to the extent possible given the constraints (heavy curve).

A quantitative genetics analysis of frequency-independent selection starts with the basic evolution equation (7). An equilibrium mean phenotype, $\hat{z}$, must be a solution of $\Delta \bar{z} = G\beta = 0$. Because individual fitness is frequency-independent, $\overline{\nabla_z w} = 0$ in equation (9) (see above), so that $\hat{z}$ need only satisfy the simpler

$$\Delta \bar{z}|_{\hat{z}} = G\beta|_{\hat{z}} = G \left. \frac{\nabla_z \bar{w}}{\bar{w}} \right|_{\hat{z}} = 0 \tag{11}$$

where the notation "$|_{\hat{z}}$" means evaluated at $\hat{z}$.

Equation (11) may be satisfied in two qualitatively different ways. First, $\Delta \bar{z}|_{\hat{z}} = 0$ if $\nabla_z \bar{w}|_{\hat{z}} = 0$. In this case, $\hat{z}$ globally maximizes mean fitness, $\bar{w}$ (Fig. 13.2b, plus sign). This represents an "ecological optimum" in the sense that there is no net linear selection on $\hat{z}$. Such an equilibrium will eventually be reached, even if G varies through time, provided that there are no persistent genetic barriers to evolutionary change (such as lack of heritable variation or sufficiently strong genetic correlations; see below) and may be reached even if such constraints are ever-present, but changing (Hammerstein 1996, this volume).

Alternatively, an equilibrium could occur with the population not at an ecological optimum (i.e., with $\nabla_z \bar{w}|_{\hat{z}} \neq 0$) if there is a lack of appropriate genetic variation, as reflected in G (see below). In this case, $\bar{w}$ is not globally maximized at equilibrium; rather, $\bar{w}$ is maximized over a subset of "evolutionarily accessible" directions for the mean phenotype (filled circle in Fig. 13.2b). Evolutionarily accessible directions can be thought of as the complement of the set of "evolutionarily forbidden" directions (Kirkpatrick & Lofsvold 1992), which is the set of all selection gradients that would produce no evolutionary response in the current population. The notion of "evolutionarily forbidden" directions gives a quantitatively precise and biologically useful definition of an important type of evolutionary constraint (Arnold 1992).

Mathematically, evolutionary constraints are present whenever the additive-genetic covariance matrix G is "singular" (i.e., at least one of its rows is a linear combination of the other rows). The corresponding evolutionarily accessible and forbidden directions are described by the eigenvectors associated with, respectively, non-zero and zero eigenvalues of G. (G must have at least one zero eigenvalue if it is singular.) These constraints will limit evolutionary responses to accessible directions (the dashed line in Fig. 13.2b). Note that some authors have assumed that genetic correlations merely slow evolution but do not prevent ultimate optimization. Not only is this incorrect (e.g., see Fig. 13.2b), but even small genetic correlations may be consistent with equilibrium populations that are far from their ecological optima (Dickerson 1955, Via 1987, Gomulkiewicz & Kirkpatrick 1992, Kirkpatrick and Lofsvold 1992).

For a given set of fitnesses and constraints, how similar are the equilibria predicted by optimization and quantitative genetics approaches? The two approaches give quite similar results, at least under some circumstances (Charnov 1989, Charlesworth 1990, Iwasa et al. 1991, Taper & Case 1992, Abrams et al. 1993a). Specifically, the function that describes individual fitness, $w(z)$, must be *analytic*, which is to say it can be represented by a Taylor series that converges to $w(z)$ for every z (see, e.g., Marsden & Tromba 1988). If, in addition, terms above a certain order in the Taylor series are small, then an equilibrium predicted by one approach will be close to that predicted by the other. The rationale in the case of a two-component character, $z = (z_1, z_2)$, goes as follows. By assumption, $w(z)$ can be expanded in a Taylor series around the current population mean $\bar{z} = (\bar{z}_1, \bar{z}_2)$:

$$w(z) = w(\bar{z}) + \left.\frac{\partial w}{\partial z_1}\right|_{\bar{z}} (z_1 - \bar{z}_1) + \left.\frac{\partial w}{\partial z_2}\right|_{\bar{z}} (z_2 - \bar{z}_2)$$
$$+ \frac{1}{2}\left[\left.\frac{\partial^2 w}{\partial z_1^2}\right|_{\bar{z}} (z_1 - \bar{z}_1)^2 + 2\left.\frac{\partial^2 w}{\partial z_1 \partial z_2}\right|_{\bar{z}} (z_1 - \bar{z}_1)(z_2 - \bar{z}_2) + \left.\frac{\partial^2 w}{\partial z_2^2}\right|_{\bar{z}} (z_2 - \bar{z}_2)^2\right] + \ldots$$
$$\tag{12}$$

Substituting (12) into equation (2) leads to the following expansion for $\bar{w}$:

$$\bar{w} = w(\bar{z}) + \frac{1}{2}\left[\frac{\partial^2 w}{\partial z_1^2} P_{11} + 2\frac{\partial^2 w}{\partial z_1 \partial z_2} P_{12} + \frac{\partial^2 w}{\partial z_2^2} P_{22}\right]\Bigg|_{\bar{z}} + \ldots \tag{13}$$

where P_{ii} is the phenotypic variance of component z_i ($i = 1, 2$) and P_{12} is the phenotypic covariance between z_1 and z_2. The derivation of (13) relies on the facts $\int(z_i - \bar{z}_i) f(z)\, dz = 0$, $\int(z_i - \bar{z}_i)^2 f(z)\, dz = P_{ii}$, and $\int(z_1 - \bar{z}_1)(z_2 - \bar{z}_2) f(z)\, dz = P_{12}$. From (13) it follows that $\bar{w} \approx w(\bar{z})$ if all terms involving products with second and higher derivatives of $w(z)$ are small. Thus, under these conditions, a mean phenotype that maximizes population mean fitness $\bar{w}$ will also approximately maximize individual fitness $w(z)$, and vice versa. This correspondence is shown by the similar positions of the global optima in the upper and lower panels of Fig. 13.2.

The preceding argument can be extended to analyses involving evolutionary constraints. Continuing with the above example, suppose that $z_2 = h(z_1)$. For example, this might describe tradeoffs between call duration and intensity imposed by an organism's energetic capacities. If $h(z_1)$ is differentiable, the optimal phenotype satisfying this phenotypic constraint can be determined by solving the equation

$$\frac{dh(z_1)}{dz_1} = -\frac{\partial w/\partial z_1}{\partial w/\partial z_2} \tag{14}$$

for z_1 (Charnov 1989). Adapting the methods of Charlesworth (1990), it can be shown that given the constraint $z_2 = h(z_1)$, an equilibrium mean phenotype for the quantitative genetics model must satisfy

$$\left.\frac{dh(z_1)}{dz_1}\right|_{\bar{z}} = -\left.\frac{\partial \bar{w}/\partial \bar{z}_1}{\partial \bar{w}/\partial \bar{z}_2}\right|_{\bar{z}} \tag{15}$$

If higher-order terms in the expansion (13) of $\bar{w}$ are small, then $\partial \bar{w}/\partial \bar{z}_i \approx \partial w/\partial z_i|_z$ for $i = 1, 2$. Thus, any $\bar{z}$ that satisfies (15) will also approximately satisfy (14) and vice versa. This shows that, with or without constraints, optimization and quantitative genetics methods will predict roughly the same equilibrium phenotype when appropriate mathematical conditions are met.

13.3.2 Frequency-Dependent Fitness

When individual fitness depends on the distribution of phenotypes—in particular, on the mean $\bar{z}$—an equilibrium phenotype can be predicted on the basis of being an "evolutionarily stable strategy" (ESS) or a stationary point of the quantitative-genetics model (7). These two approaches will be discussed in turn. Individual fitness will be denoted $w(z, \bar{z})$ to emphasize its dependence on $\bar{z}$.

The concept of an ESS was developed as an extension of game theory to evolutionary biology (Maynard Smith 1982, Parker and Maynard Smith 1990). Briefly, a mean phenotype $\hat{z}$ is an ESS if it is its own "best response" (Bulmer 1994). (For simplicity, assume this best response is unique.) The best response to a mean phenotype $\bar{z}$ is the phenotype z that maximizes individual fitness, $w(z, \bar{z})$, holding $\bar{z}$ constant. If $w(z, \bar{z})$ is differentiable with respect to its first argument, then a best response to $\bar{z}$ can be found by solving $\nabla_z w(z, \bar{z}) = 0$ for z. In this symbolism, a phenotype that is its own best response (i.e., is an ESS) must be a solution $\hat{z}$ of

$$\nabla_z w(z, \bar{z})\big|_{z=\bar{z}=\hat{z}} = 0 \tag{16}$$

A graphical illustration of ESS analysis for a two-component trait $z = (z_1, z_2)$ is shown in Fig. 13.3. Note that an ESS defined by (16) may not be an equilibrium for the "standard" game-theoretic model discussed above [equation (5)] if $\beta \neq 0$ when $\bar{z} = \hat{z}$.

In the quantitative genetics approach, determining evolutionary equilibria when fitness is frequency-dependent again begins with equation (7). Assuming phenotypes are normally distributed, an equilibrium mean phenotype is a solution $\hat{\bar{z}}$ of

$$\Delta \bar{z}\big|_{\hat{\bar{z}}} = G\beta\big|_{\hat{\bar{z}}} = G\,\frac{\nabla_z \bar{w} - \overline{\nabla_z w(z, \bar{z})}}{\bar{w}}\,\Bigg|_{\hat{\bar{z}}} = 0 \tag{17}$$

[see equations (7) and (9)]. As for frequency-independent fitnesses, there are two qualitatively different ways equation (17) may be satisfied. First, $\Delta \hat{z}|_{\hat{\bar{z}}} = 0$ if $\nabla_z \bar{w} = \overline{\nabla_z w(z, \bar{z})}$ when $\bar{z} = \hat{z}$. Such a solution represents an equilibrium that would be reached in the absence of genetic constraints. Although $\hat{\bar{z}}$ will not maximize mean fitness if $\nabla_z \bar{w}(\hat{\bar{z}}) \neq 0$, it is an "ecological optimum" in the sense that there is no net force of linear selection acting to change the mean when $\bar{z} = \hat{\bar{z}}$. In contrast, $\hat{\bar{z}}$ may be

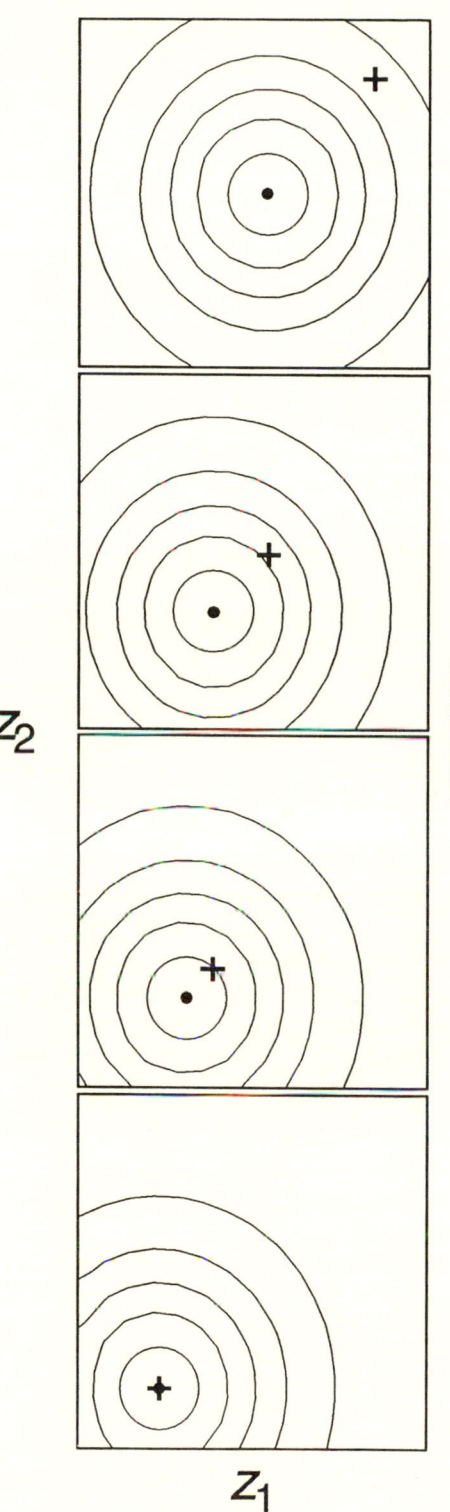

z_2

z_1

Figure 13.3. ESS analysis for a two-component character $z = (z_1, z_2)$. Individual fitness surfaces, $w(z, \bar{z})$, for four mean phenotypes (plus signs) are shown. On each surface, the filled circle represents the "best response" to $\bar{z}$. In the bottom panel, $\bar{z}$ is its own best response, i.e., it is an ESS.

a solution of (17) even though $\nabla_z \bar{w} \neq \overline{\nabla_z w(z, \bar{z})}$ at equilibrium because of genetic constraints indicated by the singularity of G. The net force of linear selection on the mean is not zero (i.e., $\hat{\bar{z}}$ is not at an ecological optimum). At such an equilibrium, selection will favor changes in evolutionarily forbidden directions but have no net effect in evolutionarily accessible directions.

ESS and quantitative genetic analyses have been compared in several theoretical studies (Charlesworth 1990, Iwasa et al. 1991, Mangel 1992, Taper & Case 1992). The following generalizes the approach used by Abrams et al. (1993a,b) to multivariate characters. Assuming that the individual fitness function $w(z, \bar{z})$ is analytic in the argument z, then

$$\beta = \frac{\nabla_z \bar{w} - \overline{\nabla_z w(z, \bar{z})}}{\bar{w}} = \frac{\nabla_z F(z, \bar{z})|_{z=\bar{z}}}{\bar{w}} \tag{18}$$

where $F(z, \bar{z})$ is defined as

$$F(z, \bar{z}) = w(z, \bar{z}) + \tfrac{1}{2}\left(\sum_i P_{ii} \frac{\partial^2 w(z, \bar{z})}{\partial z_i^2} + 2\sum_{i<j} P_{ij} \frac{\partial^2 w(z, \bar{z})}{\partial z_i \partial z_j}\right) + \dots \tag{19}$$

F has the property $F(\bar{z}, \bar{z}) = \bar{w}|_{\bar{z}}$. If the terms of expansion (19) involving second and higher derivatives of $w(z, \bar{z})$ are small, then $F(z, \bar{z}) \approx w(z, \bar{z})$ so that $\nabla_z F(z, \bar{z}) \approx \nabla_z w(z, \bar{z})$. This implies that, at least under these conditions, a phenotype satisfying the ESS condition (16) will approximately satisfy the equilibrium equation (17). (In addition, this shows that an ESS defined by (17) will only be an approximate equilibrium for the "standard" game theory model described above [equation (5)] because it is generally only approximately zero at an ESS.) The above arguments can be extended to cases in which phenotypic constraints are present (see Charlesworth 1990). Once again, ESS and quantitative genetic equilibria will be close under the appropriate mathematical conditions.

Taken together, the results of this section demonstrate that, at least under certain mathematical conditions, an optimization or ESS analysis will predict roughly the same equilibrium as the comparable quantitative genetics analysis, with or without phenotypic constraints. The next section will consider the extent to which these conditions might or might not hold in practice.

13.4 Dissimilarities

The last section showed that optimization or ESS methods will predict equilibria similar to those using quantitative genetics methods provided that three conditions hold: (1) The function describing individual fitness, w, must be analytic, (2) terms in the expansion of $\bar{w}$ or $F(z, \bar{z})$ involving higher-order derivatives of w and their coefficients must be small, and (3) constraints that occur at the additive-genetic level must also appear at the phenotypic level. The extent to which an evolutionary equilibrium can be considered a common prediction to quantitative genetic and optimization (or ESS) analyses depends on how often the above three conditions hold in situations of biological interest. (Technically, the previous section only showed that the three conditions are sufficient since the methods may predict similar equilibria under other circumstances.) In this section I argue that there are many biologically realistic situations in which at least one of these conditions fail and that, in those situations, the different methods generally give widely different results. This suggests that the extent to which optimization/ESS and quantitative genetics results agree may be substantially limited. For simplicity, only one-component characters will be considered in this section, although the situations described below can easily arise for more complex characters.

The outwardly most innocuous of the above three requirements is that the individual fitness function must be analytic. Mathematically, this means that the Taylor series of the fitness function must converge to $w(z)$, or $w(z, \bar{z})$, for every value z (e.g., Marsden & Tromba 1988). Although analytic functions enjoy widespread use in the theoretical and statistical literature, this requirement is not met in a number of biologically important circumstances, of which just three examples will be considered.

The first example is a "threshold character" model for the evolution of strategies in a two-person, two-strategy game, such as the Hawk–Dove game (Maynard Smith 1982). A threshold character is a character with discrete states that are not inherited in a simple way (Falconer 1989). If the inheritance of strategies is not simple, then it is reasonable to model the set of strategies as a threshold character. In such a model, the expression of each character state (strategy) is assumed to depend on an underlying continuous "liability." Consider, for example, a two-strategy game with pure strategies A and B. Let z denote the liability. Assume that an individual with $z \leq T$ plays strategy A and plays strategy B otherwise.

If the distribution of z is normal with a fixed variance P, then the proportion of individuals playing strategy A or B is a function of the mean liability, $\bar{z}$ (Charlesworth 1990). In particular, the proportion playing A is $\Theta[(T-\bar{z})/\sqrt{P}]$, where $\Theta(\cdot)$ is the cumulative distribution function of the standard normal distribution. Now suppose E_{IJ} is the fitness payoff to strategy I in a contest with an opponent playing strategy J. Then the expected fitnesses for strategies A and B in a population with mean $\bar{z}$ are, respectively,

$$w_A(\bar{z}) = E_{AA}\Theta\left(\frac{T-\bar{z}}{\sqrt{P}}\right) + E_{AB}\left[1 - \Theta\left(\frac{T-\bar{z}}{\sqrt{P}}\right)\right]$$

(20a)

$$w_B(\bar{z}) = E_{BA}\Theta\left(\frac{T-\bar{z}}{\sqrt{P}}\right) + E_{BB}\left[1 - \Theta\left(\frac{T-\bar{z}}{\sqrt{P}}\right)\right]$$

The (frequency-dependent) individual fitness function for the liability z is thus

$$w(z, \bar{z}) = \begin{cases} w_A(\bar{z}) & \text{if } z \leq T \\ w_B(\bar{z}) & \text{if } z > T \end{cases}$$

(20b)

(see Fig. 13.4a). Provided that $w_A(\bar{z}) \neq w_B(\bar{z})$, $w(z, \bar{z})$, is discontinuous at the threshold point $z = T$ and cannot be analytic. Moreover, the ESS analysis for the continuous

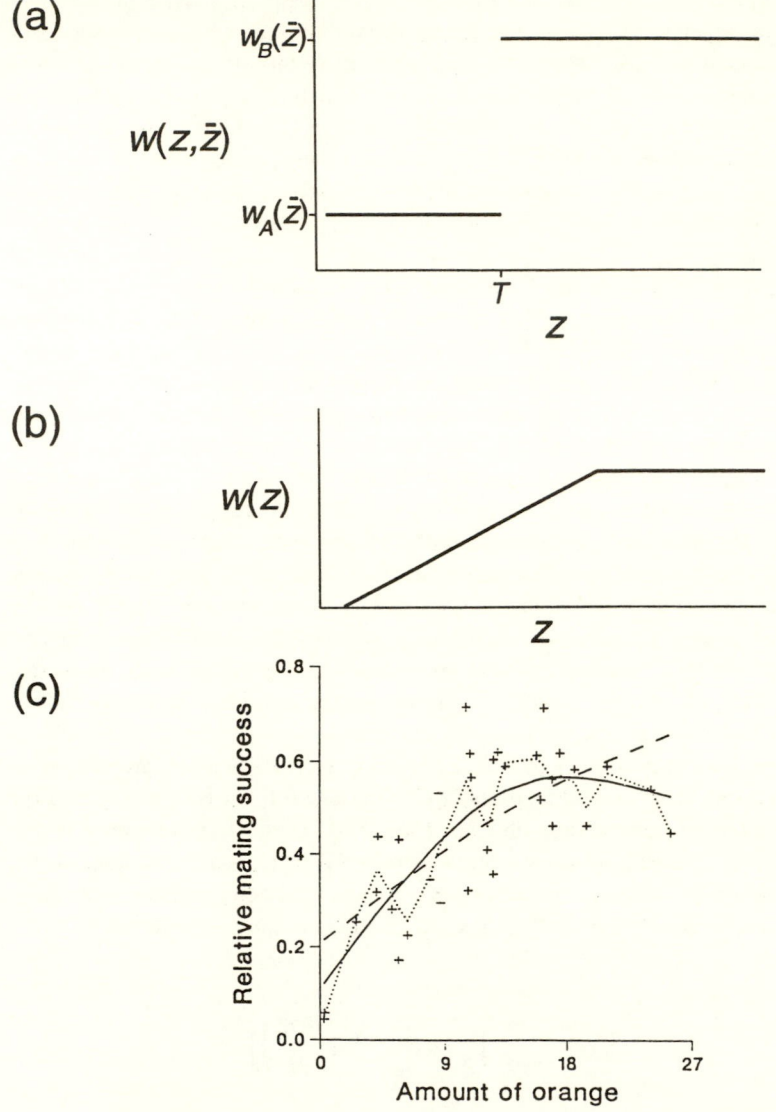

Figure 13.4. Individual fitness functions, $w(z)$ or $w(z, \bar{z})$, that are not analytic. (a) Fitnesses for a two-person, two-strategy game with pure strategies A and B as described in the text (eq. 20). (b) A continuous fitness function with a discontinuous first derivative. (c) Fitness functions estimated using nonparametric regression. Taken from Figure 2 of Schluter (1988), which is based on data from Houde (1987). Shown is mating success of male guppies, *Poecilia reticulata*, as a function of the percentage of body area that is colored orange. Curves correspond to fitness function estimates obtained using different levels of a smoothing parameter. See Schluter (1988) for details. Figure (c) used by permission of The Society for the Study of Evolution.

trait z [see equation (16)] is inconclusive because $\partial w(z, \bar{z})/\partial z = 0$ for all $z \neq T$. By comparison, the associated quantitative genetics equilibrium analysis [equation (17)] requires that an equilibrium $\hat{z}$ must be a solution of the equation $d\bar{w}/d\bar{z} = \overline{\partial w/\partial \bar{z}}$, where

$$\bar{w}(\bar{z}) = w_A(\bar{z})\Theta\left(\frac{T - \bar{z}}{\sqrt{P}}\right) + w_B(\bar{z})\left[1 - \Theta\left(\frac{T - \bar{z}}{\sqrt{P}}\right)\right]$$

and

$$\frac{\overline{\partial w}}{\partial \bar{z}} = \frac{dw_A(\bar{z})}{d\bar{z}}\Theta\left(\frac{T - \bar{z}}{\sqrt{P}}\right) + \frac{dw_B(\bar{z})}{d\bar{z}}\left[1 - \Theta\left(\frac{T - \bar{z}}{\sqrt{P}}\right)\right]$$

The equilibrium condition for $\hat{\bar{z}}$ reduces to $E_{AA}\hat{q} + E_{AB}(1 - \hat{q}) = E_{BA}\hat{q} + E_{BB}(1 - \hat{q})$, where $\hat{q} = \Theta[(T - \hat{\bar{z}})/\sqrt{P}]$ is the proportion playing strategy A at equilibrium. This is exactly the proportion predicted by the more familiar "discrete" analysis of this game [Maynard Smith 1982, equation (2.5)].

The above threshold model was, of course, chosen to illustrate how widely different ESS and quantitative genetics analyses can be when a fitness function is not analytic. It may be possible to overcome problems, like an inconclusive ESS analysis, if it were based on a different phenotypic model or scale (Charlesworth 1990). For instance, an alternative continuous trait model might let z be the probability of playing strategy A and $1 - z$ the probability of playing B. Then individual fitness takes the form $w(z, \bar{z}) = zw_A(\bar{z}) + (1 - z)w_B(\bar{z})$, which would produce similar results whether using an ESS or quantitative-genetics analysis. In any case, the main point is simply that one should not assume by default that ESS and quantitative-genetics analyses of a given model will yield similar predictions.

The discontinuous relationship between fitness and phenotype in the last example may seem like an exceptional case with the awkward property that the fitness function is not analytic. In fact, there is an extremely large class of continuous—and even smooth—fitness functions that are not analytic. Figure 13.4 shows two examples. In Fig. 13.4b, fitness increases monotonically over lower values of z and is constant for larger z. This might describe, for example, how reproductive success depends on some measure of courtship display intensity. The function in Fig. 13.4b is continuous, but not smooth. It is not analytic because it has a discontinuous first derivative. Schmid et al. (1994) present methods for estimating nonsmooth functions like Fig. 13.4b, and they describe several empirical examples of such functions. They suggest that nonsmooth relationships are common in biology. The fitness functions in Fig. 13.4c were estimated from data using nonparametric regression methods (Schluter 1988, Schluter & Nychka 1994). Such estimates, while smooth, are not analytic because they are cubic splines. (Cubic splines are smooth but have discontinuous second derivatives.) Consequently, equilibria predicted using quantitative genetics or optimization/ESS methods based on these fitnesses may differ substantially. Other biological situations might conceivably involve even smoother fitness functions that have discontinuities in their higher-order derivatives and, thus, are not analytic. The difference between quantitative-genetics and optimization/ESS methods need not decline with increasing degrees of discontinuity. So, even for cases of very smooth fitness functions in which only a high-order derivative is discontinuous, large differences may exist between equilibrium analyses.

Optimization/ESS and quantitative-genetics approaches may predict very different equilibria even if a fitness function is analytic. This will occur if the terms involving derivatives of second and higher order in the expansion of $\bar{w}$ or $F(z, \bar{z})$ [see equations (13) and (19)] are not small. For example, $w(\bar{z})$ will not be a good approximation of $\bar{w}$ if the higher-order terms, such as $\frac{1}{2}[P_{11}\partial^2 w/\partial z_1^2 + 2\partial^2 w/\partial z_1\partial z_2 + P_{22}\partial^2 w/\partial z_2^2]|_{\bar{z}}$, are not negligible [see equation (13)]. For such terms to be small, not only must the higher-order derivatives of $w(z)$ not be too large, but the magnitudes of the phenotypic variances and covariances cannot be large. It is not difficult to construct hypothetical, but biologically plausible, fitness functions and phenotypic distributions in which these terms are large—as are the resulting differences between optimization (ESS) and quantitative-genetics analyses (Kirkpatrick & Gomulkiewicz, unpublished results). The "corridor model" of adaptation analyzed by Bürger (1986) is an example involving frequency-independent selection on more complex characters in which higher-order terms are not negligible. In that model, phenotypes that maximize $\bar{w}$ do not even approximately maximize in the absence of constraints.

Finally, optimization and quantitative genetics methods may predict widely different equilibria for fitness functions and phenotypic distributions that do not suffer from either of the above "problems." This can occur whenever evolutionary constraints (as reflected in G) are not apparent at the phenotypic level (as reflected in P). Charlesworth (1990) showed that if characters have more than two components, there is no simple relationship between genetic and phenotypic correlations. In fact, these correlations may have opposite signs for a particular pair of traits. This implies that the correlations underlying phenotypic constraints may often not correspond to correlations that are responsible for evolutionary constraints.

In addition to this lack of correspondence between the form of genetic and phenotypic constraints, it is possible (and even likely with a more complex character) that certain genetic constraints will be completely masked at the phenotypic level. (This is the extension to complex characters of the situation in which a phenotypically variable trait is not heritable.) Conversely, every phenotypic constraint must also appear as a genetic constraint. These properties follow from Pease & Bull (1988), who proved that if P is singular, then so is G, but not vice versa. (Technically, the "null space" of G contains that of P.) Taking their results a step further, it can be shown that G can actually be "more singular" (has a larger null space) than P, for traits with more than two components. That is, there may be fewer evolutionarily accessible dimensions associated with G than with P, even if both matrices indicate at least one evolutionarily forbidden direction. In this situation, equilibrium predictions made using optimization/ESS methods that rely on phenotypic constraints could be greatly different from those made using quantitative-genetics methods that use additive-genetic constraints. The magnitude of such a discrepancy could be quite large under biologically realistic conditions. Because the potential for constraints increases with the dimensionality of a trait (Dickerson 1955, Gomulkiewicz & Kirkpatrick 1992), this source of dissimilarity should be increasingly important for a more complex character, like behavior.

To summarize, there appear to be many biologically plausible and important circumstances in which equilibria predicted by an optimization or ESS analysis on the one hand and a quantitative genetics approach on the other can differ greatly. This argues strongly against assuming by default that the approaches will provide similar equilibrium predictions. Establishing the conditions under which the analyses are assured to give similar results would involve verifying that the fitness function is analytic, that higher-order terms are negligible, and that genetic and phenotypic constraints are the same.

13.5 An Empirical Strategy for Detecting Adaptation and Constraint

Given the potential for disparity between distinct theoretical approaches, empiricists may wonder if there are methods available that would help them to independently assess the influences of adaptation and constraint in natural populations. In fact there are. Most of the methods discussed here were developed (originally by Lande & Arnold 1983) with quantitative genetics analyses in mind; however, many of them do not require genetic data. The volume by Boake (1994) contains an excellent introduction to, and survey of, these methods as applied to behavioral characters. See Brodie et al. (1995) for a succinct review.

This section will outline an empirical strategy for resolving the roles of adaptation and constraint in an equilibrium population, similar to one proposed by Gomulkiewicz and Kirkpatrick (1992). The strategy's main advantage is that it is structured so that the least data-intensive steps are completed first; if a satisfactory explanation is attained with the relatively simpler tests, the subsequent more laborious steps can be avoided. It is crucial to bear in mind that this scheme applies only to populations that are known to be, or can reasonably be assumed to be, at equilibrium. The procedure shares many similarities with the more general proposals of Reeve and Sherman (1993).

Step 1: Test for adaptation. At a minimum, this step requires data on the relationship between phenotype and fitness. It may also require information about the phenotypic distribution. To assess adaptation and constraint in a equilibrium population, it is simplest (though not usually simple!) to begin by testing whether or not the population's mean phenotype is experiencing directional selection. One way this can be done is to determine the selection gradient, β, which can be estimated as the vector of partial regression coefficients of relative fitness on phenotype (reviewed in Arnold 1994, Brodie et al. 1995). One could also estimate β using equation (9) if an estimate of the fitness function, based on naturally occurring or artificially created variants, is available (e.g., Schluter 1988, Schluter & Nychka 1994, Brodie et al. 1995) and if phenotypes in the population are normally distributed. If $\beta = 0$, the mean is under no selection to change, which suggests that it is at an ecological optimum. Alternatively, one could determine if the distribution of phenotypes is consistent with the predicted ecological optimum. For example, Reeve and Sherman (1993) suggest that the most adapted phenotype should be predominant. If either alternative is satisfied, a reasonable conclusion is that the population occupies an ecological optimum. That is, constraints are probably playing a minor role, compared to adaptation, in maintaining the current population distribution. If β is significantly different from zero or the population deviates from the expected distribution, then constraints are probably having an important effect.

Step 2: Detect phenotypic constraints. This step requires an estimate of the population's phenotypic covariance matrix, P, which can be estimated directly or inferred from a known constraint function (see, e.g., Charnov 1989). Phenotypic constraints are implied if P is singular. Note that determining whether or not the true P matrix is singular is a mathematically nontrivial task since *estimates* of P may fail to be non-negative definite. This problem can be partly circumvented using a procedure developed by Shaw and Geyer (1993) that constrains estimated covariance matrices to be non-negative definite.

If P is singular, then genetic (evolutionary) constraints must be present (Pease & Bull 1988). However, the phenotypic correlations may not correspond to the constraining genetic correlations (Charlesworth 1990). Despite this limitation, detecting the presence of evolutionary constraints may be of great value, even if the exact causes are obscure.

If phenotypic constraints are detected, constraints revealed by P may not provide a sufficient explanation for equilibrium, since G may be "more singular" than P (see above). Given reasonable estimates of P and β, one could test this question for the quantitative genetics approach by computing the product $P\beta$. If $P\beta \approx 0$, then the population is probably at an ecological optimum given the constraints indicated by P. If, however, $P\beta$ is significantly different from zero, then important genetic constraints may be hidden at the phenotypic level.

Step 3: Determine genetic constraints. This level of analysis requires knowing additive-genetic variances and covariances, which can be estimated using individuals of known relationship (such as parents and their offspring or sibling groups). For overviews of estimation techniques, as well as references to more specialized sources, consult Falconer (1989), Simms and Rausher (1992), and Arnold (1994). The result will be an estimate of the additive-genetic covariance matrix, G, for components of the character z. As in Step 2, genetic constraints are detected if G is singular. In the quantitative genetics framework, these constraints would provide a reasonably sufficient explanation of the equilibrium if the matrix–vector product $G\beta$ were indistinguishable from zero.

Step 4: Explore other explanations. If the roles of adaptation and constraint are not sufficiently resolved in Steps 1–3, then a number of other factors (apart from sampling error) merit consideration. First, the population may in fact not be at equilibrium. Second, the characters under consideration may be constrained by traits that have not been measured. Third, other evolutionary forces, such as migration, mutation, or parental care, may be strongly opposing selection.

At worst, a statistically powerful study that follows some or all of the above steps can rigorously establish that certain *a priori* reasonable explanations for equilibrium do not apply. (Moreover, it may be possible to use the parameter estimates to predict future evolutionary changes. See Grant & Grant 1995.) However, if all goes well, such a study would provide a clear quantitative assessment of the importance of adaptation and constraint in maintaining a population's equilibrium.

13.6 Conclusion

This chapter has attempted to compare and contrast three methods for analyzing adaptive evolution of behavioral traits: optimization, game theory, and quantitative genetics. First, it was pointed out that only game-theory and quantitative-genetics approaches are appropriate for studying evolutionary dynamics. Provided that the genetic basis is understood, these two approaches are basically identical (except for the terminology). All three approaches can be used to predict evolutionary equilibria that result from natural selection given information about fitness and constraints. Optimization and quantitative-genetics methods are used when fitness is frequency-independent, while ESS and quantitative genetics approaches apply when fitness is frequency-dependent. Given that certain mathematical conditions are satisfied, equilibria predicted by an optimization or ESS analysis versus a quantitative genetics analysis will be similar. However, if these mathematical prerequisites are not met (as probably occurs in many biologically plausible situations), then their respective equilibrium predictions may be substantially different. Finally, an empirical strategy is proposed for detecting and quantifying the roles of adaptation and constraint in maintaining equilibrium populations.

There is another distinction between game-theory/optimization and quantitative-genetics approaches that needs mentioning. Game theory and optimization thinking may be especially useful for understanding the ecological and behavioral bases of individual fitness. In contrast, individual fitness is always input to (rather than output from) quantitative-genetics analyses (Mangel & Ludwig 1992). That is, quantitative genetics does not provide a framework for predicting individual fitness functions or selection gradients from ecological and behavioral first principles (although it provides methods for measuring such fitness inputs). Quantitative-genetics methods do, however, provide powerful means for deducing evolutionary constraints and for examining the evolutionary consequences of natural selection. Still, the time horizon over which quantitative-genetics estimates remain accurate is not certain (Turelli 1988), whereas there is some evidence that optimization approaches provide reasonably good predictions of evolutionary patterns over very long time scales (e.g., Charnov 1993). This suggests that optimization, game-theory, and quantitative-genetics approaches all have important roles to play in the development of a more complete understanding of evolution by natural selection.

ACKNOWLEDGMENTS   I thank Marc Mangel and Mark Kirkpatrick for many stimulating discussions on the subject matter of this chapter. I am grateful to M. Mangel, H. K. Reeve, and an anonymous reviewer for providing helpful comments on the manuscript. Support for this work was provided by National Science Foundation grant DEB-9528602.

References

Abrams, P. A., Harada, Y. & Matsuda, H. 1993a. On the relationship between quantitative genetic and ESS models. *Evolution,* 47, 982–985.

Abrams, P. A., Matsuda, H. & Harada, Y. 1993b. Evolutionarily unstable fitness maxima and stable fitness minima of continuous traits. *Evol. Ecol.* 7, 465–487.

Arnold, S. J. 1992. Constraints on phenotypic evolution. *Am. Nat.,* 140, S85–S107.

Arnold, S. J. 1994. Multivariate inheritance and evolution: A review of the concepts. In *Quantitative Genetic Studies of Behavioral Evolution,* C. R. B. Boake, eds., pp. 17–48. Chicago: University of Chicago Press.

Barton, N. H. & Turelli, M. 1987. Adaptive landscapes, genetic distance, and the evolution of quantitative characters. *Genet. Res. Cambridge,* 49, 157–173.

Boake, C. R. B., ed. 1994. *Quantitative Genetic Studies of Behavioral Evolution.* Chicago: Chicago University Press.

Brodie, E. D., Moore, A. J. & Janzen, F. J. 1995. Visualizing and quantifying natural selection. *Trends Ecol. Evol.,* 10, 313–318.

Bulmer, M. 1994. *Theoretical Evolutionary Ecology.* Sunderland, MA: Sinauer Associates.

Bulmer, M. G. 1971. The effect of selection on genetic variability. *Am. Nat.,* 105, 201–211.

Bulmer, M. G. 1985. *The Mathematical Theory of Quantitative Genetics.* Oxford: Clarendon Press.

Bürger, R. 1986. Constraints for the evolution of functionally coupled characters: A nonlinear analysis of a phenotypic model. *Evolution,* 40, 182–193.

Charlesworth, B. 1990. Optimization models, quantitative genetics, and mutation. *Evolution,* 44, 520–538.

Charnov, E. L. 1989. Phenotypic evolution under Fisher's fundamental theorem of natural selection. *Heredity,* 62, 113–116.

Charnov, E. L. 1993. *Life History Invariants: Some Explorations of Symmetry in Evolutionary Ecology.* Oxford: Oxford University Press.

Dickerson, G. E. 1955. Genetic slippage in response to selection for multiple objectives. *Cold Spring Harbor Symp. Quant. Biol.,* 20, 213–224.

Falconer, D. S. 1989. *Introduction to Quantitative Genetics,* third edition. New York: John Wiley & Sons.

Gomulkiewicz, R. & Kirkpatrick, M. 1992. Quantitative genetics and the evolution of reaction norms. *Evolution,* 46, 390–411.

Grant, P. R. & Grant, B. R. 1995. Predicting microevolutionary responses to directional selection on heritable variation. *Evolution,* 49, 241–251.

Hammerstein, P. 1996. Darwinian adaptation, population genetics, and the streetcar theory of evolution. *J. Math. Biol.,* 34, 511–532.

Hastings, A. 1990. Second-order approximations for selection coefficients at polygenic loci. *J. Math. Biol.,* 28, 475–483.

Houde, A. E. 1987. Mate choice based upon naturally occurring color-pattern variation in a guppy population. *Evolution,* 41, 1–10.

Iwasa, Y., Pomiankowski, A. & Nee, S. 1991. The evolution of costly mate preferences. II. The "handicap" principle. *Evolution,* 45, 1431–1442.

Kirkpatrick, M. & Heckman, N. 1989. A quantitative genetic model for growth, shape, reaction norms, and other infinite-dimensional characters. *J. Math. Biol.,* 27, 429–450.

Kirkpatrick, M. & Lofsvold, D. 1992. Measuring selection and constraint in the evolution of growth. *Evolution,* 46, 954–971.

Kirkpatrick, M., Lofsvold, D. & Bulmer, M. 1990. Analysis of inheritance, selection and evolution of growth trajectories. *Genetics,* 124, 979–993.

Kohn, L. A. P. & Atchley, W. R. 1988. How similar are genetic correlation structures? Data from mice and rats. *Evolution,* 42, 467–481.

Lande, R. 1976. Natural selection and random genetic drift in phenotypic evolution. *Evolution,* 30, 314–334.

Lande, R. 1979. Quantitative genetics analysis of multivariate evolution, applied to brain:body size allometry. *Evolution,* 33, 402–416.

Lande, R. & Arnold, S. J. 1983. The measurement of selection on correlated characters. *Evolution*, 37, 1210–1226.

Lofsvold, D. 1986. Quantitative genetics of morphological differentiation in *Peromyscus*. I. Tests of homogeneity of genetic covariance structure among species and subspecies. *Evolution*, 40, 559–573.

Mangel, M. 1992. Descriptions of superparasitism by optimal foraging theory, evolutionarily stable strategies and quantitative genetics. *Evol. Ecol.*, 6, 152–169.

Mangel, M. & Ludwig, D. 1992. Definition and evaluation of the fitness of behavioral and developmental programs. *Annu. Rev. Ecol. Syst.*, 23, 507–36.

Marsden, J. E. & Tromba, A. J. 1988. *Vector Calculus*. New York: W. H. Freeman and Company.

Maynard Smith, J. 1982. *Evolution and the Theory of Games*. Cambridge, UK: Cambridge University Press.

Moore, A. J. & Boake, C. R. B. 1994. Optimality and evolutionary genetics: Complementary procedures for evolutionary analysis in behavioural ecology. *Trends Ecol. Evol.*, 9, 69–72.

Nagylaki, T. 1992. *Introduction to Theoretical Population Genetics*. Berlin: Springer-Verlag.

Parker, G. A. & Maynard Smith, J. 1990. Optimality theory in evolutionary biology. *Nature*, 348, 27–33.

Pease, C. M. & Bull, J. J. 1988. A critique of methods for measuring life history trade-offs. *J. Evol. Biol.*, 1, 293–303.

Reeve, H. K. & Sherman, P. W. 1993. Adaptation and the goals of evolutionary research. *Q. Rev. Biol.*, 68, 1–32.

Schluter, D. 1988. Estimating the form of natural selection on a quantitative trait. *Evolution*, 42, 849–861.

Schluter, D. & Nychka, D. 1994. Exploring fitness surfaces. *Am. Nat.*, 143, 597–616.

Schmid, B., Polasek, W., Weiner, J., Krause, A. & Stoll, P. 1994. Modeling of discontinuous relationships in biology with censored regression. *Am. Nat.*, 143, 494–507.

Shaw, F. H., & Geyer, C.J. (1993). Constrained covariance component models (IMA Preprint Series No. 1189). University of Minnesota.

Simms, E. L. & Rausher, M. D. 1992. Uses of quantitative genetics for studying the evolution of plant resistance. In *Plant Resistance to Herbivores and Pathogens: Ecology, Evolution, and Genetics*, R. S. Fritz and E. L. Simms, eds., pp. 42–68. Chicago: University of Chicago Press.

Taper, M. L. & Case, T. J. 1992. Models of character displacement and the theoretical robustness of taxon cycles. *Evolution*, 46, 317–333.

Turelli, M. 1988. Phenotypic evolution, constant covariances, and the maintenance of additive variance. *Evolution*, 42, 1342–1347.

Turelli, M. & Barton, N. H. 1994. Genetic and statistical analyses of strong selection on polygenic traits: What, me normal? *Genetics*, 138, 913–941.

Via, S. 1987. Genetic constraints on the evolution of phenotypic plasticity. In *Genetic Constraints on Adaptive Evolution*, V. Loeschcke, eds., pp. 46–71. Berlin, Germany: Springer-Verlag.

Wilkinson, J., Fowler, K. & Partridge, L. 1990. Resistance of genetic correlation structure to directional selection in *Drosophila melanogaster*. *Evolution*, 41, 11–21.

HUDSON KERN REEVE
LEE ALAN DUGATKIN

Why We Need Evolutionary Game Theory

14.1 Introduction

The original game-theoretic models and their extensions discussed in this book potentially shed light on a tremendous range of social behaviors. Despite the work outlined in this volume, surprisingly few game-theoretic models (other than sex-ratio models) have been rigorously empirically tested during the more than two decades that have elapsed since game theory became a part of evolutionary biology. The scarcity of explicit tests of game-theoretic models contrasts markedly with the extensive empirical testing of frequency-independent, fitness-maximization models (such as most optimal foraging models). Why is this?

One possibility is that such models are difficult to test—for example, because it is difficult to demonstrate "equality of fitnesses" (or "equality of marginal fitness returns") for discrete behavioral variants selectively maintained in a stable polymorphism or as parts of a mixed evolutionarily stable strategy (ESS). However, the latter answer isn't satisfying for two reasons: First, frequency-independent optimization models (henceforth called "FIO" models), like game-theoretic models (henceforth called "GT" models), make predictions about, and thus can be tested by comparing, the relative fitnesses of alternative behavioral variants (e.g., Gomulkiewicz, this volume). The empirical difficulties that arise in measuring and comparing fitnesses in tests of FIO models are the same as, or complementary to, the difficulties in testing GT models. Second, both GT and FIO models can be tested without measuring fitnesses at all, by observing whether the predicted behavior (or distribution of behaviors) occurs under the appropriate environmental and social conditions; the latter have been described as "forward" tests of evolutionary hypotheses as opposed to the "backward" tests involving fitness comparisons of previously observed behaviors (Sherman and Reeve 1997). We see no consistent difference between FIO or GT models in the ease with which either forward or backward tests can be performed.

14.2 The Skepticism Surrounding Evolutionary Game Theory

We suspect that the infrequency of explicit tests of GT models results from a hazy, but persistent, skepticism in their utility. The very term "game theory" may connote a parlor room exercise that is remote from biological reality, fostering in some the view that GT models provide an overly complicated representation of nature, one that succumbs to a high-level version of Occam's Razor (i.e., "don't multiply theories unnecessarily!"), and in others the exactly opposite view that GT models are overly simplistic, ignoring as they do the crucial details of genetic architecture. The possibly pervasive, implicit belief that "game-theoretic models are not (and have not proved) useful" therefore might reflect multiple criticisms, which we outline and examine in order of increasing plausibility:

Criticism 1: One possible criticism is that theory of any sort is unnecessary and researchers should be content simply with the description of behavioral diversity. This objection is fundamentally unscientific in outlook and, moreover, is rejected by the numerous cases in which otherwise inexplicable behaviors have become rigorously understood and even predictable within theoretical evolutionary frameworks (Parker and Maynard Smith 1990). Within the scope of game theory alone, such cases include at least a general evolutionary understanding of the conventional settlement of animal contests by uncorrelated asymmetries (Riechert, this volume), honesty in communication (Johnstone, this volume), the sex ratio, ideal free spatial distributions of animals (Sih and Brown, both in this volume), maintenance of mixed or polymorphic strategies (Gross and Repka, this volume) such as producer–scrounger systems (Giraldeau, this volume), cooperation despite the temptation to cheat (Dugatkin, this volume and Stephens and Clements, this volume), patterns of conflict among siblings (Mock et al., this volume), the modulation of reproductive skew in social groups by relatedness and ecological factors, and the surprising absence of nepotism within many animal societies (Reeve, this volume).

Criticism 2: A second possible criticism is that natural selection has not molded behavioral phenotypes, so that neither GT nor FIO models are successful in predicting or explaining which behaviors are seen in nature. This claim seems to us to be simply false, given (1) the tremendous success of selection models in illuminating the existence of otherwise puzzling behaviors (see above) and (2) the nearly universal fulfillment of the sufficient conditions (i.e., heredity, variation, and differential reproduction) for natural selection to operate on behavioral variants, as demonstrated by both field observations and artificial selection experiments (Falconer 1981, Endler 1986). Many claims that natural selection is ineffective in driving behavioral (or even most phenotypic) evolution reflect logical misunderstandings about what kinds of hypotheses truly compete with selective hypotheses as explanations for the existence of observed behaviors (Reeve and Sherman 1993).

The concern about GT's ignoring the details of genetic architecture is another expression of Criticism 2. We believe that this concern is unwarranted for three reasons. First, theoretical work has lessened this worry by showing that populations will, in the long run, tend to closely approach game-theoretic ESSs, even given

strong initial genetic constraints (e.g., due to dominance, pleiotropy, epistasis), because over long periods of time the genetic system itself will evolve (Hammerstein,
this volume).

Second, we argue that while genetic constraints may be powerful when only one
or very few mechanisms can generate the behavioral phenotype, they may become
greatly weakened or even vanish when large segments of the genome can influence a
phenotype via distinct, parallel mechanisms, as is probably often or always the case
with macroscopic phenotypes like behavior. Suppose a single phenotype P can be
produced by at least two distinct, parallel mechanisms, I and II (Fig. 14.1), each
mechanism influenced by many (nonoverlapping) genes of small effect. For example,
a level of some aggressive behavior can be raised in a given context to some value
$a*$ if (1) a specific population of neurons becomes more easily excited by steroids
(which itself might be mediated by multiple mechanisms such as increases in receptor
density, decreases in steroid-deactivation rates, changes in resting membrane potential, increases in number or efficacy of synaptic inputs, etc.) or (2) a different population of neurons in *a parallel pathway leading to the same behavior* becomes excited
in the same or different way(s). Of course, many such parallel mechanisms (e.g.,
distinct groups of functionally similar neurons) may exist.

Genes producing P through mechanism I are genetically correlated with a finite
set of other traits, all of which are members of the set Q_I; the additive variance–
covariance matrix for these traits is given by G_I. Genes affecting P through the very
different mechanism II are genetically correlated with other traits in the set Q_{II} (another set sharing only the element P with Q_I), and the additive variance–covariance
matrix for these traits is given by G_{II}.

Suppose now that the matrix G_I is singular (i.e., its determinant is zero, such as
when all the corresponding elements of two rows or two columns are proportional to
each other by the same amount), with the result that some directions for evolution
are prohibited (Gomulkiewicz, this volume). At evolutionary equilibrium:

$$G_I B_I = 0 \tag{1}$$

where B_I is the vector of selection gradients measuring the direct forces of selection
on Q_I. As Gomulkiewicz points out, when G_I is singular, this equation can be satisfied
without $B_I = 0$ (the latter giving the classical ESS), and thus the evolutionary equilibrium can be quite different from that predicted by classical game theory. However,
suppose there is at least one additional, distinct and parallel mechanism II capable of
producing the ESS phenotype (P = $a*$), whose matrix G_{II} is nonsingular. Then at the
joint evolutionary equilibrium, two equations must be simultaneously satisfied:

$$G_I B_I = 0 \quad \text{and} \quad G_{II} B_{II} = 0 \tag{2}$$

In this case, since G_{II} is nonsingular, it must be that $B_{II} = 0$, meaning that, at equilibrium, the phenotype P *must* take on its ESS value (so too could all the other traits in
Q_I and Q_{II} if each of these similarly had multiple, distinct mechanisms). Obviously,
as the number of distinct mechanisms affecting P increases, *the probability that at
least one of the corresponding genetic variance–covariance matrices is nonsingular*

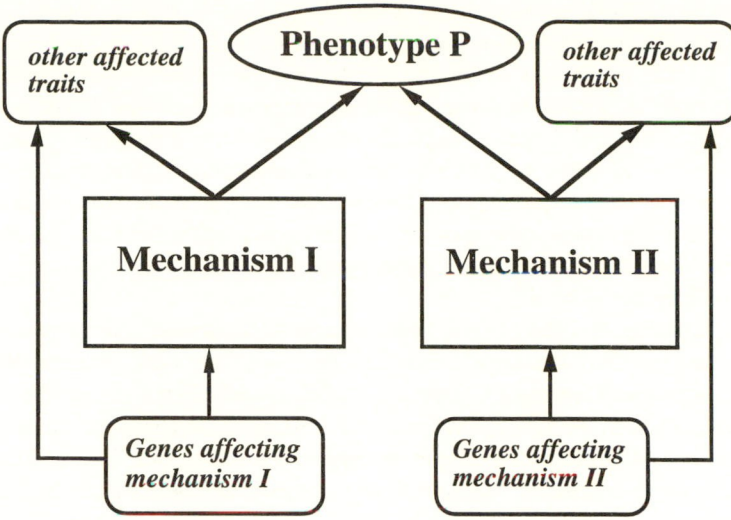

Figure 14.1. Genotype–phenotype relations for the "parallel mechanism" model.

increases, and thus the likelihood that P will have *only* the classical game-theoretic equilibrium increases. This model does not depend on the sets Q_I and Q_{II} sharing only a single trait P; the intersection of the sets could include multiple traits, each of which will have only the classical game-theoretic equilibria if at least one of the variance–covariance matrices corresponding to the sets is nonsingular.

It is not difficult to imagine that there are many parallel mechanisms capable of producing any given behavioral variant, and thus that the most reasonable behavioral ESS is just that predicted by classical, asexual GT models unfettered by genetic constraints. Thus, we suggest that GT models that make the simplest genetic assumptions (asexual inheritance; no constraining genetic correlations) may be the *most,* not *least,* realistic models, when organisms are properly seen as a complex aggregate of both serial and parallel physiological mechanisms. This "parallel mechanism" view of phenotypic evolution thus reinforces the "streetcar" model (Hammerstein, this volume), with the two views jointly emphasizing that the long-term evolution of phenotypes of complex organisms should be strongly attracted to classical game-theoretic equilibria. (It is tempting also to conjecture that the existence of parallel, multiple mechanisms also would lead to a "speeding up" of the approach to these equilibria.)

Finally, Gomulkiewicz (this volume) has suggested a method that can be used to detect departures from game-theoretic equilibria that do result from constraining genetic intercorrelations among multiple phenotypic traits, including behavioral traits. The essential point here is that, far from being rendered useless by the possibility of nonadaptive genetic correlations, GT models can, at the very least, be used to assess the evolutionary potency of such correlations, just as measuring the deviation of an arrow's landing spot from the center of a painted target requires knowing the location of the target's center!

Criticism 3: The third possible criticism of GT models is that fitnesses of behavioral variants are usually frequency-independent, so that FIO models are sufficient for understanding the evolution of behavior. This clearly cannot be generally true for behavioral traits affecting outcomes of social interactions, because, as pointed out repeatedly by Maynard Smith (1982), the fitness of such traits will depend on the actions taken by interactants, which in turn will generally depend on the frequency of the given trait in the population. Construction of a GT model of social behavior does not begin with the *assumption* of frequency-dependent fitness, but rather with the *insight* that the social interactions being modeled will inevitably lead to frequency-dependent fitness.

It should be made clear that "frequency-dependent fitness" has two senses, *both* of which require game-theoretic approaches. First, the phrase can mean that the fitness of a behavioral variant is a function of the relative frequency of the gene promoting that trait (this is the usual meaning of "frequency-dependent fitness" in population genetics). Alternatively, the phrase may refer to the fact that the fitness of a behavioral variant depends on the frequency of *other* behavioral traits in the population, even if the given variant's fitness is independent of the frequency of its own underlying gene. As an example of the latter kind of frequency dependence, consider the joint evolution of the reproductive strategies of a dominant and a subordinate in groups consisting of just two individuals. Let *s* and *s'* be alternative strategies for the subordinate and let *d* and *d'* be alternative strategies for the dominant (the probability of being in the dominant versus subordinate role is assumed independent of these strategies). Given a fixed strategy by dominants (*d* or *d'*), the relative fitness of the *s'* (versus *s*) strategy can be independent of the frequency of the *s'*-promoting allele in the population: Since *s'* strategists never interact with each other, increases or decreases in the frequency of an *s'* allele will not alter the payoffs to *s'*-strategists. However, the relative fitness of the *s'* strategy may depend strongly on the frequency of the *d* (versus *d'*) strategy—that is, on the frequency of a *d*-promoting allele, which can belong to a genetic locus completely unassociated with that for *s'* or *s* alleles. Within the second meaning of "frequency dependence," game theory can still identify the evolutionarily stable states, which are given by the pairs of dominant/subordinate strategies representing Nash equilibria—that is, "best replies to best replies" (see Hammerstein this volume). In general, the first kind of frequency dependence will tend to apply to symmetric games and the second kind to asymmetric games (games in which interactants occupy distinct roles); it is also possible that both kinds of frequency dependence will apply simultaneously. The crucial point is that GT models can predict evolutionary equilibria for both kinds of frequency dependence. Next we argue that GT, not FIO, models are *necessary* to generate the correct predictions.

Criticism 4: The fourth (and most subtle) criticism is that, while fitnesses of behaviors are often frequency-dependent, the frequency dependence typically isn't strong enough or of the right kind to make the predictions of GT models essentially different from those of similar FIO models; thus, GT models aren't really necessary. This objection is not so readily dismissed, and we consider it in some detail here.

Consider the following example: Let *x* refer to the probability that some behavior is performed and $w = f(x, x')$ represent the fitness change of a rare mutant playing *x* in a population (or subgroup of the population) playing *x'*; this is a common first step in the construction of a GT model. The GT procedure for finding the ESS is to compute $\partial w/\partial x$, then set x and x' equal to x^*. Call the resulting expression $g(x^*)$. If the $g(x^*)$ is always negative, then the ESS is $x^* = 0$; if it is always positive, the ESS is $x^* = 1$. If $g(x^*)$ can be zero, a solution x^* of the equation $g(x^*) = 0$ is a candidate for an intermediate ESS (its stability must be checked).

To take a simple case, let w be proportional to the product xx' ($x' > 0$). In an FIO model, x' is (by definition) viewed as irrelevant to the evolution of x, and it is not explicitly included in the fitness function f. Any effect of x' will be entered as a (nonzero) *constant*, say c, to yield the fitness function $y = f(x, c) = xc$. Thus, since $\partial y/\partial x = c > 0$, the FIO model predicts that x will evolve to the maximum value of 1. What does the GT model predict? Clearly, the ESS is $x^* = 1$, because any rare mutant playing an x below this value will have a fitness less than that of individuals playing $x = 1$ in a population where nearly everyone plays $x = 1$. (This solution is formally obtained by noting that $\partial w/\partial x = x' > 0$). Thus, in this case, the FIO and GT models make exactly the same prediction, and the GT model has not added any new insights.

However, now suppose that $w(x, x')$ is proportional to $x(1 - bx')$, where b is a true constant ≥ 1. The corresponding FIO fitness function will *still* have the form $y = xc$, and the optimal x again will be predicted to be 1. However, the GT model predicts an ESS of $x^* = 1/b$ (since $\partial w/\partial x = 1 - bx'$, and $x^* = 1/b$ satisfies $1 - bx^* = 0$). If b is large, the predicted equilibria of the FIO model and GT model will be $x^* = 1$ and $x^* \approx 0$, respectively!

Why do the predictions of the GT and FIO models diverge in the latter case? The key is that in the latter (and not the former) case, the fitness of the rare mutant playing some x *declines* as the population x' increases, "braking" the evolution of higher values of x to such an extent that x ceases to evolve upward when x' equals $1/b$ (the constant b reflects the strength of the "braking effect"). The FIO model is completely insensitive to this braking effect and thus can yield a strikingly wrong answer.

This point can be made much more general. In the Appendix, we show that GT models will tend to predict (a) lower equilibria than FIO models if $\partial^2 w/\partial x \partial x'_{x'=x}$ differs in sign from $\partial y/\partial x$ and (b) higher equilibria if their signs are the same. In other words, in general there will be the divergence in predicted equilibria whenever frequency dependence generates "braking" or "acceleration" effects not accounted for by the FIO model [see equation (A3) in Appendix 1].

14.3 Conclusions

Our conclusion (however unappealing to some) is that there is no good reason for ignoring game theory. Models of behavior, particularly social behavior, that ignore frequency dependence will often be wrong, and data on social behavior collected without regard to the precise predictions of GT models will often be uninformative. Correspondingly, we see two important ways that tests of evolutionary models of social behavior can be sharpened: First, GT modelers must ensure that their models are accessible, their assumptions are explicit (and realistic), and their predictions are clear. We hope that the present volume provides a step in this direction. Second, field researchers (if they are not themselves modelers) must learn the assumptions and

predictions of these models and design their experiments and data-collection strategies to sensitively test the appropriate predictions. Such efforts will rapidly advance
sociobiology as a rigorous science, certainly much more so than will hiding behind
such currently popular platitudes as "sociobiological theory has outstripped the data"
or "sociobiology is top-heavy in theory."

ACKNOWLEDGMENTS   We thank Richard Gomulkiewicz for comments on this chapter.

Appendix 14.1

Let $w = f(x, x')$ be the fitness function for the GT model, and let $y = f(x, c)$ be the
fitness function for the corresponding FIO model, as in the text. The FIO modeler
erroneously incorporates x' as a *constant* equal to c. A first-order Taylor expansion
of $\left. \dfrac{\partial w}{\partial x} \right|_{x'=x}$ about the point $c = x_0$ yields

$$f^{(1,0)}[x_0, x_0] + \{f^{(1,1)}[x_0, x_0] + f^{(2,0)}[x_0, x_0]\} \ (x - x_0) + O[x - x_0]^2 \qquad \text{(A1)}$$

where $f^{(i,j)}$ refers to the partial derivative $\partial^{i+j} w / \partial x^i \partial x'^j$ and $O[x - x_0]^2$ refers to
higher-order terms that are assumed negligible (e.g., if selection is weak). Similarly,
a Taylor expansion of $\partial y / \partial x$ about the same point yields:

$$f^{(1,0)}[x_0, x_0] + f^{(2,0)}[x_0, x_0](x - x_0) + O[x - x_0]^2 \qquad \text{(A2)}$$

Now both (A1) and (A2) approximate the derivatives of fitness with respect to the
value x of the behavior as linear functions of the form $b + m(x - x_0)$, where $b = f^{(1,0)}$
$[x_0, x_0]$ and m is $f^{(1,1)}[x_0,x_0] + f^{(2,0)}[x_0,x_0]$ for the GT model and is just $f^{(2,0)}[x_0,x_0]$ for
the FIO model. At internal equilibria (the only equilibria we consider here), $b + m$
$(x - x_0)$ will equal 0; that is, the equilibrial values of x are given approximately by
$x^* = x_0 - b/m$. Increasing m will increase x^* if $b > 0$, and increasing m will decrease
x^* if $b < 0$. The GT model has a higher m if $f^{(1,1)}[x_0,x_0] + f^{(2,0)}[x_0,x_0] > f^{(2,0)}[x_0, x_0]$,
i.e., if $f^{(1,1)}[x_0, x_0] > 0$, and it has a lower m if $f^{(1,1)}[x_0, x_0] + f^{(2,0)}[x_0,x_0] < f^{(2,0)}[x_0,x_0]$,
i.e. if $f^{(1,1)}[x_0, x_0] < 0$. Thus, the GT model will predict (a) a lower equilibrium than
the FIO model if $f^{(1,0)}[x_0, x_0]$ and $f^{(1,1)}[x_0, x_0]$ are nonzero and have opposite signs
and (b) a higher equilibrium if they are nonzero and have the same sign. Letting
$f_{1,1} = f^{(1,1)}[x_0,x_0]$, $f_{10} = f^{(1,0)}[x_0, x_0]$, and $f_{20} = f^{(2,0)}[x_0,x_0]$, the difference between the
equilibrium in the GT model and that in the FIO model will be approximately equal
to

$$\frac{f_{11}(f_{10})}{f_{20}(f_{11} + f_{20})} \qquad \text{(A3)}$$

Only in the special cases of $f_{10} = 0$ or $f_{11} = 0$—that is, when the chosen c just happens
to be the true ESS (yielding $f_{10} = 0$) or there are no "acceleration" or "braking" effects
($f_{11} = 0$)—are the predicted equilibria guaranteed to coincide.

References

Endler, J. A. 1986. *Natural Selection in the Wild.* Princeton; NJ: Princeton University Press.

Falconer, D. S. 1981. *An Introduction to Quantitative Genetics.* London: Longmans.

Maynard Smith, J. 1982. *Evolution and the Theory of Games.* Cambridge: Cambridge University Press.

Parker, G. A. & Maynard Smith, J. 1990. Optimality theory in evolutionary biology. *Nature,* 348, 27–33.

Reeve, H. K. & Sherman, P. W. 1993. Adaptation and the goals of evolutionary research. *Q. Rev. Biol.,* 68, 1–32.

Sherman, P. W. & Reeve, H. K. (1997) Forward and backward: Two approaches to studying human evolution. In *Human Evolution: The Critical Reader,* L. Betzig, ed. Cambridge: Cambridge Univesity Press.

Index